98

D1038474

282.092   Kelly, George A. CENTRAL
K29i   Inside my Father's
            house.

NEW BOOK

INSIDE MY FATHER'S HOUSE

Inside My Father's House

Msgr. George A. Kelly

DOUBLEDAY

NEW YORK · LONDON · TORONTO · SYDNEY · AUCKLAND

3 1116 00932 5678

OCT 3 0 1989

282.092
K29i

Published by Doubleday, a division of Bantam
Doubleday Dell Publishing Group, Inc.
666 Fifth Avenue, New York, New York 10103

DOUBLEDAY and the portrayal of an anchor with a dolphin are trademarks of
Doubleday, a division of Bantam Doubleday Dell Publishing Group, Inc.

Library of Congress Cataloging-in-Publication Data

Kelly, George Anthony, 1916–
Inside my Father's house/George A. Kelly.—1st ed.
p.   cm.
Includes index.
1. Kelly, George Anthony, 1916–   . 2. Catholic Church—New York
(N.Y.)—Clergy—Biography. 3. Catholic Church—New York (N.Y.)
History—20th century. 4. New York (N.Y.)—Church history—20th
century. I. Title.
BX4705.K373A3   1989
282'.092'4—dc19
[B]   88-36618
CIP

ISBN: 0-385-26227-2
Copyright © 1989 by George A. Kelly
All Rights Reserved
Printed in the United States of America
September 1989
First Edition

DEDICATED

TO

MISS CAROL HAND

Requiescat in Pace

The First Secretary of The Fellowship of Catholic Scholars
Seventeen Years a Devoted Professional Assistant
at St. John's University
New York City

CONTENTS

vii

CONTENTS

tion. The Commission for Inter-Parish Financing. Reform and Resistance. Cardinal Cooke and Public Aid. The Fleischmann Commission. His Finest Hours.

INTRODUCTION

THE GREATER GLORY OF GOD and the salvation of souls were the approved motives of priestly activity when I was ordained in 1942. They are still good reasons, even to write a book about one man's priestly experience. The hope is, of course, that he has something to say of interest to others, but then others will be the final judges of that. The period between 1939–89 is only a small slice of Church history, but it has been an interesting time for this priest. In 1939 so many seminarians were bulging Dunwoodie's supply of rooms that Cardinal Hayes wrote to pastors asking if they could use an extra curate. He did not know what to do with the fifty-four scheduled for ordination in 1937. Now in 1989 we look back on John Paul II's Extraordinary Synod, convoked in part to deal with the present-day priest shortage.

Much has been written since 1939 about the Church and the priesthood, most of it upbeat if written in the pre-World War II period; some of what was written after 1961 treats the Church as if she were a scarlet woman, hardly the Mother Church we all loved a generation earlier. A strange psychology moved some priests to claim super-love of the Church by denying her claims or by tearing down institutions that were built by saints with the pennies of the poor. While the only archive in which the full story of a priestly life is properly recorded is God's eternal mind, the busy priest is well remembered by people he served as long as he lives, and well beyond the grave, if he is a legend. Few priests who have served the parish life of the Church as long as I have are afforded the opportunity to tell that story as they lived it. I am grateful for the life and the telling of an ordinary tale.

Still, such history becomes interesting when it involves great men or those close to important thrones. There is something to be said about telling a story while memories are still fresh and some documents are extant. Too much history is written by professional gossip mongers pouring over long-since-dead documents for lessons they retroject into the lives of people they did not know and may not like because of the things for which they stood.

It has been my privilege to work with many great Bishops and great priests. Indeed, the U.S. Church has been blessed with some of the finest clerics to be found anywhere in the Church at any time. It is not a privilege but a pain to have lived through the blurring of Catholic identity and the belittling of its sacred persons, places, and things. What follows is the story of one priest's experience and reactions to all that has happened to him, while he enjoyed every minute of these fifty years.

Of course, not everything that happens to a priest is personal. If he happens to serve the Church during a period of Catholic turbulence, his life will be radically affected. Surely, World War II, the Korean War, the Cold War, the Second Vatican Council, the Vietnam disaster, dissent within the Church and liberation theology, the tension between Rome and national hierarchies, helped change the face of the American priesthood. I was involved in many of the controversies and with much of the ecclesiastical infighting that has gone on within Catholic circles in recent years, with Roman as well as American prelates. Here is another story to be told—about Catholic revolt, about the sex changes in Catholic habits, about Curial Cardinals and two Popes. The issues facing the American hierarchy and how its leadership faced up to them will interest Church historians long after we are all dead. And there remains the question still searching for an answer: Where does the Church go from here? So, *Inside My Father's House* will have a sequel, *Keeping the Church Catholic—With John Paul II,* published naturally by Doubleday. The second book will be an extension of this volume.

The following pages contain the names of priests and laity without whom this priestly life would have been shallow. As the tale unfolds, others—too numerous to name—inspiring priests and laity across the country, medical apostles of the various Catholic Physicians Guilds, the great married couples of the Christian Family Movement during the years they made Chicago's Msgr. Reynold Hillenbrand proud, the parish people of many places who helped their young to grow up fully Catholic—will find their place in the story of this priest's life and will sense how much and with what affection they still live in memory. Because the account is highly personal, based on my own lived experiences over half a century, drawn from years of parish and other Church assignments, from reams of private and official correspondence, and from proximity to ecclesiastics who make history, I have tried to keep the narrative as informal as possible, referring to published documents where and if necessary. In all respects I owe a great deal to many Bishops, priests, religious, and parishioners whose contribution to a very satisfying and happy life can only be acknowledged. It is not possible even to do more than thank them for what they have meant and still mean to me.

Closer to home, words of appreciation belong to the Catholic Community of St. John's University for its small-town warmth in a big city; to the Vincentian Fathers, Father Joseph T. Cahill, C.M., Father Joseph I. Dirvin, C.M., Father Joseph O'Donnell, C.M., especially, for the good example they set and the religious commitment they demonstrate daily before a student body of almost twenty thousand young people; to Father Ronald Lawler, O.F.M. Cap., and Msgr. Eugene Clark for their companionship and stimulating intellectual discourse. To Mrs. Gloria Lombardo and Mrs. Terry Archer—the sole staff of a busy office who made all of us look good, even when we deserved to look bad. And, not least, a profound expression of gratitude, hardly sufficient in itself, to Miss Alice Patricia Hand, who, after the death of her sister Carol, kept reshaping this text through many versions and who used a computer so well that Doubleday's senior editor Miss Patricia Kossmann received from her hands a fairly clean manuscript. Miss Kossmann, a protégé of the late great John Delaney, from the first day of our renewed acquaintance to the moment of publication has provided invaluable counsel and technical assistance. Needless to say, the shortcomings of the book must be laid at my door.

GEORGE A. KELLY

ONE

The Odyssey of a Priest: A Manifesto

A HUSH CAME OVER THE ROOM when "Wild Bill" Donovan knelt down before Father Frank Duffy for the priest's blessing just before the "Fighting" 69th went into battle. It was an impressive act of faith on the part of two American military heroes, only the scene was not Flanders fields in 1916 but Dunwoodie Seminary in 1939. Pat O'Brien sounded like the real Father Duffy, but he was only one of many actors in those days who made a good living by playing priests. A few years earlier Spencer Tracy showed himself to be Oscar material with his portrayals of Father Flanagan in *Boys' Town* and the brawniest priest in *San Francisco*, pugilist enough to knock some Christian sense into Clark Gable. By 1944 Bing Crosby was showing the nation what it meant to be *Going My Way*. The priest seemed to be every-

1

where, in the movies, on the stage, lionized by novelists. Even the whiskey priest in Graham Greene's *Power and the Glory* ends up as a martyr and Willa Cather created American folklore with her *Death Comes to the Archbishop.*

When one thinks that hardly ten years earlier Al Smith was roundly rejected because the American people did not want a priest-ridden President in the White House, the rise to public affection of the priesthood was little short of remarkable. The interesting aspect of this rise from infamy was that the celluloid clerics merely fictionalized the real men most of us saw in our boyhood parishes. Father Frank Duffy, pastor of Holy Cross Church on Forty-second Street, was bigger than anything Pat O'Brien could make him. I was in my second year at Cathedral College, New York's minor seminary, when he died in 1932. His priestly accomplishments, recounted at the time, were so impressive that today Chaplain Duffy is immortalized in stone, on Broadway no less, looking down the road at Times Square itself. He is the only priest so honored by a city which knows a hero when he comes its way. But, then, though only sixteen years old myself, I shared in the tribute from the knowledge that Duffy's boss in Flanders fields was my pastor, Msgr. James Nicholas Connolly, chief Catholic chaplain to the American Expeditionary Forces, and a recognized hero himself. Though by 1932 Connolly was seventy years of age, he was still giving out report cards quarterly to more than fifteen hundred children at Our Lady of Good Counsel school and, when I brought him my Cathedral College report for countersigning, he would take time to instruct his young parishioner on how easy it was to master Latin and Greek.

During these private sessions I learned that he had been secretary to Archbishop Michael Corrigan and, in that capacity, he had a large role in shaping and financing Dunwoodie Seminary, the pride and joy of the Corrigan administration. Msgr. Connolly might have risen higher on the ecclesiastical ladder had he not been a rival of his contemporary, Patrick Hayes, who was easily the favorite of Corrigan's successor, John Farley. Of such happenstance choices, life's fortunes are made or unmade, and being pastor of Our Lady of Good Counsel parish seemed to suit him just fine. A man small of stature, he stood tall nonetheless.

But, then, all the priests in Our Lady of Good Counsel seemed to stand tall, not the least of whom was one Arthur Edward Murphy, ordained to the parish in 1918, assigned there as a curate in June of the same year, made pastor in 1935, where he remained until he died in 1959. What in hindsight is remarkable about the parish is the realization that from 1918 to 1945 one, two, or three priests celebrated their first masses there every year. Somehow it was taken for granted that Good Counsel would ordain a new priest each year. In 1930, for example, thirteen of my fellow graduates from the school took the entrance exam for Cathedral College, an indication of how many boys wanted to walk in the footsteps of Father Murphy. On my wall today is a picture of him with three of his Dunwoodie seminarians in 1938, taken during a summer boat ride up the Hudson. Murphy, then in his fifties, was handsome in his straw hat and linen collar, the quintessence of priestly dignity as we came to know it.

It is fashionable, nowadays, to pay too much attention to sociologists and psychologists after they dissect the psyches of priests from a purely unbelieving point of view. Priests were firstborn, they say, or only children, or dogmatic characters, or mother's pets, or conformist types, or members of large families, and so forth, hardly suggesting a relationship of vocation to faith. Fortunately, none of us at the start knew we were any of those things. We did not even know we were part of a Catholic subculture and were using the priesthood as a stage in upward mobility for our entire ethnic group. When we played saying Mass as kids, in a secret corner of our parents' flat, we were only copying the men in the neighborhood we admired most. And without being able to explain it, we sensed the most important aspect of the priest was his ability to say Mass. Deeply imbedded in our being by this time—no older than ten or eleven—was the understanding that the most important task for a priest was saving other people's souls. So, we fought to serve Mass, even at five-thirty on a dark wintry morning, disturbing our poor mothers who needed more sleep than we knew. Yet we had to compete with at least a hundred other boys for the privilege. Backsliding or tardiness was out and mastering the *Suscipiat* was in. There were earthly compensations, to be sure, such as getting out of class to serve funerals, or the dollar bill for being on for weddings, and occasionally orchestra seats courtesy of Father Murphy for *The Student Prince*. The sight of a half-dozen ragamuffin boys from the East Side sidling their way into the aisle of a Broadway theater must have caused a little eyebrow lifting to many a second-nighter in 1926.

It was drilled into us from the first day we entered Our Lady of Good Counsel school. We were told to be quiet in church, approach Holy Communion with great reverence, and to confess our sins regularly, usually to Father Murphy. Why did we want to be priests? Perhaps to be like him. But it went deeper than that. We were proud little Catholics and we got the idea early that the Church spoke for Christ and He, of course, was God. You could not beat speaking for God. To spread that kind of faith was reason enough to leave father and mother. Fifty years later, Pope Paul VI would call a Synod of Bishops to discuss this very thing and on the first pages of *Evangelii Nuntiandi* (1975), one of his best exhortations, he said, "Christ first of all proclaims the Kingdom of God; Christ proclaims salvation, this great gift of God which is above all liberation from sin and the Evil One, in the joy of knowing God and being known by Him, of seeing Him and of being given over to Him." That was it. We could not put this into words like the Pope. But salvation, preaching salvation, saying Mass, was the kind of faith which made leaving father and mother a rational act. Indeed, that kind of faith was the only reason we would have taken such a giant step.

We must not, however, give too much credit to Msgr. Connolly and Father Murphy. There were also father and mother, father as well as mother. Anyone who has been a priest long enough has seen situations where the mother, not the son, had the vocation. Well, my mother was having too many babies too fast to think what she wanted Number-One Son to be. If anything, perhaps she hoped he would grow up fast enough to bring another salary into the house. Eight children in thirteen years, six of whom survived to adulthood, were more than enough to keep her busy. The

Mister, too, having the need to work at night in a second job during the first twelve years of parenting, was hardly in a position to care what his twelve-year-old would do twelve years hence.

They both came from the small town of Birr, in Ireland of course, and never met until one night at an Irish dance hall on East Fifty-ninth Street. He was the extrovert. She the private little Irish lady who was known on the street only as Mrs. Kelly. He was Charlie to everyone. Inside the house, however, that little woman who left home at seventeen, her mother dead, was like steel, shakes and all. One night in 1924, while Charlie was lugging trunks for the American Express Company (his day job was bookkeeper for the city's railroad), one of her four children, we will not mention who, knocked over an oil stove in the front room of a third-floor cold water flat on East Ninety-fourth Street, setting the room aflame. From the kitchen, five rooms away where she was ironing, Mother Kelly yelled, "Open the window!" And the ninety-eight-pound demon she was, with the safety of her brood in mind, came running through the rooms taking a blanket off any bed she could reach, throwing all of them on the fiery stove, picking up the whole kit and caboodle in her arms and throwing stove and flames out into the snow down below. And, then, socked her miscreant son.

We never knew Mom and Pop were so pious until we were older, and we did not know enough theology to realize that piety meant doing what you were supposed to do. More than talking about it, even to God. Still they both talked to God, my father seemingly more than my mother, although she was a good prayer in her own right. He could be seen at night in the corner of the front room, all alone, going through his prayer book and the many death cards of friends for whom he always felt some intercession was necessary. And when he had nothing to do between or after the two jobs—he was Holy Naming or K of C'ing (sometimes running guns for the IRA), with enough regularity that eventually he became trustee of Our Lady of Good Counsel and a delegate, too, for the Transport Workers of America-CIO. She ran the house and the kids hour by hour, day by day, until or unless he got mad, which was only now and then. The genes on

5

both sides were good, those mysterious hereditary units which predispose good and bad health, looks, intelligence, personality, industry, and whatever else makes life easy or hard. Later on in life, a priest friend, with ample opportunity to observe the Kelly clan at play, asked rhetorically: "How come there are no Indians in that family, only chiefs?" It was a family trait going back to the three generations I saw. Mother outlived father by twelve years, perhaps proving that the weaker sex—and she was chronically sick, he almost never—has the greater survivability and a bit more. At his wake, her Number-One Son, standing nearby, heard her say to him before the coffin lid was closed: "Good-bye, Charlie, we had a good life. I'll see you in Heaven." They left behind six individuals, none of whom was sorry he or she was born, none of whom, as far as I know, she was sorry to bear.

Home, school, neighborhood, parish, streets, peers—which institution better than another makes the priest, presuming that God plants the seed? The parents may not have had the religious vocation, but they surely encouraged high marks in school, which did not always come. But, then, the neighborhood and the pastor placed low value on failure of any kind. Both Cathedral College and Dunwoodie expelled classmates with ruthless regularity to prove they meant business with their fairly high academic standards. Considering the complaints made about seminary education after Vatican II, most New York priests would judge their training was pretty good—not perfect, but good.

Some years after 1965 I got into a mild argument with a Bishop who, before a group of university academics, knocked the seminary training he received. I knew only that the Bishop in question came from a small diocese and a small seminary. He complained how he was once put out of a library by a professor who thought he would be better advised to spend his spare time in Chapel. The Bishop was feeding into a myth popular in some academic circles that the Church preferred pious ignoranti in the priesthood more than scholarly types. He was quickly reminded that had he been educated in Dunwoodie (New York), Overbrook (Philadelphia), Brighton (Boston), Mundelein (Chicago), Kenrick (St. Louis), or Menlo Park (San Francisco), the chances are that he would be chastised for his academic failure, not for lack of piety. Indeed a "reign of terror" in Dunwoodie after 1937 eliminated the surplus of candidates then oversupplying the Archdiocese. The number of priests ordained for New York fell from fifty-four in 1937 to eighteen in 1940. The scholastic average, not lack of piety, determined the rate of depopulation.

Seminaries, major or minor, like colleges, are better big than small. They provide variety. While we wondered how some of the faculty ever got there, there were enough great teachers to inspire and make you work. In Cathedral College Father John Monaghan was one. But there was also a young Father Ed Waterson, whom everybody hated young but admired old. He taught us Latin against our will and even how to use the English tongue. Waterson was a great one for making students memorize rules, many of which they never forgot. " 'Farther' is for distance, 'further' is for everything else." Then, we were moved by Father Henry Gebhard, a first-rate orator, who taught us how to debate. There was a stutter in my speech and he noticed that it was absent whenever I sang or talked loud. He said: "Let your voice ring out!" and so I joined Gebhard's public debating team and have been talking ever since. Indeed, the memory of those teen days evokes the question I once asked my father's mother on her eighty-second birthday: "Granny, how will we know you're dead?" Her response was characteristic of that delightful lady: "If the tongue's not wagging, I'm dead." Speech making runs in the family.

Dunwoodie had its share of mediocrities on the faculty, but also some real winners. One unsolved mystery, however, is why those "winners," some of whom were very learned, almost never acquired scholarly reputations. Something in seminary life seems to inhibit the scholarly writing necessary for this recognition. Father Jeremiah Toomey was one of the finest moral theologians of his day, but died suddenly in 1939. Hardly more than forty years old, Father Toomey wrote almost nothing. Neither did McMahon, who had the makings of a first-rate church historian and surely did inspire a class to do scholarly work. The only scholarly writer was Father William O'Connor ("Bucky" as he was called), who achieved recognition as a superb dogmatist, one of the clearest teachers in Dunwoodie's history and by virtue of his written productivity later elected president of the Catholic Theological Society of America. Those of us who went from Dunwoodie to graduate study were well prepared by good teachers, if not by recognized scholars, for whatever the likes of Catholic University had to offer.

It would be a mistake, however, to think that schools by themselves made the man or the priest. In my time the streets contributed a great deal. There were four hundred kids of all ages on every block, drawn from the fifty four-story story walk-ups of nine apartments each. From 3 P.M. till dusk during the week and throughout large pieces of time on weekends, play was the thing. Any kind of game for all ages and sexes was available—on stoops, sidewalks, sewer to sewer, even in the areaway of tenements. And it was free, no CYO, no Little League, no adults involved. You organized yourself for tag, Johnny-on-the-Pony, potsy, jacks, poker, dice, punchball, stoopball, stickball, and when you were old enough to play baseball, you learned to raise your own money for uniforms. Selling chopped wood at ten cents a basket or working for James Butler at five dollars a week, caddying at city golf courses for the princely price of one dollar a round of eighteen holes, running late-teen dances and blackjacking local store owners to take an ad in a journal we thought beautiful, but which really was second rate, were all exercises in free enterprise by youngsters who learned quickly to become self-starters. It was a good training ground for a future priest who would be called upon to work in a laissez-faire parish world.

Playing, at least the way we did it on East Eighty-ninth Street, was not simply a display of athletic prowess or proof that some of us should stick to crossword puzzles. It was an exercise also in sustained relationships. Paul Hanly Furfey would have called it "the gang age" in action, except that there were no nefarious connotations to our get-togethers in Yorkville. We had a few roughnecks around, to be sure, the tough guys who had been left back in school once or twice and who took delight in harassing younger kids. None of our wide group ever saw the inside of a police station.

8

Interestingly, I cannot remember any "tramps" on our block, the unceremonious word we reserved then for bad girls. There were none. In the earlier teen years by-play between boys and girls took place but by and large the play was sex divided. When there was a coming together it was innocent. Spin the bottle and post office were harmless exercises in growing up, and if any boy got rambunctious, some little sixteen-year-old lass would put him in his place. Her mother saw that she was amply prepared for that sort of warfare. Such was the Catholic nature of the neighborhood that even minor seminarians were accepted as being different, outside the pale even of that innocent sexual horseplay. No one minded, least of all the seminarians. Those who became over-involved were likely to quit the college, although a few daredevils survived to become outstanding priests.

What was remarkable about "the gang" was its continued stability as sixteen became eighteen and courting began in earnest, again somewhat chastely. It was the age of the local baseball team and the neighborhood league composed of eight teams from a geographical area of no more than one mile. That was how packed Yorkville was with budding athletes. Out of this group Eddie Lopat came to go on to become a super-Yankee star. Vince Lombardi may have pushed his maxim too far by insisting that winning was the only thing. Yet, winning was better than losing, especially if the prize was worthwhile, a good lesson for those interested in salvation. The girls followed the athletes throughout the season. It was the beginning of the beer-drinking age, but there were no drunks (yet), girl-chasing, but no shotgun weddings, great man-to-man, woman-to-woman friendships, but not a homosexual in the lot. I was twenty, about to enter Dunwoodie, when some of the gang dared to try out the burlesque houses on East Forty-second Street. How embarrassed "the gang" became one day when our right fielder reached into his pocket for a pack of cigarettes and out fell a condom. No one in that circle had ever seen that packet before and most were somewhat relieved. He was a non-Catholic.

Many of those relationships continue to this day, fifty years in the growing. Not every member of that gang became a star in the game of life, yet all who married stayed married, went to war, and lived to raise fairly decent Catholic children. The memories are still precious because the relationships turned out to be so long-lasting, made possible by the natural cohesiveness of the neighborhood, something no longer likely to be found in a city of towers and managed populations, except perhaps in the ghetto. Whereas those old ghettos were halfway houses to success, the new ghettos are more like jails.

These recollections may seem like dreamy nostalgia to some, but such was the nature of the times. We were poor but did not know it and saw light at the end of every tunnel. It was a nice time to be young. Psychiatric wisdom, drawn from the testimony of the sick or chronic complainers, with its hostility to ties that bind, had not yet enlightened women to leave their husbands, or mothers not to have children, or the normal young to blame their parents for their own failures. The Catholic ethos dominated and the various segments of the community reinforced each other. You never came home with a complaint about what they did to you in school because you would find yourself in trouble all over again. And if, for some reason, the cop on the beat picked you up, he did not take you to jail, but upstairs to your mother. Mom was always there. By the time we were twenty, however, neither the cop nor mother could find us. We had learned the art of staying out of both their ways.

By 1936, going to Dunwoodie seemed the most natural thing in the world. Graduation from Cathedral College was over and the time had come to move on to something else. (One of my classmates went off to fight in the Spanish War on the side of the Communists!) It was time to take a breather, so throughout the summer I dawdled a bit, but by August Dunwoodie became the objective.

What a strange place it turned out to be. Fifty new aspirants, mostly ball players of one kind or another, each crowded into a small room in the seminary wing, sometimes in pairs because of the shortage of space. We did not have the least idea of what we were getting into. A lot of crazy rules, we soon found out, especially the one which permitted you to have your family visit the week after you arrived, not in the middle of the semester when you and they would have enjoyed seeing one another. Up at 5:30 A.M., prayers at 6, Mass at 6:30, class at 9, Chapel at 12, handball at 3, bed by 10, and no talking above the ground floor. It was a structured life and part of the adventure was beating the system without getting caught. Cardinal Hayes made one of his rare visits in 1937 and, finding cigarette stubs in the quadrangle near a statue of Our Lady, banned all smoking (which up to then was permitted in the ballfield area). Msgr. Arthur Scanlon, the Rector, tried to enforce that for a week and his sorties around the campus became hilarious. The would-be smokers outwitted him at every turn. He gave up and persuaded Hayes to withdraw the ban.

Johnny-come-latelys think that old system was a corrupting influence on the lives of future priests. They feel this way possibly because their permissive training denied them the opportunity to develop the skill to live within any system, even to develop a sense of humor doing so. Beating the system, while leaving it intact, was often very funny. Professors coming upon real or imagined offenders directed them to "drop cards," each of which was added to others as points against us, when we came up for faculty evaluations or calls to orders. But for every card we dropped there were probably ten or twenty violations which went undiscovered. What turned out to be amusing were the compulsive law abiders, "goody-two-shoes" they were called later, who were forced to drop a card for an offense they did not commit. Professors did not always see what they thought they saw.

Dunwoodie had no infirmary then, nor does it now, so that if you really became sick, you went home or to the hospital. Veterans in the seminary soon instructed juniors that the winter was long, dark, and holiday-less. Late January was a good time to catch a cold and a ten-day rest at home. It was always fascinating how the nose breathed better in winter once you passed through the Dunwoodie gate. In May 1938, when I walked into the Rector's office for my first call to the clerical state (tonsure), I was reminded that because of my two midwinter "vacations," the faculty was afraid my health was somewhat fragile. I knew a

11

veiled threat when I heard it and managed to spend my winters at Dunwoodie through the next four years.

Strangely, I do not remember any serious complaining about the Dunwoodie structures, that bugaboo which agitates so many youngsters who never lived under strict dominion. The recent joke about the pastor who vehemently asserted that those six seminary years were the happiest in his life has the ring of credibility to it. The two young curates had complained bitterly in his presence about their own seminary life. Upon hearing the old man say he would love to relive those years, they asked impatiently, "Why?" To which the pastor indecently answered, "Because if I knew I was going to get two jokers like you for curates, I would have quit the place." Few of us in 1939 had any deep psychological hostility either to the place or to the faculty, although it was student complaints to the Apostolic Delegate that forced the "retirement" of the Rector and one professor. The food was bad and one of my classmates one night took a piece of what he called "diseased liver" from the supper table and sent it on to the Yonkers Board of Health! We considered such conduct as prankish and went on eating the bad food for several more years. At twenty-one, the ball player in us looked upon food, any food, as a delicacy. There was grousing during "the reign of terror," when the weekly classload increased from fifteen hours to eighteen to twenty. But that was all it remained, grousing. We fitted into the new schedule rather nicely, once it became a fact of life.

Marks were a big thing in Dunwoodie. It was hard to judge a seminarian's faith or predict his performance twenty years hence. Some seminarians were eventually rejected because the faculty did not like their attitude, which could be seen in the curl of a lip, the manner of walking, the fresh answer, or the sloppy appearance. However, a "goody-two-shoes" demeanor or long-suffering subservience did not prove to be a reliable guide either to future performance or sustained respect for authority. Neither were exam marks. If the norm is effectiveness in the parish priest's role, then many of those preferred by faculty for their academic accomplishments later turned out to be less than adequate pastors, even as teachers. Yet, marks were often the major indexes of brains, industry, compatability, agreeability, and so forth. Indeed, the faculty usually saw students only in class. In our first two years the Rector, when he interviewed the student at year's end, spent most of the time on marks, supplying the average mark for the year and the student's class standing. This procedure, later abandoned, may have begun with a desire to encourage competition and it might well have done that. I was a member of what became known as "the Grand Class," a silly name given to us in our first year because a young professor, unsure of himself in dealing with sixth-year deacons, only three years his junior, asked them pointedly why they were not like the first philosophers. "Now, that's a grand class," he opined with anger in his voice. The name stuck. And, truthfully, his newest seminarians did hit it off rather well with him, partly because the class of 1942 had a large number of individualistic and industrious members.

Marks came easily to me, and when in 1938 two members of the class were chosen to go to Rome for continued study and early ordination, it occurred to me and some others that we could do better. So the next four years saw more involvement with libraries and term papers, and in the burgeoning new apostolates sparked in one way or another by Pius XI—catechetics (CCD), the poor (The Olier Guild), workers (ACTU), apologetics (Catholic Evidence Guild), liturgy (Orate Fratres), Negroes (Interracial Councils), Catholic Action (YCW)—and softball. A great deal was made later that prior to Vatican II the Church was interested only in the salvation of souls, not in the salvation of the world. Not so in the Church after *Rerum Novarum* in 1891, not in Dunwoodie by 1941. Strangely, there was no course on parish life or how to run a parish, not even how to start the CYO or the CCD, two basics for the newly ordained, as we would discover. When one considers how doctors, engineers, and junior lieutenants are interned, it is amazing how little time—no time at all, really—was spent on parochializing the priest, on whom the diocese was to depend most of all. Of course, it was the era before methodology courses *sans* content for teachers, so diocesan authorities might have felt that the system itself would do the teaching. They miscalculated.

In 1942 the young priest was thrown out into a very wide sea, to sink or to swim, on his own.

But what a day Ordination Saturday, May 30, 1942, turned out to be, with the Sunday First Mass just as awesome. Forty-seven years later the memory of the events is still warm. Riding by bus to St. Patrick's Cathedral from Yonkers, the Imposition of Hands by Cardinal Spellman, my mother and father kneeling before their priest son like children for *my* blessing, and the first *Hoc Est Enim Corpus Meum.* There can be no feelings, in this person at least, equal to the emotions of that original thirty-hour period of priesthood. Years later Father Robert Ford would toast his priest friends at dinner: "Here's to the greatest fraternity in the world." He was not toasting the men as much as the priesthood. By and large most of the priests with whom we lived were good men, happy to be priests. A few found out early that they did not belong, others were hurt by bad experiences or became overly friendly with John Barleycorn. Following Vatican II large numbers left the priesthood, some with dispensations, but there were always a handful before that who just wandered away. What fascinates, however, is how the priesthood continues to preoccupy the attention of those who are no longer part of the fraternity. In the presence of former classmates, their questions usually relate only to what they left, questions even about the Bishop. The "character" of Holy Orders perdures in more ways than one.

The priests who remained faithful to their commitment are still what they were on ordination day—idealists, good to people, celibate, and, until recent years, reaching seventy years of age without money. For most of my years the average priest received hardly more than fifty dollars a week. Priests enjoyed, of course, a fully financed rectory life and if they were effective parish priests, they were loved by the people, who showered good will and favors upon them. These priests, too, will never be lonely because into their old age they will still be marrying, baptizing, and burying old friends. What is the most satisfying aspect of a priest's life are those families and individuals who attribute their faith, their spirituality, their good family life to "their" priest. It would require one fat volume to compile the influence of a good priest on the lives of those whom he served well. The jobs he secured, the marriages he saved, the families whose love relationships he deepened, the babies he encouraged them to have, the parents he buried, the converts, the religious and priests he inspired, the piety he initiated—the list is endless.

Good priests worked hard. The myth of "the golfing priest" or "the Palm Beach priest" survives because some priests (mostly young) played golf and some priests (mostly older pastors) spent too much time in the Florida sun. But those who "were the parish" had a hard time finding time to play golf, although it was a delightful diversion from their daily routine, especially since those activists often did double duty by outside involvement in various diocesan apostolates. Teaching in a labor school or giving a four-hour Cana Conference somewhere in the middle or at the end of a sixty-hour week was seen as a broadening experience. Consider what those early priest teachers at one of Spellman's diocesan high schools did in a given week—teaching one hundred sixty teenagers in a given day, management of a school "club" until five o'clock, and parish work on Saturday and Sunday.

However beloved they were by parishioners or students, those priests never indulged their flock or made undue concessions to their weakness or sinfulness. It was one thing to love them, but forming them into fully believing Christians was a first responsibility, to lift their religious sights, and to help them carry the usual crosses. Betty Ann and her mongoloid baby, Irene and Mickey through their twenty years of Sunday Mass without communion because she was married once before (rectified finally), finding a foundling for Paul and Gladys, who could not have children, Gina, who gave up money and status to become a nun, Bill, who wanted to commit suicide but did not, Richard, who was kept out of jail and became a cop, and so on. Perseverance and God's grace were the keys that unlocked a mind or the character of someone whose faith was all but dead or whose morals hardly qualified him for membership in the parish choir. You might visit an unregenerate sinner three and four times and get nowhere. The fifth visit (perhaps) cleaned up the forty-year absence from the sacraments or merely prepared the way for the next priest who might call on him, perhaps in a hospital.

If I summarized what the priests of my time did best, I would say it was reinforcing Catholic identity and keeping a watchful eye on anything that might subvert the faith or betray the faith, those scandals of which Christ Himself spoke. In other words, the faithful did not have to shift for themselves to know what being a Catholic meant, and while parish scandals existed, they were limited in their ecclesial nuisance by the direct action of priests unafraid to make tough decisions. And what priests could not or did not do, the Bishop frequently did. The discipline made Catholic life easy for everyone, which is what discipline is supposed to do. Parish acrimony was minimal and even the lukewarm Catholics wanted their children educated by nuns. The post-World War II Church came as close to "gold" status as any other segment of our two-hundred-year Catholic patrimony. And priests sure of their role, and the faithful who believed in one Lord, one Church, one priesthood, were happy about that.

Catholic identity was shaped by the Mass and the sacraments as the faithful were constantly reminded. The Mass was not an option, and the state of grace was absolutely necessary to receive most of the sacraments. Even though the rituals were in Latin, the people seemed to get the message. It would be unthinkable that anyone living in mortal sin would receive Holy Communion. No priest would condone it and few laity would be so presumptive of God's forgiveness as to try it. Probably the only sacrament that was poorly administered was Penance, the one sacrament that had a great deal to do with "Catholic identity." The numbers seeking absolution had something to do with the overroutinization of the penitential discipline. But the increasing speed of American life also contributed to quick absolutions without spiritual direction. Yet, the faithful continued to have a good sense of sin and priests were generally kind, so that the overall effects, psychological as well as spiritual, were expected Catholic bonuses. The fact that the lines were long said so. If sexual sins dominated the confessions of certain age groups, it was for the reason that sexual sins were their most serious violations of God's law. Few were gangsters or high-grade crooks. Venereal pleasure was fun and it was private and it was cheap. But in the Catholic ethos one of the signs of Christian character was mastery over lustful impulses. Priests were usually permissive to teenagers who masturbated and to married couples who used contraceptives, without ever leaving the sinners to believe that their conduct was acceptable Catholic behavior. In many cases personal difficulties had to be faced with a priest, but then Christ's contemporaries had their troubles with Him for similar reasons. They wanted what they wanted and His blessing, too. Refused absolution, like the displeasure Christ reserved for the hard-hearted, set the limits of toleration within the Company. Even tales about denial, never favorable to a priest, had a positive effect on Catholic conduct. Other Catholics heard the message and believed the Church meant what it said.

Of course, it was the "nuns" who enhanced Catholic identity in the neighborhood. Fifty School Sisters passed through the parish school in my time, and whether they spent three years or ten, they had an incredible effect on positive feelings for the Church on the East Side. Just to have them walk through the parish streets, or shop on the local avenues, or jump rope with girls during recreation time, one hand on the skirt, the other on the veil, tickled the hearts even of the lukewarm. Their schooling and their liturgies affected the parents as much as the children. Their involvement in human problems—a broken arm or the lack of milk at home—made them truly beloved. First communion days became parish celebrations, as did Our Lady's feast days, name days, culminating in the Christmas and Easter liturgies. Even the Sunday nine o'clock Mass for children was planned to maximize what was special to the Church—the worship of God. As far back as 1946 the Mass was dialogued with a priest in the pulpit every Sunday. Even parents heard the message because there was no way out of sending their child to Sunday Mass. The vision of parishioners gathering in the courtyard prior to Christmas midnight Mass to serenade the School Sisters still lingers as a high point in the parish year. Whoever sold nuns on giving up their veils and their community life was not speaking for Catholic parents or for the nuns' own best interests.

Many of the School Sisters departed the parish before they could see the fruits of their endeavors. I saw them all the time and still do. Some years ago, after addressing the New York City police Holy Name Society, I was invited by the commissioner into the VIP room for a drink. There I found waiting for me about twenty-five of my former altar boys, all cops, some already lieutenants and captains. As I approached them, the best I could muster up, as a response to their warm greeting, was: "And to think that Sister De Padua and I expected most of you to end up in jail."

The forging of a strong faith was easy in those days because the Church was really one in faith, in worship, in law. There were the grousers, to be sure, not all of whom were laity, but the enthusiasm of some, the hard work of others, and the watchful eye of Chanceries meshed to allow enthusiasts to fan the fires of ardent faith and to keep deviance to a manageable minimum. Scandals were few. Priests' weaknesses were not entirely hidden from view, but there were few Judases. No Archbishop of New York would tolerate false teaching or public licentiousness among clergy and religious. Father John Courtney Murray told a young band of New York's finest ordinandi in 1941 how his Jesuits kept their worst misbehaviors from public view. Such was the nature of the period. Pastors had no difficulty getting rid of scandal-mongering priests. Good priests were sufficiently numerous to fill any void without delay. Zealous priests also managed local scandals involving laity. At times, parish affairs scandalized the neighborhood because of the amount of drunkenness tolerated on Church property. To cure that situation one pastor banned alcoholic beverages for five years. No one seemed to mind except the drunks. Then, the chronic reappearance of "collection clippers," those trusted "pillars" of the Church who cannot resist improving their weekly income at the expense of the parish treasury, always caused embarrassment because the last one who seemed to know was the pastor. But it was gossip about them that did the greater damage. In one parish, whose main body of Sunday churchgoers was Italo-American, the leading parish officials were superannuated Irish-Americans who did not seem to recognize that the parish no longer was theirs. Breaking their stranglehold on the parochial organizations involved knocking some heads together, but the last state of the parish turned out to be better than the first. Had something not been done, bitterness between two otherwise decent ethnic groups would have festered needlessly.

When the Church is functioning well, the priest is called upon to make tough decisions which may not sit well with somebody, not infrequently a local nabob or an entrenched holdover from another regime or simply the village troublemaker. Whatever the source of the difficulty, it is the priest's responsibility, not necessarily the pastor's, to forge unity, but if that is not possible then someone must be fired. My first pastor, John Moylan, was a gentle soul but he was not above saying to a troublemaker: "I'm your pastor, but you have my permission to take your special cause elsewhere, where it will do us the least amount of harm." That usually was the end of the matter. In any event, there was little internal dissension in the first twenty-five years of my priesthood, either at the parochial or diocesan level. Malcontents might have felt quashed by the system, but malcontents have no special claims on the system. Admittedly, those in authority make mistakes in deciding complicated issues or in dealing with personnel. But they make greater mistakes when they are indecisive or postpone dealing with evil. Evil, like disease, contaminates the innocent. It is the job of officeholders to protect the innocent, who are helpless before terrorists of one kind or another.

If "Dollar Bill" is not remembered as a kindly pastor, regardless of the debts he paid off, neither is "Good-Time Charlie" nor "Easygoing Jim." These latter may come down to posterity as "nice guys," but they had no great influence on the religious lives of their people. The most mystifying pastor of all was "Everybody's Friend, Joe," the pastor who agreed with everybody because he could not stand any controversy which made him look bad. Priests like him usually ended up with few friends, little respect, and enemies on both sides of every border. On the other hand, "Doc" is remembered because he put his being where his wise voice called his flock to go. "Big Bill" was not exactly lovable, but he dominated a neighborhood populated with as many

Catholics as some dioceses. He was Msgr. Catholic. Even the Jewish storekeepers had the good sense to respect his influence over the masses of "the people." "The Chief" was another type to command following. If he did it his way, it was for the reason he was more right than some of his critics. The Chief never doubted he spoke for the people. Usually, such leaders, while speaking for themselves, do speak for their country or for their Church.

Strangely, obeying the law or following the directions of pastors or Bishops was once taken for granted. It was the given of priestly life. Few of us felt oppressed, because we also had ample room for our own initiative or creativity, whatever this might have been. Undoubtedly, not every diocese provided the latitude to priests that was commonplace in New York. If you could not organize the CYO, which became dearest to your heart precisely because a pastor said no, you still became the hero of the parish by spending a lot of time in the school or in the local hospitals, usually with no one minding, least of all a penny-pinching pastor.

In the course of time most good priests developed a decent relationship with Church authorities. If they did not, the failure might be theirs or perhaps no one was at fault. Life begets unexplainable situations. If they did, they might even make it to the episcopacy. Most priests took life as it came, rarely complaining about their lack of recognition "downtown" and generous to a fault when ecclesiastical favors fell to their peers. Priests are not noticeably a jealous lot. They are not unmindful of "climbers," those who lust for the purple or the beanie with an unusual desire, whether they are capable of bringing honor to the advancement or not.

It was not difficult to become a monsignor in Spelly's time. As a pompous prelate was heard to say one Friday morning upon reading the new list in the *Catholic News:* "My God, now he's making anybody." And sometimes he did.

Becoming a Bishop was trickier business, however. There were fifty thousand priests and about three hundred Bishops. Some unfortunates never learned that the odds were against them, that most who yearned lost. One friend of mine in another diocese was something of a favored son at a time when his Ordinary was a noted Bishop-maker. Suddenly, he found himself next in line. He could almost feel the silk of the miter. Just as suddenly his patron dropped dead and my friend never made it with the successor. He died years later, a sad and disappointed priest done in by overweening ambition. Several priests I treasured lingered too long in their disappointment or in their envy of those who made it. They did not seem to appreciate the value of their own priestly life or the important role they had or would have, or the handicaps of being a Bishop. Not every Bishop is successful, not even happy, and the fall from a high perch is never a small fall. For good or for ill, especially in times of crisis, the well-being of the Church depends on Bishops, their vision of the Church and their ability to implement its policies. However, most priests who were aggressive on behalf of the Church did not lust for the episcopacy. Nor did they become depressed by remaining a priest. Francis Spellman, who was visibly ambitious, and Terence Cooke, who never sought advancement by design, would have been successful priests even if the Cardinal's hat had gone elsewhere. The tragedy lies with those who lack sufficient piety to accept the role God assigns them.

All in all, over forty-seven years, the priesthood has been a great adventure. It is a little harder in 1989 than it was in 1942, but that only makes it a new kind of challenge. Those aggressive on behalf of the Church were once called upon to spread the word, now the urgency is to defend the word. It is a recurring event in the Church's long history. In 1942 we never thought about anything but spreading the word. Disobedient priests or secularized laity never occurred to us. Yet, what did we expect? An easy life? Status with comfort, freedom without rejection?

I think frequently of those priests who really spent themselves for Christ without ever counting the cost and never posed a problem to anyone, least of all to their people—Arand, Coogan, Furfey, Conlin, Ford, Kapusta, Lynch, Costello, Frawley. Their numbers are legion, those whose names will never be cut on a diocesan tombstone and, lacking family, have no one to pray for them. These are the priests who went along with the Church rather easily. *Sentire cum ecclesia* was their life's reason for being. They did not merely think with the Church, or feel with the Church, they acted for the Church. They walked with the Church. The ones I have in mind did not look upon the Church as a museum piece or a relic or as something that ceased living a full life at Constantinople, Paris, or Trent. Their Church was living, taking on new forms as it shed old customs and older pieties. They were wed neither to Latin, nor to tiaras, nor to monkish habits. Only to one true faith, to the Mass, to their parishioners. And their followers were not simply the saved but all the people they could reach. They were not neglectful of those who paid the parish bills, but if you look at their converts, the marriages they validated, the names of the hospital patients visited, you will find a goodly number of lost sheep. And if you walk through the parish streets which were their favorite hangouts, you will find how kindly Jewish storekeepers, Protestant bank guards, and anybody's barber thought of the Church because of them. Many of those priests were ecumenical long before the word appeared in a university catalogue.

These priests dealt with purists in their ranks every week, sticklers for the canon law, who never learned about commutations, dispensations, or epikeia. They understood the pressures on their people and were patient with their weaknesses, as well as their sins. But they also knew their role as pastors. They were ordained to shepherd their flock into the fold, not to let them go their own way with the feeling that the fold was wherever they happened to be. As John Paul II had reason to remind the U.S. Bishops on September 5, 1983, compassion is not indulgence. Most of the priests of my generation believed that. We worked to get people to face the realities in their lives, we spoke the truth to them, proposed guidelines for them to live by, and we offered them a helping hand. We did not mislead people about the need for virtue nor did we support them in a life of sin, if that happened to be their choice. Going down in a quagmire with the sheep to wallow in their errant behavior or their illicit way of thinking was not our idea of pastoring. Christ did not celebrate the prodigal son because he was prodigal, but because he put his wasteful life behind him.

But if the best priests of those times were models of *sentire cum ecclesia,* they were also highly "critical" of the Church. People forget that the word criticism in its root means discernment and judgment. Since most good priests were idealists and knew the Church system better than anyone else, it was inevitable that they would be dissatisfied with second-rate performance or abuses. Many of them disturbed the smugness of higher ecclesiastics who seemed satisfied with a status quo which was failing in its worship of God, in the quality of priestly performance, or in outreach to the most helpless of our society. Granted the remarkable works of the Church, and they were remarkable, there were also serious lacunae and shoddy practices which cried to Heaven for relief and reform. Most priests knew these things. No Archbishop of New York was ever denied access to the solid criticism of Church management by his interested priests. Those criticisms came through the system, either orally through diocesan officials or in articles for magazines like *The American Ecclesiastical Review.* Do you know what was the most commonly discussed subject in Catholic magazines of the 1930s? "Leakage from the Barque of Peter," as Pittsburgh's Father Thomas Coakley called it in 1936. Is anyone interested in this subject today? My first article there in May 1944 (with L.A.'s Father Thomas Coogan) suggested that somewhere out there were 10 million Catholics hiding, whom pastors seemed not to want to know. Such self-criticism was commonplace and was good for the Church, as it had been in the days of St. Jerome or St. Catherine of Siena.

On the other hand, we were not Savonarolas with a will to destroy our superiors and the Church, too. We were not parading our dirty linen before non-Catholics, nor taking out ads in *The New York Times,* nor picketing the Bishop's house. That reckless conduct shows no respect for the Church and treats her more as the Whore of Babylon than the Bride of Christ. We understood the human limitations of our superiors but they remained our Christs. Whatever their shortcomings in intelligence or character, we presumed their good will and our own patience to await proper results in God's due time. Saul Alinsky would become a household word in Chicago, but ACTU chaplains did not want his kind or his deeds in New York, and to our credit he had no following here, until recently, that is.

What we could not foresee, however, was the destructive impact of Alinsky-type priests on the lives of religious and good laity. The revulsion against the institutional Church, against Church authority, and against Rome especially, which followed Vatican II was unpredictable in 1962. Somehow and suddenly we permitted norms set by those of no faith to dominate the minds of those with great faith. Mysteriously, great faith became little faith, modernity undermined tradition, "holy disobedience" became the vow of liberated religious, and the Church found herself in the dock, forced to defend her right to be Catholic, with Jesuits and erstwhile holy women becoming her chief prosecutors. The Church's trial is not yet ended.

It is consoling to remember during times of Catholic crisis that in the fullness of time God sends a saint or two or a Pope or two to save His Church from the alleged wise men of a given age. Elites seemingly take delight in trying to bring the Church down, as they brought Christ down. The message of Christianity is too much for them—too otherworldly, too impractical, too irrational, interferes too much with passion, lust, pleasure, and power. And it also depends on faith. The Church usually is oversupplied with the uneducated, who take too many myths for granted. Disdain for "little ones" is as old as the agora of Athens when Paul first preached there. It has also been present at the University of Paris during the French Revolution and can be found today in those theology departments of leading Catholic universities, where the opinions of elites count for more. Sages frequently prefer their own religion and, when they prefer it at all, they do so without a Church, at least without a Church that is one, holy, Catholic, and apostolic. Know-it-alls tolerate the existence of folk-religionists in their midst, those who follow the simple teachings of John Paul II, but predict (and frequently they are wrong) that the future belongs to the postconventionals, i.e., those who believe in the pure gospel of "love your fellow man" without the cultural baggage that developed after Christ—myths of Mary's Virginity, Christ's transsubstantiation, Peter's infallibility, or the Church's priesthood.

Today's elites are no different from earlier dissenters. They look down on Polish or Irish Catholics because their faith is so fierce. But, then, we must remember that one of the arguments against Christ was that his followers were "uneducated laymen" (Acts 4:13). Looking over the breadth of the Church's membership, converts, especially intellectuals, must pause to ask, if they seek something new after Baptism, what they are doing to themselves or to the Church which they recently joined. The chances of being "priest-ridden" surely look ominous to some. Entering a despised minority from an esteemed position in upper-class Anglicanism gave John Henry Newman momentary pause. G. K. Chesterton was already in when he began to realize that "the Church is much larger inside than it is outside."

Father Henri de Lubac, S.J., once wrote a book about his Church. He called it *The Splendor of the Church* (1953). If ever a book was written in faith by a first-rate scholar, this is it, by a priest who suffered with the faith, as much as for it. The splendor he spoke about attached to the body itself, to Christ the Priest, and to all who shared in that priesthood by Baptism, as by Holy Orders. He draws on St. Augustine's *Confessions* to close out his book. In the Great Doctor's time, a famous thinker, Victorinus by name, believed but did not wish formally to identify with the Church. He had much to lose by so doing, this philosopher whose statue stood proudly in the Roman Forum. But nagged sufficiently often by his friend Simplicianus, Victorinus succumbed: "Let us go to Church. I wish to be made a Christian." De Lubac pauses here and then writes the last sentence of *The Splendor of the Church:* "If Victorinus had not made up his mind to take this decisive step and lose himself among the humble flock of the practicing faithful [he would still be admired as a thinker but], he would not deserve to be called by a name which is common indeed and in the eyes of many without distinction, yet is the finest of all when its significance is understood. He would not have been a Catholic."

On that note de Lubac ends his book. If that ending was good enough for a priest who is now a ninety-year-old-plus Cardinal of the Church, it is good enough for me.

TWO

Learning the Church, Spellman-Style

THE FIRST INAUSPICIOUS MEETING

WHEN I PROSTRATED MYSELF on the altar of St. Patrick's Cathedral May 30, 1942, prior to promising "reverence and obedience" to my Bishop, I had no idea that I was being initiated into the service of one of the most important prelates in the history of the U.S. Church. World War II had just begun and Francis Spellman did not look like much. He had been in New York three years but had yet to make his mark. The forty of us who lay there that day did not care much about things like that, so excited were we about becoming priests. But by the time we celebrated our silver jubilees, the year he died (1967), most of us were proud of what he had accomplished for the Church.

My first face-to-face meeting with Archbishop Spellman came almost two and a half years after he ordained his fourth class of New York priests. The year was 1944, the month was November, and the occasion was his presence in the nation's capital for the annual Bishops' Meeting. Spellman had been asked by President Roosevelt to return home from Europe only a month before, to cut short his extended visits to military forces and with Pope Pius XII. Four months earlier (June 4) the defeat of German forces and the fall of Rome to Allied forces resulted in growing starvation and high mortality rates in the occupied Italian territories. Spellman arrived in the United States on October 16 to help with the relief problem, in time for FDR's fourth election and the 1944 Bishops' Meeting, besides.

Spellman's decision to meet with his nine student priests at the Catholic University of America came as a surprise. The suspicion, then, was that he had time on his hands and so decided to catch up with the new priests he had earlier sent on for graduate study without ever having met any of them personally.

The first impression he made that November day was that of a grand inquisitor. Asking questions, we soon discovered, was his favorite device for handling new situations. But to those trained to hold a Cardinal in awe, the staccato-like inquiries hardly made the first interview easy. Only weeks before I had returned from Florida to begin my third and last year in pursuit of a doctorate in social science. After saying hello, the remainder of the fifteen minutes was spent discussing why I chose to go to Florida. In March of that year Joseph P. Hurley, Bishop of St. Augustine, a diocese with jurisdiction over almost the entire state of Florida, invited a Los Angeles priest, Father Thomas F. Coogan, and me to organize and conduct a door-to-door census of the entire diocese. We leaped at the offer. Not only was it an opportunity to make a first-time visit to the Sunshine State, but the data collected could become the basis of a solid Ph.D. dissertation. We surmised that three months of home visitations in Florida and Washington's IBM machines would help us complete our work at the university by the summer of 1945. Hurley agreed. What made the offer especially attractive was the Bishop's decision to cancel all diocesan business for the three months, to place at our disposal all of his hundred plus priests, and to pay for the statistical computations we would need. This was a heaven-sent gift to two young priests as anxious to return to parish work as they were to become scholars.

Naturally, to engage in the project we needed permission of our respective Ordinaries. Early in May 1944, a letter to Spellman's Vicar General, Bishop J. Francis A. McIntyre, requesting such authorization brought the countersuggestion that the study be done in Harlem. The request was impossible to reject out-of-hand, especially by a youngster. It was also obvious that the New York Chancery could not provide the guarantees already made by Hurley. Furthermore, four-floor walk-ups in Harlem on a summer day would create insurmountable difficulties for priests, whereas the house-to-house visitation of one-family homes in wartime Florida might be enervating but viable. (Actually, the 1944 diocese of St. Augustine comprised only 108 parishes and 146 priests, less than half of whom were diocesan, and served, as it turned out, 50,000 permanent residents identifiable as Catholic.) When McIntyre learned that the study would cost ten thousand dollars, he gave his blessing with the advice: "Go get the experience before we try Harlem." Whether the Vicar General felt mousetrapped into saying yes, and whether he conveyed irritation to the Archbishop, is difficult to say. But it was obvious that Spellman was not pleased with the Florida sojourn, even though he was assured that the research shortened his priest's tour of duty in Washington by a year. But then again, Spellman's pique, if that is what it was, might not have been due to the project at all, but to the association of one of his priests with Bishop Hurley. Young priests did not suspect that some Bishops did not like other Bishops, and apparently Spellman did not like Hurley. The Florida Ordinary had taken his place (1932) in the Vatican's foreign service, when the then Boston prelate returned home as Auxiliary Bishop. Hurley was also a critic of Spellman's Roman performance. When Hurley, a Cleveland priest, was sent to Florida as Bishop in 1940, he became a voice overnight for American intervention in the recently declared war against Germany, some say at the urging of

Pius XII. This set him against most American Catholics, including Bishops, who were opposed to our involvement in the European war. The fall of France and the all-night raids on London, commonly called "The Blitz," brought conscription to the United States, but public opinion was still isolationist.

Hurley was seen as a maverick, and one who bad-mouthed Spellman besides. Compared with Spellman, the Florida Bishop was an insignificant force in the hierarchy, but he was young, smart, had his own Roman connections, and was a better communicator than the New Yorker. (Two years later, in 1946, Hurley became the Vatican's Apostolic Delegate to Tito's Yugoslavia.) Archbishop Spellman would have been more annoyed if he knew that, as the Florida census ended, Hurley attempted to persuade me to stay with him in Florida: "There are many opportunities in a young diocese like this," he said. This New Yorker had no interest in Florida as a permanent place of ministry, and I probably said the right thing when I told the St. Augustine Bishop: "Archbishop Spellman would not be amused."

Another tête-à-tête with Spellman would not take place for ten years. Yet that one meeting was sufficient to leave an impression that here was a "boss" who did not take kindly to being ignored. And he may have thought that was what had happened in my choice of Florida over Harlem for a census. He was not unkind but, as would become clear in time, he was ever alert to the outside entanglements of his priests with other Bishops, unless he was the prime mover.

THE FLORIDA ADVENTURE

In 1948 shortly before he was elected President in his own right, Harry Truman met at the White House with a large group of Catholic prelates and priests. After saluting the Eminences and Excellencies, he paused to end his introduction with the line: "—and just plain fathers who do all the work." He won a few votes with that one but also struck an important truth about the Church. The priests who serve where people live are the ones who keep the Church alive. And there is no better way to learn about the Church firsthand than to go among Catholic people where they live and work with priests who are never going to be bishops. And if, while a tyro, you come eye to eye with a Bishop like Joseph P. Hurley, one cut from the same cloth as the Spellman I was to discover, you enjoy a heady internship in Church ministry and Church politics. The work was sweaty but to a baby priest it was lots of fun.

Indeed, every young priest should be an apprenticed census-taker. Few are fortunate enough early in the priesthood to conduct a census of an entire diocese, as were two graduate student priests whose only real interest at the time was writing a dissertation. I later published *Catholics and the Practice of the Faith* and L.A.'s Thomas Coogan wrote *Catholic Fertility in Florida*, all based on Bishop Hurley's pioneer study of the Catholic population of Florida. His skeptical pastors said he was doing this only to collect names for a future diocesan fund-raising campaign, not for scholarship; and their suspicions were later proved to be correct. Yet the Bishop was also responding sincerely to a complaint heard at a Family Life Convention held in March 1944 that no one in the Church knew anything about the Catholic population in the United States, not even its size. The Catholic Directory reported 23,000,000 Catholics for 1940, but its recorded 550,000 infant baptisms also suggested that the real Catholic population may have been as high as 30,000,000. The point was not lost on Hurley, who that day made the decision to do a complete census of his diocese. It was a first of its kind, and perhaps the last door-to-door canvas of a diocese since then, at least one which went beyond religious statistics to study education and income levels, fertility patterns, generational comparisons, etc.

Oliver E. Baker, a prominent sociologist, who specialized in demographic studies for the U.S. Government, was particularly intrigued by the patterns of Catholic behavior revealed in the study, especially the high fertility rates and the extraordinary religious observance of Florida Catholics. Two thirds of those Catholics had been born in the Northeast and Middle West, indicating that these Catholics might have been typical of the U.S.

Church at large, which in 1944 was highly concentrated in those regions. At least, they were not "Crackers," the name Northerners gave to home-grown Floridians. Nine out of ten Florida Catholics had been married by a priest, eight out of ten attended Mass every Sunday. Their teenage sons and daughters were as regular in religious observance as their parents. Particularly significant was the fact that native-born Catholics practiced their faith better than foreign-born, the rich and better-educated Catholics, especially Catholic college graduates, were the best of all. The data also pointed up how deleterious was the effect of mixed marriage on religious observance and fertility. Religious performance was also negatively influenced when married women worked outside the home.

What especially surprised Baker were the prewar fertility patterns of Catholics. In view of the crisis that was to overtake the Church a generation later over birth control, the 1944 Florida statistics look impressive, even at this late date. Not only the high fertility generally but the fact that the upper-income and better-educated Catholics had larger families than the middle class. This was precisely the opposite of the secular American trend, where rise in education and income meant fewer children. Catholics alone in the U.S. were replacing their numbers, which probably explains why the country's Paul Blanshards began to be fearful of rising Catholic power.

The Florida census demonstrated further how far immigrant Catholics working through the Church's evangelization process had come from that day in 1840 when John Hughes, later New York's first Archbishop, bemoaned the immigrants landing on East River piers as "the offscouring of the Irish nation."

In the long run of my priestly life (Father Coogan was killed in 1947 in an auto accident), the unique nature of the study and the data themselves were less memorable than the human experience of working with a Bishop and his priests on the systematic visitation of Catholic homes in an entire diocese. Census-taking or the regular visitation of parishioners in their own homes by 1944 had fallen into desuetude in most large dioceses. Some of the better New York parishes were doing sporadic parish censuses during the 1930s, but not by priests. The Florida priests were taken by surprise, if not by shock, at Hurley's edict about a compulsory census. The prospect of a seven-day work week in the hottest season of the Florida year was hardly attractive to priests accustomed to a restful summer. The war even prevented Irish pastors from visiting relatives in their homeland.

But summer heat alone was not so much the problem as a certain resentment against the Bishop. The leader of the opposition was Msgr. William Barry, former Vicar General under his brother Patrick, Hurley's predecessor. Bill Barry, as he was called, was Msgr. Miami Beach, pastor of St. Patrick's Church, the Cathedral of lower Florida. Not only was he a handsome man, but his dynamic personality acquired him more priest friends in Florida than his brother ever had. Under the two Barrys Catholic Florida was the land of FBIs (Foreign-born Irish), where Church business was conducted on a handshake, where dispensations from impediments to marriage were granted on the telephone without special scruples about the formalities or record keeping. When Bishop Hurley, the outlander, imposed the "Roman system" on this freewheeling diocese, he encountered immediate resistance. Many pastors, and not a few curates, were prepared to stand against anything that came out of St. Augustine's Chancery under Hurley's name.

The interesting thing, in hindsight, however, is that when push came to shove, Florida priests did what the Bishop told them to do. They complained, but they took the census, a tribute to their self-discipline and to Joseph P. Hurley, Rome's episcopal choice to bring order into a disordered diocese.

Hurley was no ordinary Bishop. Though a protégé of Detroit's future Cardinal Mooney and secretary during the latter's assignments as Apostolic Delegate to India and Japan, Hurley by nature was not "second man." He was bright, creative, and an obvious leader with potential to be anything he cared to be. And his eight years as Spellman's successor in Rome were not wasted. Later, he would lose the confidence of Rome, a regrettable development since his appointment as Apostolic Delegate to Yugoslavia in 1946 suggested great promise. He performed courageously during the trial of Archbishop Stepinac, for which he was elevated to titular Archbishop in 1950, the first such honor bestowed on a Florida prelate. After his return home he was never the same, so they say. Yet, today, the seven Florida dioceses, all cutoffs of St. Augustine, owe a large part of their Church properties to this Bishop, who had the foresight to plan for the future. He bought acreage all over the state, property which would have been over-priced and perhaps unavailable by the time those dioceses were erected. In 1944 he was at his wartime best, the associate of generals and admirals. Once scheduled to appear at an official banquet at the Jacksonville Naval Station, he disappeared for the day to bone up on military history, going back in his study to the days of the Caesars. When the conversation that night turned to the recent American landings at Anzio, Hurley startled his com-panions with specific views of how best the Allied Forces might reach Rome with the least damage. At the end one general re-marked: "You would have made a great military strategist, Bishop." To which Hurley replied: "Well, had I not gone to the seminary, I would have set my eyes on West Point."

Bishop Hurley did his homework equally well whenever dioce-san interests were involved. Shortly after he was named Bishop, he traveled the length and breadth of Florida familiarizing him-self with the geography and the pastoral problems. During one stop at West Palm Beach in the off-season, he was given a Cook's tour of St. Ann's parish, then the only parish in town. All went well but, as he was about to depart, he casually said to the Jesuit pastor: "What about your mission church?" A beautiful St. Ed-ward's Church and rectory had been erected shortly before, with financial aid from the likes of Mrs. Randolph Hearst and Colonel Bradley of racetrack fame. The church was situated across the bridge in Palm Beach itself, only steps away from the ocean. Obviously, the Jesuits wanted to keep their mission. Hurley, told in advance that the mission was closed during the off-season said, "Well, let's open it." So, across the bridge they went to look at the "mission," at the end of which visit Hurley said to the Jesuit pastor: "I think we'll make this a parish and the winter residence of the Bishop."

Similar determination went into the organization and administration of the diocesan census. Assaying the opposition, he
brought his two census-takers to the annual priests' retreat at St.
Leo's Abbey immediately after D-Day. Here men only a few years
ordained faced the slings and arrows of Florida's veteran clergy.
The Bishop's motivational exhortation carried the day, and after
some testy questioning the opposition spent itself quickly. The
priests were instructed how to train their lay enumerators and
how to conduct their priestly visits to each home. Father Coogan
was sent to St. Paul's Church in Jacksonville and I to St. Mary's
Church in Miami (now the Cathedral), there to supervise the
northern and southern sections of the diocese respectively.

The parish visitations themselves were tiring but exhilarating.
Priests left their rectories at 9 A.M. In the larger parishes the
priests managed thirty house calls in a given day. Thinking back,
it is remarkable that hardly more than a hundred priests covered
a state of that size (after lay leaders identified the Catholic homes
block by block). Time has not dimmed the memory of how remarkable Hurley's accomplishment was and how intact was the
priestly discipline in a diocese many thought was unruly. But this
was not the only or the best side of that diocesan census.

Those old enough to remember the tales of great affection between old Catholics and their pastors sometimes forget that most
of the late nineteenth- to early twentieth-century priests were
street priests. The era of few rectory telephones (and none in the
homes of most churchgoers) forced priests to go out to the people.
The significance of priestly visitations to parishioners' homes
came into focus during the Florida census, when one experienced
firsthand not only what such visits meant to the people, but what
they did for priests.

One day, having driven to Hialeah without my census cards, I
was forced to return to the rectory, a twenty-minute ride away. As
I entered the empty house, the phone was ringing. An angry
voice, later discovered to be that of a French-Canadian apostate,
wanted a priest to attend his wife dying in a hospital at the south
end of Miami. The nurse could not find the neighboring priests,
because they were all out census-taking. "Why can't a pious Cath-

olic like my wife have a priest?" the angry husband asked. The wife had been badly burned when a kitchen stove using propane gas exploded. How to find an unfamiliar hospital in a strange city was only part of the problem. Administering Extreme Unction to a comatose lady in an oxygen tent, swathed with gauze from knee to brow, carron oil oozing from every cover, was the other. She was literally anointed on the seemingly raw flesh of her forehead. With the hysterical husband mumbling in French, I and a nurse continued saying the prayers for the dying. No one succeeded in soothing the savage beast that was the husband, though the remainder of the afternoon was spent trying. The doctor said the lady would not survive the night. Three months later that lady was released from the hospital without a single scar on her new baby face. She wept unashamedly and told me: "My husband Jean has returned to the sacraments last week—after thirty years. It's the miracle for which I have been praying ever since we were married." If it was a miracle, it was a fortuitous act of Providence which brought together a prayerful woman, an exploded gas tank, and a priest who did not have the sense to keep his census cards in the car.

The inexplicable ways of Providence came to the surface during another census call. This time to a twenty-nine-year-old mother whose husband was on his way overseas. Teresa, lying in bed after delivering her fourth child, was still far from recovery. She asked to receive Holy Communion, so I arrived the morning after my visit to be greeted by a twenty-two-year-old soldier (her brother) holding the traditional lighted candle. Kneeling along the walls of the hallway were her other children (aged ten, eight, and five), also holding candles. After the sacrament was received, we sat discussing her family. She told an interesting story. After the birth of her third child, a routine examination disclosed what was diagnosed as a cancerous tumor. An operation was scheduled that year for October 15, the feast of St. Teresa. Her mother visited her the evening before to say that she was completing a novena to their patroness saint, asking God to spare her young daughter for the sake of those three babies. The mother apparently asked in prayer that whatever cross in God's good reason

36

was to be borne, let it be borne by the mother, whose life was already well spent. As Teresa reached this part of the story, she began to sob. The room became very still. One hardly knew what to expect next. With tears streaming down her face, she cried: "When they opened me up they found my tumor was benign. A year later my mother died from a cancerous tumor in the same place."

The mysteries of Providence did not end even there. One day coming toward the end of a street, the visit fell to an aging Irish lady, who had lived in St. Mary's parish for twenty years. She knew everybody and everything there was to know about the parish. The census-taker usually checked his cards for each street with someone having local knowledge. Asked whether there might be Catholics on the street whom the parish leaders might have missed, she said no. But pausing, she added, "There's something suspicious about the woman in the street's corner house. She, her husband, and four children attend the local Protestant church, but when we women gab about religion on our way home from the A&P, she always seems to be familiar with 'Catholic' saints." On the basis of that suspicion, I crossed the street to be greeted by a frosty-faced matron. "You'll pardon me for intruding," was the opening gambit. "I've been visiting homes all day and I'm thirsty. Could I bother you for a glass of water?" She quickly replied, "I'm not a Catholic." To which she received as a rejoinder, "It's only water, and water is neither Catholic nor Protestant." Courteously, she moved toward the kitchen and through the door she left ajar I sidled.

The conversation was strained, mostly chitchat about New York. By this time we were both sitting down, perhaps for as much as ten minutes. Suddenly she broke into tears, then spoke, "You're the first priest I've talked to in twenty-five years." Her story gushed out: A young Boston girl found herself pregnant in 1930 by the Protestant man now her husband. Disowned by her family, she eloped to Florida to avoid a neighborhood scandal, but she was always disturbed because she had abandoned her faith. By the time the 1944 diocesan census was completed in September 1944, the couple was married by me. A year or so later she reported that her husband was even thinking of becoming a Catholic.

Visiting homes for reasons of evangelization was not all peaches and cream. This was the land of Florida Crackers, where wartime Catholics were a distrusted minority, where Bing Crosby, playing Father O'Malley in *Going My Way,* wore a Roman collar inside the state's theaters, but a tie on all the public billboards. The public had to pay for the knowledge that the movie was about a Catholic priest. Even Catholics did not like Yankee priests from the North or West preaching at them in foreign tones. Some of this alienation appeared during interviews, especially in the Latin Quarter of Tampa, called Ybor City.

During the first week of the census it was discovered that priests were not welcome in the Spanish homes. Six Mission Helpers of the Sacred Heart were brought in from Baltimore to deal with the usual insoluble problems (bad marriages mostly) or with someone's bitter experience with a priest or a teacher. These were often recounted to the census-taker in colorful language.

Two women—blood sisters—were particularly incensed, twenty-five years after one of them fell afoul of a change in the Church's marriage legislation. The 1907 decree called *Ne Temere* required, for the first time in the United States, that marriage before a priest was necessary for Catholic validity. Up to this time a Catholic married by a justice or by a minister was considered by the Church to be validly married. The United States was considered a missionary country, so universal Church law did not apply, that is until 1908. These two sisters, separated by three or four years in age, married on both sides of that dividing line. Both marriages ended in divorce. The younger sister, having married outside the Church after 1908, was free to remarry in the Church; the older sister was not. Their fury at the Church survived two wars and one diocesan census. Neither sister saw anything divine about being trapped by the Church's sense of timing. However, at the end of a long visit, they acknowledged the humanness of Church Law, which cannot take into account the gains and losses falling on people merely because they are born on a certain day or are married in a certain year. For more than ten years thereafter they sent me Christmas cards, that is, until they both went to their eternal rewards and *with* the sacraments.

In the early years of his episcopate, Bishop Hurley believed that things should be done well or at least done the way he said. Not once during the four months of census-taking did he bother with the details of what was going on all over the diocese. The census directors reported regularly to Father Thomas McDonough, later Archbishop of Louisville. Hurley presumed things were going according to plan. In late September 1944, at the very end, he was told that two pastors, one in Miami, an Irish contemporary of Cardinal Spellman's Roman days, the other a Jesuit in Tampa, refused to take the parish census. Before the month was out, Hurley rode down Florida's East Coast picking up young curates wherever he could, and then up the West Coast doing the same. Into each rectory he marched with an appropriate number of healthy priests to inform the pastor, "You are assigned these curates for two weeks. If the census is not completed by then, I will remove you from the parish." In both places and within the time allotted the census was completed.

When our work in Florida was done Father Coogan and I returned to Catholic University to tabulate our findings, write our books, take our doctoral diplomas, and return home. Neither of us ever had dealings with Bishop Hurley again.

NEW YORK PRIEST

Return to New York in 1945 from Catholic University for a parish assignment would have been less than memorable except for a few twists of fate. Bishop McIntyre denied me permission to remain for the summer to finish the dissertation, a recognized risk since some graduate students, once home and engrossed in local ministries, never completed their dissertations. Though Vicar General McIntyre said no by letter, Chancellor Edward Gaffney by telephone said, "Stay until the book is finished," implying he would be my angel guardian from the Vicar General's wrath. The delay amounted to a month, no more. On July 4 two priests departed CUA, I going to New York for a parish assignment, John Tracy Ellis to Baltimore to explore the life secrets of James Cardinal Gibbons. Despite the twelve years difference in our ages, we had become close friends, although at the time he was somewhat alarmed at my addiction to the New Deal. FDR had died only a short time before, providing Ellis with the opportunity to counsel me to keep an open mind on the dead President's defects. The Church historian was furious over the U.S. "giveaway" of Poland to the USSR at Yalta.

At this juncture, Msgr. Gaffney, protector of priests from diocesan ogres, reentered the picture. During those years (and after McIntyre's departure for Los Angeles) he symbolized the administrative flexibility within the Spellman operation. Later the *National Catholic Reporter* "exposed" alleged institutional cruelty at the hands of people like Spellman, its post-Vatican II paradigm of the ecclesiastical bully. This was a myth fed to the hinterland by malcontents within the "Big Apple," some of whom later left or degraded the priesthood.

The real New York Archdiocese under Spelly was something else. Gaffney explained to me that the Ph.D. was qualification for an assignment to Catholic Charities, where a director for Youth Counseling Services was needed. Hayes High School was also in the market for a Dean of Social Studies. Very early in his administration Spellman sought to lure priests into volunteering to teach in Hayes High School, only to be told by the older among them that they had not become priests to teach in a school. The new Archbishop reacted to the rebuff by turning to his younger men, so that when Hayes opened in 1941, the first faculty comprised forty-five priests, forty-five brothers, and one layman, an athletic director. To the Chancellor's offer of those several options, my answer was a simple: "Whatever you think." Gaffney thought a parish assignment was in order, suggesting first my home parish, Our Lady of Good Counsel on East Ninetieth Street. That struck me as a bad idea, since my father was one of the parish trustees there. On October 20, 1945, Spellman assigned me to St. Monica's parish on East Seventy-ninth Street, within walking distance of my parents, my home near home for the next eleven years. It would not take long to discover that New York was basically a "laissez-faire" Church. The Archbishop presumed that parishes ran effectively without his interference. A parish priest came to his attention only if he did something special or something wrong.

Several months later (1946), on a visit with John Tracy Ellis to New Rochelle College, the Dean, Mother Ignatius, offered me a part-time position as a lecturer in social science. The pastor approved the idea, but Bishop McIntyre demurred. He had something else in store for me, he said. Actually, once notified of the New Rochelle opening, the Bishop called Mother Ignatius to say he had someone else in mind for that post, a priest stationed at St. Patrick's Cathedral. The Dean was properly agitated at the Vicar General's interference, but took the change of plans in good grace. McIntyre's choice proved to be a good lecturer. In hindsight, however, the pass-over turned out to be a blessing for me. However attractive the academic post appeared at the time, it would have been a distraction. The next fifteen years of parish work were to have an enriching effect on my life. Besides providing a network of friends that would last a lifetime, parish life brought a down-to-earth view of the Church and experience in motivating people to live their faith better. Making the most of what the Bishops assigned one to was a learning experience in obedience. The Church lives on obedience.

In 1948, Father John S. Randall, editor of Rochester's *Courier-Journal,* telephoned St. Monica's looking for a popular analysis of the Taft-Hartley Law to be used in the country's labor schools. The law had been vetoed by President Truman earlier on June 20, 1947. This commentary, once completed, was sent to the New York censor as *A Primer on the Taft-Hartley Law* for the usual *imprimatur;* but it was discovered that the book did not need one. The censor, Msgr. John M. Fearns, suggested that the Bishop's permission to publish was still necessary. The request went, routinely, to Bishop McIntyre, who turned the manuscript over to the diocesan moral theologian, Msgr. Frank Murphy, at the time secretary to Cardinal Spellman. Murphy telephoned from the Cardinal's residence to say there was no reason for delaying the publication. Still, because McIntyre did not wish the Archdiocese to be identified with the pro-union views of the book, he delayed publication three months. His personal and diocesan contributions to ACTU and to Dorothy Day's *Catholic Worker* were well known, but his judgments about what was permissible to priests in the public forum were tightly drawn. No one questioned his right to supervise the public activity of clergy and religious, since this is what Bishops were supposed to do.

What became a problem was his narrow view of what was permissively Catholic. On one occasion, he called theologian William R. O'Connor to a meeting with officials of the National Conference of Christians and Jews, ostensibly to uphold New York's ban on participation by priests in the activities of that organization. To the Vicar General's surprise, Father O'Connor used Rome's latest instructions on intercredal cooperation to favor such participation. From that moment in 1947 on, the Archdiocese officially cooperated with the NCCJ, usually through the Secretary for Education. But left to himself McIntyre would have sought a more cautious role for clergy in public affairs.

Spellman's view of priestly activity was much broader than McIntyre's, perhaps because "the Little Man" liked public involvement himself. People went over McIntyre's head to "the boss" on occasion and found him willing to overrule his Vicar General. On the other hand, McIntyre lived in "452," the Cardinal's House. Across-the-breakfast-table conversation between the two often settled diocesan policy early in the morning. Years later, the Los Angeles Cardinal, still sure of himself, boasted that had he remained in New York, Spellman would never have drowned himself in hot water over cemetery workers or Mrs. Roosevelt. McIntyre was probably right. His conservative public instincts would have restrained Spelly's impetuosity.

The vaunted "powerhouse" numbered 452 Madison Avenue never meant a great deal to parish priests. Chancery officials who worked across the street thought differently. But pastors and curates out on the fringes were usually on their own. New York-haters frequently resent New York just for being itself, and they do not understand why Spellman was well respected by his own, even liked after a fashion. The words "after a fashion" take into account Spellman's reserve. In spite of his world travels, the Cardinal visited more parishes, more schools, and attended more boring dinners than the average Bishop anywhere. On or offstage, he was gracious and available, a people-toucher but Yankee-style. The boyish grin, the stumbling tongue, which annoyed media, merely ingratiated him to churchgoers. When he came to the people, he often brought with him a few goodies—a subsidy for the institution, a papal medal for a layman, a monsignorship for the pastor, or a new diocesan post for a curate. On those hegiras around the Archdiocese, he discovered many a young Chancery official. So he did make many friends.

On October 24, 1954, the Cardinal came to St. Monica's parish for its seventy-fifth anniversary. Rumor had it that I was still in Spelly's "doghouse" because of the Calvary strike, which is treated at length later in this chapter. You would never have known it that day. The aging pastor was not up to par, so the "doghouse" priest celebrated the Solemn Mass and supervised the luncheon which followed. Thousands of longtime parishioners and old-timers crowded the Church before Mass and the streets afterward. During the luncheon Spellman managed to leaf through my *Story of St. Monica's Parish,* a book which traced the Church's growth on the East Side through five Archbishops and fifteen mayors. Walking back to his car that afternoon, the Cardinal was friendly yet typically pointed out some errors in the book. With an impish grin, he told me the word "fiscal" was misused. A priest friend standing nearby said to me: "I think you have risen from the dead." Eleven months later—on September 17, 1955, the Cardinal appointed the "doghouse" priest the Archdiocese's first Family Life Director.

The journey, however, from Seventy-ninth Street to Fifty-first Street was not as simple as the mere announcement made it out to be. It never occurred to anyone in 1954 that my assignment at St. Monica's would end the way it did. Two years earlier (1952) Paul Hanly Furfey invited his former student to teach three summer courses at the Catholic University of America, a request which called for the Cardinal's permission. CUA had been a delightful place to be a graduate student, but after seven years in parish life, campus life as professor turned out to be a bore. The chitchat of CUA professors in Curley Hall was less than scintillating, sometimes petty as it often is in large institutional settings, and remote from the Catholic world where people lived. Rising from the Caldwell Hall Chapel that first summer Sunday morning was not exactly exciting for a priest whose Sundays were the most exhilarating day of the week, the day when three priests met their thirty-five hundred churchgoers face to face. And if one were lucky enough to be in a family parish like St. Monica's, the feeling was good, indeed. At the end of August 1952, it was a pleasure to return from CUA to East Seventy-ninth Street.

Eight years later, the Vicar General Bishop John Maguire told the story of how that summer teaching assignment really came to be. My original letter to Spellman seeking permission to take Furfey's offer brought a return note from Maguire asking me to visit him. He was only a name to most priests at the time (his popularity came later), but proved himself to be a formidable questioner in his own right. Why did I want to go to CUA? What would I teach? Toward the end of the conversation, "Suppose you can't go?" My answer was equally direct: "Whether I go or not is not a necessity. The offer looks like a good change of pace for a parish priest, a chance to get back to the books. But, no sweat, I'm quite content where I am." At this point Maguire said: "Okay, go." So this young curate got another crack at academia, explaining to graduate students how the new McCarran-Walter Law worked and hearing Adlai Stevenson give one of the finest acceptance speeches ever given at a presidential nominating convention. But on a January Sunday night in 1960, minutes after Spellman had made me a "little" monsignor, Maguire told me that in 1952 Spellman had tossed him my letter about Catholic University with this directive, "Call that man in and tell him he can't go." Apparently, the Calvary strike "doghouse" really existed. But Spellman's Chancery Office had none. Maguire did not believe that ACTU chaplains should be made scapegoats for that strike, so he overruled Spellman and let me accept the Furfey invitation. The permission spoke reams about John Maguire, then not yet twenty-five years a priest. It also said something for the latitude Spellman allowed his Vicar.

Before that CUA summer ended, Msgr. Maguire asked me how the Archdiocese could go about doing a survey of the Puerto Rican population, then emigrating to New York at the net rate of fifty thousand per year. The study which he appointed me to direct began in September 1952 and was completed by the spring of 1953 in a report entitled, *The Puerto Rican Population in the Archdiocese of New York 1953*. One by-product of my involvement was an increasing number of Hispanic meetings, whenever Puerto Rican leaders sought contact with the Archdiocese. This was an impossible situation given the time-consuming duties of a full-time curate. More importantly, the Puerto Rican leadership, which deserved better from the Archdiocese, should have been dealing with a status ecclesiastic. The problem was explained to Father Thomas Donnellan, later the Archbishop of Atlanta, out of which discussion came the name of Msgr. Joseph F. Connolly, who at the moment was awaiting assignment after a stint in Beirut for the Catholic Near East Welfare Association. He was tapped in 1953 for the first major appointment of its kind in the United States—Coordinator of Spanish Catholic Action.

During the Puerto Rico survey, there was no need for me to deal directly with the Cardinal. As the data unfolded he reacted only once, the day he marched across Madison Avenue, annoyed at the finding that no diocesan priest spoke or was learning to speak Spanish. When finalized, the report brought no reaction from him one way or another. The lead in sending young priests to Puerto Rico for special tutoring in Spanish culture and language was assumed by Maguire. More immediately, the report was responsible for bringing official recognition to the Spanish presence in New York. Msgr. Connolly inaugurated the annual parade and rally up Fifth Avenue on the Feast of San Juan Baptista (June 24, 1954). It was not much, but at the time it was a valuable symbol of Catholic interest in New York's most recent immigrants.

The next and almost immediate contact with the "powerhouse" came through the intervention in my life of the Colombian ambassador to the Holy See, who invited me on a Saturday in 1953 to a Waldorf-Astoria lunch. There he suggested that the Cardinal Archbishop of Bogotá was about to ask Spellman to release me for an appointment as Rector of the Catholic University of Bogotá. (The two had been made Cardinals together in 1946.) When I showed no interest, the ambassador intimated that Spellman had already consented to Bogotá's choice of any New York priest. The Archbishop of Bogotá must have misunderstood, I explained; New York's Cardinal would never send an unwilling priest to Bogotá. The ambassador ended our meeting abruptly, leaving the impression that the matter was still open. I walked the one block to the Chancery Office to tell Father Tom Donnellan, the Vice-Chancellor, that any request of this kind was to be rejected, because I would not be party to it. Nothing happened after that conversation and the incident was quickly forgotten. Seventeen years later, as the newly inducted Secretary for Education, I was sitting at one end of the Cardinal's luncheon table, when a question directed to Spellman mentioned Bogotá's Cardinal. Suddenly, as if reacting to something that happened the day before, Spellman turned in my direction and said: "That's the fellow who wanted you for Bogotá." It was a classic example of his remarkable recall. And of how little concerning his vital interests escaped him.

PRIESTS IN LABOR

No parish priest in my lifetime wore one hat, if he happened to be a friend of John Patrick Monaghan, Staten Island pastor, Fordham University professor, and founder of the Association of Catholic Trade Unionists. "My God, man," he was likely to yell, "no one under forty is entitled to be tired," if you dared try to get out from under one of his fiery demands. "The poor need you, and not just those in your parish," was enough to cow the most overworked curate. This explains how some of us ended up as associate chaplains to his ACTU.

And while ACTU was hardly a priority interest of New York's

famous Archbishop, "labor priests" would prove to be an ongoing source of discomfort to him in the early years of his administration.

The Association of Catholic Trade Unionists was born February 27, 1937, in the home of Dorothy Day's *Catholic Worker*. Eleven laymen and Father Monaghan met to provide the Church with a new dimension. Martin Wersing, Edward Scully, Roger Larkin, John Cort, and George Donohue were among the workingmen in those depression years who achieved prominence in Catholic circles for their labor activity. While ACTU always remained a laymen's organization, it was "Doc" Monaghan, as he was called, who lit the fire that sparked this little local group of activists into a national Catholic force. ACTU grew to be a national organization with nine chapters: in New York, Brooklyn, Boston, Chicago, Detroit, Gary, San Francisco, Pittsburgh, and Bayonne. Their two best-known newspapers were New York's *Labor Leader* and Detroit's *Wage Earner*. The Chicago chapter broke away later to establish a new organization called the Catholic Labor Alliance, with a new newspaper called *Work*.

ACTU began as a study group and ended up as a partisan defender of rank-and-file workers. It appeared first on the downtown campus of Fordham University with a labor school, not far from the famed Woolworth building, the first of such schools that were to spread across the nation. The unique thing about these schools was the appearance in classrooms of painters discussing Terence Powderly, of steam fitters instructing peers on how to speak up at union meetings, and of laundry workers giving a course on labor ethics.

ACTU's founders were firmly convinced that the labor union was vital to worker well-being. The economic conditions of 1937 are hard to recapture so as to be meaningful to a 1989 audience. Forty dollars a week was good pay for the father of a family, and beginners' pay in many nonunion occupations, even when jobs were available, amounted to forty cents an hour. The cushions against job loss or major illness to the family breadwinner were few. Most industrial leaders were antiunion and American business was largely unorganized. ACTU's founding fathers saw their

Church by its inaction in the public forum standing, as it were, alien to the worker's need for a living wage and for job security. Not only did they want the Church to assume responsibility for spreading the good news of her social teaching, but they hoped to see Catholics use their influence on the side of justice, to help workers organize good unions, to help them clean up unions riddled with racketeers and Communists. Even as ACTU was coming off the drawing board, its pioneers immediately threw themselves into a strike against the Woolworth's Five and Ten stores. Barbara Hutton was charitable to a fault, but ACTU following Pius XI opposed her workers receiving in alms what was their due in social justice.

Pius XI's *Quadragesimo Anno* (1931) became the ACTU's bible. The Pope, who had said, "Go to the poor," who defended unions and profit sharing, also wrote a prescription for Catholic trade union leaders:

> Side by side with these unions there should be associations zealously engaged in imbuing and forming their members in the teaching of religion and morality so that they in turn may be able to permeate the unions with that good spirit which should direct all their activity.[1]

With this as its charter ACTU began to raise the knowledge level of ordinary workers, first by giving uninitiated workers a sense of their own past and a wider knowledge of the economic realities of their time; then, by teaching parliamentary procedures and rules through which they could make or keep their union democratic; and finally, through courses on labor ethics to enlarge their understanding of Catholic social doctrine and its moral principles. If they were to make sound judgments concerning the proper conduct of both, they needed to know more than what they learned in catechism class. And since knowledge of itself did not solve problems in the industrial jungle where they worked, ACTU went one step further. A Labor Defense League, comprised entirely of lawyers, assisted small unions in defending themselves against employers and supported union members against the racketeers and Communists in control of their unions.

Those were the days before civil rights organizations and government watchdog committees. It was not an uncommon event for rank-and-file complainers to find their heads bashed in or their stomachs ripped open by a stevedore's hook if they tried to overturn an election or remove an established union leader. Muscular unionism was so in command of certain industries, shipping and building especially, that ACTU found itself fighting union leaders as often as it confronted employers. If racketeers did not intimidate idealistic social reformers, Communists and fellow travelers did. During the depression, the Red penetration of electrical workers, of transport workers, of seamen and longshoremen was serious. Not until the late 1940s, with prosperity well on its way and a successful war behind, did the American trade union movement purge itself of leading Soviet loyalists.

So, early in its career ACTU discovered that, while "thieves" in Horn and Hardart cheated underpaid cooks and waitresses with low wages, "thieves" also roamed the longshoremen's and teamsters' unions. Helping workingmen see the importance of good wages through trade unionism became only one plank of ACTU's platform. Labor schools might enlighten the depression poor about their rights under law, but securing those rights from employers or trade union gangsters was another story, indeed.

The simple faith and the goodness of those early ACTU lay leaders is memorable. Most of them were daily communicants with their Christian priorities in good order. Ten years after their initiation as social actionists, John Cort could still say, "It is only through reforming individuals that we can reform institutions."[2] This was the ACTU secret. Good people were needed to make good institutions and to keep them good. Hand in hand with the programs of social reform went ACTU's religious and moral formation, which itself was fairly simple: Workers had the right to a steady job, to a wage sufficient to support their families in decent comfort, to collective bargaining through representatives of their own, freely chosen, to share in profits where feasible, to strike and picket peacefully for a just cause, to humanitarian working conditions, and to a just price for the goods they bought. In return, the ACTU expected workers to give employers a full day's work, to respect their property, to abide by union agreements, to strike only as a last resort, to refrain from violence; and to worship God. If ACTU was looking for a new type of employer in the 1940s, it was also hoping that enlightened workers would give birth to a new type of labor leader.

Yet it was not the programs so much as the quality of the lay activists that made ACTU an influence on the local labor market, men and women who labored on their own time for workers they did not know, some of whom they did not even like. In Chicago and Detroit Ed Marciniak and Paul Weber were better known than most priests, perhaps because they edited papers. In Detroit and Pittsburgh, priests like Father Raymond Clancy and Father Charles Owen Rice quickly attracted a public following. But, as it was supposed to be from the beginning, it was the local lay leadership who made people sit up and take notice that the Catholics finally were taking their Pope's social encyclicals seriously.

In New York City, where ACTU began, the laymen and their priest chaplains were quite numerous, but rarely noticed, in the larger world of Gotham, not even by the Church. In the center of the ACTU circle stood John Patrick Monaghan, all five foot five looking mighty big. If lawyers were the ACTU's brains and trade unionists its brawn, Father Monaghan was the soul and the humor. This Irish far-downer was a master at coining a phrase, and equally adept at keeping his protégés in their place, even as he inspired them to do what many thought they could not do. He told members of the Labor Defense League that the health of any labor situation could be measured inversely by the number of lawyers at the negotiating table. More lawyers made things worse. Cajoling his Midland Beach parishioners (most of whom in 1939 were Italian and on welfare) to clean up the mess that was their streets, he said: "Slums are not places; they're people."

When Spellman expressed outrage to Monaghan over the incarceration of Archbishop Alois Stepinac by Yugoslavia's Marshal Tito in 1946, Monaghan rejoined by telling his Ordinary that the spiritual life of the Church was never better than when Bishops were in jail. In August 1943 Monaghan met his friend Bishop Bryan J. McEntegart in Grand Central Station. McEntegart, newly consecrated, was on his way upstate to take possession of the Diocese of Ogdensburg: "Bryan," Monaghan said, "in six months you'll find yourself surrounded by so many sycophants that you'll never find the truth about anything, even if you try."

The same flip and funny Monaghan was nonetheless the common man's uncommon spokesman, and a good pop psychologist besides. This side of his character appeared whenever he dealt with people's serious problems or when he spoke for the Church. Why did he get involved in labor's problems? Because people asked his help. As a professor at Fordham University he was in touch with intellectual currents but, literary though he was, Father Monaghan never ceased being an involved parish priest, the role which taught him about social problems long before he founded ACTU. Much to the consternation of English teachers, he insisted you could not teach people anything until you first learned them. Monaghan the teacher knew his boys and he taught them to think as well as to know. To answer his questions they might have to read Ralph Waldo Emerson or Lord Acton and, under penalty of failing his course, satisfactorily explain why an "institution is the lengthened shadow of a man" or why "absolute power tends to corrupt absolutely." Two years before ACTU, he led his eighteen-year-old pupils into the mystery of Norman Thomas' latest book, *Human Exploitation in the United States.* It was with the "Doc" that young aspirants to the priesthood were exposed to a kind of poverty that they, as poor sons of poor immigrants, never had to face personally.

Father Monaghan, himself a worker, had an Irish farmer's love of work. A man's job was his life, he told us, the most important thing in the world if he was poor. He wanted a worker's mind and muscle recognized as being no less important to economic prosperity than the money of investors or the moxie of entrepreneurs. What concerned him most, however, was the fact that the minds of workers were seldom molded with the ideas of Christ. In his view the two enemies of the working class were pragmatism and Marxism, both of which had infiltrated the AFL and the CIO as readily as the Chamber of Commerce. He said once: "Pragmatism is very pious looking and is frequently found at Communion

Breakfasts. Marxism is anti-Christ, the enemy of Labor and America."

So this labor priest (a title he did not like) went to workers on behalf of the Church. He saw the wages of workers as the real wealth of the Church, the foundation supporting our novitiates, our parishes, our hospitals, and our homes. While neither Leo XIII nor Pius XI ever approved trade unions as ends in themselves, Monaghan was disappointed that the Church's apostolate to the worker was still so immature that its record of involvement could be written on less than a page.

It was Father Monaghan who persuaded Cardinal Hayes to endorse the newly formed Association of Catholic Trade Unionists. The Cardinal of Charity could hardly do otherwise, although Monaghan brought Msgr. John A. Ryan up from Washington to be his final persuader. Ryan had written the 1919 Bishops' *Program of Social Reconstruction,* of which a younger Hayes had been cosigner. But ACTU's daily fortunes rested on the good will of Msgr. J. Francis A. McIntyre, Hayes's Chancellor, later Spellman's Bishop-Vicar General and ultimately the Cardinal Archbishop of Los Angeles. McIntyre was never comfortable with trade unionism, but because of Monaghan accepted it as a legitimate Catholic interest. If the Pope endorsed unions, who was he to fight them, although temperamentally he was disposed to try.

Monaghan taught most of his disciples to respect McIntyre ("His bark is not his bite."), to stand up to him when necessary but with respect ("He'll never agree with you but he may surprise you by doing what you want or even by changing his mind."). Asked later what Archbishop Spellman saw in McIntyre, Monaghan replied: "Absolute loyalty. If Spelly asked him to stand on his head in the Cathedral, Frank would do it—with dignity." McIntyre supported ACTU as regularly as he supported Dorothy Day's *Catholic Worker.* When Monaghan heard that McIntyre was going to Los Angeles, he said to a friend: "My God, he'll scare every Irish pastor on the West Coast." He probably did, much to the advantage of the West Coast. While still in New York, however, he also tried to scare or at least keep young priests in their place. In 1947 New York's ACTU priests learned they were in trouble with the Chancery Office because its lay activists supported a strike of Wall Street clerks against Stock Exchange bosses; smack in the middle of a 1947 Catholic Charities campaign for their contributions. The next year (1948) McIntyre telephoned St. Monica's rectory to find out if I would represent the Archdiocese that night at a meeting of two thousand striking telephone workers. "Our girls," he said. Advised that I might not say what the Bishop would say if he were representing the Archdiocese, McIntyre retorted: "I don't care what you say. They tell me some Jesuit from Brooklyn [Father William Smith] is going to appear there, and if anyone is going to get credit for being on the side of the workers, it isn't going to be a Jesuit from Brooklyn." When years later that event was recalled for the retired Cardinal, McIntyre laughed and said: "Don't tell that story in Los Angeles. I'm in trouble enough."

These small experiences are instances of how older Catholic actionists, lay and clergy, fared in New York. ACTU was a risky enterprise and there were no built-in guarantees of propriety or success. Even though its people always showed proper respect for the authority of Bishops, ACTU leadership never sought advance permission from its chaplains when it lent support to controversial causes. Father Monaghan insisted that Bishops could not be expected to give a blank check to untried or debatable organizations. He also recognized the legitimate freedom of lay apostles to act on their own initiative in favor of what they perceived as a sound Catholic interest. (Clergy and religious, he knew, as officers of the Church had an entirely different set of obligations from their religious superiors. Like public officials they were subject to the public law of the Church.) Free exercise of Christian responsibility also liberated Bishops of blame for blunders or offensive actions by overzealous or irresponsible activists. Church authority was free thereby to disown the activists or legitimize the cause, as circumstances warranted. In 1946, for example, when the newly created Cardinal Lercaro, the Italian prelate whose reputation in postwar Italy as a "workers' priest" brought him worldwide fame, inquired of McIntyre what the Archdiocese was doing for the workers, the Bishop proudly pointed to ACTU, to a seminary course on labor economics, and to a weekly column "A Look at Labor" by A. C. Tuohy in the *Catholic News*, activities which up to that moment existed without official endorsement. The latter two projects, courtesy of Father Monaghan, were my babies.

The Association of Catholic Trade Unionists enjoyed both friends and enemies. Godfrey Schmidt, the lawyer for the Archdiocese, categorized those enemies during the Calvary strike as follows: "The greatest opposition to the activities of the ACTU comes from within the household of the faith, the hierarchy, the clergy, and a large segment of the laity; . . . Another group of persons violently opposed to the activities of ACTU is made up of the thieves, racketeers, reactionaries and autocrats that constitute a large part of the hierarchy of the AFL. ACTU is a threat to their security and power." *(Catholic News)*. Schmidt oversimplified, of course, but he did point to two main sources of complaint against activities like ACTU's: (1) establishments which are subject to strikes and boycotts; (2) establishments which are corrupt or oppressive.

Strikes surely disrupt public equanimity, sometimes the public order. Immediately after World War II regional and nationwide strikes were called to secure good wages, good working conditions, or some form of social insurance against sickness and old age. These big strikes had popular support and few needed ACTU's support, save in cities like Detroit and Pittsburgh, where the auto and steel unions were fighting the corporations which dominated the local economy. ACTU support, therefore, was given to particular strikes, usually at local rug factories and department stores. Opposition to strikes surfaced through right-to-work laws and opposition to the unionization of government workers. Prior to the war, activist unions of public workers were almost unthinkable. So "sacred" was the concept "government," that laws against government unions with the right to strike or to a closed shop were increasingly looked upon with favor.

Congress passed the Ball-Russell-Wherry rider to several appropriation bills in 1946, which provided that no government money would pay the salary or wages of any person who engaged in a strike against the federal government or who belonged to a union which advocated such a strike. In April 1947 Governor Thomas Dewey signed the Condon-Wadlin law, which outlawed all strikes by public workers in New York. By this time there were as many strikes in private industry in a given year as there had been of government workers over a century.

Public hostility against strikes by civil servants was occasionally engendered by lurid headlines and by the specter of cities in flames or of citywide epidemics. To bolster his approval of the Condon-Wadlin bill, Governor Dewey raised the bogey of strikes by policemen and hospital staffs. Yet, the right to strike was seen by most Americans as a human right to reject proposed conditions of work. ACTU opposed the Condon-Wadlin law on the principle that striking per se is neither intrinsically good or bad. Purpose and circumstance determined its rightness or wrongness. Others assumed that the evils attendant on strikes by public workers were so great that no cause was sufficient to justify them. However, the harm done to public order depended largely on what society conceived to be a function of government. Factually, government role-playing had gone beyond anything conceived by the Founding Fathers. In 1947 public officials (1) enforced laws concerning the order, security, and peace of society and the rights of legislators, judges, police, etc.; (2) performed public services which private groups did not supply, e.g., waterworks or railroads, hospitals, schools, etc.; (3) provided nonessential public services in parks, museums, libraries, etc.; and (4) sometimes engaged in profit-making industry, e.g., lotteries.

The further the worker was removed from essential government role-playing, the less justification there was to limit his right to strike. Condon-Wadlin made no such distinctions. However, the growing political power of public unions and the general irreverence of citizens toward government made restrictive laws unenforceable and generally a dead letter. Government workers flouting public order was one indication that legislation was meaningless without civic virtue.

THE CALVARY STRIKE

On January 13, 1949, 240 employees of Calvary Cemetery, a diocesan enterprise, walked off their jobs. This became the most embarrassing eight-week period in the twenty-seven-year tenure of Cardinal Spellman. A powerful ecclesiastic in confrontation with ditch-diggers was just what the media needed to make Spellman the ogre many of them thought him to be. Many of the cemetery workers, all men, were Catholic immigrants, earning little more than a dollar and a quarter an hour. Even though Spellman was considered a master diplomat in sensitive matters of Church and state, this was bad public relations of its very nature.

Three years before (1946), Cardinal Spellman had recognized the union of his cemetery workers, a breakthrough of its kind because nonprofit organizations like St. Patrick's Cathedral's Trustees, the real cemetery owners, were exempt from the requirements of New York State labor laws. However, labor relations in Calvary were strained from the very beginning, a result of forces that were not purely economic. Wages were not great—less than sixty dollars for a forty-eight-hour week—but they were in reasonable line with average pay for similar work. What made the men unhappy was the six-day week (considered necessary by management because people died every day and because no burials were held on Sunday). Management was also insensitive to the sometimes hazardous difficulties of grave-digging. One parishioner of Yorkville's St. Monica's parish, Patrick Sullivan by name, was felled by a tombstone while digging a grave. He suffered a permanent spinal injury and for more than a year was unable to do any work at all. Sullivan eventually used up all of his earned and unemployment income, but was capable of doing light work. Calvary Cemetery, while sympathetic, was unwilling to make room for him in one of its "soft" jobs, even though he had given twenty years of his life to the work. After a year of attempted mediation, I appealed over the head of the cemetery director to Msgr. Edward Gaffney, the New York Chancellor, who saw that the injured employee was restored to his job on a limited basis until his retirement. Unfair labor practices like this, when multiplied, only increased dissatisfaction in the ranks of simple but hard-working cemetery workers.

Another complicating factor was the decision of the United Cemetery Workers to affiliate with the Food, Tobacco, Agriculture and Allied Workers. This CIO union was seen as Communist-dominated, a difficult charge to prove at any time. Quite evident, however, was the fact that its officers gave diocesan leaders a hard time. They certainly did not approach "burying the dead" as a corporal work of mercy. They demanded a 30 percent increase in pay, and when they received no for an answer, they went on strike in mid-January 1949, less than two weeks after the expiration of the previous contract.

The strike and its aftermath can be explained only by inexperience and false expectations on both sides. It was settled by an 8 percent increase with the five-day week sent to arbitration. The postwar ambitions of the working class were eminently proper, especially their desire for a good living and decent working conditions. "Commies," prevalent in many CIO unions, were agitators by definition and at work stirring the cemetery workers beyond their normal boiling point. The union lawyer publicly complained that it was more important to pay a just wage than to bury the dead, hardly the best form of dialogue with a religious leader.

What nettled Spellman more than anything else was the charge, played to a drumbeat by the priest cemetery director, that his Catholic cemeteries were held hostage by Commies. The Cold War mentality of the time is difficult to recapture, but it existed. President Truman and his FBI director, J. Edgar Hoover, were its chief warriors, but Spellman was not far behind. His anti-communism had been fired five years earlier by his annoyance with FDR's failure to take stronger action against Stalin in Eastern Europe. The North-South Korean tensions were also beginning to boil, as Spellman knew from his military travels. In his hatred of the "Red Menace," he wanted his men out of that CIO union, and in the end the settlement involved the workers' shift to the AFL's

Building Service Union. President David Sullivan of BSU later claimed that the strike would not have occurred had there been "responsible union leadership." Maybe, maybe not. The Cardinal had a long-standing friendship with AFL leaders. He dealt with them regularly during his many building projects, which often involved an outlay of $50 million in a given year.

The "Commie" question in New York cemeteries was intertwined with efforts elsewhere to clean Communists and fellow travelers from the CIO. Philip Murray, CIO's national president, had recently expelled from the national federation several of his Communist-dominated unions. J. Edgar Hoover was vigorous in his surveillance of suspected unions, including the bugging of a meeting of cemetery workers. Spellman heard himself denounced in colorful terms, with disbelief that such language would be used by Catholics describing their Bishop. The FBI helped reinforce his conviction that here truly the Archdiocese was dealing with a radical fringe. But this time Spellman's tendency to support his staff led him into one of his worst decisions.

The role of the Association of Catholic Trade Unionists in the strike also infuriated the Cardinal. ACTU was involved in the strike from the very beginning. The cemetery workers' lawyer was an ACTU member. There were ACTU signs on the picket lines. ACTU chaplains, of which there were many, and all Spellman's priests, supported the strike, although not publicly. What seems strange in hindsight is why Spelly did not seek enlightenment from them or why they on their own did not pursue more vigorously a meeting with the Cardinal. But then, Spellman was not close to those priests and his fury almost made discussion a waste of time.

Once aroused, Cardinal Spellman was a formidable foe. Not only was his judgment on the line but his person, even to the extent of him dealing on a one-to-one basis with the workers, and later with their wives. Perhaps he thought he would charm them or gain an advantage from the respect they obviously held for him. But he lost. The men rejected his offer (183–0). Then the Cardinal undertook a bold but most controversial step. When he found that a thousand bodies were stored in cemetery vaults, he decided to bring in his Dunwoodie seminarians (Maryknoll Brothers also helped), then well over two hundred in number. He convoked a meeting of diocesan consultors for advance discussion of the move, but the meeting turned out to be a *pro forma* performance. Any consultor who advised caution or delay was brushed aside. Newsreels of ditch-digging seminarians subsequently made their way throughout Europe, then digging out of the wartime rubble, making the strike a great propaganda foil for the very Communist agitators Spellman thought he was burying in a Calvary plot. The Cardinal's second mistake only made the situation worse.

By and large diocesan parish priests were untouched by the strike or by the tensions Spellman managed to create. Not so the environs of Madison Avenue, St. Patrick's Cathedral, or Dunwoodie Seminary. In these diocesan centers no one dared criticize the strike. A. C. Tuohy's column, "A Look at Labor" (which I wrote) for the *Catholic News* infuriated the Cardinal because it defended the right of workers in nonprofit occupations to organize unions and bargain collectively. The column was read at the strike meeting held in Cathedral High School and was reported to Spellman. Subsequently, the column was dropped by the diocesan newspaper, as was my course on labor economics at Dunwoodie. Later, several seminary professors received new assignments, and a few others remained in the Cardinal's "doghouse" for many years.

Three months after the strike ended, Spellman went to the three annual priests' retreats at the Dunwoodie Seminary, there to tongue-lash the priests who were disloyal to him during the Calvary strike. It was the only time he ever did this kind of thing to his priests. Those priests heard the message, but the Cardinal walked out of the prayer hall that evening a pathetic figure without the usual applause from priests who over ten years had come to be proud of him. Pitting the seminarian sons of workingmen against workers no better off than their own fathers was not viewed by priests as an appropriate way of confronting a disagreeable labor situation. In this respect Spellman suffered the temporary fate of President Truman with whom he had something in common, personality-wise. Harry Truman freely confronted corporation presidents and union leaders in the interest of a perceived American good. Spellman, a Churchman par excellence, never asked anyone to run interference for him. When he was good he was very good, so that his mistakes looked as awful as his victories were awesome.

He was a leader, one of a kind. His blunder in the Calvary strike was picking on little people. Had he stood up to the Teamsters or the Bricklayers, he might have made friends for himself, since those larger unions were involved in enough chicanery and were vulnerable to criticism from public figures. But the Calvary contest was lopsided. Even the Cardinal's straightforward personal meetings with grave diggers and their housewives did not help his cause, although they demonstrated the certain courage he was known to possess. They also violated an established custom. Prominent leaders are regularly warned by mediation experts to avoid personal involvement in labor negotiations because they can be unduly pressured into unwise, precedent-setting concessions.

As bad as this situation was, John Cooney provides some humor with the silliest description of the Cardinal's meeting with the strikers: "Spellman heightened the effect by sitting on the throne in the reception room. He was dressed in ermine and scarlet . . ."[3] For a prelate who did business sitting on a footstool or on a mailbag in a B-52, these lines border on the ridiculous. There was no throne in 452, and Spellman never conducted business except in "civvies." However, the Cooney venom does indicate how much passion exists over Calvary forty years after the fact.

Whatever happened to ACTU? By the early 1950s it was going the way of most voluntary associations which fail to make it in the larger society of which they are a part. For all its alleged monolithic character, the Church has more free associations than the most democratic states. Groups exist everywhere in parishes or dioceses, serving a variety of Catholic causes, many of them independent of and outside of the ambit of episcopal authority. Indeed, the Catholic Church is the only major institution in the

United States, including government, with an "office" of some kind in every neighborhood of the country, staffed by volunteers and low-paid professionals. Some of these groups become part of the official household, eventually supported by hierarchy (e.g., religious communities, parochial schools, Opus Dei); others exist on the fringe of the Church or pass out of existence like ACTU and CFM. (In those years not even the fringe movements would think of attacking Church authority.)

Some blame incidents like the Calvary strike for the declining interest of priests and workingmen in ACTU. Stated another way "the hierarchy's at fault." This is not quite a fair judgment. Bishops who had little to do with its rise did not suddenly achieve power over ACTU. Catholics were still lower middle class, large family-minded, and Bishops were engaged more in Catholicizing the faithful than improving their social status. This was a time, too, when people were expected to help themselves. This benign neglect by Bishops had its dysfunctional aspects, of course, because trade unions needed not only support but internal reform, two aspects of the ACTU program which are now buried in the limbo of yesteryear.

Father John Cronin, one of the better informed economists attached to the older National Catholic Welfare Conference (predecessor of the present United States Catholic Conference) inclined to the view (1967) that prosperity did these apostolates in, that during the 1950s interest in Catholic social teaching declined "because we believed that poverty was becoming only a matter of history in this prosperous nation." From the vantage point of forty years later (including Vatican II's stress on peace and justice), Cronin's observation is dated. But the optimism of the 1950s partially explains the sudden drop in ACTU's activity and eventually its extinction.

However one explains it, the tragedy of the loss was not realized by ecclesiastics at the time. Had ACTU survived to greet Vatican II, the Church would have been enriched by an abundance of experienced social activists, whose acquired wisdom might have helped Church authorities maintain better after 1965 the balance of their own priorities. Whatever else can be said about ACTU, it was above all a religious organization dedicated to forming the consciences and the conduct of union members in order that they might better improve the lot of fellow workingmen through decent and democratic trade unions and by labor-management collaboration. Priests provided the inspiration and the formation but priests never made the tactical decisions for laymen. Nor did they appear on picket lines doing laymen's work. Some priests were more influential than others, but even then, one with the stature of Father Monaghan backed off in the face of a decision by the lay-dominated ACTU board, although it was destined to cause him embarrassment before his old schoolmate, Francis Spellman.

A new breed of Catholic activists are not above battling the Church over the meaning of the Apostles' Creed. But it was not thus forty years ago. Adult American Catholics of that day were mostly New Dealers; they favored trade unions, and wanted FDR to keep the United States out of war. The Bishops' statements were paraphrases of *Quadragesimo Anno* or similar documents, instructing churchgoers how as Christians they ought to think about social issues, but leaving the pragmatic working out of norms to their faithful. Bishops were not reluctant to spell out in detail what those same faithful must believe and do to enter God's kingdom and eternal life. Catholic unity, built around the hierarchy and their preachments, was not affected by the inevitable divergencies over economic and political interests.

Those Catholic divisions were clearly to be found within the ACTU movement. Some were merely tactical, but the more severe ones were ideological. In the Washington or labor circles of the 1940s, the great heresy was to vote against, even to speak against, Franklin Delano Roosevelt or U.S. labor. Differences over what or how much ACTU should teach, whether there should be an overarching national ACTU organization, whether non-Catholics should become voting members, etc., were tactical disagreements and so relatively harmless. The substantial and bitter argument was this: Should Catholics as Catholics do more than exercise free speech in favor of unions? In practice this argument was rephrased as follows: Can Catholic organizations properly demand as much rectitude of trade unions as they demand of corporations? No one raised these questions in 1937 when ACTU was founded, but by war's end organized labor itself was highly politicized and so was American Catholic Action. Laissez-faire was out for corporations, government controls were in for business, industry was to be democratized through labor power, and political action was to supply the votes which would keep FDR and organized labor in power. Insofar as ACTU supported these objectives it was welcomed as part of the new liberal consensus, whose headquarters for the nation was Washington, D.C. The growing federal bureaucracy, the leaders of the national research institutions and billion-dollar foundations, the national press, and the bully Presidents of both the New and Fair Deals were part of this apparatus.

At the local level, however, especially in New York where labor racketeering was notorious in the building industry and in Detroit with more than its share of Communist union infiltrators in the auto and electrical unions, members of ACTU, all unionists themselves, developed an independent consensus of their own, viz., that racketeers and Communists must be uprooted from their dominant positions in vital American industries. But when ACTU went beyond expressing this pious wish and offered its facilities or technical assistance to critics of established union leadership, howls of protest began to be heard from international union leadership. AFL leaders damned ACTU activity as "outside interference." Daniel Tobin, later to serve a jail sentence for his criminal activities as president of the notorious Teamsters (and a predecessor of Jimmy Hoffa once removed), wrote his local unions warning them not to allow religious groups to interfere in their internal affairs. Communists, facing ACTU opposition, also raised the red flag of "divisiveness." As early as 1939 James Matles, organizational director of the United Electrical Workers, a union ultimately driven out of the CIO by Philip Murray, charged that ACTU was "divisive" and wrote a pamphlet on the subject. The criticisms of Tobin and Matles ultimately found a home among certain Catholic social actionists.

Controversy over lay apostolic activity, Catholic or otherwise, is a necessary by-product of political involvement. There are no ready-made panaceas for social problems and large differences of opinion between equally competent intervenors. ACTU's founders were prepared for opposition from clergy uninformed about modern Catholic social thought, from industrial leaders, and even from union presidents embarrassed by demands of their own rank and file. But ACTU reformers resented charges of "outside interference" and "divisiveness," when they began to be mouthed by officials of the Social Action Department of the Bishops' NCWC, whose first director had been Msgr. John A. Ryan. Ryan was what he was later called, a "Right Reverend New Dealer," but he was not captivated by the daily doings of labor officials. The same could not be said of those who came after him—Father Raymond McGowan, Father John Cronin, S.S., Father George G. Higgins, and Msgr. Francis Haas, mentor of the other three. Haas, later Bishop of Grand Rapids, and his protégé, Higgins, were quite involved with the labor establishment, especially with the many Catholics who several years before led the CIO revolution against the AFL. The NCWC personnel were friendly with ACTU leaders in many places, but they were closer to their Washington labor circle.

Word reached local chapters that the complaints made against ACTU—of interfering, of dividing unions along religious lines— were being mouthed or repeated by one Washington priest or another. Sometimes bluntly made, sometimes more slyly raised as questions worth pondering, but never with any strong defense of ACTU against the complaining labor leaders. Chicago priest George Higgins, hardly out of graduate school and four years a priest, publicly posed such unanswered questions in *Commonweal* in 1944. Father John Monaghan was sufficiently annoyed to take the matter up with Msgr. Ryan, who told the New York priest not to pay attention to criticisms coming out of Washington. Monaghan, the carver of pointed phrases, explained his distress with the remark: "We send priests to Washington to represent the Church and they end up representing Washington to the Church." Four years later (1948) Father John Cronin repeated the same doubts about ACTU in his *Catholic Social Action,* impelling Father Monaghan to persuade the editors of *Commonweal* to allow me to answer the charges. This was done in an article entitled "ACTU and Its Critics."[4] Neither Father Cronin nor Father Higgins regretted their remarks, choosing to consider the New York ACTU leaders overly sensitive and reasserting their view that the real source of the complaints was ACTU activists in other cities. The NCWC priests particularly resented New York's charges that the Washington priests were more in tune with national labor leaders than with rank-and-file members of crooked and Red-dominated unions. New Yorkers stand on their judgment to this very day.

The Chicago chapter of ACTU withdrew to form a distinct Catholic Labor Alliance with less controversial objectives. Nonetheless, the NCWC priests had allies but critics, too. Father Paul Hanly Furfey, a social actionist of a different sort, held the opinion that as far as NCWC was concerned, anyone unconnected to the Social Action Department was deemed to know little about Catholic social action.

The Furfey comment expressed a certain truth about ideologues in academia and vested bureaucrats, whose reference center was always removed from that of field workers. Ideology (pro- or antibusiness, pro- or antiunion, pro- or anti-laissez-faire/welfare state) does not work in the field. The same arguments which began over ACTU in 1942 surfaced in 1962 over the relationship of Chicago's Christian Family Movement with the rest of the Church. CFM today lies dead and buried for the same reason as ACTU—influential priests with more concern about outside opinion than the needs of their own people.

The strange thing about NCWC's Social Action Department was its relative alienation in those years within 1312 Massachusetts Avenue. The chief officers and large numbers of Bishops were often at odds with what came out of the Social Action Department, whose directors filtered the Church's social teaching through the spectrum of the Democratic Party and Washington think-tanks. These latter supplied the intellectual underpinning of the welfare state with its double standard about private and public morality. More than one observer witnessed the "bullying" that regularly accompanied their brand of activism. But if the old Social Action Department was a stranger in its own house prior to Vatican II, its one-sided political positions came to dominate its successor, the USCC. Call to Action, conceived as a search conducted by the Bishops' bureaucracy for rank-and-file Catholic opinion, ended up as a congress slanted to reflect the same "liberal consensus."

One should not transpose history to suit the needs of current events. But the ACTU controversies of the 1930s to 1940s uncovered what would be the seeds of a future Catholic problem: political priests. Priests tend to be absolutists, even when they favor relativism in Catholic doctrine. By the time Father John Cronin was writing Bishops' reports about the menace of U.S. Communists, he was also reporting that sixty-five Catholic action centers existed in forty-three major cities promoting trade unionism, social legislation, welfare programs—hardly any of which exist anymore. What neglected groups like ACTU once did well, recent Popes now say must be done more than ever. But at present there is no significant coordinated lay apostolate on behalf of the poor. We have Bishops' statements, but nothing like what ACTU might have been.

IN A FAMILY WAY

My eleven years as Family Life Director (1955–66), half of which were spent as a full-time parish priest, may well have been as exciting as any of my priestly experiences before or since. The period in question was a high point of modern Catholic interest in matters of family life. The appointment itself came as a total surprise. It also involved a lesson in how Church bureaucracies grow.

Following Pius XI's 1930 encyclical on Christian Marriage *(Casti Connubii),* the U.S. Bishops established a Family Life Bureau within the National Catholic Welfare Conference. Its purpose was to carry out the Pope's instructions concerning family life education, by then considered a desirable addition to the usual

Church programs. The attacks made on the Christian family by socialist states and other irreligious movements were having their effects on Christians. Free love, divorce, and contraception were just beginning to make headway among Catholics. NCWC's Family Life Bureau remained a national service organization until World War II, structured to compile suitable literature for professionals and to arrange an annual meeting of such Catholics. The FLB was not duplicated at the diocesan level, nor did it involve those Catholics directly concerned with family life, viz., married couples.

From out of nowhere came the Cana movement, mostly as a result of Jesuit involvement in Family Renewal Days by Jesuits John J. Delaney and Edward J. Dowling, which began as early as 1941. Other Jesuits, Joseph Cantillon and Gerard Murphy in particular, followed immediately. Cana, as a parish-based couple movement, proved effective and popular. In short order diocesan authorities showed interest, enough to prompt the NCWC's Administrative Board by 1949 to ask diocesan Bishops to place someone in charge of family life education. By reflex action Spellman turned responsibility for this work over to the Family Division of Catholic Charities, an agency fully involved in the psychosocial needs of poor families. Father Robert A. Ford, already overwhelmed by casework, undertook to organize Cana and Pre-Cana Conferences out of the Charities' office. Only when Father Ford became totally swamped by his double burden, did Msgr. Maguire arrange to create a separate office exclusively devoted to family life education.

By this time (1955) John Maguire had begun to play the role that Spellman once allowed only J. Francis A. McIntyre to exercise. He was made a Bishop in June 1959 and, as the Second Vatican Council was ending (December 8, 1965), Spellman announced that Paul VI had made him the Coadjutor Archbishop of New York. A man of few words, Maguire enjoyed the respect of priests and religious. He would remain relatively unknown to the public, but he knew the needs of the Archdiocese better than anyone. Personal friendship with Msgr. Gaffney originally brought him to Spellman's attention. His talents were recognized in their own right in a very short while.

Maguire's particular skill was finding reasonable answers to tricky problems, whether they concerned priest personnel, the division of parishes, new Church programs, or diocesan finances. He and his aide, Msgr. Leonard Hunt, played a creative role after World War II in finding an economical way to pay for the new North American College buildings in Rome. Costs had far outpaced the $4 million budgeted for the project by the U.S. Bishops. Maguire and Hunt, discovering that the Italian Government had frozen the assets of Paramount Productions, released the Bishops' U.S. money to the Hollywood producers in exchange for frozen Italian lire, 25 percent above the Roman market rate. This was enough to pay for the college overruns. Needless to say Spellman was impressed.

Once Vicar General, Maguire launched almost all the new archdiocesan movements—the Spanish apostolate, approval for the Christian Family Movement, housing programs for the poor, marriage counseling, continuing education for priests, etc. It was he who enrolled Cardinal Spellman as a life member in the National Association for the Advancement of Colored People, to the surprise of Roy Wilkins, its national president. Maguire transferred all the assistant pastors, designated assignments for most pastors, named new monsignors, suggested or approved new building sites, dealt with religious communities of men and women, assisted in funding poor parishes, and supervised the health and welfare of priests. When the Diocesan Board of Consultors was divided, it was usually the convictions of Bishop Maguire that carried the day.

However, Spellman was no passive partner in his own diocesan administration. This would have been a psychological impossibility. But confidence in Maguire and his acquired ability to delegate managerial authority freed Spellman for larger issues of diocesan and national concern which were his special interest. The Cardinal could not possibly have established his worldwide network of civil and ecclesiastical alliances if he allowed himself to be bogged down by the details of diocesan management. He sometimes had occasion to regret the scope of this delegation, especially when things did not work out to anyone's satisfaction. Many appointments that went out over his signature, for example, were Maguire's, not his, sometimes of some priests he would not have chosen. Spellman himself might not have been a perfect chooser, but the Coadjutor became vulnerable when his appointees fell down on the job or betrayed his trust. However, Maguire had many well-earned victories to his credit. Twenty-two years after Spellman's death, the Archdiocese of New York conducts its affairs from offices in a twenty-one-story building at 1011 First Avenue. This complex of administrative offices, high school, and parish church replaced the Chancery Office at 451 Madison Avenue (which had become too small), an aging Cathedral High School on Lexington Avenue (Fifty-first Street), which had become hazardous, and the declining parish of St. John the Evangelist on Fifty-fifth Street. Cardinal Cooke ultimately saw the project to its conclusion in 1972, but the idea was not his nor was it Spellman's. The complex was the brainchild of John Maguire.

The Family Life Bureau got its start in the old Chancery attic (there was no other space available) with a five-hundred-dollar bank account. "When you need more, ask for it," said Maguire. From that point on New York's family life movement grew like Topsy. There were no vested interests to interfere with growth and the Catholic people were ready. Spellman provided support from a distance. If he had anything to say, he said it through Maguire.

One Sunday morning at the Waldorf-Astoria, a *New York Times* reporter sought comment on Governor Nelson Rockefeller's "overnight" remarriage to Mrs. "Happy" Murphy, the young mother of four children by a doctor employed at the Rockefeller University. Because Rocky was a close friend of the Cardinal, it seemed propitious to evade the question by professing ignorance of the fact. The indefatigable reporter, looking for a quotable quote from a Catholic spokesman confided, "Episcopal Bishop Horace Donegan says, 'Rockefeller's remarriage is the governor's private business.'" My response seemed innocent, "Nothing a governor does is private." But the Monday *Times*'s report, which featured the remark, prompted Spellman to tell Maguire, "He needn't have made that statement." Rocky was special to the Cardinal, no matter what he did. Later Spellman gave me his private counsel, "When in doubt, say nothing." This was not advice he always followed himself, especially with his one-liners. Most of those were rather funny, although the one-line remark that Eleanor Roosevelt was guilty of "discrimination unworthy of an American mother," would have been better left unsaid. Reno's Bishop once described St. Patrick's Cathedral to a reporter as ostentatious. Asked by a TV newsman whether he had anything to say about the Bishop's remark, the Cardinal snorted, "He must want to stay in Reno." On another occasion he sent fifty thousand dollars to the Archbishop of Bombay to defray the cost of a Eucharistic Congress. Cardinal Gracias' return letter of appreciation contained an inappropriate phrase, "because, as Your Eminence knows, every little bit helps." Spellman's tart reaction was, "That's the last little bit he'll ever get."

The Family Life Bureau was not one of Spellman's main priorities during its first five years of existence (1955–60), and there was almost no contact between the priests involved and their Archbishop. Pre-Cana Conferences began with a rush of engaged couples, followed shortly by the growth of Cana Conferences for married couples. The pent-up need for the Church's support was satisfied, at least for those Catholics who were anxious to raise good Catholic families. The New York priests, especially those ordained between 1945 and 1960, volunteered their services liberally, wandering the Archdiocese to give conferences, even though they were also the Church's busiest parish priests. They were also remarkably unified about what Catholics entering or already in marriages should be taught—what the Church always taught about marital ideals, mutual love, roles in marriage, childbearing and child rearing, moral norms, etc.

By 1960 the New York Family Life Program reached over 50,000 Catholics per annum, and the volunteer staff grew to include 150 priests, 150 medical doctors, and 1,000 married couples devoting many hours each week to this apostolate. If Cardinal Spellman was a distant figure during the formative stage of FLB, so were most Bishops, save perhaps St. Cloud's grand old man, Peter Bartholomé, NCWC's episcopal moderator. Bishops did not sense the urgency of these instruments, as once they did the need for parochial schools. But the virtue of the Spellman administration was that family life activities went on with approval, encouragement, and money.

The Cardinal's diocesan interests lay more with Catholic soldiers, Catholic hospitals, and Catholic schools. Between 1939 and 1967 the number of hospital beds passed the 5,000 mark, while student enrollment in Catholic elementary and high schools doubled from an initial base of 120,000. The largest segment of New York's churchgoing body twenty years after Spellman's death involves the children and grandchildren of Italian immigrants. Few people today even know that it was Spellman's prodding of Italian pastors to build parochial schools, and his own high schools, which explains the rise in Italo-American religious observance. Mention must also be made of the fine staffs of priests and religious he managed to assemble, all of whom up to Vatican II taught that attendance at Sunday Mass was vital to Catholic life. On the other hand, the diocese's detached view of lay apostolate, family life, sodalities, etc., caused them to be neglected by pastors too.

Still, for a time, family life programs were the most exciting activities in the U.S. Church. They received their impetus from a Pope alarmed about the vices appearing in married life. By 1962 the Cana movement was quite vigorous on its own. Every level of the Church was encompassed—parishes, high schools, colleges, and Newman Clubs, public school officials, even newspaper and TV editors. Family life was not only a mission of the Church *to* and *for* the family, but it was a movement *by* Christian families for the Church and for the nation.

A 1960 survey of engaged couples attending New York's Pre-Canas (75 percent attending Mass every Sunday, 58 percent being married at a Nuptial Mass) confessed to the inadequacy of their preparation for marriage. One Staten Island man, asked to evaluate his parental training, said: "I refuse to answer on the grounds that I might incriminate my father and my mother." Three quarters of the couples said they received no training for marriage at home, except about money matters. While the young couples may have underestimated the educative force of their parents' example, they also had the felt conviction that they were ill-equipped for responsible roles in Christian marriage. Those who had been public school products felt especially vulnerable. In spite of some obvious facts, about half the New York parishes were doing nothing for such couples, not even taking advantage of the diocesan conferences.

Little by little Cardinal Spellman became interested in what was going on, mostly through the interventions of Msgr. Maguire. In 1957, at the annual Clergy Conference, he encouraged priests to promote attendance at Pre-Cana Conferences. Later that year he expanded the staff of the Family Life Bureau. With the Cardinal's blessing Family Consultation Service was instituted to provide marriage counseling and to deal with petitions for separation, as well as a Pastoral Life Conference to update the theological competence of senior priests, and Bethany Conferences for single Catholics. At the outset of Vatican II the Archdiocesan Clergy Conference was reorganized to involve participation by priests. The Pastoral Life Conference—a two-year course for future pastors—became an immediate success when at its first graduation Cardinal Spellman announced that seven of their number were appointed new pastors, all of them at the time ordained at least thirty years.

Probably the most direct personal involvement of the Cardinal came in 1960 when he participated in the first Catholic Family Day. This marked the beginning in New York of annual awards in St. Patrick's Cathedral to couples married fifty years, and in parishes for those celebrating their silver anniversary. His enemies never credit him with the personal touch, but on occasions such as this, Spelly was at his best. Perhaps because he was depicted as having ten-foot-tall power, seventy-year-olds on the other side of the Cathedral's main altar steps were captivated by his short stature, soft voice, and boyish grin. At these events he was good, reaching down to hold up or lift a man his own age who was trying to kiss the Bishop's ring.

That first event in January 1960 was particularly moving because the Cathedral was filled with twelve hundred married couples, the vast majority Italian-born, each couple having brought with them at least ten of their relatives. The Cardinal was obviously moved by the people, as they were by him, because he made me a Very Reverend Monsignor on the spot. He also arranged for me to take a six-week tour of European air force bases in four countries to give Cana and Pre-Cana Conferences. There was nothing particularly demonstrative about these gratuities, because by this time Spellman conferred favors offhandedly. The European tour resulted from the Chief of Air Force Chaplains telling the Cardinal that he was sending Msgr. John C. Knott, Hartford's director, on a similar tour of Far East bases. Already a dyed-in-the-wool New Yorker, the Cardinal rejoined: "What about Father Kelly?" So was it done.

The first Catholic Family Day occasioned such a surplus of couples that several upstate celebrations in county seats were necessary to take care of the overflow. The outpouring of affection for the Church was in itself an inspiration to those organizing these events. One Italian patriarch telephoned the Chancery so often about his seating that by the third call we were chatty. I asked him why so many Italians survived together for fifty years, while the golden jubilarians among the Irish were so few. His answer in broken English was classic: "Most of us from the old country had to fight our bosses every day to make a living. But when I went home at night, I was the boss. The Irish papa, he fight the boss all day and the wife all night. He die at sixty."

Catholic Family Day represented a development in the relations between family life leaders and their Archbishop. It took four years for him to approve the Christian Family Movement, which he did on August 31, 1959, in a letter which read in part: "The New York Christian Family Movement is one of the recognized and approved forms of the lay apostolate in the Archdiocese of New York. This organization of married couples, working in our parishes under the authority of the pastor, in the Archdiocese works under the authority of the Family Life Bureau." The reason for his earlier reluctance was the complaint he heard from some Bishops that CFM units were being organized in parishes without pastors' approval and that the movement's national officers were making end runs around Bishops. There was also some dissatisfaction that CFM was overpromoting its couples' potential by directing their activity toward political life, rather than toward family life, which was the immediate responsibility of couples who were still young. At one point a wag translated CFM to mean "Can't Find Mother." Spellman needed assurance that these criticisms would not be leveled against CFM couples in his diocese.

Other difficulties began to appear within the Family Life Bureau of the National Catholic Welfare Conference. Msgr. Irving A. DeBlanc, a Lafayette, Louisiana, priest, had performed yeoman-like service in Washington from 1955 on, persuading Bishops to establish diocesan bureaus and tying those far-flung local units into what was an incipient national family life apostolate. He succeeded admirably in spite of sniping from Chicago priests and despite Chicago CFM's unwillingness to consider itself part of the family apostolate. During these controversies Bishop Christopher Weldon of Springfield, Massachusetts, became Episcopal Moderator, to be shocked almost immediately at evident anticlericalism in his first appearance in 1959 at a Cana Institute in Chicago. It is not clear what motivated Spellman, but when he read the 1959 annual report which ended with a description of New York's relationship with NCWC, the Cardinal sent word that we were to have nothing more to do with the NCWC agency. Spellman was once heard to say that he paid his dues to Washington so they would leave him alone. The ban was revoked within the year when Msgr. John C. Knott assumed the Washington post.

One of the most bizarre events during my dealings with Spellman came in 1965, as the Cardinal was nearing fifty years as a priest. For a man his age he seemed to be in good physical shape, considering the fact that he never seemed to rest.

By 1964 the controversy over contraception had reached a boiling point. *Humanae Vitae* was still four years away and the first meeting of the papal Birth Control Commission had ended. Paul

VI told the Catholic people (June 23, 1964) that traditional norms on contraception were still in force. He reaffirmed these norms again on October 19, 1964, asserting anew that the Church had no doubt about them, no matter what some Catholic theologians were saying. A few European Catholic Bishops were actively promoting unorthodox views which received wide coverage in the American press. Not surprisingly Catholics were unsettled. Earlier the same year in a private audience the Holy Father said plaintively to a few members of the Birth Control Commission: "Where are our loyal sons?" He also cautioned Cardinal Suenens to cease his public remarks on birth control, which the media were using to give aid and comfort to contraceptionists.

The Pope's plaint was brought from Rome to Bishop Maguire with the suggestion that Cardinal Spellman take the lead for U.S. Bishops by speaking out on Catholic marriage and the Church's norms. Spellman agreed to address the subject during the celebration of Catholic Family Day, scheduled for January 10, 1965, then departed for Vietnam with the advance text already in hand. The sermon was designed to present Catholic doctrine on family life and the regulation of births in a pastoral way. In the presentation Catholic doctrine on marriage would be restated authoritatively. The theological sections of the sermon stated only the exact teaching of the Church on two important items (contraception and the pill), leaving the free issues on family limitation open to further discussion. The contemplated sermon, corrected to suit his style, would also announce his support for counseling services for married couples facing difficult reproductive decisions.

The key paragraphs in a talk by a priest ordained in 1916 to couples married in 1915 (including my mother, who was present as a guest) were the following:

> There are many aspects of the problem of family regulation, and the scientific studies on this subject are quite extensive. While the Church is ever ready to accept the established findings of science, she must always evaluate these data whenever a moral issue is involved. She has the duty, given by the Lord, to teach and propound His law before the people of God. And, however much she sympathizes with those who intimately face the problems involved in regu-

lating the size of the family, she must speak when methods offered as a solution violate moral order and God's holy law.

The position of the Catholic Church on contraceptive birth control is unmistakably clear. His Holiness Pope Pius XI solemnly stated that any attempt on the part of the husband and wife to deprive the marital act of its inherent force or to impede the procreation of a new life is immoral and, furthermore, that no matter how great the need may be it cannot change an intrinsically immoral act into a moral and lawful one (Encyclical *Casti Connubii*, December 31, 1930).

His successor, Pius XII, reaffirmed this teaching in an address delivered in 1951. There he stated, "This precept [of Pius XI] is as valid today as it was yesterday, and it will be the same tomorrow and always, because it does not imply a precept of human law but is the expression of a law which is Natural and Divine." The natural law cannot be changed, because, as His Holiness declared later in the same address, it is something "from which the Church herself, as you well know, has no power to dispense!" (Address to the Midwives, October 29, 1951.)

Perhaps some persons are entertaining false hopes that Catholic doctrine on contraception will change, probably because of certain widely publicized, even imprudent, statements concerning the so-called antiovulent pill. Concerning the use of such pills, Pope Pius XII spoke quite plainly in 1958. He taught that while they may be taken for certain medical purposes, it is wrong to use them if the direct intention is to prevent conception. (Address to Hematologists, September 12, 1958.)

In commenting on this statement, our present Holy Father, Pope Paul VI, declared: "We do not have sufficient reason to regard the norms laid down by Pius XII on this matter as superseded and, therefore, no longer binding." Catholics, therefore, must abide by the teaching of the Holy See in this matter. They are not free to follow contraceptive birth control practices or to use antiovulent pills for a directly contraceptive purpose. Opinions to the contrary may not be followed by Catholics in good conscience.

And without minimizing the human problems that people face—whether they concern poverty, racial injustice, the threat of nuclear war, or the regulation of family size—experience does show and history can demonstrate that men best solve their problems by obeying God's law.

You, our golden jubilarians here today, witness in your own lives the truth that marriage best fulfills itself when it is lived under God and for God. It was by harmonizing your will and God's will that you achieved the contentment and the joy that today are yours."[5]

During the Christmas hiatus Spellman toured the military bases in Vietnam, no mean accomplishment for a seventy-five-year-old. The media were informed that on Sunday, January 10, 1965, at 2 P.M. Cardinal Spellman would make a notable statement during Catholic Family Day Services in St. Patrick's Cathedral. More than five hundred couples were expected to participate that day along with five thousand friends and relatives gathered in the Cathedral and around the neighboring plazas. By 1965 Catholic Family Day had become an emotionally packed day for hundreds of Catholic families. The procession assembled as usual behind the main altar, with a half-dozen Bishops and more than a hundred priests standing at attention. When Spellman emerged from the sacristy below (it was a rainy day), it was my task as host to approach him and to extend a greeting. The words were hardly out of my mouth when he bluntly said: "I can't give that sermon. You give it." The words had the force of a knockout blow. All those strategy and writing sessions up in smoke, the Pope forsaken, the media outraged by what would look like deceit! As soon as I finished gulping, I replied: "I can't give that talk, it's a Bishop's sermon." The Cardinal peremptorily ordered: "Get the procession started."

God only knows what those poor old people heard that day from this bedraggled Family Life Director, but they did not receive the meticulously honed words of their Archbishop. They did, however, encounter an imperturbed and kindly Cardinal, who carried on as he always did on these occasions, with typical grace, an inspiration to aged couples whom he earlier had been scheduled to call "saintly heroes" of the Church. The ritual ended, attending Bishops and priests recessed to their original place, waiting for the slower-paced Cardinal to reach them and bestow his blessing. Conscious of smoldering fury and in no mood to say "thank you," I approached "the Little Man" with carefully chosen words: "Your Eminence, they loved it," a true but sanitized remark. Spellman, hardly looking in my direction, turned to go down the sacristy steps with a parting shot: "You gave me bad advice." Then followed what those priests looking down the stairwell considered a bizarre sight, indeed. Down the same steps went the forty-nine-year-old Family Life Director asking: "What do you mean I gave you bad advice?"—"The Pope rapped Suenens's knuckles for talking on marriage."—"The Pope rapped Suenens because he appeared to be speaking against the Pope."—"You still gave me bad advice."—"The people who gave you bad advice were the ones you talked to last night." So the argument went.

At this point in the "dialogue" we reached the black door leading to the Cardinal's house. He walked through it, slamming the door with seeming violence. Standing before that door for a few seconds, staring at the blackness with thoughts worthy of censorship by the Legion of Decency, seemed an eternity. Suddenly, the door reopened and there Spellman stood again, this time saying: "I forgot to tell you the Holy Father has made you a Right Reverend Monsignor." Off he skirted into his residence.

In a daze my retraced steps brought Bishop Maguire into view. I said: "You can't beat him." (The assumption that Spellman was atoning for the obvious distress he caused proved to be wrong. He had arranged for the prelacy a month earlier.)

Later on, it was learned that the Cardinal stopped off on his way home from Vietnam for a few days' rest in Florida with old-time priest cronies and his secretary. They read the sermon and they told him he was too old to become involved in another controversy. (This was not true, as future events made clear.) But at this moment Spellman bought the advice, evidence that carefully worked out official strategies can be upset by the casual interference of uninformed friends, sometimes by Bishops' inexperienced secretaries. This is particularly true with officeholders who lose their zest for daring adventures as they grow older.

The real issue was whether one or the other of his intimates was pro-contraception. By joining his silence to that of U.S. Bishops on a doctrinal matter of major importance, about which Paul

VI would continue to speak until he published *Humanae Vitae* in 1968, Spellman ceded the public forum to the Church's dissenters, giving them three peaceful years to change the consciences of Catholics against Church teaching.

The sermon was eventually published as "The Sermon that Cardinal Spellman Never Gave" in Father Paul Marx's *The International Review—Natural Family Planning,* thirteen years too late to do any good.

THE SECOND VATICAN COUNCIL

In spite of his reputation, Cardinal Spellman was not by personal preference given to public crusades. Yet on a given issue, if he thought a Church interest was at stake or if he was prodded to exercise leadership on some issue, he was capable of taking a strong stand, even if it was not often eloquently expressed. Participation in the recent Council made him more sensitive to social issues. In 1963, for example, Martin Luther King praised Spellman for the support given by New York to the Baptist minister's March on Washington that year. Prior to this march, Spellman, a life member of the National Association for the Advancement of Colored People, published a devastating critique of the race problem, one which became must reading in every one of his four hundred churches. Forgotten now are the strong words of July 11 that year.

> There is simply no reason—there never was and there never can be—why the color of a man's skin should limit his opportunities in a society that boasts of freedom.
> Americans who risked their lives for America—for you and for me —are denied the right to vote, the right to receive an adequate education, the right to live where they desire and their means enable them to live and to receive the normal courtesies befitting their dignity as human beings. They are denied these rights for only one reason—the color of their skin. How lamentable that some Americans who would die together today, will not eat together, will not travel together, will not live together. This is an outrage which Amer-

ica cannot tolerate. Doors cannot continue to close in the face of Negroes as they search for jobs, as they strive for membership in some unions, as they seek the chance for specialized job training.[6]

Less than two years later he came back to his priests and the people with a more urgent call for their personal involvement in the question of racial harmony. On March 14, 1965, he wrote:

> The frightening disturbances in Selma, Alabama, culminating in the martyrdom of the Reverend James Reeb, are a tragedy for America and must awaken the consciences of all who are fair-minded and against the evil of violating the basic rights of men. Racial and civil injustice are a cancer attacking the very life of our nation and society. Their eradication is the urgent concern of all Americans and we cannot disassociate ourselves from this great challenge.[7]

If in January 1965 Cardinal Spellman found himself unsure what he could or could not say about Catholic marriage, he was acting out of character. Normally, as if by instinct, he responded "yes" or "no" when faced with a request of any kind. His uncertainty in this case was due in part to what had been going on at the Second Vatican Council for two years. More than Spellman were rattled by what the media reported from Rome after 1962. Commentators of the day liked to portray Spellman as anti-Council, even anti-John XXIII. But the aging Cardinal was too much of a Churchman to be explained in these simple terms. Likely, because by temperament he was more activist than legalist, he was bored by long sessions devoted to wrangling over theological points and documentary language. Furthermore, as a good organizer himself, he would have been discombobulated by what seemed to be a lack of planning in the management of the Church's first ecumenical meeting in ninety years.

John XXIII went into Vatican II with a plan devised by his Curia, and Spellman would have been briefed about those proposals by his Auxiliary Bishop James H. A. Griffiths, once my pastor, and a member of the Council's Preparatory Commission. Griffiths was one of the hierarchy's most scholarly theologians (in seven languages), but the original design for the Council on which he worked for two years was quickly sidetracked by well-organized

French and German Bishops, who wanted more radical changes in Church priorities and ecclesiastical structures (without diluting the Catholic faith in any way). And John XXIII let them do it. From that moment on—and in the absence of a papal backup plan—the Council ran its own course with only occasional interference from the Pope. Before 1963 was half gone John XXIII (and Griffiths) were dead and the diplomatic Paul VI fundamentally left the Council in the hands of the troops. This quasi-anarchy would not have pleased Spellman, especially when the media began to become a para-Council in its own right, interpreting the future Church in ways not contemplated by the most radical Bishops, whose actual numbers were few.

The New York Archbishop, who ran an effective diocese, sensed that the efforts to decontrol the papal office would have long-range dysfunctions for pastors everywhere. You cannot dismantle hierarchy at the top without rattling its ability to manage way down the line. In this concern he was surely correct and the innovators were certainly shortsighted.

St. Louis' Joseph Cardinal Ritter and Chicago's Albert Cardinal Meyer, who were considered "reformers" by the press (in contrast to Spellman), did not live long enough to experience the long-term effects of decentralization. Ritter, who died in 1967 before Spelly, ran into troubles of his own upon return from the Council. He fired three diocesan officials who wanted to run away with the diocese in the name of Vatican II. Cardinal Meyer, who died in 1965, left behind him one of the most internally divided Archdioceses in the U.S., one which caused untold problems for his two successors.

"The Little Man" may not have been a devotee of a vernacular liturgy, but he was not a dog-in-the-manger either. His friends might joke with him about favoring English for the priests' breviary but Latin in the lay people's Mass, yet New York was one of the first major Archdioceses to revise its liturgy according to Vatican II norms. There were more altars turned around in the short time left before Spellman died than his Building Commission could find contractors to make the changes correctly. He would not be in favor of Mass facing the people in his own Cathedral

81

and became annoyed in 1966 when the Christmas Midnight Mass, which was televised across the country while he was in Vietnam, was so celebrated in St. Patrick's. Archbishop Maguire was not about to offer Mass before a nationwide audience with his back facing the camera—one year after Vatican II. Yet, not even Spellman anticipated the total wipeout of the Latin Mass, the Church's liturgical language for most of her life, so completely that to ask for one was considered *prima facie* evidence of Lefebvrite tendencies. Almost thirty-five years later John Paul II is trying to restore the Latin liturgy with its majestic music as a legitimate option, precisely what the Council intended and what Spellman would have considered right. By the time of his death many of the reforms decreed by the Council were in place in New York—new ecumenical regulations, the updating of religious life begun, a Priests' Senate, and better consultation procedures.

As for the Council itself, Cardinal Spellman was not without influence in matters about which he held strong convictions. Through his interventions the Council document on religious freedom was perfected, placing the Church on record against government coercion in religious choices. He was also an outspoken supporter of the Conciliar statement on anti-Semitism and a leader in the effort to place the world's Bishops behind government aid to religious schools. These contributions to the Council were not insignificant and reflected not only his good relationship with American Jews, but his commitment to the country's political system and the parents' right to educate their children in schools of their own choice without undue handicaps from the state's exclusive support of public education.

CARDINAL OF EDUCATION

"Cardinal of Education" is a title that never has been appended to his name, although Spellman did more for Catholic education than any ecclesiastic before or since. He surely did more than his predecessor ever did for the Church's charitable works, that which earned for Patrick Hayes the identity "Cardinal of Charity." He also journeyed from Boston fully conscious that the New York to which he had been named contained a few "personal empires," which would resist, as if by instinct, any overview by an outsider. One fiefdom was "Catholic Charities," a mega-organization of welfare institutions, already bloated with the inflow of federal money. The other was "Education," which Spellman knew from Roman sources was below standard, at least below the accomplishments of the Chicago and Philadelphia Archdioceses. The tug of war began almost the day he arrived. Both empires became his in short order but not without some infighting.

On the day he was installed as Archbishop of New York (May 23, 1939), three powerful holdovers from the Hayes administration—Msgr. J. Francis A. McIntyre, Chancellor; Msgr. Robert Keegan, executive director of Catholic Charities, and Msgr. William R. Kelly, superintendent of schools—had prominent positions in the ritual. The onetime Boston prelate faced his first test in deciding how to handle three influential strangers. Robert I. Gannon's *The Cardinal Spellman Story* tells how he took charge of New York from the moment he crossed the state line. McIntyre had been co-opted some weeks earlier in Boston where he came to resign and remained to become Spellman's Chancellor, later his right hand in running the Archdiocese, close friend, and a future Cardinal. Kelly was known as an independent operator of the school system. At Rome's urging the Archbishop would launch the largest school-building program in New York's history. Eventually he bypassed Kelly by creating the super-post of Secretary for Education, and making its first nominee, William A. Scully, a Bishop. If Kelly, named pastor in 1946, never figured in the Spellman biography, neither did Robert Keegan. Msgr. Keegan was perhaps the most powerful ecclesiastic during the declining years of Cardinal Hayes, a likely Bishop had the Cardinal's death not intervened. Endowed with unusual organizational ability, he made New York Charities a model of social service under religious auspices. The New Deal brought friendships with both President Roosevelt and Mayor La Guardia. Hardly fifty years old at the time of Spellman's accession, Keegan almost single-handedly controlled the political postures of the New York Church and was an established king-maker in Church affairs, if the number of priests who owed their pastorates to his interventions are counted. He was also as powerful a personality in his own right as Spellman, and the new Archbishop knew it. The Charities' director probably made his first mistake when he told his staff to draft an installation sermon for the new boss, something he did regularly for Hayes. Spellman did not use it. A year later (March 12, 1940) when the new Archbishop received the pallium, the symbol of his supervising authority over the Bishops of the state, Msgr. Keegan was Archpriest at the Solemn Mass, a role which befitted his position in the Archdiocese. At the end of the service when the officers of the Mass had repaired to the Cardinal's Residence, Spellman thanked Philadelphia's Cardinal Dougherty first, then Msgr. Keegan. Standing before his Archpriest, the new Archbishop went out of his way to point out the significance of the vestments he was wearing. They originally belonged to Pius XII and were first used in 1917 when the Pope was consecrated a Bishop, and again fifteen years after that when Pacelli officiated at Spellman's consecration. Who was Keegan to fight that combination? From that moment on the Archbishop dominated the Charities' organization and, during his lifetime, all of Keegan's successors were made Bishops, one a Cardinal (Patrick A. O'Boyle).

In matters educational Cardinal Spellman was much more eclectic. By virtue of his involvement in the politics of Catholic education, he became a fierce combatant on behalf of nonpublic school parents' right to government assistance. Somewhat legendary were his moral and financial efforts for the Catholic University and for Manhattan College and for Fordham, which in 1941 he called "the apex of the Catholic educational system in the Archdiocese of New York." His friend Nelson Rockefeller helped Mercy College relocate to a $9 million complex at Dobbs Ferry and Spellman himself relocated Manhattanville College to Purchase, New York, from its run-down quarters on the West Side. Not only was he light-years ahead of the Religious of the Sacred Heart in purchasing the new property in the name of the Archdiocese, while reluctant nuns were making up their minds, but the skill of his archdiocesan lawyers obtained a $9 million settlement for the old property, three times what the religious by themselves would have obtained. (He would not be happy with any of these institutions had he lived longer.) During his tenure he built a major library at Dunwoodie Seminary, launched two new Catholic Encyclopedias, and doubled the enrollment of Catholic school students from 120,000 to 240,000. In spite of these impressive accomplishments, he never seemed to become involved in the nitty-gritty of what went on within this system, except to complain about this or that aberration whenever someone complained to him.

By 1965 Cardinal Spellman was presiding over an educational empire. The scores of institutions aside, he was chief Administrator of a vast array of diocesan agencies involved in catechetics, adult education, formation in the lay apostolate, public information, and political action, providing services to eighteen Catholic and twenty-three secular colleges, and a number of seminaries within his jurisdiction. Major appointments to many of these bureaus were his to make and a large part of their operating expenses he financed. The Cardinal was always the court of last appeal when things went wrong, but as a day-to-day operation Catholic education was a laissez-faire enterprise, every director a lord unto himself. Furthermore, when prelates spoke of education they meant Catholic schools. Not only did this make the Superintendent of Schools prominent among educators, but by nature of the system, he alone was able to develop income (books, book contracts, testing, etc.) independent of the Archbishop, and often unreported to high authority. (This accounted for William R. Kelly's status under Cardinal Hayes.) In contrast, the Confraternity of Christian Doctrine, which theoretically was responsible for a comparable number of Catholic public school children, was a diocesan stepchild. The CCD director had the more difficult role of trying to provide religious instruction to children who could only be reached after school, but more often than not he was a beggar of funds for new projects or overruns on his allotted budget.

There were other serious problems. One department frequently did not know what the other was doing, or two departments were

engaged in similar work. When I was appointed the first Family
Life Director in 1955, Msgr. Charles Walsh, then one of the country's most respected CCD directors, asked me to take over some of
his family programs for which his staff had no time. While CCD
and the School Office shared the same building and the two staffs
enjoyed good personal relationships, CCD programs often suffered in the field because of obstacles placed in their way by local
parish school personnel.

It was also obvious to an interested bystander that few Chancery officials really knew what was going on within this education
complex. No one person or office had charge of supervising or
coordinating the growing empire. This would have been a matter
of little account in a small diocese where the Bishop, like a neighborhood storekeeper, knew everything there was to know about
his operation. If Cardinal Spellman wished information or judgment concerning a hospital, a child care institution, adoptions,
family counseling service, or old age homes, he needed only to
call the Catholic Charities' director. Not so if the matter were
educational. Such an inquiry would be directed to this or that
office or, more likely, be routed through the Vicar General, who
already was overburdened with running the day-to-day details of
the Archdiocese. Not everyone was unhappy with this decentralization. Chancery officials were reluctant to cede what by tradition
was part of their hegemony. School and seminary officials considered themselves elite, entitled to a direct line to the Archbishop
without the mediation of anyone, save perhaps the Vicar General.

The dangers of isolated compartments of learning did not begin
to be taken seriously until the post-Vatican II period arrived,
when Catholic colleges began to forswear their allegiance to the
Bishop, when religious sisters declared their independence of pastors, when religious educators set themselves up as the new teaching authorities in the Church in defiance of magisterium, if need
be.

By the Council's end (1965) Coadjutor Archbishop John
Maguire was the *de facto* manager of Catholic education in New
York. He made most of the appointments to educational posts,
approved all of the subsidies for educational efforts, authorized all

of the construction of schools, and dealt with most of the major superiors whose communities staffed diverse educational apostolates. That so many archdiocesan problems were related to education troubled him for many years. First, there was the growing deficit-financing of archdiocesan high schools. Secondly, parishes with schools began to expect the Archdiocese to subsidize their operations, if costs outran income. Thirdly, the impression was spreading that the size of the financial problem was due partly to inefficient management. Finally, the instruction of children in public schools, of young Catholics in secular colleges, and of Catholic adults seeking specialized Church training was being short-changed.

Twenty-five years earlier Cardinal Spellman created a super-educator role for a Secretary for Education and placed one of his pastors in the post. The Secretary was then and remained what the title suggested—a secretary. He performed specific functions on request, e.g., representing the Cardinal at public events, drafting speeches for him, acting as liaison with colleges and public officials, and speaking officially with the superintendent of schools whenever it seemed appropriate. But he had jurisdiction over nobody and was bypassed whenever it suited the purpose of anyone in authority. No one in any education enterprise was obligated to consult him, save on the basis of a personal relationship.

It is noteworthy that after 1946, when William R. Kelly departed in favor of this pastorate, Spellman forgot his original reasons for creating the Secretaryship and began automatically to promote the standing superintendent to Secretary, almost as an *emeritus.* Any supervisor role over education was thus abandoned and the idea further institutionalized that when you said "education" you meant "schools." The School Handbook described the Secretary for Education as "the coordinator between the various levels of Catholic education on the one hand and the public and private educational agencies on the other. In effect he is the public relations officer of the Archdiocese in educational matters." But actually he had no supervising authority over the School Office.

The system really called for a Vicar for Education, an alter ego of any Bishop of a large Archdiocese who takes seriously his responsibility for the catholicity of education. The Vicar becomes the *de facto* ecclesiastical supervisor, not necessarily a professional schoolman.

Archbishop Maguire understood this and finally persuaded the Cardinal to appoint me to the post of Education Secretary. Spellman's written instructions, given on January 28, 1966, asked me "to coordinate all the educational programs of the Archdiocese of New York." Then, after so instructing the new Secretary in person, and as if to indicate that the Cardinal did not fully understand what "coordination" meant in the concrete, he called in the superintendent, equivocally apologized for going outside the school system for a Secretary, and assured him that nothing had changed. Everyone knew that the new Secretary was a Maguire appointment, even though Spellman signed the letter. Then, as evidence that the Cardinal acted out of the old framework, he sent the new Secretary to Albany to discuss ways for amalgamating two small Dominican Colleges (Sparkhill and Blauvelt) to the satisfaction of the New York State Department of Education.

Forging the disparate elements of education in the large Archdiocese of New York is a story in itself. Before 1966 was far gone, reorganization of departments took second place to the Cardinal's political involvement in parochial school aid. Cardinal Spellman had long relished his involvement in the politics of Catholic education. In 1949 he attacked the Barden Bill, calling it a "Brewer of Bigotry." This first proposal to provide federal funds for education, traditionally considered a function of the states, excluded nonpublic school children from its benefits, even from bus transportation, which the Supreme Court already approved. The bill never became law but not before Eleanor Roosevelt intervened on the side of Barden, not once but three times. Spellman took after the late President's wife, accusing her of anti-Catholicism. Later, Mrs. Roosevelt's one-time secretary, Joseph Lash, wrote of her in *Eleanor: The Years Alone* (1972): "Somewhere deep in her subconscious was an anti-Catholicism which was part of her Protestant heritage." But in 1949 a Catholic Cardinal was not supposed to say that, in public at least, and for so doing Spellman ate a certain amount of crow, probably at the bidding of his mentor, Pius XII.

In 1960 Spelly demonstrated once more that his anger over discrimination against Catholic school children extended even to the Catholic President-elect. When John F. Kennedy's task force on education proposed a $9 million package for education, without considering a penny for any of the 6,500,000 pupils in nonpublic schools, Spellman counterattacked in an address (January 17, 1961) to his Archdiocesan Education Committee.

Three years later (1965) when the first signs of the Cardinal's advancing age were beginning to receive public attention, President Johnson signed the Elementary and Secondary Education Act, drafted to aid disadvantaged children in nonpublic as well as public schools. The new President evaded the trap that snared Barden and Kennedy by focusing on poor children in ghettos. Fourteen percent of the disadvantaged students in New York City attended Catholic, Protestant, and Jewish schools. A proportionate amount of the $100 million appropriated by the federal government for New York City was expected to provide remedial reading, writing, mathematical, and counseling services to nonpublic school children. At the state level Governor Nelson Rockefeller was distracted from ESEA by his own textbook loan program, which required local school boards to purchase books with state funds and to lend them without prejudice to parochial as well as public school students. (The state textbook law was declared constitutional by the U.S. Supreme Court in 1968. In 1985 the Supreme Court required that aid to nonpublic school children exclude instruction on church property.)

The implementation of both these laws was bottled up almost immediately in administrative boondoggling. ESEA was a Johnson breakthrough, a Texan's finesse of the antiparochial school forces by making such education aid part of his Great Society's War on Poverty. Who was bold enough to say that poor blacks and Hispanics were not part of that war, simply because they attended a parochial school? In like fashion Nelson Rockefeller, facing a demand from public school superintendents for increased state aid, refused to increase the state formula (based on average daily attendance). He was not about to saddle the state with a fixed annual budget increase. But he was willing, so he told the superintendents of public schools, to accept some form of categorical aid (a single item which he could, if necessary, excise at a future date), leaving them to choose the specific form it should take. They opted for textbook aid. Until 1965 the cost of textbooks was a local school board responsibility. After some legislative byplay a bill was drafted authorizing an allocation by New York State of twenty-five dollars per child for the first year, and ten dollars for every year thereafter, with local school boards to administer the program. Politician that he was, Rockefeller added nonpublic school children to the bill, which in 1965 he signed into law.

One year later Catholic school students still had not received their due federal services nor their state textbooks. The New York City Board of Education blamed the federal government for the default of ESEA money. State Commissioner James Allen, who immediately released state money to public school boards, held back money for nonpublic school books awaiting a court test of the constitutionality of this section of the law. Hugh Carey, then a Brooklyn congressman, was the *amicus curiae* for nonpublic schools in the federal case. He discovered that the first $25 million (more than $3 million of which belonged to parochial school children) had already reached New York City but had been used by Mayor John Lindsay to cover new pay raises for public school teachers. Few officials seemed embarrassed that federal funds were diverted to satisfy local political needs. After much haggling, however, federally funded services were provided Catholic, Jewish, and Protestant children in their own schools.

John V. Lindsay was not perceived as a friend of Catholic causes. He assumed office as New York City's mayor on January 1, 1966, following a campaign which deliberately avoided association with Cardinal Spellman. Customarily, ritual required major campaigners to pay a courtesy call at 452 Madison Avenue. This Lindsay did not do. Shortly into the New Year, however, Lindsay telephoned the Cardinal's house seeking a meeting for himself and his wife Mary. Spellman invited them to lunch the following

Saturday. Minutes before the mayor's arrival, Spellman briefed his chief officials on the uncertain purpose of the visit but advised them to assist him should the need arise. As it turned out outside assistance was totally unnecessary. Spellman, along with Rabbi Lovis Hollander and Episcopal Bishop Horace Donegan, was an experienced spokesperson on religious and civic issues, and even at seventy-six, the Cardinal was recognized as a master of the political fencing arts.

Before dessert was served, the Cardinal asked Lindsay, who sat across from him: "Is there something we can do for you, Mr. Mayor?" Lindsay replied that he wanted to appoint a New York priest as chairman of his contemplated Police-Civilian Review Board, a major political commitment during the campaign. The priest he had in mind was Msgr. Gregory Mooney, a longtime servant of the Harlem poor. The Cardinal expressed appreciation for Lindsay's confidence in one of his priests, then said to Lindsay: "I am willing to give you Msgr. Mooney—" But before he could complete the sentence, Lindsay became so excited that words of gratitude were poured in the Cardinal's direction. Those watching the scene saw the problem for the Church—an Irish-American priest becoming chief judge of cops' conduct vis-à-vis the city's poor. The cops were mostly Irish-Catholic, the poor involved blacks and Spanish Catholics. As Lindsay drew breath Spellman continued: "—on one condition." Lindsay said, "Anything." To which the Cardinal replied: "If you persuade Rabbi Hollander and Bishop Donegan to be co-chairmen." The suggestion fell on the table like the dud bomb it was. Lindsay did not anticipate the counteroffer and it was not a step he was prepared to take, politically. No political advantage accrued to the mayor from the Spellman plan. Lindsay pursued his quest of Mooney once more. Spellman replied that Vatican II asked Bishops to be more ecumenical. Lindsay persisted. Spellman continued: "Mr. Mayor, you would not want me to violate the decrees of Vatican II." John Lindsay was beaten by a master and knew it. He would have to solve his interracial problem without using the Church as a foil. After that luncheon Catholics had difficulty acquiring status jobs in the administration of John V. Lindsay.

Spellman's ability to go to the heart of the matter became evident again, not many months later, during his first luncheon meeting with the new Provincial of the New York Jesuits. He was into his twenty-seventh year as Archbishop but very little escaped him even now. During the meal Father Robert Mitchell announced he was thinking of moving Woodstock Seminary, the world-renowned Jesuit training center, from its rustic settlement in Maryland to New York City. What did the Cardinal think of that? Spellman did not think much of it. He wondered aloud why the Jesuits wanted to do that in view of Woodstock's great reputation, John Courtney Murray's presence there, *Theological Studies*, etc. Mitchell explained that Vatican II made rethinking necessary about the continued value of large institutional living, isolating trainees from the mainstream of modern urban living and from the ecumenical outreach, which was eminently possible in New York. Spellman asked if Mitchell had examined the files of his Provincial's Office before coming to this meeting. The Jesuit did not seem to know what the Cardinal was talking about. After an embarrassed silence, Spellman said: "Well, if you had, you would know that your predecessor, Father McQuade, sat in that same chair twenty-five years ago and gave me the opposite reasons for going to Shrub Oak. I wish you people would make up your minds."

As Mitchell was leaving the Cardinal's residence, I asked him why he would break up a successful operation. His explanation was that new psycho-social studies suggested this to be a preferable new direction for a post-Vatican II Jesuit ministry. When reminded that those studies were iffy at best, in both methodology and conclusions, and not necessarily a boon to religion, the Jesuit Provinical merely shrugged.

Woodstock Seminary was slipped into New York after Spellman's death. The transfer turned out to be a disaster. The Jesuit superiors deceived Archbishop Cooke about their life style and their underground liturgical practices. Two of their prominent officials left the priesthood. Major faculty became notorious dissenters. *Theological Studies*, replanted in Washington, turned into a sourcebook of anti-Roman theology. The bad influence of the new Jesuit ideology and theology, apart from their influence on the conduct of religious women, cannot be calculated. A few weeks before his death (August 16, 1967) John Courtney Murray in a conversation with me bemoaned the aberrations already going on in Maryland, a year before the Jesuits moved to New York. Murray himself by this time was *persona non grata* to the new Jesuit breed. Had Spellman lived, one may believe, the Jesuits would have had to go elsewhere than New York. But considering the acquired anti-Roman bent they had already manifested, it is not likely that the results would have been any different.

Once the federal problem seemed to be resolved, Spellman was impatient about what happened to our textbooks. Rockefeller had pulled a political coup, the first of its kind in New York since the Supreme Court's approval of released-time religious instruction for public school children (1952). Without prejudice nonpublic school children enjoyed government-paid bus rides and discount fares. Why the delay of textbooks?

One good reason was the acrimony stirred up by *The New York Times*. What was proposed by the public school establishment as a public school bill ended up being called a Catholic school bill, because *The Times* week after week said it was. What began as a noncontroversial political move, to the advantage of money-strapped public school boards, was depicted as a hotly debated issue, uncertain of passage—and/or court action, because *The New York Times* said so. Organizations like PEARL (Public Education and Religious Liberty) entered the fray like vultures, stimulated by *The Times* (perhaps one agitated the other). PEARL was a coalition of the major antireligious forces in the state. The American Civil Liberties Union, the American Jewish Committee, Protestants and Other Americans United for Separation of Church and State were the prominent foes of textbooks going anywhere but to public schools. Even though Orthodox Jewish and Reformed Christian children would also benefit from the new law, *The Times*'s headlines stressed the Catholic school advantage. Many readers came to believe it really was a Catholic school bill. Few knew its public school origins. The Education Secretaries for the three local dioceses protested this anti-Catholicism and were invited to meet with four members of *The Times*'s Board, including Turner Catledge, Fred Hechinger, Clifton Daniel, the latter being former President Truman's son-in-law. The editors denied bias, defended themselves for the reason that the newsworthy aspect of the Textbook Bill was its "Catholic" component. The meeting became a futile exercise, but as the conversation proceeded, the three priests realized that most of the men arguing *The Times*'s case were Southerners, offspring of the Bible Belt. In spite of the starched cuffs and manicured hands, they were overly preoccupied with any advantage that might accrue to the Catholic Church. Cardinal Spellman was hardly their favorite clergyman.

Foot-dragging over textbooks for nonpublic school children continued in New York State's Department of Education, headed by James Allen. This proved to be particularly annoying because Nelson Rockefeller, the boss, assured Spellman that the books were forthcoming. The religious leaders decided to wait no longer. Each Secretary for his own school system directed a strong telegram to James Allen threatening court action to force his hand. Routinely, a copy of the telegram was sent to the Cardinal's residence. The following day I was on Spellman's carpet. Who was I to send such a telegram to his friend, Jim Allen? By what right? It was the best tongue-lashing a priest might receive in his priesthood. Nothing assuaged the Cardinal. The three Secretaries thought it was necessary. That counted for nothing. The rabbis agreed. That counted for less. "Don't do that again," was his final word. As he helped me on with my coat, Spelly added, "There's nothing personal in this." With hand on the door, I turned for a last word. "Your sources are better than mine. Find out whether Jim Allen's Education Department is a friend of ours. We will recheck our sources. If we made a mistake, not only will we apologize to you, but we'll fly to Albany and apologize to Allen." So ended a stimulating experience for someone only three months Spellman's Secretary for Education.

Not many weeks later the Cardinal dedicated a Paul VI Residence for Retired Priests, in which more than a hundred priests participated. Later, at the reception, one of the staff said: "The Cardinal is coming this way. Is he looking for you?" There was only one sensible rejoinder: "He's not even talking to me." But, sure enough, there he was calling me out for a private confab. "How's your mother?" he asked. "Fine, how's Your Eminence?" "I could be better. I just came over to tell you Jim Allen's Department of Education is no friend of ours." With that terse comment he turned and walked away. We received our textbooks.

THE BLAINE HUMILIATION

Every man ought to be allowed to die in peace. Not so Cardinal Spellman. He carried the cross of his office right into the grave. For the last six months of his life, though not well, he was in the center of the biggest political fight of his life. And he lost badly. It was more a defeat for the entire Church of New York State, than a personal failure. But since he was the titular head of the eight Bishops who ran the state's Catholic dioceses, the inability to remove from New York's constitution the Blaine Amendment prohibiting aid to nonpublic schools was a bitter blow to him. Within four weeks of that November 7, 1967, debacle, he was dead.

The story itself has its own fascination, demonstrating perhaps the ineptness of clergy in dirty politics, but more the depth of hostility in high places to religion itself, and to the Catholic religion in particular.

The Catholic Church never overcame, not even in this alledgedly liberated era, the fear of Catholicism engendered early in both Protestant and Jewish communities. The oft-cited dictum of Arthur Schlesinger, Sr., that anti-Catholicism is the most deep-seated bias of the American people is probably true. As is the other adage, attributed to several, that anti-Catholicism is the anti-Semitism of Americans who function as self-declared "political liberals."

The anti-Catholic bias rarely bares its ugly head more openly than when questions of public aid for nonpublic schools reach center stage either in the halls of Congress or before the U.S. Supreme Court. When the cause of "nonpublic schools" is presented, everyone from justices down to the local newspaper editor, unconsciously or otherwise, substitutes the adjective "Catholic" for "nonpublic," without regard for the obvious insult this does to the ministers, rabbis, and independent schoolmasters who also operate religious or private schools.

The greatest failure of the Catholic Church during the life of the so-called American experiment, if one can call it that, is its failure to obtain some measure of public support for parochial schools.

Originally, religious schools existed before public schools, perhaps fifty years earlier. After 1842 they coexisted with public schools during the period when local governments paid for the public schools. Voluntary donations and contributed services by religious made it possible for Catholic schools to keep pace with public schools until World War II. Indeed, the U.S. Church assembled the largest private school system ever seen anywhere—five million students by 1965, one out of every six American school children.

But, as the price of public school education rose, due first to the influx into local schools of state, then of federal monies, academic standards rose, salaries rose, and expensive educational machinery became available. Nonpublic schools found themselves in a disadvantaged position. The constitutional right of parents to choose private rather than public education was now in jeopardy. The Church looked on while many of her colleges abandoned their religious identity in the alleged pursuit of public monies. Within the past twenty years the parochial school system, too, has been cut in half—down to two and a half million students—largely the result of inability to cope with rising costs. Catholic schools, which once were relatively free schools, have now become relatively expensive. In a country boastful of its free enterprise and of the protection it gives to endeavors important to national well-being and/or security, something more than the law of supply and demand is now at work. If open competition really prevailed, nonpublic schools would prosper. But a deep-seated desire in high places for the parochial school system to wither away keeps interfering with possible growth of that system, which has been praised in every decade for its contribution to U.S. well-being. The course of nonpublic education is now downward, except among the upper classes.

How this state of affairs came to be can be understood only if we grasp the significance of the name "Blaine."

THE BLAINE FACTOR

Although nothing in the U.S. Constitution established the public school as *the* American school, the present domination of lower education by city and town governments grew almost certainly because the Catholic Church went into the school business in a big way early in the nineteenth century. Protestants did not need their own schools because the *public* schools *de facto* were thoroughly Protestant and were financed with public monies. Catholics were not going to tolerate this situation for long, and since there were not enough Jewish parents on the scene at the time to challenge the Protestant control of the American culture, it was left to Catholic Bishops alone to challenge this monopoly, first by seeking public aid, then by creating their own school system. The Protestantization of millions of young Catholics through public education was a serious threat to a young Church whose membership was mainly immigrant.

At the first sign of a threat to their hegemony, Protestant zealots moved immediately to penalize Catholic parents who exercised their constitutional rights over children's education by restricting the flow of tax money to *their* schools. A prominent leader in this crusade was James Gillespie Blaine, a Republican congressman from Maine. When Blaine lost his Speaker's post in 1875 under a rising tide of Democratic victories, the Republicans who had become used to power sensed they were in political trouble. Low-life Democrats were beginning to carve out big and little Tammany Halls amid the rapidly proliferating city slums. Republicans had neither the issue nor the leadership to offset those inroads. Who could save the Republican Party? And how? These became important questions for the heirs of the Lincoln mantle. Congressman Blaine galloped to the forefront with the issue that would rally the still Protestant majority to his party. Cut the ground from under the Catholic Church's potential for Americanizing city youth away from the dominant Protestant ethos. Make Catholic parents pay for their own schools and for the public schools as well.

Blaine's first effort to harness the country's Protestant vote came in 1875 with a proposed sixteenth amendment to the U.S. Constitution excluding aid to religious schools. The tactic failed to pass the U.S. Congress but not without impressing the Republican President with the political significance of the issue. In an effort to gain oneupsmanship on James Blaine, Ulysses Grant joined the chorus in 1876 denouncing parochial schools. The political mood against the Church was established for Democrats as well as Republicans. Amendments outlawing public money for religious schools were introduced into the House of Representatives twenty times between 1876 and 1929, and each time they were defeated. On the state level, however, nonpublic schools under religious auspices were not so fortunate. By 1918 "Blaine" had passed into twenty-nine state constitutions. New York fared no better. Although an unsuccessful effort had been made in 1867 (prior to Blaine), the New York State Constitution (Article XI, Section 3) was amended finally in 1894 to include the following stipulation:

> Neither the State nor any subdivision thereof shall use its property or credit or any public money, or authorize or permit either to be used, directly or indirectly, in aid or maintenance, other than examination or inspection, of any school or institution of learning wholly or in part under the control or direction of any religious denomination, or in which any denominational tenet of doctrine is taught.

The Constitutional Convention of 1938, which was marked by hospitality toward church-related schools, amended this to add the following clause: "But the legislature may provide for the transportation of children from any school or institution of learning."

This most restrictive of all such enactments was drafted by one of the country's most skillful lawyers, Elihu Root, to ensure that public monies would never be used, not even for religious orphanages.

Did the Blaine effort help the Republican Party? Unquestionably. From 1876 to 1912 Republicans controlled the White House, save for the two terms of Grover Cleveland, who defeated Blaine in 1884. The Republicans lost then by only sixty thousand votes, due to Blaine's ill-timed bluster over "rum, Romanism, and rebellion."

The 1894 amendment does not ban aid to private schools as such, only to those schools which teach religion. Cornell University professor Andrew Hecker evaluated the public mood as it evolved toward the end of the nineteenth century:

> The primary motivating force behind its initiation and passage three quarters of a century ago was frank Protestant animosity toward Catholic education. To have such a sentiment in the State's basic law was an understandable cause for concern on the part of its Catholic citizens.[8]

The only comparable exclusionary statutes born of bigotry were those enacted in the 19th century against blacks and the so-called "yellow peril." These restrictions have now been eliminated.

The educational problems created by the Blaine Amendment after 1894 were legion. Handicapped children could not receive home teaching unless they were full-time public school pupils: remedial reading paid for with state money was not possible for parochial school students, who also could not use public school gyms or swimming pools (but they could use those owned by public parks). They could not take a driver training course, even on Saturday, or lease a football stadium, or obtain physiological services or speech therapy (although basic health services were permitted). This hodgepodge casuistry was the direct result of a dual standard, depriving services at the state level that were perfectly permissible under federal law. "Blaine" also discouraged state courts from reviewing restrictive regulations established by local Boards of Education.

While the conflict between Catholics and Protestants helped

condition public opinion, especially that of the intellectual community, to accept government neutrality in public education, no polemicist of the nineteenth century, neither James G. Blaine, nor New York's Bishop John J. Hughes, the first major Catholic protagonist of aid to nonpublic schools, anticipated that the result would be neutrality against all religion, traditionally understood. Certainly, it was inconceivable to those antagonists that even the most bigoted anti-Catholic of that time would have approved the Supreme Court decision in the Torcaso case of 1961, which equated religion not only with faith in God, but with Secular Humanism and its denial of God's existence. What resulted from a healthy contest between competing religious bodies has been the banishment of religion itself to the fringes of the American culture. Before the U.S. courts today religion is a private matter and of little public consequence to any institution operating with government money. Not even the Founding Fathers, granted their suspicions of revealed or established religion, would have anticipated such a turn of events.

SPELLMAN AND BLAINE

Cardinal Spellman's campaign to repeal the Blaine Amendment to the New York State Constitution has been called his last hurrah and, indeed, it was. This, after one of the most highly organized political activities, and likely the most expensive, of his twenty-eight-year archepiscopate.

The 1967 State Constitutional Convention, in which the Church became embroiled, came about as a result of a decision by the power brokers of the Democratic Party to solidify and perhaps extend its political power throughout a state controlled in recent years mostly by Republicans. The Constitutional Convention was not called specifically to repeal the Blaine Amendment, nor as a favor to the Catholic Church, although later on voters would be led to think so by the propaganda aimed at discrediting parochial schools. The basic motivating force was Democratic politics and the seizure by Democratic power brokers of a substantial state

100

issue. For years reformers had been arguing over how, and when, to update the state's fundamental law—the court system, the election procedures, welfare arrangements, etc. Some of the old articles were unchanged since the days of Al Smith. Republican Nelson Rockefeller was the governor in 1966, but it was Democratic Speaker Anthony Travia and his Assembly leadership who decided to use a Constitutional Convention as a way of expanding the power and patronage of downstate Democrats. The popular Rockefeller, and before him the efficient Tom Dewey, had managed to eviscerate Democratic power statewide. Speaker Travia happened to be interested in nonpublic schools, but he was more committed to Democratic politics and his own future as a potential successor to Rockefeller. Once the formal call to a State Convention in 1967 became a *fait accompli,* Travia made it clear that a key plank in his platform for Democratic success was to be the repeal of the Blaine Amendment. This, he thought, would lock in for the Democrats the Catholic vote, which in New York State was considerable. His thinking was exactly the same as Blaine's a century before: appeal to a religious voting bloc to enhance the power of a political party.

From Cardinal Hayes's time onward, the Church's political think-tank in New York was the state Catholic Welfare Committee. The tradition of Church involvement in politics was even longer; John Hughes politicked Albany legislators in the 1840s to free him from harassment by lay trustees; Patrick Hayes sought welfare reforms in the 1920s. The issue in 1964 was textbooks. The Catholic Committee, as it was called, stood as the instrument through which political decisions on behalf of Catholic interests were processed. Until 1960 the concerns were chiefly welfare-oriented—child care, mental health, nursing homes, etc., mainly because the Bishops in 1894 traded away school aid as the price for holding onto constitutional aid to their charitable agencies. In that year churches generally had a vested interest in this compromise, because they were all into welfare care in a big way. Unless they agreed to the compromise about schools, they could have lost aid to their homes and hospitals, so hostile were the antireligious forces. At that time the parochial school movement was only beginning to gain momentum. Those nineteenth-century Bishops could hardly have foreseen that by the end of Spellman's life Catholic welfare agencies because of substantial state aid would be quite secularized, or that their chief concern then would be an educational empire far greater than anything they imagined in 1894. The trade-off had another ominous feature. Originally, the strings attached to money grants to child care or nursing homes were few. But, as time went on, the same antireligious bigotry which denied aid to parochial schools would also have the walls of Catholic institutions stripped of their crucifixes and their hiring policies adjusted to meet secular norms, not those of the Church, e.g., nondiscrimination against homosexuals.

In spite of the implicit dangers in the nature of the situation, the Catholic Committee was happy in 1966 to follow Tony Travia's lead. His interest was ours, so we decided. In short order the Catholic Committee began to work closely with a statewide Superintendent's Council, its monthly agenda crowded for the first time with education's concerns. Even the word "Welfare" was dropped from the committee's name. As soon as the Travia plan was endorsed, Charles Tobin, the executive secretary, conveyed the approval to all the Bishops, including Cardinal Spellman, who was not anxious to lead another controversial crusade in the public forum. It was not true, as John Cooney suggests,[9] that Tony Travia was "one of Spellman's conveyor belts." Spellman was not the type to evade his responsibility to lead, even if controversy awaited him, but by 1966 he was too tired to go looking for trouble.

Anyone who looked upon Tony Travia as a dupe of Cardinal Spellman was badly informed about the Brooklyn power broker. Travia was a friend of Brooklyn clergy, but a relative unknown in New York. Indeed, his first meeting with Cardinal Spellman was arranged by me and the Education Secretary of Brooklyn, Msgr. Eugene Molloy, who was a close friend of the Speaker. At a luncheon in the Cardinal's Residence Travia explained his plans for the convention and for Blaine. He impressed all his listeners with the need to present the constitution to the people as one package, with the Blaine repeal only one of its parts. The Blaine repeal out there by itself as a separate amendment, he argued, would elicit the same bigoted attacks that brought the amendment into the constitution in the first place. By nestling "Blaine" among "welfare goodies," Travia hoped to forge a coalition which would defeat any opposition the Republicans might muster. Not only was he persuasive, but at that luncheon who, appreciating his concern for "Blaine," was competent to fault his carefully honed political strategy? The voters would later prove him wrong. Church leaders, too, would discover too late the mistake of tying their interests to those of a political leader. There was no malice, to be sure. Anthony Travia was a son of his party, and of the Church. And when he spoke to the Cardinal about tying "Blaine repeal" into one package, he sincerely thought he was doing the best, as much for the Church as for the party.

The basic trouble, however, was that on a day-to-day basis Travia was more involved with his party than with his Church. The country was then experimenting with Lyndon Johnson's plan for a Great Society, and there was hardly a social cause Travia was not about to have New York State finance, especially if the programs advanced Democratic voting strength. His background in Brooklyn's clubs made it easy for him to give priority to re-aligning the balance of political power in the state to the advantage of his party. By the time the Travia strategy was clear in Albany, if not in New York, Lieutenant Governor Malcolm Wilson, a Republican power broker in his own right, was telling Spellman to get the Blaine Amendment out of the "one package." Republicans, he said, would support its repeal, but they were not going to pay through increased taxes for Travia's goodies, nor would Republicans contribute to any increase of Travia's power throughout the state. Spellman nodded his head, as if in disbelief. But he heard the message: the Republicans would kill "one package" at the polls. Charles Tobin, legal counsel to the Catholic Committee and a veteran lobbyist, could not budge Travia. The Church's fate was locked into the political wisdom (or its lack) of New York's Democratic Party.

Faced with this ukase, there was little for Tobin to do other than proceed with the Catholic Committee's program of supporting the one package, all the goodies and the Blaine repeal. He established a Research Institute for Catholic Education under the aegis of Msgr. Edgar McCarren, Rockville Centre's Secretary for Education. RICE's function was to provide research material and Catholic spokesmen to the media. Msgr. William O'Brien, the 1989 president of Daytop International, Inc., created a statewide network of Fairness to Children committees, mostly parish-based, to deliver the message to Catholic parents about Blaine and about the contributions their schools were making to the economic and political well-being of the state. A preelection rally in Madison Square Garden capped the effort to create grass-root support in New York City. Breakfast meetings were held with influential opinion-molders such as Senator Robert F. Kennedy (who was pleasant and noncommittal), and gubernatorial candidate Frank O'Connor. Luncheons with labor leaders George Meany, Harry Van Arsdale, Ray Corbett, suppers with various media stars, were carefully planned. Very little was left to chance.

Charles Tobin, acting for the Catholic Committee, undertook the largest advertising campaign ever undertaken by the Church, with the $1 million which the committee raised. TV/radio spots, public advertisements on the sides of city and suburban buses were brilliantly conceived, but they focused exclusively on the unfairness of Blaine to nonpublic school children. The advertising firm decided against involving the Church publicly in the grab bag features of the new constitution, lest they prove to be unpopular. The public relations people followed the lead of a Princeton poll, one which had been commissioned by the Catholic Committee. This showed that a majority of New York State voters favored Blaine's repeal.

As the ads began to appear, the Democrats sensed they had bitten off more than they could chew. Six weeks before Election Day, Steve Smith, Bobby Kennedy's brother-in-law, telephoned to ask for a meeting with me. We met in his Waldorf Towers suite, Smith saying that the senator would like to do some TV ads in support of the new constitution, but lacked money for his effort. Would we pick up the tab? Earlier someone had tried to interest Kennedy in participating but to no avail. Better his help late than never, we thought, since he was the most popular Democrat in the state. What were Kennedy's projected costs? I asked Smith. His answer was a hundred and fifty thousand dollars. With Smith's night telephone number in hand I headed for Spellman's Residence. All of the committee's money, except a hundred thousand dollars, had been contracted out. Where would the other money come from? These were troubling questions for anyone about to face Spellman, who always demanded decisive suggestions. (No one expected him to be dead four weeks after the forthcoming Blaine vote.) He tottered into the room, literally tottered, and sat down on the end of a chair with difficulty. Briefly he received the story. When the point of Kennedy's lack of money was reached, the Cardinal looked over the rim of his glasses and smiled: "Hmph, the Kennedys never have money when you want it." The final word placed before him was: "If we put money up for the senator, we are overspent by fifty thousand dollars and somehow you're likely to be stuck for it." He hesitated only a moment. Then with his knees groaning as he rose from the chair, he stood and said: "Father, in a million-dollar-ball game, what's fifty thousand?" Then he walked out. Steve Smith was called, so was Charlie Tobin, and Bobby Kennedy was in business without my having the least idea how Spellman would find the money.

THE CONSTITUTIONAL CONVENTION

The 1967 convention actually produced a fairly decent new constitution, one that was simpler, modern, and half the length of the existing document. Among its attractive features were: a bill of rights which guaranteed citizens the right to test the constitutionality of any statute or expenditure and to inspect the public records; strict control of wiretapping; a preamble that called for the state to eliminate inequality and poverty, to assure legal, social, and economic justice and for cooperation between government and private enterprise in community development; the transfer of all welfare costs, including Medicaid, to the state; financial aid for needy citizens seeking a college education; the establishment of new criteria for state aid to local communities; a shift of the tax burden to the well-to-do. The Blaine Amendment was dropped and in its place the new constitution used the language of the First Amendment: "Congress shall make no law respecting an establishment of religion or prohibit the free exercise thereof." The Blaine repeal was passed by the delegates to the convention by a vote of 132–49, just the reversal of the vote which enacted the amendment in 1894 (130–50).

All but the Democrats had problems with it—mostly Republicans, but Catholics and anti-Catholics, too. The Republicans said it would increase state expenditures by 80 percent over the next decade. Rockefeller's budget director said the repeal of Blaine would double state taxes. They also saw the provision for redistricting county boards as a threat to their political power outside New York City. At one point, the governor openly discussed the possibility of the Church softening its position on Blaine, promising he would use his unquestioned influence to repeal Blaine through the legislative process. This promise was persiflage. Rocky would have liked to see the constitution presented to the voters in eight separate packages, enabling Republicans to pick and choose the ones they wanted to kill. His own Minority Leader, Earl Bridges, considered this impractical, given the complexity of the new constitution. About six weeks before the scheduled vote of the delegates (August 15, 1967), the Republicans decided to call for a separate vote on Blaine (to protect their Catholic constituency) and one package for the remainder, which they promised to kill and so frustrate the Democratic grab for statewide dominion.

The Republican ploy to divide the Travia package failed just about the time Catholic schoolmen began to suspect that Blaine would go down to defeat if it remained in that single package. They also began to ask: Would, therefore, Blaine be better presented alone? What would happen to Church credibility if she won a separate Blaine vote (and future money for her schools) but helped defeat the other package—the heart of the new constitution—and in so doing damaged the interest of legitimate constitutional reform? It was a Catch-22 situation. However, it was late in the game to be asking these questions, forcing the Catholic Committee to acquiesce on Travia's one package (and take the consequences), although some educators insisted that in so doing Catholic education was once more being sacrificed to the interests of the Catholic Charities complex (as had been done in 1894) with its strong support for the social "goodies" the Democrats had included.

Once the "one package" was voted in by the convention to be delivered for a popular vote in November, the political campaign for and against the new constitution began in earnest. The anti-Catholics pulled out every stop. Blaine repeal, they argued, meant the end of the public school system, the rise of religious conflict, the flight of whites to Catholic schools, and the end of separation of Church and state. These were the very arguments used by nineteenth-century bigots, this time mouthed by Protestant and Other Americans, the American Civil Liberties Union, the United Parents Association, and a number of Jewish groups. Mayor John Lindsay feared a mass exodus from public schools. Leo Pfeiffer, counsel for the American Jewish Congress, saw the repeal of Blaine as a concession to the bigotry of white parents who did not want their children to sit with blacks. Seymour Graubard of New York's Anti-Defamation League thought the separation of Church and state would be weakened and the public school system pauperized.

These allies, even during the convention, tried desperately to hamstring parochial schools in every way possible. At one point they wanted the Blaine repeal to carry a rider which would still deny public funds if the religious school discriminated for racial or religious reasons. This in itself was an absurd proposal, intended if possible to subject religious schools to harassment by antireligious forces. The rider was also absurd because at the time Catholic schools were bulging to the breaking point. There were 900,000 nonpublic school students in the state (greater than the total public school enrollment in thirty-two states), 450,000 in New York City alone. Furthermore, though only 18 percent of the city's Catholic population were members of minority groups, 52 percent of the Catholic enrollment in Manhattan were minority,

30 percent in the Bronx. In Manhattan and the Bronx there were thirty-five racially mixed areas, where the parish school was better integrated than the neighborhood public school.

Nothing infuriated the anti-Catholic enemies of Blaine repeal more than the Catholic Committee's TV ads. One filmstrip showed a tow truck hauling away a wrecked auto. The voice intoned:

> A funny thing happened to Steve Carroll on his way to school today. He just never saw the other guy. A driver education course might have taught Steve to be on the alert. And the irony is that he wanted to take such a course at the public high school in his neighborhood. But our State Constitution said "no" because Steve attends a parochial high school a few blocks away. Unlike the public school, Steve's school receives no funds for driver education and, worse, kids are forbidden what could very well save some lives. Unless we have a new Constitution, one out of every four kids in New York State—Catholic, Jewish, and Protestant—may never be taught to drive safely. Does that make sense? Let's teach safety to all our children. Vote "yes" on Proposition No. 4. New York needs a new Constitution.

This TV ad, like others dealing with black Catholics disqualified from remedial reading, brought cries of foul from the anti-Catholics. Florence Flast, president of the public schools' United Parents Association, cried "scurrilous advertising," "an outrageous lie." But the ad only highlighted the institutionalized discrimination against children who attended religious schools.

Two weeks before Election Day (October 25, 1967), *The New York Times* on behalf of the Florence Flasts and Leo Pfeiffers sermonized by: (1) identifying the issue "mainly" as a concern of Roman Catholics, (2) describing the advertising campaign as "mawkish and misleading," (3) raising the specter of middle-class pupils fleeing public schools, and (4) suggesting that public schools would become "havens for the children of the ghetto."

The new constitution was roundly rejected on November 7, 1967. If Spellman accepted this defeat with detachment, others in the Catholic world did not. Monday-morning quarterbacks could be found everywhere on Wednesday morning. We should never have consented to one package; the advertisements should have stressed the constitution, not just the Blaine repeal; New York/ Brooklyn ran a big-city show leaving upstate and Long Island Catholics (the Republican power base) looking like poor country cousins. The Catholic educators who complained the most on November 8 were those whose parishioners abandoned the Catholic cause in the greatest numbers. A number of imponderables also came into play. Only two years after Vatican II anti-institutional- ism was surprisingly virulent in some dioceses, especially among religious educators and members of religious orders. To pursue a narrow Catholic institutional interest was a cause of shame to some Catholics. "Why aren't we more concerned about the poor?" "Or about public school children?" "Why are we strain- ing ecumenical relations by pursuing a course non-Catholics obvi- ously resent?" One other imponderable was the extent to which the institutional needs of the Church's well-subsidized welfare agencies were really involved in burying the repeal of Blaine. Was Catholic Charities responsible for tying Blaine into one package? Tony Travia's package had a lot of "goodies" for their agencies. College administrators also queried: "Why did we not seek in- stead a partial repeal of Blaine (making possible monies for Cath- olic colleges)?" This approach would not have aroused non-Catho- lic animosity. (A few years later when so-called Bundy money became available, Catholic colleges seized it voraciously, even though the price they paid was the legal abandonment of their Catholic affiliation.)

It may be offensive, at this late date, to those good-willed par- ticipants in the Blaine repeal who contributed their money and substance to the crusade on behalf of Catholic school children to assign blame for the rout of the Catholic forces; but without preju- dice it is possible to explore the factors which contributed to the political disaster.

First, Catholic leaders underestimated the anti-Catholic ani- mus. The Princeton poll during the summer of '67 provided hope that a significant majority of New York voters, Protestant as well as Catholic, favored the repeal of the Blaine Amendment. Harry

Truman, however, was more correct in his claim that polls predict nothing, except about the pollsters. The voting results demonstrated that the anti-Catholic bug still bit poisonously, especially in the so-called "liberal" community, for which *The New York Times* was the official spokesman. Albert Shanker's United Federation of Teachers, Leo Pfieffer's American Jewish Congress, and Hubert Humphrey's Americans for Democratic Action joined with the Protestant National Council of Churches to explain how Blaine's repeal meant the end of the country as it had been known. PEARL, the coalition group, headed by William Haddad, a spokesman among Jewish leaders, and Percy Sutton, Borough President of Manhattan, the most visible black politician of the day, were outraged by the Catholic "ads" which highlighted poor Catholic children as objects of discrimination, including the increasing number of blacks in parochial schools. The counterattack of the public school establishment depicted parochial schools as havens of the privileged, and deceitfully so. But there was a bite of antireligion, too. While Orthodox Jewish and Protestant schools were fully involved, PEARL stressed "Catholic" throughout the campaign. Citizens for Educational Freedom suddenly became a Catholic front. Since PEARL gained no mileage from the interfaith nature of CEF, it appealed to bigotry. If CEF had responded by saying that PEARL was a Jewish front, there would have been an uproar. Yet PEARL suffered no damage from its outrage.

The most disconcerting experience in efforts to alleviate intra-Church tensions over Blaine came during "dialogue" with leading officials of the Anti-Defamation League, an affiliate of B'nai B'rith. Jewish leadership sought to dialogue with the three downstate Secretaries for Education on ways of reducing hostilities between religious groups during the campaign to the minimum. "Dialogue," an American panacea for resolving differences of opinion, never works when deeply held convictions are involved, as Solomon learned when he was asked to cut the disputed baby in half. The "dialogue" with Jewish leaders, led by a persuasive Hollywood mogul, Dore Schary, who flew into New York for these breakfast meetings, was pleasant. Conversation was open and enlightened. No item was taboo. By the third or fourth week, a breakthrough over nonpublic schools, many of which were Orthodox Jewish, seemed to be in the offing. One morning the dialogists awakened to a story on the front page of *The New York Times* which informed the country that the local chapter of B'nai B'rith opposed the repeal of Blaine. The dialogue with the top brass of the Anti-Defamation League came to its predestined end.

The second, and equally important, lesson from the Blaine disaster was, of course, the precarious nature of Democratic and Republican politics, and of Church involvement with either brand. People, they say, vote their bellies more than their creeds. As a general rule, this is probably true. Certainly, for him to win, Tony Travia had to make inroads on Republican bastions upstate and on Long Island. And he could not do this effectively without the help of the "liberal" community, which was basically anti-Catholic. Tony Travia lost on all fronts.

Finally, there was the political rivalry between Malcolm Wilson and Tony Travia. Had Travia passed his constitution, he would have become the natural candidate of his party to seek Nelson Rockefeller's job. Malcolm Wilson, the lieutenant governor, had an important stake in shooting down a dangerous political rival. For a dozen years he lived in the governor's shadow, even though he was the politician who made the Rockefeller machine run. Now that Rocky was to retire he was the heir apparent. Here was the Church caught between two practicing Catholics and the two smartest politicians in the state. Under the circumstances it is difficult to see how the Church could have won under either scenario. Would anything else have worked? Perhaps on the Catholic side a more modest goal of repealing Blaine partially (for college students). But in 1967 this was unacceptable to the Catholic Superintendents Council, which was interested only in parochial and diocesan schools. On the other hand, partial repeal might have eased the financial burden on Catholic colleges without exacting an abandonment of their religious identity. On the politicians' side, compromise by Travia and Wilson on the "goodies" in the new constitution would have been necessary—and that was not likely in 1967. Travia went on to become a federal judge in 1974.

Wilson was defeated for the governorship by Congressman Hugh L. Carey, buried in political history along with the repeal of Blaine.

And so would be Cardinal Spellman. The Cardinal, who on election eve called the new constitution "a document worthy of support by the people in New York State," was dismayed two days later "to think that they would have over-whelmingly supported the new Constitution were it not for the fact that it repeals the ban on parochial aid." But "the Little Man" died with one satisfaction. Two weeks earlier (November 17, 1967) the Second Vatican Council approved its *Declaration on Christian Education* which included the following sentence in section six: "The public authority, therefore, whose duty it is to protect and defend the liberty of its citizens, is bound according to the principles of distributive justice to ensure that public subsidies to schools are so allocated that parents are truly free to select schools for their children in accordance with their conscience."

This was a fitting last will and testament for Cardinal Spellman, who was the prime mover of that codicil.

On December 2 he brought this latest defeat, and his many victories, to the Lord he served with so much diligence. That afternoon Spellman's consultors elected Archbishop John J. Maguire as Administrator of the Archdiocese by a vote of 22–4. Auxiliary Bishop Terence Cooke was the other candidate. The Spellman era had ended.

THE SPELLMAN OF HISTORY

Many years later, when hardly anyone spoke of him any more, a young priest sitting at a priest's meeting with a group of pastors made a disparaging remark about the late Cardinal, whom he never knew, "Well, they didn't call him 'the Little Man' for nothing." A battle-scarred veteran of the Spellman era, a retired pastor, turned on the young curate with a look of scorn and sputtered: "Sonny, for your information when that 'Little Man' walked out into the daylight he threw a shadow ten feet tall." The point was well taken. Spellman did not look like much but he was.

Francis Cardinal Spellman will surely be more than a footnote in U.S. Catholic history. The scholars will dissect him, psychoanalyze him, report his doings, criticize from hindsight his worst mistakes, perhaps even credit him with some creditable performances. But they will not pass over him.

When John Cooney sent me a copy of *The American Pope,* his muckraking biography of Spellman, as a token of appreciation for giving him an interview, the autograph scrawled across the flyleaf was preceded with the line "Save the Church from the Spellys." This prayer, if that is what it can be called, was as misplaced as was Cooney's bigoted understanding of the Churchman.

What kind of man was Spellman? What kind of a Bishop? His bishoping may have evoked hatred from the world's John Cooneys, but he was the greatest Archbishop New York had seen since John Hughes, who died a hundred and three years before him. If one has to define him in one word, Yankee, Boston Yankee that is, might be the word. Spellman showed annoyance with people who did not take for granted that he was Irish, but he was about as Irish as his one-time boss, William Cardinal O'Connell. While "the Little Man" was not without emotion or humor, his human relations by and large were businesslike and impersonal. Critics often asked what special talents he had, as if he had none. He was not a great mind to be sure, nor did he have unusual oratorical abilities, nor was he a handsome figure of a man. It would not be far from the truth to admit the contrary. But, like Eddie Stanky of the old Brooklyn Dodgers, who it was said could not hit or field, Spellman might have been the most important man on anyone's team. In the twilight of his life and in a rare moment of open emotion, Spellman confessed to having been afraid of the New York assignment, because "I thought the priests there might not accept me." The reflection itself was hard to believe as he said it, because from the moment of his takeover (May 23, 1939), he acted as if he was afraid of no one. Although he never pandered to his priests and occasionally scolded them, most New York priests were proud of him and he was good to

113

most of them. When he died the morale of priests in the Archdiocese was high indeed, no matter what Church's malcontents later would tell John Cooney. Many years after Spellman's death Jesuits at Marquette University expressed outrage at funny but flattering stories told about Spelly. In the post-Vatican II Church of those Jesuits nothing good was to be said about his likes. But when the news spread abroad on December 2, 1967, that "the Little Man" was dead, there was a certain sense of loss felt at his passing, a feeling that would have made him uncomfortable, had he to face it in life.

Cardinal Spellman loved prominence and power and sought both from an early age. But he used them well. It was not simply that he took over a diocese with an alleged debt of $28 million and left it the most prosperous See in the United States. New York's outside debt at the time was only $400,000 (less than many parishes), enough to maintain an outside credit line for the Archdiocese, if ever he needed one. He never did. Everything in New York was better because he came—parishes, seminaries, schools, convents, and hospitals. He created trouble for himself because he was direct with his friends and his enemies alike, calling bigots bigots, in language hardly used in public anymore. But he also had more non-Catholic friends, who liked and admired him, than any Archbishop before him. They laughed when he condemned *The Miracle* and *Baby Doll,* but now parents ask, "Why aren't Bishops condemning dirty movies the way Cardinal Spellman did?" They say he was too money-minded, too close to the wealthy, and truly he would pursue a million dollars with the ease of a hobo putting out a hand for a loose quarter. But for himself? In one period alone, 1955–59, he erected fifteen churches, ninety-four schools, twenty-two rectories, sixty convents, and thirty institutions at a cost of $140 million. He is charged with being arrogant, and he surely could be blunt; but he never took anything that was not his to take and he could manifest unusual shyness at too much praise. Yes, he did love his Church, his country, and his soldiers. Yes, he lacked great intellectual depth, was uncomfortable with abstract discussions, was a very poor public communicator. His bad relationship with the press was mostly his own fault, the result of his discomfort in having to respond to adversary questions. Nor was he a "consensus builder," because he expected people to follow any lead he took, once he took it. But then he could surprise outsiders. Spellman was not uncomfortable with John Courtney Murray, impressing even on Murray that Bishops, not scholars, made Church decisions. He commissioned a scholarly biography of John Hughes at great expense, only to be let down by scholars who spent his money but produced nothing. And for a resolute personality, he could eat crow with equanimity, as during the meeting with the Calvary workers he was berating or his peace-making with Eleanor Roosevelt, who was the anti-Catholic he called her.

The New York Cardinal reached for influence almost by natural impulse and without second thoughts about whose lines he crossed. In 1952 I happened to be returning from the dedication of the new St. Mary's Cathedral, Ogdensburg, New York, in the company of Boston's Archbishop Richard Cushing, who had roared his way that morning as preacher of the occasion. There was hardly anyone on the small plane but the two of us, and Cushing was at his delightful best. He did not know me save that I was a New Yorker, and for all he might have sensed, I could have been one of Spellman's Chancery staff. Unconcerned about who I might have been, he roared, all in great humor, for the better part of two hours about his friend "Frank." They were more than close associates, of course, Spellman having intervened with Rome in 1944 to secure Boston for the impulsive Cushing (as later in 1958 he did to ensure that the Cardinal's hat came Boston's way).

The gist of Cushing's riotously funny description of his relationship with Spelly was the effort he spent in those early years trying to keep New York's nose out of the Boston tent, even to tap wealthy friends therein for moneys to promote the interests of the Archdiocese of New York! Said Cushing at one point: "He even tried to get me to do some of his errands. I had to change my private phone number on several occasions simply to avoid his phone calls at two or three o'clock in the morning, usually with some new idea for me, once telling me I ought to be supporting a particular mission in South America." Boston's Archbishop must have enjoyed tweaking Spelly for my benefit because when we finally rattled into La Guardia Airport, he drove me home to my rectory at midnight, an hour out of his way. But that expansiveness was Cushing at his normal best, and his tale telling was Spellmania *au naturel*.

How would Spellman fare in today's Church? His critics and enemies say he would not make it, nor get away with doing what he did during his lifetime. Who can really answer this question? Spellman was too pragmatic to give Frank Skeffington's answer in Edwin O'Connor's *The Last Hurrah*. When asked at the end of his life whether he would do things differently if he had to do them over, said Boston's fictional mayor: "I wouldn't change a thing." That would not be Spelly. More likely, his possible answer was given by a New York priest who mused over the question: "If it were possible to ask Spellman now how he would fare in today's Church, his likely answer would be 'Let them try me.'" That certainly would be in character.

If a man's measure is to be gauged by the kind of enemies he makes, then Spellman achieved greatness merely by defending Catholic interests. He was dead only a few days when *Harper's Magazine*[10] conducted its own burial services. A Harvard-trained *New York Times* reporter put him down as the Church's "Shirley Temple," then scorned him for his interventions in New York politics. Speaking of the new divorce law which was broadened in 1966 to allow six grounds, not just adultery, correspondent Corry rejoiced: "What really got the divorce bill off the ground was a man named John—Pope John." John XXIII, he said, did to traditional Catholic power what FDR did to Tammany Hall. Maybe so, but while Spelly was alive, there was still some power left in "the powerhouse."

Msgr. Florence D. Cohalan, author of *A Popular History of the Archdiocese of New York*, in his review of John Cooney's life of the Cardinal, best framed the scope of what the historian of the future must assess:

Cardinal Spellman had a long, interesting and exceptionally active life. Long before the Council made collegiality almost a common term he was aware of his responsibility to the Universal Church. His career was unique not only in this country but in the contemporary Church and it deserves and will repay a serious full length study. When it comes it will not claim that he was a saint, or that he never made mistakes, or that all who opposed him had unworthy motives. Let us hope that, unlike this book, it will be written objectively, with genuine understanding, accuracy, balance, and perspective and will avoid a minor obsession with ecclesiastical finery and purple passages.[11]

NOTES

1. *Quadragesimo Anno,* no. 35.

2. *Commonweal,* May 23, 1947.

3. John Cooney, *The American Pope* (New York: Times Books, 1984).

4. *Commonweal,* December 31, 1948.

5. *The International Review—Natural Family Planning,* February 18, 1978.

6. This address is part of the Spellman papers in the Archives of the Archdiocese of New York at Dunwoodie Seminary.

7. Ibid.

8. *New York Times Magazine,* October 1, 1967.

9. Cooney, *The American Pope,* p. 311.

10. *Harper's Magazine,* December 1967.

11. *Newsletter of the Fellowship of Catholic Scholars,* June 1985.

THREE

The Heir Non-Apparent:
Terence J. Cooke

THE INTERREGNUM as it is called—the length of time between a death and the replacement—was comparatively brief, four days short of a hundred days. And Archbishop John J. Maguire reigned supreme, the popular choice of priests to succeed. These turned out to be fun days, and Maguire enjoyed the role. Shortly after the Cardinal's burial, a nationally known pastor in the Bronx, hoping to build a "Cathedral" overlooking the Long Island Sound, received a letter from the Archdiocesan Building Commission instructing him that his new church could contain only eight hundred seats. He rushed into Maguire's office one day explaining that in a private conversation the month before with his now deceased Ordinary, he was assured he could build to almost twice that capacity. Maguire, terse as always, responded:

118

"I guess you haven't heard. Spellman is dead." Others soon found that out, too.

During this three-month hiatus, conversation about the future of New York was wide and free—about whether the Archdiocese should be divided, whether the Brooklyn diocese properly now could be reunited once more with New York, whether the future Archbishop might move away from Madison Avenue so that he might live with more privacy where he did not work, whether the Cardinal's House and St. Patrick's Rectory should be razed so that the beauty of the Cathedral might be as visible on Madison Avenue as it was on Fifth, whether the Cathedral ought to be redecorated and its main altar moved forward to conform to the new demands of Vatican II, and, of course, there were lots of guesses about who would succeed. During the interregnum a few unexpected things happened.

One day, hardly more than a fortnight after the funeral, William Vanden Huevel, an aide to Robert Kennedy, telephoned me to say that the New York senator would like to pay a courtesy call on Archbishop Maguire. Could I arrange it, he asked. The Administrator was more than willing and so one afternoon in February 1968, Bill and the senator met in Maguire's office. I was the only other person in the room. I had been involved with the senator the previous year because of the fight over the repeal of the Blaine Amendment, but both Maguire and I were well aware that Kennedy was ready to displace the faltering Lyndon Johnson and to take the presidency unto himself, if he could. The senator might have known or guessed that Johnson would refuse another term (as he did on March 31, 1968), so he was in the process of mending his Catholic fences, an important consideration in New York, where the "Catholic vote" was large and erratically dispensed. Upon entry to Maguire's office, Bobby was properly respectful of the Archbishop. Unlike his brother Jack, he was considered a practicing Catholic and, with wife Ethel, a model Catholic couple, too. Archbishop Maguire, who often played a Buddha role with strangers and was apolitical if any prelate ever was, made Kennedy come to him. After the customary greetings, the Archbishop left it to the senator to explain why he was there.

119

Bobby Kennedy did not let him down. "I'm here," he said, "to initiate better relations with the Archdiocese than my family enjoyed during the late years of Cardinal Spellman. Once we were quite friendly, but as the Cardinal grew older he became, as you know better than I, testy and difficult to deal with." He paused just long enough for the dead-panned Maguire to interject: "Oh, just like your old man?" The directness of the riposte stopped Kennedy cold. He seemed stunned—but only for a second—and then broke into the typical Bobby Kennedy laugh: "Touché," he rejoined. From that moment on the conversation was the talk of "big" men, about the state of the nation, about the civil rights issue, the role of the Church, and about how "we" could cooperate. The meeting lasted an hour with Kennedy and Maguire hitting it off quite well. As we repaired to the courtyard of the Chancery Office, a longer trip than necessary because the secretaries fawned over the senator at every step, Kennedy stopped to say good-bye and said to me: "Now there's a Bishop I could deal with." He never got the chance. Four months later he was assassinated, and Maguire never became Archbishop of New York.

Cardinal Spellman was no sooner dead than speculation began as to who would take his place. No one really expected Auxiliary Bishop Cooke to be that man.

Two days after the death *The New York Times* headlined a story by its religion editor, Edward B. Fiske: "U.S. Bishops to recommend Spellman's successor to Vatican." Fiske deduced this from the fact that a committee of seven Bishops was established after Vatican II to reach a consensus about candidates for important Sees. Fiske's likely candidates included Bishop John Wright of Pittsburgh, Detroit's Archbishop John Dearden, and Archbishop Fulton Sheen of Rochester. The elected Administrator of New York during the interregnum, John J. Maguire, was "not regarded as a likely candidate." Cooke's name was mentioned by no one. Indeed, during this period Chancery officials speculated that Cooke would get something, perhaps a small See like Poughkeepsie if the large New York See was divided upon the naming of a new Archbishop. The gossip mongers, including those in the national press, reckoned without "the Little Man," the popular inside name for Spellman. By prearrangement with Paul VI, the dead Cardinal succeeded in having Cooke named his successor, from the grave as it were. Three months later (March 6, 1968), Cooke was appointed Archbishop, and a Cardinal a mere year later. (Coincidentally, several other Spellman favorites were promoted within the twelve-month period—George Guilfoyle to Camden, Thomas Donnellan to Atlanta.)

The only one who ever predicted the Cooke succession was Msgr. Joseph O'Brien, later his Vicar General. At the close of the Council (December 8, 1965), on the occasion of the elevation of Maguire to be Coadjutor Archbishop of New York, Spellman indicated to both Cooke and O'Brien that Maguire would not be his successor. Six months before his death, at a luncheon for his Board of Consultors, the old man openly spoke of his end, as if he sensed it was not far away. The Cardinal reminisced how in the normal course of events he would have been Archbishop of Boston, a prospect that did not displease him. Once named to New York, however, he became anxious, fearing that priests there would never accept an outsider. Now, sensing he was nearing the end, Spellman sentimentalized that he had come to admire New York priests as the best body of its kind in the country. Most of his listeners that day were surprised at the amount of emotion he was betraying. Then he prophesied, "I can tell you this. When my time comes to go, the Holy Father this time, unlike in 1939, will not have to look outside for my successor." It was a startling statement, but one that was made with the usual Spellman certitude. Archbishop Maguire was seated immediately across the table from him. Nearby sat Auxiliary Bishop Guilfoyle, head of New York's prestigious Catholic Charities organization, also Bishop Broderick, Rector of Dunwoodie Seminary, and, of course, Terry Cooke. Since only four of the twenty-six consultors listening to him that day would after his death vote for Cooke to be Administrator during the interregnum, it is fair to say that in any guessing game Cooke was not seen as a front-runner.

Months later, when the old man's body was interred below St. Patrick's high altar, some of Cooke's intimates suspected that even by the time of that July luncheon Spellman had given his young favorite some indication that he would succeed to the New York See. Nonetheless, the appointment, when it came, surprised even the initiated. One-time Apostolic Delegate Vagnozzi later asked what Spellman saw in Cooke to choose him as successor, only to be reminded that Paul VI actually did the choosing. But from the grave Spelly was still the respected proposer and Cooke the type of personality likely to have enjoyed the favor of Montini. Obviously, too, those stories of Spelly being out of favor with the new Pope were somewhat exaggerated.

"The Little Man's" predilection for Cooke was that of an old man who late in life found a son. Spellman never wore his heart on his sleeve and in the early years the Cardinal's tastes favored the McIntyres, O'Haras, O'Boyles, Griffiths, Maguires—priests of varied talents but all with a common thread of Spelly's toughness. Cooke was a boy. He was gentle. And he loved the old man, who reciprocated the affection to the extent this was possible for a Boston Yankee. Recommended by Msgr. Charles Giblin, himself a one-time favorite, for the post of procurator at Dunwoodie Seminary (actually to take Giblin's place), Cooke quickly proved himself to be competent, tireless, and a master of detail. The irony was that Giblin would later find himself in the doghouse over the Calvary strike, even as his protégé was taking a first step toward the Cardinal's hat.

For a young priest Cooke was very sure of himself with Spellman, who ordinarily kept subordinates at arm's length. "The Little Man" was by no means a palsy-walsy Administrator, but from the beginning his relations with Cooke were warm. From 1956 onward the rise was fast—Vice Chancellor, Chancellor, Bishop, Vicar General. More and more, Terry began to speak for the Cardinal, to lead him around, to put him to bed. And in spite of the fact that the young man had been operated on for cancer of the lymph nodes only months before (and given three years to live by the surgeons), Spellman proceeded to consecrate Cooke Auxiliary Bishop on December 13, 1965. It was said that Paul VI was impressed with Cooke's handling of the papal visit to New York two months earlier (October 4). Whatever the personal chemistry with Spelly, Terry Cooke also fitted comfortably into the vision of a Pope who himself played the assistant role for twenty years in the larger than life of Pius XII. Cooke's warmth and geniality would gain him great affection from the masses of people he would later serve. In spite of the medical problems, he reigned over New York's Catholic life for the next fifteen years and died with such equanimity in the face of severe pain that the word "saint" appeared in many of his obituaries.

Although the promotion was a pure case of nepotism, Terry's appointment was accepted with great calm. Five days before the actual announcement a rumor, with his name on it, floated through the Chancery by way of an Italian pastor well connected in Rome, but it was not taken seriously. Yet, when reality set in, the traditional poise of the diocese prevailed. There were no protests, no bitterness from any quarter. Cooke was a good man, well experienced, and, though for many priests not a hail-fellow-well-met, was liked by most and disliked by few. He knew the Archdiocese as well as anyone, and New York was used to its own in the Chair. In the previous century four of five Archbishops (Spellman excepted) were New York-born diocesans. Surely, in Cooke's mind, there was no doubt that he would be accepted. (It probably did not enter his mind that the two outsiders—Hughes and Spellman—were by far the more historic Churchmen.)

Indeed, the reception was exceedingly warm. Adjectives in the press about him were correct: "approachable," "genial personality," "pastoral rather than administrative." What was not evident then, as it later came to be recognized, was his capacity for work and his dislike of bad feeling and confrontation. In his first press conference Cooke was asked how he expected to fare with the newly created Priests' Senate, known to be headed by antiestablishment priests/"rebels." He responded, "We have no rebels among us here. We share in the greatest fraternity in the world."

Indeed there were rebels in New York, but he was not prepared to admit it. Irenicism—and its name was Cooke—would be the mark of his episcopate. He had received in quick order so many approvals from his predecessor and from Rome that he oozed confidence. His charm would carry him through the most difficult circumstances. In the beginning some said he did not know much about finances, but he certainly proved them wrong. Cardinal Spellman left a prosperous Archdiocese, but Cooke left New York even better off. His ninety-nine-year lease of the Madison Avenue Chancery's property to Harry Helmsley for the Palace Hotel guarantees the Archdiocese a million-dollar income annually and a return of the property toward the end of the next century. He established a long-delayed pension system for religious and lay employees on a pay-as-you-go basis without placing the diocese into debt. And the new twenty-one-story administrative complex at 1011 First Avenue at a cost of approximately $1 million a story, when it opened for business in 1973, was fully paid for.

Such was the priest installed as Archbishop of New York on April 4, 1968, who took immediate command of his Cathedral pulpit in what was one of his two finest hours (the other would come fifteen years later—October 6, 1983—when he climbed into his bed of pain to die a saintly death from cancer). That first archepiscopal sermon was magnificent. In a thunderous voice, rarely heard again, he told thirty-four hundred listeners, "We seek to achieve a happy wedding of the new and the old. Our task is to perfect and adapt what we have and at the same time move forward into new areas of concern. Progress builds, it does not destroy." The remaining remarks touched all the right issues— racism, the Vietnam War, concern for the poor. It was pure Terry Cooke—"we must be flexible," "there are no simple solutions," "no magic formulae." And then, "I pledge the resources of this Archdiocese to uplift the poor."

It did not go unnoticed that his inaugural presentation stayed with generalities. He was coming to power at a perilous moment in Church history and some had sought a more pointed sermon. The Charles Curran debacle at Catholic University the year before had rattled the New York Church, as elsewhere, and April 4, 1968, was less than four months away from *Humanae Vitae*. The first Synod of Bishops only a short time earlier had deplored the doubts about the truth of the Faith that were being raised within the Church by priests and religious. It had called for "the firm exercise of authority" in dealing with those responsible for such deviations. "Those who are pertinacious should be removed from office." Was Cooke prepared for this role? What did he mean by "flexible"?

Yet it was unfair to expect a new leader to lay out the specifics of his administration in a first address. Those who heard him that day were moved by his youth and his idealism. That was precisely what the moment called for.

What did the people expect of him? No one could say and, as Harry Truman once noticed, the polls would never really say for sure. Catholics usually accept the Bishops given them by the Holy See. In Cooke's case this was especially true. The media, however, had their own idea of what a new Archbishop of New York ought to be, or what they wished he would become. It took Ted Fiske, former minister and *New York Times* religion editor, six months to put it into writing.

The Times, of course, always has its own norms for the news it deems fit to print about the Catholic Church. The mind of the secular establishment and its grand design for a "reformed" Catholic Church was amply represented by Editor Fiske. His article in *The New York Times Magazine*[1] amassed all the "inside" gossip which would make Cooke appear to be a predestined mediocrity. *The Times*'s best informants were disgruntled priests who defined their Chancery Office as "the ecclesiastical equivalent of the smoke-filled room" and "government by crony." Fiske's would-be church, which Cooke could create if he were pressured enough, would accept contraception, marital dissolubility, underground liturgies, doctrinal dissent, and management by public opinion. Authority was out because it meant paternalism and obedience, and because it had been outlawed by the Second Vatican Council. Fiske's ideal priests were those who promised to give Cooke a hard time. *The Times*'s analysis came close to the truth only insofar as it highlighted the forces within the Church that were waiting to move against the Archbishop whenever he failed to follow the so-called "liberal agenda." This proved to be the case. There was little that Cooke, or any Bishop, could do to assuage that establishment's lust for change or to persuade it to have a more Catholic view of the Church's mission or nature. Cooke made several moves in its direction, e.g., by appointing almost immedi-

125

ately a black priest as his Vicar in Harlem. This office was created to evoke a front-page story but was against the advice of all his trusted advisers. Terry gained the headline and still another when the man in question later abandoned the priesthood. It was a lesson that he never fully learned, viz., that appointments are properly given to those and those alone who can be expected to implement the policies of the Church.

When the celebrations ended, diocesan business picked up where it left off the month before. A new era was dawning. At the end of the Spellman era there were three "powerhouses" on Madison Avenue, 452 where the Cardinal lived, 455 where Archbishop Maguire lived, and 451 (the Chancery) where Bishop Cooke had grown to be a power unto himself. Most Chancery officials had been Maguire appointees and were used to the Coadjutor's thinking and style—Cooke was friendly with all these appointees but once on his own he elevated his intimates immediately to the power roles once centered only in Maguire. Furthermore, Cooke was a detail man, who involved himself in decision-making at the lowest levels. Those accustomed to wide latitude and quick decisions characteristic of the Spellman-Maguire era had some adjustments to make.

The new Archbishop reconfirmed all diocesan officeholders as custom in the Church dictated, although it was suggested that he might wish to make some immediate changes. There really was no reason why he should suffer for several years with holdovers who did not fit into his plans or style of operation. In one sense the corporate and political practice of high officials going out of office with their mentor made better management sense. Typically, Cooke said he did not want anyone to think he did not get along with his predecessor's choices. Many of them, however, were already at that age when assignment to a pastorate was the most understandable move to be made.

Even so, there is a religious aspect to Church decisions and Providence does play its proper role, if one lives long enough to recognize God's fine hand. Father John Monaghan used to moralize, "The worst thing that can happen to a priest is that God gives him what he wants." In the lifetime of those in this generation that was a rare occurrence, and most priests seemed to prosper in going, like the Apostles, where they were sent. You could always ask later to be relieved of a painful situation and in New York, at least, such requests were usually granted. But it was also understood that priests were to serve the mission of the Church, not their own fantasies. For the most part the system worked as much for the priests as for the cause of evangelization. In 1968, however, I did ask for the parish of St. Monica, where I had spent my early priesthood with much satisfaction and happiness. Cooke demurred. A year later, when it became open, he said I could have it if I wanted it, but then changed his mind and gave it to someone else. Monaghan was right. Something more interesting lay ahead for me unbeknown to anyone.

For two years beginning with his installation Cooke and I dealt together mostly with matters of education. But not entirely. It did not take long for the media to badger him the way they badgered Spellman. Whereas Spelly froze the press out (he was never to agree, for example, to a meeting with the Editorial Board of *The New York Times*), Cooke wanted to be agreeable. He paid a price for that effort. *The New York Times Magazine* did such a hatchet job on him that two of his closest friends were forever excluded from the episcopacy. Even Rome read the signs of *The Times*. *Commonweal* editor, John Deedy, also wrote an impertinent article. *The New York Daily News*'s correspondent Bill Reel, who later turned out to be an admirer, was an early non-friend simply because Cooke would not allow himself to be interviewed by Reel. Such is the freedom from the press denied to prelates.

In those early years Cooke appreciated those of his staff who came to his defense. He did not wish to be known as a "bad guy" but recognized that he had few defenses against the media's unfriendly scrutiny conducted under the rubric of news gathering. Unlike a governor or a president, an Archbishop has no power to punish those who injure him. As time went by Cooke's media image improved, but the early criticism made him as wary of the press as his predecessor, and not so newsy.

Cardinal Cooke had one other attribute in common with his predecessor. He was more comfortable handling the internal affairs of his own Archdiocese than making headlines. However, unlike Spellman, he had no thirst for power in the national affairs of the Church. And although personally compatible with Paul VI and later with John Paul II, the New York leader never became a Bishop-maker, nor an ecclesiastical power, nor was he one likely to make a name for himself in U.S. Church history. Sensitivity to complaints, even about bad appointments made by his Personnel Office, and discomfiture in the face of public disputes of any kind made him an unlikely warrior, even in the most worthy of controversial causes.

"HIS PORTION OF GOD'S PEOPLE"

The diocesan portion allotted to Terry Cooke was ten counties of New York State, 150 miles long with 1,825,090 Catholic people. Some thought the numbers were too many for one Bishop to mind. Talk about dividing New York began in the days of Cardinal Hayes when the upstate counties were relatively depopulated. Later Archbishop Spellman, on his coming, is alleged to have offered the Bishop of Brooklyn a "trade"—Staten Island for Queens where peripatetic New Yorkers lived by the hundreds of thousands. On Spellman's death I suggested to Apostolic Delegate Luigi Raimondi that the five counties of Fun City be reunited to form a single Archdiocese, if only for political reasons. None of these proposals went anywhere in Rome, probably because New York Cardinals give up turf reluctantly. Ten counties certainly provided priests with variety in ministry and social classes, although the idea of New York City with two Bishops did not make the same sense in Cooke's time as it did in 1853, when the only links between the upper Bronx and Coney Island—about thirty miles apart—were ferries and horse-drawn cars.

Still, when on the completion of his tenth year Terry Cooke described for Rome the state of his "portion of God's people," 409 parishes and 535 chapels remained an extraordinarily large benefice for one Bishop to manage. He had a lot of help from 1,700 priests and 6,000 religious. Even so, he alone stood before

God responsible for the manner in which those aides treated the 32,000 families who came each year for baptism, the 10,000 couples who were married by his priests, and the 17,000 families who buried their dead. New York's support systems, schools, social agencies, and hospitals touched, in the Church's name, 1,000,000 lives annually. Cooke's job also was to make sure that all those institutions paid their bills. New York's parishes spent several hundred million dollars each year, while Catholic institutions raised even more to provide the services people demanded.

One of Cooke's special concerns was the Hispanic population, which comprised at least a third of the Catholics under his care, most of whom preferred to worship in Spanish. Hispanics were especially important to the future of the Archdiocese because they were young (35 percent under sixteen) with a high birth rate. During Cooke's lifetime they were the poorest segment of the diocese, taxing his genius to keep their parishes solvent and maintain service to them at an appropriately high level. Most New York Hispanics related to the Church positively, though the vast majority were not regular churchgoers.

It is not easy to evaluate the effectiveness of a Bishop's ministry. Church historians usually credit or discredit his record on the basis of the ecclesiastical or political leadership he exercises. But this norm hardly ever tells much about what goes on under him out in the parishes or institutions where Catholic people live. To look at this side of his day-to-day labors, it is necessary to go to extant reports, which also do not tell the living story. Yet once every five years the Bishop must go to Rome to give an account of his stewardship to Curial Cardinals and to bring with him what is known as "the Quinquennial Report."

Cardinal Cooke's 1977 report is of interest, therefore, not for the statistics, which are never completely accurate, but for the issues which he thought complicated the Church's and his evangelization efforts. The poor and the disenfranchised were not his main problem. These newcomers, he said, enriched the Church with their wholesome values. "Secularization"—the identity of morality with civil law—bothered him more. The rising tide of abortion, pornography, and homosexuality were three social evils lowering moral standards and debilitating family life, so he told the Holy See.

No report to superiors is ever total and rarely is it blunt. And in his most tense moments Cooke was never likely to be blunt. Yet he did say to Rome what he never said aloud to New Yorkers, complaining about biblical scholars who compromised the reliability of the scriptures as a source of God's revealed Word. He asked Rome "to reaffirm and clarify authentic teaching on the doctrine of inspiration and the place and function of Sacred Tradition." He was also critical of the "misemphasis on Christ's humanity alone by some theologians" and the deleterious effect of this on religious education. He further blamed a "misunderstood ecumenism" for the lost or lessened appreciation of the Church as *the vehicle* of salvation.

The most forthright sections of Cooke's "Quinquennial Report 1977" dealt with subjects about which Bishops, individually and collectively, are still relatively mute in public. Cooke decried to Rome the lack of "proper formation of a correct Catholic conscience," the distortions about the Church as the *locus theologicus* in that formation, the "undue and uncritical attention given to sociological surveys," the disparagement of the magisterium as mere "official teaching," and the detrimental effect on the practice of the Faith by theological personalities who fostered "an alleged right to dissent." In this report Cooke is especially critical of those who falsely distinguish between individual and social morality.

He saw the greatest sin of his time to be the loss of the sense of sin.

Cooke was a fan of Vatican II but he was not unmindful of its dysfunctions—the lessened emphasis on the Church, a false freedom of conscience, the distortions of the Council by secular media and by some theologians. He had strong words for theologians who thought progress consisted in theological advocacy, and called upon the Pope to spell out the responsibility of theologians within the *Communio Ecclesiae* and the nature of their academic freedom within the Catholic context.

Had Cardinal Cooke taken these concerns to the Church's public forums, where his remarks might have been timely and influential, he might have exercised some of the national influence enjoyed by his predecessor.

But this was not Cooke's forte. The internal affairs of New York were his specialty. Back in his graduate study at the University of Chicago and at the Catholic University of America, he specialized in community organization and group work. His talents in this direction were never more evident than while administering the multifaceted agencies of the New York Church. Here he was at home, confident in group meetings, rarely flustered, hardly ever cornered. He loved flow charts and chains of command, as long as they did not interfere with his direct access to any diocesan official down the line. No one was ever allowed to forget who was Archbishop and he was never so friendly as to blur the lines of his authority, even when he was being insulted by an obstreperous underling. A 1973 internal study of diocesan administrative structures changed the system very little, although some departments were strengthened due to his attention being drawn to operational deficiencies.

The Marriage Tribunal was a good example. In 1974 New York had 170 formal trials compared to Brooklyn's 725, with the disparity explained by Cooke's allotted budget of $170,000 compared with $405,000 across the river. More staff costs money and Cooke was importuned to make it available. Quite oppositely, the Office of Vicar for Religious remained unaffected by the review because Cooke did not know what to do with his rebellious religious. Indeed, he introduced into his own machinery the Archdiocesan Conference of Women Religious, an advocacy group with which he had no sympathy, a move which was intended to appease but never brought about conformity to Church norms. The Office of Religious Education had been chartered in 1969 but ceased to function when a demanding director was transferred and never replaced, leaving religious education totally under the control of the professionals who by 1975 had begun to graduate religious illiterates. This represented a retreat from the earlier decision to take final control over what went into catechesis out of the School Office, where publishers more than Roman norms decided what would or would not be taught about the Church.

Cardinal Cooke's "Quinquennial Report" also contained a few footnotes for the history books—one concerning the feeling of most priests that social action was a "relatively unimportant" element of their ministry, another that almost half of Cooke's Education Committee (the curates and diocesan workers especially) felt that the parochial school system had no future.

A cursory glance at these 182 pages of data ought surely impress even the most uninterested reader with the scope of the New York Church's secular involvement. The first public accounting by Cooke of the use of Church monies (November 5, 1976), though criticized by chronic complainers who always do everything better, must have startled those Roman prelates who had the patience to read it line by line—$143 million expended in the preceding year for education, health, and social services that went far beyond what the world usually called religion. Two thirds of those funds were accumulated by local pastors through Sunday contributions or tuitions. No other private institution provided so many services in every nook and cranny of New York State (and elsewhere) at a ridiculously low cost, and as much by the contributed services of priests and religious as by money.

Cardinal Cooke's Roman report reflected particular pleasure with the new ministries which he as Archbishop had encouraged —the prayer groups (142 as of 1977), the marriage encounters (reaching 16,000 couples a year). He was also high on the many consultative groups functioning cooperatively with him—the Vicariates, the Priests' Senate, the consultors, the Coordinating Committee of the Laity, the Priests' Personnel Board. He told Rome that "the relations between the Ordinary and the clergy are open and the morale in general is rather high." He mentioned differences among the clergy and the Due Process Procedure he initiated although, as events would prove, it was rarely used. He acknowledged the diocesan debt to foreign-born priests for pickup of the slack resulting from the shortage of new native clergy, without mentioning the difficulties caused the laity by their oft-inability to speak understandable English. He informed Rome that all of the renovations in the liturgy authorized by the Holy See were in place and used strictly in conformity with the letter and spirit of Church Law. New York had its proper share of lay Eucharistic ministers, but they never became substitutes for priests at the altar rail, as occurred in some places. With the change in penitential rites, communal penances increased in number as Rome intended, but not general absolution. Cardinal Cooke never countenanced violations of the liturgical norms and in this he was a model Bishop. Nor did New York priests demonstrate any desire to test Cooke's filial piety by blatant violations of Church Law. The Sacrament of Penance fell into desuetude and Rome was told that there were forty-six thousand fewer people at Sunday Mass than five years before, but these shortfalls were the result of circumstances beyond the Cardinal's control.

The 1977 report contains two short paragraphs on the St. John Neumann Residence, inaugurated that year for college students seriously considering the priesthood. It was a halfway house, as it were, not a seminary. But in an era of fewer priests, the Neumann Residence, in the capable hands of Father John McIvor, became a very successful feeder for Dunwoodie Seminary. During the five-year period covered by this report, only forty-five men were ordained, an inadequate replacement for the hundred and twenty-seven who died, retired, or otherwise left the priestly ministry in that time. Yet, today Dunwoodie Seminary is enjoying its largest enrollment in years, in large part due to the Neumann Residence and the leadership of John McIvor.

An example of how a report can cover up an evil in a mass of innocuous-sounding words is evident in the way Cooke spoke to Rome of the "Church-related colleges." Fourteen of the fifteen he cites (St. John's University excepted) had by then abandoned their Catholic identity in order to receive financial aid ("Bundy money") from New York State. This was more than a juridical move. In practice it meant that these colleges, led by Fordham University, no longer could favor the interests or the teachings of the Catholic Church and her people. By abandoning their institutional commitment to the Church these colleges came to house teachers and administrators who frequently were hostile to Catholic definitions and norms. The negative effects on the thirty-seven thousand matriculating students soon became a matter of concern to parents and local pastors, but none of these concerns made their way into Cooke's report to Rome. The Cardinal alerted Rome to the fact that on New York's secular campuses there was a "general reluctance on the part of most [students] to identify religiously" and that they "appear not to be particularly proud of their religious heritage." These lacks were also noticeable on the campuses of one-time Catholic colleges, which traded on the Church's name without any more delivering a Catholic product. But Cooke did not mention this.

MODERNIZING CATHOLIC EDUCATION

The restructuring of Catholic education became Archbishop Cooke's first administrative effort. As early as 1964 Archbishop Maguire wished to end the laissez-faire way of doing things Catholic educators seemed to prize. Schools were becoming costly and their managers, be they pastors or religious, were turning to Bishops to make up deficits or to help them raise money. In New York under Spellman, John Maguire had been the *de facto* diocesan treasurer. He knew where there was waste and where there was incompetence. He also knew the areas of Catholic education that were being neglected because schools were gobbling up the available moneys. (No one in 1964 was the least bit worried about the Catholicity of those schools.)

But the long Blaine campaign, the fight over the Elementary and Secondary Education Act and the Textbook Law, and Spellman's declining years forced reorganization onto the back burner. At last the earlier proposals once more came front and center under Cooke. Two years earlier Msgr. William O'Brien, Associate Secretary for Education, had created a committee of distinguished Catholic laymen to help bring to reality John Maguire's vision of what the diocesan education machinery ought to be. O'Brien quite correctly argued that the time had arrived for Catholic laity to take positions of leadership and to become spokesmen for Catholic learning. One of those who emerged to prominence from his potential leader group was T. Murray McDonnell, then the head of a prominent Wall Street brokerage firm, one of whose sisters was married to Henry Ford II, by Bishop Fulton Sheen no less.

Up to then New York's most distinguished Catholic laymen—John A. Coleman, John Burke, Joseph McGovern, Porter Chandler, and others of their class—all with considerable political clout in the state, had achieved public influence while serving the charitable interests of both Cardinals Hayes and Spellman. Coleman, one-time president of the New York Stock Exchange, was, as far as city politicians were concerned, "Mr. Catholic." His close friend John Burke was president of Altman's. McGovern became chairman of the state's Board of Regents, while Porter Chandler achieved national prominence with his successful defense before the Supreme Court of the constitutionality of the New York State law which paid for textbooks in both public and parochial schools. So important to archdiocesan affairs was the Catholic Charities organization that in 1965 the chairman of the Archdiocesan Education Committee was the head of Charities, not the Secretary for Education. Indeed, there was no home-grown lay leadership in New York's Catholic education circles, no indigenous and recognized spokesmen for the rights of Catholic parents. There were few prominent lay apologists for Catholic higher education, and hardly any Catholics in public education who identified themselves as such in the civic community.

The lack of lay leadership was only one aspect of the Catholic education problem. More fundamental was the general ignorance of why the system was as good as it was or why suddenly after Vatican II it was under attack from within. Greeley and Rossi had only recently published (1968) their report of the academic achievement of parochial schools and their remarkable religious effects. *The Education of Catholic Americans*[2] summarized the latter as follows:

> Sunday Mass, communion several times a month, Catholic education of children, financial contributions to the Church, acceptance of the Church as an authoritative teacher, acknowledgement of papal

and hierarchical authority, informality with the clergy, strict sexual morality, more detailed knowledge about one's religion . . .

These are not only the apparent effects of Catholic education, they comprise as well a reasonable description of what the American Church expected of its laity during the years when it was still concentrating on the preservation of the faith of the immigrant and his children and his grandchildren.

An effort was made in 1966–67 to uncover certain basic facts about the Catholic school system in New York, the per capita cost, the racial mix, average class size, etc. These were highly political years during which religious schools came under fire from civil libertarians and public educators. Accusations against nonpublic schools flew high and wide—they were elite and upper class, they discriminated, they were inferior, etc. Louis Gary, then a research assistant at Columbia University, conducted a parish-by-parish school study for me in New York and for Msgr. Eugene Molloy in Brooklyn. (With a 450,000 enrollment in both dioceses, the Catholic school complex of New York City was the third-largest education system in the United States, behind the cities of New York and Chicago.) Gary exploded the myth that Catholic schools were havens for rich parents and for racists. The average salary of the parents was under $150 per week, placing them in the middle and lower middle class of their day. And in New York counties where minorities abounded, the Catholic schools were better integrated without busing than were the public schools. In 1966 Manhattan Catholic schools were 60 percent black or Spanish, and 30 percent of the Bronx schools were minority. Since blacks were rarely Catholic, it was clear that non-Catholics in places like Harlem were attracted by the quality of the education being provided in local Catholic parishes. From the vantage point of 1989, Catholic parents a generation ago surely obtained high-quality education for children at little economic cost to themselves. It seems incredible today that the average pastor's school cost then amounted to $5.00 per child per week ($200 per year), compared with a public school's comparative outlay of $35 per week ($1,400 per year).

The Gary study was the beginning of a long series of efforts to bring order out of the mounting chaos in Catholic education, brought on mainly by the flight of religious sisters and brothers from the classroom in favor of nonteaching apostolates; or, as happened frequently, by exclaustration from religious life completely. Imagine the pastor accustomed to paying a religious teacher $1,200 a year suddenly forced to hire her lay replacement at $12,000 a year; or the parent who up to this moment enjoyed free parish education called upon overnight to pay $200 a year. Even principals of Catholic high schools, where lay teachers were numerous, agonized over asking their parents for an additional $50 a year beyond the prevailing rate of $100 to $150. (Today parish school rates may be as high as $750 per annum, high schools $1,500.)

Louis Gary proposed the first "Ten Year Development Plan for the Archdiocese of New York." This never really moved off the drawing board, partly because the Archdiocese was unprepared to restructure education, partly because of personality conflicts between Mr. Gary and some diocesan educators, but mostly because of diocesan preoccupation, to the point of obsession, with the looming financial crisis. By June 1967 the decision was made to study the situation further, a move commonplace in every bureaucracy when no one knows what to do or when the courage to do what has to be done is lacking. One hidden motive for another study was (as my June 14 memorandum stated) "to prepare the climate for new methods of financing." Several management firms were actually interviewed—McKinsey and Company; Cresap, McCormick, and Paget; later Peat, Marwick, and Mitchell—but little movement occurred because the campaign to repeal the Blaine Amendment to the New York State Constitution preoccupied everyone's attention from Cardinal Spellman down.

In Cardinal Spellman's last year of life, Gary made one final effort to move the Archdiocese to an in-depth study of its educational resources, one which would go beyond money to a reexamination of its objectives, priorities, and management procedures. He inveigled Daniel Patrick Moynihan to meet with him and me. Moynihan, a full-time Harvard professor at the time, proved to be good at chitchat about his Catholic experiences on New York's

137

West Side, but an unlikely candidate to identify with a "Catholic" cause, even if it were only a study. A few years earlier (1965) the future senator had been run out of Washington for a study he did on the Negro family while at the Department of Labor. He was not now about to take another wrong step by heading up a study commission on Catholic education. In hindsight, he would have been a poor choice. Harvard professors tend to view the world with Cambridge glasses, not the Roman spectacles such a study required.

THE McDONNELL COMMITTEE

Failure to capture Moynihan brought us back to our own devices. Cardinal Cooke decided to do an in-house study with our own leadership in command. But to do this properly we needed an important layman to lead the effort, preferably a public figure with an unusual interest in Catholic affairs. T. Murray McDonnell seemed to be the one with the potential of doing for education what the John Colemans earlier had done for Catholic Charities. After Spellman's death the Administrator, Archbishop Maguire, agreed to support the McDonnell choice. Encouraging a rival to the Coleman faction within the Archdiocese seemed to please him. "Go feel him out," he said. McDonnell grabbed at the opportunity as if he had been waiting for this role for a long time. Almost immediately he wished to seize the reigns of power in diocesan affairs, even before he was familiar with the ins and outs of Catholic education, but not before it was clear that personal aggrandizement was high on his scale of values. As he began to outline his objectives, it began to appear that he was interested in a Moynihan-type study, although he did not have the Harvard professor's competence to create an appropriate model. Maguire's reaction to my second thoughts about giving McDonnell his head was typical: "What are you looking for? A yes man?" Well, if the Administrator of the Archdiocese could live with uncertainty, subalterns surely could. Besides, when push came to shove, Maguire was no pushover. With McDonnell aboard, the next step was to propose a priest liaison between the Department of Education and the Study Commission. The choice narrowed to Father James P. Mahoney, Seminary Procurator, and Msgr. Joseph T. O'Keefe, director of the Archdiocesan Instructional Television Center. After some prodding from Cooke in favor of O'Keefe, Maguire saw to his appointment as a second Associate Secretary for Education.

The accession of Terence J. Cooke as Archbishop of New York changed the scenery almost immediately. Cooke had been a Charities' man and not so directly involved with the education world as Maguire was. McDonnell was an outsider to the inner circle of influential laymen around Cooke, but a known quantity to the new Archbishop, who was a detail man himself and, unlike Maguire, was likely to shape the study to his own purposes and liking. In an important sense McDonnell was satisfactory: he was money-minded and comfortable in dealing with Cooke on a one-to-one basis. With Cooke's approval the focus of the study shifted from Catholic education to school finances. Both Cooke and McDonnell were content. In pursuit of their common objective, the chairman assembled a blue-ribbon panel of well-known personalities, prestigious enough to make the front page of *The New York Times* on the day of the public announcement,[3] eleven days after Cooke was installed as Archbishop. Besides select members from the Catholic community, such as Bishop Broderick, John Burke, Luis Frere, the big guns of the committee included Cyrus Vance, later to be Secretary of State, James A. Perkins, Robert F. Coheen, Martin Myerson, Morris Abrams, John Fisher, the respective university presidents of Cornell, Princeton, Buffalo, Brandeis, Teachers College, and Columbia. The committee was a Madison Avenue executive's dream. Most of the panelists had no vested interest in Catholic education.

The Cardinal, in requesting their membership, asked that the appointees "develop all the facts pertinent to the entire scope of Catholic education in this Archdiocese"; that they "evaluate the policies and objectives with our available resources"; that they "propose revisions in our educational endeavors as dictated by the facts"; that they "analyze the choices available to us; and set forth the advantages of each"; and that they "use their best judgment to provide a solid basis for action."

The man who moved the study in the direction of finances was Paul McDonald, a longtime financial expert for St. Vincent's Hospital. His assumptions and his computer compiled the data which finally were encompassed in the one committee report of substance: "A Financial Study: The Catholic School System of the Archdiocese of New York." The report's urgent priority, one which Archbishop Cooke undoubtedly impressed on Murray McDonnell, was to stabilize the growing deficits in the operation of Catholic schools. Chapter One of Paul McDonald's report (page 10) urged: "A central financial office ought to be established." It was done without delay and the first officers—Msgr. Thomas A. Gartland, Joseph Robbins, and Sister Ruth Marion—proved themselves masters of cost control. Within one year the deficits of the twelve diocesan high schools were cut by one half and reduced to manageable proportions.

One other McDonald recommendation was implemented, viz., the consolidation of underused schools. Some proposals received little serious attention: (1) that the Archdiocese develop "a Catholic teachers corps," with elite volunteers supplementing the efforts of religious teachers, (2) that there be created "a wall between the finances of the parochial school and the parishes," (3) that the finance office "would report to a Lay Board of Education."

While McDonald encouraged "a massive effort to elicit aid from the federal government," it offered this caution: "Over the long term, the infusion of public funds into Church-related schools could result in such secularization of the schools that the Church would have little remaining motive to operate them. Public aid could prove to be an attenuated way of ending the Church's school system." The prophetic nature of this statement would not be recognized for several years, until the pursuit of government money encouraged Catholic colleges to abandon their religious commitment to the Church. The word "encouraged" is correctly chosen because the driving force toward secularization came from within Catholic higher education, not from the crass desire for money.

Paul McDonald's statistics had one long-range effect on Church policy—they brought about the revision of money management procedures and tuition policies. Deficit financing was halted at the diocesan level and realistic tuition policies were introduced partly to cover the substantial rise in the salaries of both religious and lay teachers. (About this time religious began to demand higher salaries.) Prior to Cooke's succession steps had been taken to increase both parochial and diocesan income. Community Counseling Services, a fund-raising organization, was invited by him as Auxiliary Bishop to make suggestions, one of which called for the expansion of the annual Catholic Charities Appeal to include education, with grossed income "shared by all" (June 30, 1967). A month later (August 14, 1967) I was asking Archbishop Maguire to consider a separate diocesan collection for Catholic education in November of 1968. The new Archbishop Cooke met with his Secretaries for Charities and Education in December 1968, independently of Murray McDonnell, suggesting one combined diocesan collection for both causes, a proposal with which I had no sympathy because the campaign would be run by Charities.

RAISING MONEY FOR EDUCATION

For more than forty years the only door-to-door collection permitted in New York was the Catholic Charities Campaign. By 1968, however, the Church's welfare causes in hospitals, nursing, and child care were so amply subsidized by government money that the annual collection for those causes began to suffer, reaching a plateau of no more than $2 million a year. It was becoming difficult to motivate Catholics to increase their voluntary contributions when they were learning that more than $100 million of tax money annually found its way into places like St. Vincent's Hospital or the Mary Manning Walsh Nursing Home. Other factors were the diminished ability because of rising crime to conduct door-to-door canvassing in metropolitan areas, and the declining interest of young priests in collections of any kind. The Catholic Charities Campaign had become by 1968 a boring exercise for many of them. About this time Community Counseling Services was telling me that a properly organized campaign for Catholic Education, using modern fund-raising techniques, could gross $6 million annually.

Archbishop Cooke, who himself had been a member of the Charities' staff, shied away from a second diocesan collection. He feared a negative reaction from the newly formed Priests' Senate and doubted his ability to reach over the head of its leadership, which at the time was negative to Church authority. The Senate was not above embarrassing its Archbishop, especially those leaders who were outspoken critics of the parochial school system. In-house bickering of this kind also handicapped those nonschool programs which were never properly financed in the first place—CCD, family life education, adult education, convert instruction, Newman Clubs on secular campuses, marriage counseling, continuing education for priests—all programs which potentially had a larger audience than schools and school-related projects. Historically, however, these were the neglected apostolates, not easy to organize, not as ready-made as school programs, which were enforced by public law, and activities which called for priest leadership rather than the disciplined life style of the nuns of that day.

Many priests were ignorant of the scope of the education problem and had been insulated too long from the realities of Church budgets. Most priests were curates, some of thirty years' priestly standing, many of whom never had been asked to raise substantial moneys, e.g., fifty thousand dollars. The crisis, therefore, was not merely educational but one of parish life itself.

One evening in 1969 following Holy Thursday services, Cardinal Cooke informed me that he had finally decided to expand the annual Catholic Charities Campaign to include the needs of education. This was not the best decision, and so he was continued to be advised. It would not attract enough money. It continued the subordination of education needs to Charities' privileged status in the Archdiocese. "Backsliding one's way through a serious problem is not a good way to solve it," I told him. To which he responded: "Sometimes it's the only way." However, his style of administration sought to avoid real or potential opposition and to deal with problems by indirection and in piecemeal fashion, always hoping that the future would take care of the problem entirely. When used judiciously this managerial style encountered less immediate resistance from dissidents. But like a bad debt, problems eventually have to be faced, usually at a higher cost. The Catholic Charities and Education Campaign became a stopgap measure, one which never contributed greatly to the reduction of education debts. In the last years of his life Cooke scrapped it in favor of a once-a-year Cardinal's Campaign, which has earned the Archdiocese more than $6 million a year ever since, the amount Community Counseling Services said they could raise in 1968.

THE COMMISSION FOR INTER-PARISH FINANCING

Deficit financing of poor parishes had also become a serious problem before Cooke became Archbishop. Traditionally, the Archdiocese subsidized new parishes until they developed sufficiently to pay their own way. Under normal conditions each parish is a self-sufficient entity and the administrative rule of life is laissez-faire for pastors, whose responsibility it is to raise the money to pay parochial bills or to contain their costs accordingly. One important accomplishment of Cardinal Spellman's regime was the creation of a "Diocesan Bank," to which pastors contributed surplus funds which were then recirculated to poor parishes as loans. The interest paid to parochial lenders or by borrowers was approximately one half the rate paid or charged by commercial banks. The "Diocesan Bank" was Spellman's device through which prosperous parishes contributed to the stability of poorer parishes. However, since it was a lender-borrower situation, the poor parishes were saddled with ever-increasing debts. The loans were never foreclosed, but neither were they erased, except under special circumstances. If the Archbishop received a bequest run-

143

ning into the millions of dollars, for example, he often used the gift to wipe out or reduce the debts of poor parishes.

Toward the end of Spellman's life something more than the "Diocesan Bank" was needed to cover the growing deficits of the increasing number of poor parishes in New York. Migration of middle-class Catholics out of the city or out of the diocese, large numbers of poor pouring into the "inner city" of the Archdiocese, rising building costs, higher teachers salaries, inflation, and the flight of religious from Catholic education forced many parishes below the poverty line. The Archdiocese itself was in good financial condition. It became common practice during the 1960s for pastors in trouble (and principals) to seek a "handout" from the Chancery Office and so to be bailed out of trouble for one more year. By Spellman's death the number of diocesan institutions on the dole was excessively high and so was the welfare dependency of many pastors who had lost their initiative as entrepreneurs and as Administrators. The single most common cause of this situation was the overnight escalation of the cost of their parochial school. An annual bill in 1958 of fifty thousand dollars was often two hundred thousand by 1968, beyond the ability to pay of many parishes whose ordinary income had not increased proportionately.

During a casual conversation one day with the new Archbishop on how best to solve this parochial problem without bankrupting the Archdiocese, I mentioned that Philadelphia's Cardinal John Krol had a plan for dealing with poor parishes. It was worth looking into. Cooke agreed, so I spent a day (October 21, 1968) with Philadelphia's diocesan officials, including my classmate, Bishop Gerry McDevitt, Vicar General of that Archdiocese. The Philadelphia plan was quite simple: Once a year Cardinal Krol asked pastors to give him outright whatever of their surplus they could afford to give. In turn he redirected those funds to parishes in need. Unlike New York with its vast potential for attracting gifts running into the millions, the Philadelphia Archdiocese depended almost completely on pastors' generosity.

Philadelphia, though a smaller diocese and far less wealthy, had a school system almost as large as New York's—205,000 children—and was tuition free at the elementary and high school levels. Unlike New York, Philadelphia had a long history of taxing parishes. For every parish child in a diocesan high school the proper pastor was taxed $150 per year. (One pastor, for example, was called upon to pay $120,000 per year for 800 of his high school students.) Additionally, a graduated income tax on ordinary parish income was levied for diocesan capital construction, e.g., a diocesan high school.

As a matter of principle, Philadelphia refused to subsidize parish deficits. After Vatican II Cardinal Krol established an Inter-Parochial Cooperative Commission, composed of elected pastors and independent of the Chancery Office, who dispensed funds to needy parishes according to norms created by the commission.

The visit to Philadelphia also disclosed that this Archdiocese was about to establish an Office of Development for Education to solicit funds from business firms of the city.

According to my memorandum to Archbishop Cooke (October 23, 1968), the Philadelphia visit led to four recommendations: (1) a diocesan takeover of parish high schools and the operation of a unified system; (2) assessment of potential diocesan resources and perchance a consideration that the Archdiocese be divided; (3) central taxation; (4) providing laymen with responsibility within appropriate guidelines.

At the next meeting of New York's Board of Consultors, the Philadelphia report was discussed. The concept of a tax on parishes was approved. Eighteen months later (April 3, 1970) Cardinal Cooke announced the creation of a Commission for Inter-Parish Financing, composed of fifteen priests, with the function of taxing all parishes (6 to 7 percent of annual ordinary income). The gross income was to be distributed to parishes with operating deficits, enough subsidy to keep them viable without stifling the pastor's initiative to raise his own parish income level. The taxed parishes contributed $1,000, $10,000 or $30,000 per year depending on their income; the receiving parishes were given $10,000, $50,000, or $100,000, depending on their need. In the early years of the program $3 million was recirculated annually throughout the Archdiocese. In working out the details of IPFC,

145

and for its successful institutionalization, Cardinal Cooke deserves the lion's share of the credit. Eighteen years later (1988) IPFC distributed more than $9 million to approximately one hundred parishes of the Archdiocese or one quarter of those which serve the Archdiocese's ten counties.

REFORM AND RESISTANCE

The McDonnell Committee finally folded its tent. The financial problems of schools were on their way to proper management. But how was the Church to maintain its enrollment in the face of higher, even though well-managed, costs? Enemies had been hoping for the demise of these schools for decades. Were they to be abandoned or depleted by members of the household? What about the quality of CCD programs? About weak programs for married couples? About natural family planning? About young collegians on secular campuses? Why were so few priests interested in marriage preparation classes when family problems were becoming so serious? How were we to find at reasonable cost adequate substitutes for vanishing religious? Where was the future lay leadership for Catholic education to come from? Public schools were militantly defended by Florence Flast, Seymour Lachman, Al Shanker. Why was it only the clergy who spoke for Catholic education?

The McDonnell Committee never came to grips with these complexities, not even to gather data on the scope of the Church's broader educational needs. Preoccupied solely with finances, the committee hardly mentioned the inner dynamics of Catholic school operations which needed as much analysis as the money issue.

Schoolmen, for one, would not greet close supervision with any warmth, although they no longer could spend money they did not have. In a small diocese they accepted the overview of the local Bishop as normal. But in a place like New York they did not have to deal with the Bishop on a day-to-day basis. The built-in ability

146

of professional schoolmen to keep outsiders ignorant of their inner workings was itself a major problem.

This self-proclaimed autonomy became a matter of concern to nonprofessionals when for the first time in memory Catholic parents and many pastors asked whether our schools were undermining the Catholic commitment of their children. The professionals replied to complaints, "the situation did not occur," "the parent [or pastor] misunderstood," "laymen are not competent to judge new educational theories or techniques." But, as public school parents found earlier when their Johnny, though schooled, never learned to read, Catholic school parents now were discovering that they had little recourse upon learning their Johnny did not know the Ten Commandments.

It was in this connection that a middle-aged Italian immigrant mother, named Rosa, challenged the Chancery Office. The Second Vatican Council had only just finished its work (1965) when she telephoned to inquire if she had done wrong. The day before, a Sunday afternoon, she had attended a school meeting at which the nuns outlined their new approach to teaching the catechism. Explained Rosa: "For two hours I listened as they explained why God did not get mad at my children, did not get mad if the kids did bad things, if they beat each other up, if they stole, or missed Mass." As an officer of New York's Christian Family Movement, Rosa *knew* something about Scripture and the teaching of the Church as well. She continued: "I could take it no longer. I went to the microphone. So okay, God doesn't get mad at my kids if they lie, steal, or beat each other up. But my kids don't go to Mass, I break their necks. Did I do wrong?"

Rosa sensed that her school was "housebreaking" her young into a value system she thought to be inconsistent with her Church. She expected her parish school to make her children better Catholics than she had been as a child, and she did not see this happening.

Parents, like Rosa, called by Churchmen the primary educators of their children, found that they no longer had any say over the formation of their young. Once upon a time they were expected to develop in their young the social virtues and some of the skills needed to advance the country's national prosperity and its external defense. Well into the twentieth century the dominant Protestant majority with its well-known "work ethic" reinforced such role-playing. The social rewards for personal virtue, industry, frugality, and patriotism were high, measured mostly in upward mobility. The social control of vice, be it divorce, contraception, drunkenness, sloth, even Catholicism, was stern. If father and mother together loved parenting and were lucky or determined to have enough children to make a family, they could influence their offspring well into young adulthood. But it was a dying art. Teachers were demanding that parents get out of their way if they came into conflict with school administrators.

What had occurred that Sunday in Rosa's school meeting was an announced shift by the nuns in their approach to teaching the Catholic religion. Whereas formerly they spoke of God the Father and the Lord God, of original sin, of Jesus the Savior and Redeemer, of Christ's commandments and Church obligations, now they wanted parents to know they would speak more of the God who loved, of the Merciful God, of Christ with human feelings who understood the shortcomings and failures of all God's creatures. They also wanted the parents to realize that henceforth they would encourage children to develop their own potential, to use their freedom responsibly, rather than do things simply because they were told. That Sunday there was much talk about a new method, but the shift being announced involved more than a new way of teaching old truths. It was a new way of teaching new "truths," which Rosa thought were no truths at all.

The reaction of one mother was no bellweather of radical protest by parents, but it was an early symptom of a grass-roots sense that an antiparent, antihierarchical attitude was developing among teachers, especially among the Church's religious. Appeal from professionalism was beginning to be *verboten*. When in 1965 and thereafter complaints were passed on to higher authority, they were usually returned to the very person or group accused of some offense. The complaint would be acknowledged, nothing more. What could one expect, when through several earlier years the Gabriel Morans, the Bernard Cookes, and the Bernard Harings, and publishers like Sadlier (whose books reflected their thinking) roamed New York's briefing sessions and religious workshops under the aegis of the School Office or some other ecclesiastical aficionado. During those early years of renewal, the only authority which heard these complaints with sympathy was the Holy See, and Rome was far away.

But more than School Office personnel or seminary faculty were offenders. The CCD Office also played an equally unsatisfactory role. Established in 1938 by Cardinal Hayes, New York's CCD surged to national prominence with the Spellman appointment of the fiery Msgr. Charles Walsh. However, by 1968 CCD faced serious problems. Its operational budget was less than a third of what was regularly allotted to the School Office ($48,000 to $170,000). Furthermore, CCD teachers were mostly parochial school teachers, so the same ambiguity appeared in catechetical programs for public school students.

At the highest levels of Church management, there was only cursory knowledge of what actually went on in the Church's classrooms anywhere. Diocesan officials heard the complaints, knew that religious communities were changing their policies and their habits, that the seminary faculty was divided, but there was no attempt to assess the scope of the new difficulties. The system had worked effectively and placidly for so many generations that presumption was in its favor. There was no desire to dig into the facts of other than school finances. As an example: Dunwoodie Seminary was radically divided as to what should and should not be taught to future priests; divisions were appearing among young priests about what was or was not authentically Catholic. Yet Dunwoodie was such an educational island unto itself that no one, not even the Cardinal, seemed capable of restoring direction to its teaching and discipline. Once when he was about to name a new Rector, I asked Cooke if he was also determined to transfer dissident faculty. He shook his head silently, no. Ten more years were to transpire before anything like teaching unity prevailed at Dunwoodie. Imagine the public outcry if such ambiguity were to prevail in medical education, enough to affect people's medical care.

Things remained confused in the Department of Education two years after it was made a department. In the spring of 1969 Archbishop Cooke called the heads of the Education Offices together and made it known he wanted a structured department under one Secretary. Later that year he visited Dunwoodie to make a similar point to the seminary Rector and his faculty. The result was a "wait and see" attitude at all levels. When conflicts of interest arose, who won the contest would determine how serious this will to reorganize really was.

Almost immediately after Cooke's stern lecture, the lay teachers in both high and parochial schools threatened to strike. The negotiating situation was muddied when it was discovered that the Vicar General was meeting with union lawyers independently of the Education team. Old habits were hard to break! This Chancery intervention occurred as efforts were being made at the Education level to work out a peaceful solution by pasting together a reasonable package of benefits. The settlement was delayed because of a late union demand that elementary and secondary teachers receive the same pay scale. That union leaders were trying to bypass the negotiators from the Education Office by appealing to the Vicar General created some uneasy moments. In the end, the system prevailed and a strike was averted when the chairman of the New York State Mediation Board, Vincent McDonnell, persuaded the union to accept the archdiocesan $3 million package, the alternative being the disappearance of teachers' jobs with the closing of many schools.

The threat of a strike, successfully managed, helped cut the umbilical cord between Education and Chancery, but not by much. The traditional habit of beating the system, of going outside of the chain of command for private ecclesiastical deals, did not die easily. One wondered if a Bishop, any Bishop, would permit it to die. Major superiors of religious communities, for instance, preferred to deal with the Ordinary, who usually was unprepared to confront notorious demands when they were made. Once upon a time this presented no difficulty, i.e., when the communities themselves were respectful of the Bishop's role and authority. But after Vatican II they became antihierarchical, even while insisting that the Bishop "listen" to them like an old friend. Bishops accustomed to saying yes to major superiors found themselves in an impossible situation, saying yes still when they should have said no. This irenicism made it impossible for lower officials to hold religious communities to their diocesan commitments.

But as harmful to the reform of education as the breakdown of religious communities was, the equally serious obstacle to a legitimate department was its inability to raise or manage its own money. Vital to any system is control—usually of money, of personnel, and the politics that goes into jockeying for rewards and patronage. Traditionally, the life or death of educational projects depended on decisions made outside the system. Educators could not create anything without Chancery help. Good news always originated with Chancery, bad news (no money, no programs) came from within Education. A minor fuss developed when the parish tax to support the Superintendent's Office (then twenty-five cents per child) was diverted to the Education Secretary instead of the Chancellor. The habit of going directly to Chancery for money is what helped balloon deficits to impossible proportions. A sympathetic Vicar General who once wiped out a two-hundred-thousand-dollar deficit for a high school principal with a nod of his head had difficulty demanding that the same principal improve his per capita income or his teacher-pupil ratios or eliminate his high-priced electives, because noneducators normally do not think in such categories.

Part of the reorganization problem was the human condition itself, that devilish conspiracy which frustrates the best planners. In education circles generally each specialty insists on its divine right to raid someone else's treasury. Schoolmen, for example, would take all the money they could get for their five hundred children, even if it meant that the five hundred public school children in the CCD program studied with outdated books or inferior teachers. Out of this state of affairs, especially in the ghetto, came antischool fireworks. One 1968 paper called *The Face of Harlem* was issued by the diocesan CCD office, declaring in part: "The Catholic Church in Harlem is just about dead . . .

151

The Church should amalgamate parish schools . . . The religious freed by this amalgamation should be used in the catechetical apostolates."

Archbishop Cooke recognized the problem. While the McDonnell Committee was riding the financial track, Cooke called in an outside firm, Peat, Marwick, and Mitchell, to design "A Comprehensive Plan for an Effective Office of Finance for the Department of Education." After this study, which lasted the better part of the year, the PMM's final report made four major recommendations:

1. A Board of Catholic Education will oversee all of the educational works of the Archdiocese.

2. The Secretary for Education is the Executive Secretary to the Board and thereby the Director of the Department. He oversees, supervises, evaluates, and coordinates the four branches of education, determines or approves policy, priorities, and budgets and raises educational funds.

3. The Department of Education is composed of four distinct divisions: The Division of Higher Education which concerns itself with 18 Catholic colleges and 23 secular colleges within the Archdiocese (the latter office headed by a coordinator); the Division of Seminary Education, headed by the Rector of the Major Seminary; the Division of Primary and Secondary Education, guided by the Superintendent of Schools; and the Division of Christian and Family Development, which operates programs of religious instruction for children and adults on catechetics and family life.

4. The staff of the Secretariat includes, besides deputies, the Directors of Finance, Research and Planning, Public Relations and Development, and Religious Education.

Obviously, this organizational chart represented a plan. The "new thing" in the plan was that one official was to oversee and direct all the defined works of education. This is what Spellman-Maguire intended in 1966. The name "Secretary" continued to be used to describe the department head because this was the title in possession since 1943. In reality, the office was ecclesiastical rather than professional, the alter ego of the Bishop in educational matters. The Secretary no longer needed to be a schoolman any more than a Bishop needed to be an educator to rule the educational machinery of his diocese. (Many years later Cardinal O'Connor understood this when in 1985 he appointed Bishop Edward Egan to be his Vicar for Education.)

Peat, Marwick, and Mitchell recognized all the danger signals. Seminary people did not like the plan. Neither did the superintendent of schools. One of the most hotly contested concepts was situating final control of religious education in the Secretariat, with a director appointed specifically to supervise the catechesis going on under the School and CCD Offices. School and CCD from the beginning had their own catechetical specialists accustomed to dealing with no one but their immediate bosses. In view of the mounting complaints about catechetics after 1965, it was necessary to do something. It was clear that the superintendent of schools and the Confraternity director by reason of good fellowship with leading religious educators and book publishers were in no position to remedy mounting defects. Indeed, they resented the complainers and anyone else who threatened to "interfere" in their operation. They also had no fear of Chancery, which would only field criticisms but could not remedy doctrinal or disciplinary shortcomings. An archdiocesan Director of Religious Education responsible only to the Secretary for Education was seen as a grave threat to their respective territories. This was an unfortunate reaction because both superintendent and CCD director had an easy way out when changes in orientation or in text material were requested. They could pass the blame "upstairs."

As far back as 1971 Rome was criticizing the "new" catechetics. Most religious educators ignored Rome. Not only that, they equivalently denied the Holy See's right to intervene. In 1971, a year after the Department of Education was established, a New York priest, recently assigned to the United States Catholic Conference, led a charge (September 23, 1971) against the General Catechetical Directory. GCD, as it was called, was an effort by the Holy See, led by John Cardinal Wright, to establish guidelines for teaching the Catholic faith. The conflict set American professionals against their Roman pastor. Cardinal Wright, the Congregation's Prefect, became so annoyed during the confrontation that he suggested that Bishops dispense with some of their experts and find one good confessor.

In spite of the Peat, Marwick, and Mitchell proposal, the first Director of Religious Education did not last long. He was timid and reluctant to face the internal opposition. The second director was not afraid to tackle the defects but was quickly promoted out of the office because of complaints from below. Once vacant, the office thereafter remained unfilled, though it is still a line office on the department's management chart. The old system was back in business.

Msgr. Theodore McCarrick, as early as 1969, thought the appointment of a Director of Religious Education might work better if it coincided with the establishment of a Diocesan Theological Commission, headed by Msgr. Austin Vaughan, Rector of Dunwoodie Seminary and a first-rate Catholic theologian. The idea was not without merit, and in hindsight it is not clear why his suggestion was not followed. Part of the reason for tabling it might have been that the names being proposed (not by McCarrick) were mostly Jesuits from Woodstock College, which by then was on its way to disaster. Such a committee would likely not have reinforced Roman demands. Indeed, even in 1989 religious educators still pay little attention to the Pope's International Theological Commission. Such a diocesan commission in 1970 probably would have merely added to Cardinal Cooke's problems.

Other elements of the PMM plan also were consigned to limbo within a few years. The Division of Higher Education practically went out of business before it got off the ground. Eighteen Catholic colleges in pursuit of New York State Bundy money declared themselves no longer Catholic. No one at the diocesan level intervened in this spoliation of Catholic patrimony. The Coordinator of the University Apostolate on Secular Campuses diminished in status once the first full-time coordinator moved on to a new ministry, leaving the appointments of university chaplains as haphazard and ineffectual as they were when there was no plan at all. The Division of Seminary Education was never really subordinate to the Secretary. After 1970 the seminary once more became the private preserve of the Chancery.

154

The Division of Christian and Family Development was dissolved into its two component parts by 1983—the CCD and the Family Life Bureau—even though both offices are engaged in the same work of catechetics, though for different audiences.

The one solid and permanent result of the study was to place the Division of Primary and Secondary Education on a sound financial footing, even if at a reduced level, and subordinate to the Secretary for Education. The Secretary's Office of Finance became Cardinal Cooke's crowning achievement in education. Msgr. Thomas Gartland took office March 22, 1969, at a time when the operational costs of the archdiocesan educational enterprise came to $163 million, more than half of which was raised by diocesan agencies of one kind or another.

In 1989 this office, now led by Father James Vaughey, not only manages an outlay of more than $30 million for the Department of Education alone but controls the budgets, the income, the disbursals, and the payrolls of diocesan high schools, large parish high schools, major and minor seminaries, parish cemeteries, and priest and student residences—a scope of endeavor hardly envisaged in 1969. It also performs similar services for the Commission for Inter-Parish Finance and for many parishes besides. Its field operation sends staff members out to parishes and to institutions to teach sound business and budgeting procedures. The Office of Finance finally handles the small amount of government money (about $8 million annually) which pays for services rendered to the state Department of Education.

Was the Office of Finance successful? It certainly was. Within two years a $2,300,000 subsidy was reduced to $1,261,741. In due course the entire system was brought under control.

Two other tools of management were planned by Peat, Marwick, and Mitchell: The Cardinal's Committee for Education and the Board of Catholic Education, one intended to provide financial advice and corporate funding for Catholic education, the other to be a think-tank composed mostly of distinguished lay men and women who would become, under the Cardinal, policy-makers for the mostly clerical and religious world of Catholic education.

155

Msgr. Theodore McCarrick, after a distinguished career as Rector of Puerto Rico's Catholic University, was appointed Associate Secretary for Education (July 1, 1969) with a view mainly to creating a fund-raising committee. Although the idea of soliciting corporate funds for education was part of the Philadelphia package, it was long discussed in New York and both Cooke and McCarrick were at home in this aspect of the Church's apostolate. By October 1969 McCarrick was well on his way to involving some of New York's most distinguished corporate leaders—Martin Shea, J. Peter Grace III, Chauncey Stillman—world-renowned public figures. The committee was patterned to some extent after the Cardinal's Committee for the Laity in Catholic Charities. The committee never quite functioned in the same way as the Charities' committee, but it evolved into what is now the Inner City Scholarship Fund, which each year distributes more than $2 million to needy students, mostly minority, in search of a Catholic education.

The Board of Catholic Education was not destined to have a long life. It first met on April 25, 1970, with such distinguished members as Msgr. John Voight, former Secretary for Education, and Bernard Butler, first black officer in the Christian Family Movement. The original plan designed this board to play a role within the Archdiocese similar to that exercised by the Board of Regents within New York State—to review performance, coordinate competing interests, and propose priorities and guidelines. Three of its members were to serve jointly on Msgr. McCarrick's committee in order to relate policy issues to financial realities. The board, too, was to develop a "brain trust" of leading Catholic opinion-molders, who would represent lay opinion to the Cardinal and Catholic opinion on the education of competent and responsible citizens to the general public. Too often the public had the impression that only hierarchy was involved in the management of Catholic institutions. The Board of Catholic Education was allowed to pass out of existence.

What the Catholic faithful, even to this day, sometimes fail to grasp is the magnitude of the voluntary contributions of the Catholic community to Catholic education. In 1970 the Archdiocese of

New York, centrally or through its parishes, was expending almost $60 million annually on educating its young. Through most
of the twentieth century cash deficits worried only those priests
and religious whose role it was to raise the money. Bishops did
the providing, the troops did the work. The task, never easy, was
manageable because the priests and the nuns worked almost for
board and keep, while dedicated lay teachers were paid just
enough to keep them from starving. But no one seemed to mind
and for most of the religious it was tiring but a lot of fun. The
children turned out by parochial schools and CCD classes were a
credit to their parents and the Church. But by 1968 annual cash
deficits of $30 to $40 million threatened the very existence of
Catholic schools for all but the well-to-do.

For the stability of what remains Cardinal Cooke deserves the
credit. Still, the future of all nonpublic education, including the
Catholic component, depended on a more favorable atmosphere in
American society. Like Spellman, Cooke would have to face that
reality. And he did.

CARDINAL COOKE AND PUBLIC AID

Although the spirits of the Catholic education world were never
lower than the morning after the defeat of the Blaine repeal, the
dynamic of public aid for nonpublic school children was still
alive. Tony Travia was on his way to political oblivion, but Nelson
Rockefeller, exhilarated by his smashing victory, was inclined to
fulfill some promises he had made to Cardinal Spellman even
after his old friend died. The first move he made was to establish
in 1968 a Bundy Committee (named after McGeorge Bundy, a
brain-truster for the Kennedy family) to search for ways and
means to aid higher education, including Catholic colleges. It is
interesting to note how the arguments used against aid to religious elementary and secondary schools received little attention
once the decision was made to give favorable consideration to
religious colleges and universities. The latter served the public
interest, direct assistance to secular institutions alone without

157

some concern for the Yeshivas, the Fordhams, and the Paces was not politically viable, aid to religious functions from state grants would be incidental, and so forth.

Many open-minded students of this question were still prepared to defend public aid for private elementary and secondary schools, including those sponsored by churches. Christopher Jencks, Bundy's Harvard associate, made the philosophical point: "The issue is whether people should be able to get what they want rather than be told they must accept what they don't want."[4] If the problem was education, not religion, why not be even-handed? If the secular education in a Catholic school was just as good as that in a public school, why not treat both systems according to their respective needs? Not necessarily equally, but with a modicum of distributive justice. If government-owned buses, books, and medical services can be made available to Catholic-educated students, why not other benefits, as long as constitutional guarantees are observed and the educational weal of the country is promoted? Why, in a word, should old arguments, old fears, old prejudices interfere with a relevant view of a very new problem—the very existence of private lower education? Those old anti-aid arguments—tragic results for the American people, end of national unity, destruction of the public school system, encouragement of racial and religious tension—were used again and again in earlier days to prevent even a bus ride for a Catholic child, with none of the dire predictions realized in actual fact.

The scope of the problem facing Cardinal Cooke in the public controversy over public aid is measured by what is to this day basically nonmeasurable—the intensity of the bigotry buried beneath argumentation based on lies, but offered to Catholics as reasonable differences of opinion. Cooke did not have any savor for controversy, nor an aptitude for going to the heart of the matter, if it happened to be bigotry. Civic action groups would never let anti-Semitism or racism against blacks be covered up the way Catholics permitted anti-Catholicism to continue on its merry way.

The kind of bitterness facing Cooke in his first year surfaced before Christmas 1969 when a prominent New York City politician, Albert Blumenthal, warned that the "public aid" argument really meant two school systems, "one for the rich and one for the poor." This was a lie, both as to the intentions of Cooke and as to the factual possibilities: There was no way parents, even with modest public aid, could fashion a rival to a system financed by government tax monies running to the billions.

Mrs. Blanche Lewis, president of the 400,000 member United Parents Association, a public school adjunct, accused Catholics of bluffing, simultaneously declaring that she would welcome back into the public school system all those students who are forced to leave parochial schools. In her view, the city would then move their former schools right into the public system and make them available for all children. Clearly, it was the very existence of those parochial schools which nettled the antagonists, not simply the picayune aid that would facilitate their continued existence.

These two officers of PEARL were representatives of a chorus that drowned out all considerations of freedom of religion, of parents' rights, of the needs of children, or even the well-being of U.S. education itself.

It did not seem possible that aid to nonpublic schools would ever be treated as the community problem it was. Even when good intentions were translated into public law, the old constitutional bugaboos prevailed. Nelson Rockefeller's objections were sincere enough, but when the Bundy Report became the Bundy Law, direct grants were legislated to private colleges on the basis of the number of undergraduate or graduate degrees conferred annually—to those colleges, that is, which were unaffiliated with a religious body. Large institutions would receive a yearly subsidy running to millions of dollars. But for Catholic colleges in New York to qualify, they had to deal with Blaine, and James G. won again. Catholic institutions could run to the public treasury for a handout—at the price of their Catholic connection. Their link with the Church must be severed. Run they did, paying the price with unusual haste, Molloy, St. John's, and Niagara excepted. (Today, only St. John's remains a stranger to the state treasurer.)

The story is oft told that when the first three "Catholic" colleges, Fordham University in the lead, received approval for

Bundy money, Malcolm Wilson called Ewald Nyquist, the state Commissioner of Education, to congratulate him for making these monies available to Catholic colleges. Nyquist responded: "Malcolm, you have it all wrong. They're no longer Catholic colleges." What was more significant in this alienation, however, was the fact that no member of the Catholic hierarchy rose to question by what right did these colleges deny their birthright or dissipate the patrimony of the Catholic faithful bought and paid for with the dimes and dollars of immigrants. In many minds they did this in violation of Church Law.

The college-aid question was no sooner "solved," than attention once more was directed to the problems of nonpublic elementary and secondary schools. Enter Rockefeller. Enter Cooke. Enter a new cast of characters, Senator Edward Speno and Assemblyman Alfred Lerner, prominent members of the New York legislature. Enter Msgr. Eugene J. Molloy, Secretary for Education for the diocese of Brooklyn. The year now was 1970. Rockefeller had fathered scholarships a decade earlier for students in private colleges by applying the principle underlying the federal G.I. Bill passed by Congress in 1944. The qualifying veteran of the World War II era used federal money in the college of his choice, even at a religiously owned college, without contest from anyone. A Speno-Lerner proposal was introduced into the state legislature in 1970, designed to extend similar grants to the elementary and secondary levels. Because of the tender age of the children, grants of $50 to $250 were to be given to parents, instead of to students. A majority of the legislators in both houses, of both political parties, of all religious faiths, and from all sections of New York State, were prepared to vote favorably for a Parent-Aid bill, if the governor permitted the bill to come to a vote. Rockefeller, however, became reluctant to extend these grants to the lower levels in education.

During the spring of 1970, and midway toward the next presidential campaign, an office on which he still cast a hungry eye, Richard Nixon to the contrary, Nelson Rockefeller asked for a private meeting with Cardinal Cooke. It was held in the Archbishop's private quarters in 452, with only three people in the room. I was the third. The governor was intent on soft-soaping Cooke about his retreat from Parent-Aid. His national image, he said, would be tarnished if he supported the Speno-Lerner approach. George Wallace had gone that route to avoid segregation and he would be compared with Wallace. Rocky was about to reject the Cardinal's request for Parent-Aid and hoped that the Cardinal in turn would bow to his political judgment. Considering the political records of Rockefeller and Wallace, it was a poor argument. Wallace created private schools to subvert desegregation, Rockefeller faced a parochial system longer-lived than public schools, situated in every neighborhood throughout the state, with fixed buildings serving local populations. The median income of Catholic school families at the time ($7,200) was below the city average, with black and Spanish children moving into Catholic schools, as whites emigrated to the suburbs. At one point in the hour-long discussion Cardinal Cooke left the room to take a telephone call, which gave me an opportunity to ask this question: "Do you think you'd get away with this line on Spellman?" To which Rocky replied with a big grin: "I'm glad I don't have to deal with Spellman." Spellman might not have known how to deal with Rocky's duplicity, but he would have expressed annoyance. Cooke was too easygoing to do even that.

THE FLEISCHMANN COMMISSION

If Churchmen have learned repeatedly not to depend on politicians to serve Catholic interests, they were to learn the lesson one more time in 1970.

After the new state constitution was defeated in 1967, James Allen, then the Commissioner of Education, proposed that the Board of Regents study the "quality, cost, and financing" of all lower education in the state, *nonpublic as well as public.* Pressures for such a study were developing in strange places. William Vanden Huevel, then aide to Senator Robert F. Kennedy, argued publicly that aid for Church-related schools be moved forward as a question from the political forum, where it could only exacerbate community relations, to a scholarly commission which would deal scientifically and constructively with the constitutional and public policy issues. As early as 1968 Assembly Speaker (later Judge) Travia reached an understanding with Rockefeller that such a study group would be appointed. A year later the nonpublic school community itself agreed to this proposal. For a variety of reasons the governor made the commission his own: "I think there is a greater crisis by far in the private schools than there is in the public schools."

On October 28, 1969, Rocky announced that, in collaboration with the Board of Regents, he was creating a commission to conduct "one of the most penetrating studies of education ever made in this state." He spoke as if he were convinced that the financial problems facing the private schools were "even deeper trouble than the public schools." The fundamental duty of such a commission, he said, would be to answer the question: "What should be the proper role of the state regarding the financial needs of nonpublic schools, particularly those serving disadvantaged neighborhoods?" Exuding confidence in 1970 that viable programs of aid for nonpublic schools were possible, he pushed forward. The commission by its existence afforded the governor an important political advantage in view of his upcoming election. The commission, not the governor, would be on the spot. Immediately prior to his fourth election, Rockefeller paid for political advertisements in the state's Catholic newspapers which read in part: "It is our belief that in a pluralistic society, the two systems of public and parochial schools must be helped in every way possible. . . . We pledge our continuous efforts to give financial assistance to meet the cost of parochial school education. You can trust us in the matter."

Although the political heat about nonpublic school aid has abated in subsequent years to a cold chill, it was still a boiling issue in 1970 in spite of the Blaine defeat. The state legislature passed another constitutional amendment repealing Blaine in 1969 and was prepared for another similar approving vote during the 1971 session, with a popular vote scheduled for November, this time as a separate issue. Throughout the 1970 interim Rockefeller was deeply concerned about that fourth term. Once elected he began to turn his hungry eyes on the 1976 White House if Nixon faltered. If Watergate had been discovered earlier, the history of the country might have been different. One Rockefeller aficionado asked in February 1971: "Who knows what kind of trouble Mr. Nixon will be in by 1972?"

Nelson Rockefeller believed in his own destiny and saw that his New York problems, particularly Catholic Church leaders, were stumbling blocks to his national aspirations. He wished to be known as a Catholic champion, but not too much so. By 1969 Catholic Bishops were no longer anxious for another bitter religious controversy. They were willing to forget Blaine in order to try a new tack: modest "Parent-Aid." Aid to college-bound G.I.s had proved to be constitutionally acceptable, even when they chose Catholic colleges, why not Parent-Aid for minor children in nonpublic primary and secondary schools?

I met with Lieutenant Governor Malcolm Wilson during the Christmas recess 1969 to be told once more that, in spite of the legislative action, Rocky was not interested in Parent-Aid. He would press for the total repeal of Blaine, which he did in the Governor's Message to the legislature at the opening of the 1970 session. Wilson wanted episcopal support for Rocky's strategy and was disappointed that the Bishops were intending instead to pressure the governor to go for Parent-Aid immediately. Rocky's office, unsolicited, went so far as to supply the Catholic Committee with data to "prove" that the costs were prohibitive. Mr. Douglass, the governor's administrative assistant, made it clear that such aid, if considered at all, would apply only to nonpublic high school students, who numbered 275,000 in the state. The aid would range from $250 to $100 per student. Charles Tobin, the Catholic Committee's executive secretary, was not interested in excluding elementary students, where the larger numbers and the more serious financial burdens rested. At an Interfaith meeting on January 5, 1970, the governor spoke of Blaine repeal, not Parent-Aid. Rocky proceeded with his public demand for the repeal of Blaine and was annoyed that the Bishops gave him no public support. In their turn the Bishops dropped the Parent-Aid initiative, believing that at this point there was a standoff.

Eventually, the governor began to assert publicly what he had said earlier to Cardinal Cooke, but with a slight difference. In private he spoke about the appearances of things, how *The New York Times* would depict aid to parents as the first step toward undermining the public school system, how it would make him out to be another Governor Wallace. When he was asked in Cardinal Cooke's quarters why he did not attack the bigotry of *The New York Times* if its editors calumniated him so, Rocky merely shrugged. Backlash from *The Times* was more his worry than the hostility of religious leaders. When Parent-Aid began to develop clout, Rockefeller began to assert categorically that such aid would destroy the public school system, "not just of our state, but of our country." He further suggested that New York's example would prompt the Southern states to keep their schools segregated. These public charges by the governor killed the Speno-Lerner chances. And to make sure that it stayed buried, he used his political muscle to see that Parent-Aid remained off the legislative calendar. He threatened a veto if it did not stay off. And it did.

A poignant moment came when State Senator Edward Speno died suddenly and was buried from St. Agnes Cathedral, Rockville Centre, in the presence of Rockefeller and five Catholic Bishops, including Bishop Francis J. Mugavero of Brooklyn, whose Secretary for Education, Eugene Molloy, was the preeminent Catholic educator in the state. Invited into the Bishop's Residence at Rockville Centre, the governor began to offer the excuses he earlier tried on Cardinal Cooke. No one knows for certain what did it, perhaps Rocky's one-liner, "Trust me." This remark brought Msgr. Molloy out of the shadows to give the governor the lecture of his life on fairness to children and the rights of common people. Gene Molloy was five foot five but possessed a profound mind and an orator's tongue when it came to articulating the political rights of the parents of nonpublic school children. In strong terms he rejected the bigoted implications of the Rockefeller position.

It is difficult in hindsight to understand why Catholic leaders trusted Rockefeller as long as they did. Rocky had asked Catholics to trust him from the moment of his first election in 1958. The only beneficiary of that trust was a four-time reelected governor. Rocky consistently mouse-trapped Catholic leadership, sold out his local Catholic constituency because of his passion for the presidency, and his arguments were all wrong. Public schools losing students to parochial schools? Nonsense. They were losing students to suburban public schools because of the crime, drugs, and bad teaching in the public system. In 1956 the city's Catholic elementary schools registered 271,000 children. Fourteen years later the school population was not smaller. Catholic schools anti-Spanish, anti-black? Only 20 of New York City's 187 Catholic elementary schools lacked Spanish children. And only 36 had no blacks, who were rarely Catholic anyway. Thirty percent of all children in Manhattan and the Bronx parochial schools were Spanish or black. Upper class or elite parents? A Louis Gary survey in 1968 of 230,000 families with children in Catholic school showed these families to be larger, with less income, than the general population. About 25 percent of New York City's 1968 Catholic wage-earning parents took home less than $100 a week, 62 percent less than $150. When LBJ's remedial programs for ghetto children began in 1965, 103 of the 187 Catholic schools were certified by the Board of Education under Title One. All the while, Catholic religious teachers were contributing approximately $100 million a year in service to ensure that children received education parents wanted. Was it good education? You bet. Science Research Associates regularly found that Catholic school children bettered the national norm in all subjects and all grades, even in the ghetto. When during the Blaine campaign Rockefeller was promising Catholic Bishops the moon, Catholic high school students were capturing 30 percent of the state's Regents Scholarships and 26 percent of the city's science awards. Were the Catholic schools divisive? Weakening the national consensus? The National Opinion Research Center of the University of Chicago's study, *The Education of Catholic Americans,* concluded: "We must report that the impressions are not sustained.

The burden of proof for the theory that Catholic education isolates its graduates from other Americans now seems to rest with those who support this thesis."

These data, however, were unpersuasive to the public school establishment or its ideologues, not even to certain post-Vatican II Catholics. A Long Island lady summarized the arguments making the "progressive" rounds of the Church. Religious training, she said, no longer centered around the old-fashioned catechism, but on loving one's neighbor. She wanted the Catholic Church to work together with the public schools for the better education of all, not for a separate system. "Let those who wanted separate schools pay for them." This was a new Catholicism.

But Rockefeller continued to speak out of both sides of his mouth. After his tongue-lashing by Msgr. Molloy, the governor announced again at a news conference that he was going to work for aid to nonpublic school children. He said this after telling public school administrators to forget new state aid because of the state's fiscal crisis. When challenged by the press on the inconsistency he did not reply, although to regain some Catholic mileage, he reaffirmed: "There is a greater crisis by far in the private schools than there is in public schools."

While waiting for the Fleischmann Commission's final report to bail him out, he resigned as governor to permit Lieutenant Governor Malcolm Wilson to realize his lifelong ambition. He himself moved on to become Vice President of the United States (1974–76). His Fleischmann study suffered from the same old built-in biases against parochial schools and other defects.

First, Manly Fleischmann, a Buffalo attorney and a trustee of New York State University, was no friend of government aid to nonpublic schools.

Secondly, while five of the eighteen members were friendly to public aid for nonpublic schools, they were also pro-public school. The majority representation for public education was hostile to Church-related schools.

Thirdly, the appointment of the commission's staff director and his ten full-time professional assistants was made without regard for nonpublic schools.

Fourthly, the public school study was budgeted at $1,500,000 and scheduled to take one year and a half. The budget for the nonpublic school study was set at less than $50,000 for a study of six months' duration. Since one of every four children in New York attended a nonpublic school, the expenditure of $30 to examine the problems of one young scholar and only $1.00 for the other fell short of what might be called public equity.

Finally, Louis R. Gary, appointed director of the nonpublic school report, was directed to balance his staff with opponents of aid to nonpublic schools. Shortly thereafter George La Noue and Leo Pfieffer were hired, men who for more than a decade fought every program of aid to children attending church-related schools, including bus rides. Who investigating the problems of blacks or Jews would have permitted their enemies to shape the study?

Nonetheless the Gary study made some contribution toward a better public appreciation of the value of nonpublic education to the people of New York State.

1. The Gary report established the fact that the nonpublic school system in New York State with its 841,378 students was the largest nonpublic system in the United States, more than twice as large as the public school enrollment of thirty states. Even if it declined to half its size, only New York's public school district would still be larger.

2. The average per pupil cost in the Catholic group was only $241, compared with $1,255 in the public sector.

3. By virtue of the existence of nonpublic schools, "pluralism is an integral part of the educational system in New York State in that alternatives [for education] do exist," leading Gary to conclude that "the vast potential which pluralism holds for creating new school types and for offering real parental options has hardly been tapped."

4. The Gary report also made clear that there was a crucial economic link between state action and Church action. The report projected that without substantial state aid the tuition in New York's elementary schools by 1975 could be over $350 per child. According to the Gary prediction, tuition had already jumped from $65 per child in New York City in 1969 to over $100. Gary stated that future tuition rises were likely to destroy the nonpublic schools as a mass system of education. (At this time Gary could not foresee how widespread the mass exodus from schools of religious women would be.)

5. The Gary report summarized the recommendations of an earlier study commission in the state of Illinois. (a) Limited Parent-Aid to most nonpublic school parents. (b) Larger grants for children of low-income families. (c) Special grants to assist joint public-nonpublic ventures in innovative secular education.

6. Finally the Gary report suggested that the commission consider various forms of voucher plans to assist the nonpublic school system.

The Gary report, however, was not without its faults:

1. It did not give proper credit to the widespread and voluntary racial mix of parochial schools. Without massive busing the Catholic schools of New York City were better integrated—that is, fewer mostly black and fewer mostly white schools—than public schools. Nor did it make anything of free choice for minority groups. Minorities complained about public schools, not about Catholic schools.

2. The Gary report discounted its earlier stress about the importance of educational plurality by emphasizing that Catholics alone really enjoyed multiple choices.

3. The Gary report was unduly nervous about the quality of Catholic education. In saying that "there is not a great difference between the over-all quality of public and nonpublic education in the state," Gary ignored the sense of many that Catholic schools, in urban and poverty areas, were superior to the better endowed public schools.

When the final advice of the Fleischmann Commission was drawn, it read as follows:

> If a public system and private system are co-existent and competitive, it is in the best long-run interest of the State to let the private

168

system wither away because anything the private system can do the State can do just as well.

Hugh L. Carey, then a congressman, responded best to this conclusion:

> Fleischmann makes fine yeast. Fleischmann distills good gin. But Fleischmann as a report is schmalz because it absolutizes statism.

The late Msgr. Eugene J. Molloy was never better as a prophet, when he wrote: "We appear to have agreed to put our trust for the future program of assistance to nonpublic schools, not in our elected representatives but in the Fleischmann Commission, which is appointed and against whose recommendations we have no recourse. We should recall the results of the Commission to Study Abortion Reform. We should also remember that to the best of our knowledge only a minority of the Fleischmann Commission is favorably disposed to nonpublic schools."[5]

The nonpublic school case suffered one other defect: The absence of an ongoing political action organization for nonpublic schools. Virgil Blum's famous dictum was ignored: "The best proposal in the world will get nowhere if there is no political organization to advance it through the legislative process." Politicians will slam the door in the face of Bishops if they know that Bishops are not serious about their politics. Ad hoc political efforts, encouraged by Bishops, tend to collapse after political defeat. Instead of understanding that their efforts were too little, too hurried, too late, clerics assembled after the Blaine defeat to beat their breasts in shame for having been involved in a sordid business of public pressure. After Blaine lay leaders once more became anonymous and passive, while clerics resumed their role of public spokesmen for parents. Andrew Greeley is not correct in demanding that ownership of Catholic schools be turned over to laymen as a way of encouraging government to provide monies to Catholic school children. But, if a repeated sequence of political defeats indicates anything, it suggests that nonpublic school parents need their own political action committees, well organized and well managed. Practical necessity created the American public school. It also brought about the secularization of that common school. But pragmatism need not decree that only public schools constitute American education.

The failure of the Gary committee to be an out-and-out pro-private school committee made it simple for the Fleischmann Commission to reach the conclusion it wished to reach. Some of its specific views make interesting reading almost twenty years later:

1. Public funds or tax revenues ought not to be used in support of the attendance of students at sectarian schools.

2. Constitutional proscriptions control this matter negatively.

3. In the short term, the State's economic interests dictate increases in the current level of support of nonpublic education.

4. We would also require nonpublic schools, as a condition to receipt of any State funds, to accept all students regardless of religious affiliation.

5. Constitutional restrictions do not apply to nonsectarian, nonpublic schools. We recommend against public support of sectarian nonpublic schools. (Except for orphanages.)

The minority members of the Fleischmann Commission, five against thirteen, were totally ignored by the media. Yet, they made a strong case for nonpublic school aid that deserved a better public hearing. They argued that the constitutionality of parent vouchers, Parent-Aid payments, tax credits, and other forms of tuition relief were yet to be submitted to a constitutional test. This was true in 1972 and is still true.

What makes the obvious bias of the commission as a whole so noticeable is the failure to take into account the fact that support for aid to nonpublic schools was generally a majority opinion of the people, even among politicians. The last President to stand absolutely against such aid was John F. Kennedy. In New York State support for such aid was bipartisan and most public opinion polls over several decades favored some kind of aid. Even the Board of Regents at the time of the hottest debates over assistance to nonpublic schools (May 27, 1971) approved such aid.

The Fleischmann Commission's minority listed several justifications for such aid, ignored by the majority. Its own Gary report endorsed the Regents' position and the rights of parents, and children too, to choose their own schools. As the cost of education rose, those rights were jeopardized for all save the affluent. Particularly eloquent was the minority position on the public benefits of nonpublic education—in the ghetto neighborhoods, in savings to the state amounting to billions of dollars, in easing population burdens on public schools, thus contributing to the improved quality of public education.

The minority accused the majority of having a closed mind to the contributions of nonpublic education, a weird preoccupation with religious schools, and an unwillingness to explore the legitimate areas of aid. They disputed the charges (1) that nonpublic schools contributed to segregation, (2) that such aid would eventually equal that of public schools, and (3) that the Catholic Church was favored by state aid. These were all untenable scare arguments, nourished in large part by religious prejudice.

What the minority report made clear was the conspiracy which concealed the possibilities still available for experiment. As a result of Fleischmann, the legislature was deterred from enacting any new and creative programs thereafter, save to pay nonpublic schools for their bookkeeping costs in meeting state requirements. It is almost an anticlimax to report that the Catholic school system of New York no longer is the third-largest in the country.

Seventeen years later (1989) bigotry reared its head once more in the Supreme Court itself. Normally Americans do not anticipate this possibility, anymore than Catholics expect Bishops to be un-Christian. In 1971 Justice William O. Douglas, helping decide the Lemon Case, dismissed the Pennsylvania and Rhode Island attempts to aid nonpublic schools as "schemes." In a footnote (No. 20) Douglas cited Loraine Boettner's book *Roman Catholicism,* which defended these theses: (1) Roman Catholicism is more dangerous to the United States than communism; (2) Catholic schools (in contradistinction to Lutheran schools) are objectionable because their teachers know only what their hierarchy tells them; Catholics take over control of public schools whenever they

171

can; the Catholic system turns out moral misfits; its members should not be allowed to teach in public schools.

Prejudice against religious schools again reared its ugly head in the most recent relevant Supreme Court decision. The case involved the 1965 Elementary and Secondary Education Act under which public school teachers entered parochial schools in the ghetto to teach remedial English and math to poor children. A 5–4 decision in the Felton Case (July 1, 1985) decreed such an application of ESEA was unconstitutional. Justice William Brennan did not question the secular success of the program, nor the good intentions of public and nonpublic school administrators. He did not provide a practical way of implementing ESEA's intent to remedy the widespread retardation in the ghetto, even among parochial school children. It was the *symbolism* of direct government contact with a religious school that he judged to be unconstitutional. Shunted to the side was the practical solution worked out after 1965 by public school professionals that poor or ghetto parochial school children should not be forced after a full day in class to travel to the public school for remedial education. Moving one teacher from school to school made more sense and saved more money than moving 40, 80, 120 children in every poor school—tens of thousands in New York City—on buses. But the Supreme Court judged this contact between the public and private sector of education was symbolically un-American, as that was allegedly understood by the authors of the Constitution.

Chief Justice Burger in his dissent wrote: "It borders on paranoia to perceive . . . the Bishop of Rome lurking behind programs that are . . . vital to the nation's school children . . . [This decision] . . . exhibits nothing less than hostility toward religion and the children who attend Church-sponsored schools." Justice Rehnquist observed: "The Court takes advantage of the Catch-22 paradox of its own creation . . . whereby aid must be supervised to ensure no entanglement, but the supervision itself is held to cause entanglement." Justice Rehnquist wondered aloud why such aid is a greater symbolic link between government and religion than the institution of legislative chaplains, which had been approved by the same Court. Justice O'Connor thought the logic of the decision "would require us to close our public schools, for there is always some chance that a public school teacher will bring religion into a school." Justice White insisted that the majority's ban was "not required by the First Amendment and contrary to the long-range interests of the country."

President Reagan's Secretary of Education, William Bennett, called the Felton decision "a new aversion to religion." In his view, "the attitude that regards entanglement with religion as something akin with an infectious disease must be confronted broadly and directly."

However, this is not what 50 million Catholics were prepared to do. They continued to act, at least their leaders did, as if they were a tiny and timid minority. The plaintiffs in the Felton Case —PEARL, the National Education Association, the American Jewish Congress—together might make for one good-sized Catholic diocese, if they were believers. Yet, their zealous determination has resulted in the institutionalization of animus against nonpublic schools by way of a Supreme Court fiat. No instrument was available to excite, or to organize, what should have been an exercise in justifiable outrage in the religious communities of the nation. Catholic leadership made a *pro forma* complaint against *Felton*, but outrage was left to public officials instead. Why should nonpublic school children leave their warm school buildings for city-rented vans stationed outside their school door, scarcely seven good strides away, because the Supreme Court feared, with no evidence at hand, that public school teachers might be contaminated by walking into a religious school, twenty years of experience to the contrary notwithstanding?

No one remains, at this moment at least, to speak for the Catholic cause but prelates. And prelates are not very good at this political game, which sometimes is immoral and always rough and tumble, when not dirty. In such contests Bishops often make the wrong decisions, and even when they are right do not know (it seems) how to make their "right" plausible to the uninitiated, certainly not to the Church's enemies. Identifying intractable enemies is a first principle of good politics. The second is to know how to deal with and beat them at their own game. Catholics never really developed a successful political agenda, at least not one which won in modern times. Education aid and abortion limits are their most ignoble failures. There is doom in any political issue once it is defined as "Catholic," but not necessarily when it is black, Jewish, feminist, ecumenical, or Hispanic. The other causes gain respect not because they are unpartisan or unselfish, but because these narrow selfish causes are better organized, better promoted, and better reinforced. Catholics often hide behind other people's bigotry to rationalize their political ineptness or their fear of not being liked.

During the course of U.S. history various Catholic defense groups have grown up without surviving their mistakes or those of Bishops' staffs. Admittedly, a hierarchic Church is always a special problem since officers have a divine right to make some decisions, and believers are likely to acquiesce even when divine right is not really involved. Additionally, the anti-Bishop and anti-Roman voices receive an oversupply of attention by the pervasive secular media, even though they rarely speak for the people who sit in the pews every Sunday.

The Church's public relations problem was never more obvious than during the Right-to-Life controversies. Shrewd laymen made abortion the cutting edge of modern politics, one which separated believers from half-believers from unbelievers. But episcopal anxiety about their aggressiveness led Bishops to blink when faced with their enemies' ridicule of the Church's absolute stand. The episcopal flip-flop from approval of the Hyde Amendment (with its general federal ban on abortion) to a Hatch Amendment (tossing the subject back to the states) was an attempt to gain a half a loaf rather than none. They won nothing. Here was a decision made *in camera* with no real consultation with the activist troops in the world's field by Bishops who support lay people in every aspect of Church life! How lay opinion in areas of their special competence is to be balanced against the responsible veto power of Bishops in their special area of rightful competence remains an unresolved Catholic problem.

If nonpublic school aid was an important Catholic issue, abortion surely is another and will always be more important. A way must be found by the Church to promote Catholic values in a nation which no longer wishes to live by Protestant values. Religious values (e.g., "One Nation Under God") cannot readily be reconciled with an utter this-world philosophy of humanist ideologues. But if in a democracy, people are to decide between such contradictory viewpoints, the issues must be clearly understood. Catholics may not always make their best case media-wise because they presume good will where there is none. But they also underestimate the general religiosity of the American people, mainly by making compromises prematurely which weaken their own best arguments. If we end up with no religious schools to speak of and abortion becomes as commonplace as contraception, the Church will not have done her job and the country will be worse for its failure. The determination characteristic of civil rights groups must invade Catholic precincts and we must learn to use correct political tactics. For this, Catholic leadership needs evenhanded treatment by the media and more *chutzpah* within Church precincts than presently is in evidence.

HIS FINEST HOURS

Terence Cardinal Cooke was not always able to direct the course of the Church affairs, but he always knew where the Church ought to be going. And he always followed the lead of the Holy See. One of his finest hours came during the November 14–17, 1977, meeting of the U.S. Bishops when the final draft of the National Catechetical Directory was under consideration. The draft was defective, mostly for doctrinal or disciplinary items that were neglected or omitted. The draft fudged doctrinal content with such statements as "formulation and memorization should be used with discretion so as not to overburden or confuse." A handful of Bishops took the lead in putting back into NCD what the staff had diligently excluded. Cardinal Cooke, prodded by Father Michael Wrenn, his leading catechetical expert, proposed an amendment, viz., that children be taught to memorize prayers,

175

parts of the Mass, the list of the sacraments, and the commandments of God and the Church. It was like asking students learning English to make sure they knew the alphabet. Cooke's amendment passed but not without the staff, and a Bishop as their spokesman, expressing fury at their defeat. It truly was one of Cooke's finest hours.

Another of Cardinal Cooke's finest hours was his work as chairman of the Pro-Life Activities Committee for the U.S. Bishops. Once the Supreme Court's *Roe v. Wade* decision (1973) legitimized abortion on demand, the National Conference of Catholic Bishops called for a constitutional amendment to protect the life of the unborn almost immediately (November 13). In no time at all Right-to-Life groups, mostly of an ecumenical nature, sprang up across the country, and in short order they developed real political clout. Within the year they were threatening to defeat pro-abortion politicians, and did win some surprising victories, mostly at the expense of Democrats, whose national party was certainly vulnerable. An outcry against "single-issue politics," initiated by affected Democrats, was heard almost overnight by important U.S. ecclesiastics. Suddenly, abortion, which at first was a bottom-line moral issue—human life in peril—which hitherto enjoyed unique political protection, became one of a smorgasbord of issues to be judged politically, relative to other contingencies with civic effects. Abruptly, a moral absolute—"Thou shalt not take innocent life"—became a political chip, a pawn in the game of political compromise. It was a radical shift, not for American politicians but for ecclesiastics.

Single-issue politics is as American as apple pie. Ask a workingman, a black, or a Jew who has to choose between politicians, one of whom is against labor unions, affirmative action, or Israel. Not even Richard Daley would have dared tell a farmer, a banker, or a fruit picker that he should not vote his pocketbook or his ethnic interests. Very few Jewish voters would be persuaded to vote for an anti-Semite because on all other social issues he was a "liberal." For convinced Catholics, too, a "seamless garment" of life issues, from relief of poverty to the sanctity of unborn life, only blurs the radical distinction between killing the unborn and executing a convicted murderer, and muddies the waters for politicians who are called upon to make pro- or antiabortion decisions. Direct abortion is an absolute no-no. Capital punishment has throughout Catholic history been considered morally permissible given the right motive and circumstance. A Catholic with an eighth-grade education knows the difference in the moral quality of various decisions relative to life, its protection, degradation, or termination. To tell a Catholic, therefore, that he should package his political choices so as to consider abortion simply as another life issue is bad theology and bad politics.

Between 1973–83 the Right-to-Life Political Action Committees, all lay directed, grew in political strength across the country simply because they persuaded their constituency to vote up or down on that issue, i.e., until Bishops began to speak of a "seamless garment" as a desirable political agenda for Catholics. By so doing they equivalently cut the ground from under a movement, which while not theirs to manage in the political arena, best represented their own 1973 intentions. Immediately after *Roe v. Wade* the NCCB called for a "well-planned and coordinated political organization by citizens at the national, state, and local levels." Such political activity was designated then "a moral imperative." Eight years later (1981), however, the conference weakened Right-to-Life politics when it walked away from its original Human Life (constitutional) Amendment to back the Hatch Amendment. Senator Orrin Hatch, deciding that a constitutional amendment banning abortion (except possibly to save a mother's life) was not feasible of passage, proposed instead one which said the right to abortion is not secured by the U.S. Constitution, that Congress and the states had the power to restrict or prohibit abortion, and remanded the issue to the several states. Per se there was nothing wrong with the Hatch Amendment since it represented an exercise in political judgment. But it was made by Bishops! Not by the Right-to-Lifers out in the trenches. Not only did it lack support in the Congress (Hatch eventually withdrew it), but it involved fifty fights instead of one, thus debilitating the united antiabortion effort which had come into being nationally. It may well be that ultimately fifty fights will become the political reality, but in 1981 the Right-to-Life cause lost its head of steam because of the Hatch endorsement, and its activists blamed the Catholic Bishops and the actively promoted "seamless garment" proposition.

Right-to-Life leadership even accused Bishops of partisanship on behalf of the Democratic Party. Entrenched pro-abortion politicos like Ted Kennedy, Mario Cuomo, Tip O'Neill, and Geraldine Ferraro (all Catholics), and Walter Mondale and George McGovern (Protestants) became fearful of the antiabortion vote. It had not yet succeeded nationally but was growing to be decisive in local elections. This development tended to favor Republicans, who were more likely to be antiabortion. Although many priests on the staff of the USCC were known to be Democratic partisans, it is not true that the Body of Bishops was. Sometimes prominent leaders—Bernardin, Roach, and Weakland come to mind—sound like Democrats because they speak on social causes with a statist bent, but Bishops generally eschew partisan politics, unless a clear Church interest is at stake. Nonetheless, the "seamless garment" concept, or the "consistent ethic," as it was later called, translated into political choice benefited Democrats. Equivalently, it told Catholics they should not single out candidates for reward or punishment simply on the basis of their abortion stance. As late as 1987 Cardinal Bernardin was still rejecting "Right-to-Life" as a litmus test for voting. His "consistent ethic," he said, "provides a grid for assessing party platforms and the record of candidates for public office." Reversing *Roe v. Wade* is one such political norm. Passing a minimum wage law is another. Are these on the same moral and political levels? One 1988 booklet, *Just Life*, using the "consistent ethic" norm, gives high approval marks to the likes of pro-abortion Ted Kennedy, low ratings to the anti-abortion Henry Hyde, indication enough of the political judgments built into this norm.

Politics aside, the moral issue is paramount. While single-issue voting is not commonplace and while voters are not necessarily called upon to make moral judgments in a voting booth, the character of a candidate or the even-handed justice of a platform are relevant to the political process, at least for Christians. Theologian Germain Grisez makes the moral case in a letter to the Fellowship of Catholic Scholars (February 13, 1988): "Certain matters do provide good tests of character with respect to justice. Abortion is one of them. For every educated person knows that each time an abortion is done a tiny and defenseless human being is killed. Nobody who is just can condone that, think it legal, or want to entangle all citizens in it by supporting it with public funds." In Grisez' judgment any individual seeking public office who supports the legality, much less the public funding, of abortion manifests character which makes him or her unfit for public office. The actual political choices may not be this clear cut and the voter may be forced to choose the lesser evil, but a pro-abortionist is very different in political potential from one opposed to a higher minimum wage.

During most of these abortion fights, the man in charge of the NCCB's pro-life activities was Terence Cardinal Cooke. No one in the hierarchy was more committed to Catholic principles and priorities than the New York Archbishop. He did not carry the day on the national scene, but home in his own Archdiocese and three years before *Roe v. Wade* he stood tall on the issue. In the first fourteen months of a new state abortion law (1970–71), he counted 205,614 abortions in New York City alone, half of which were performed on out-of-state residents who rode into the city for the service. On September 9, 1971, in the presence of 200 priests he laid out the social consequences of permissive abortion laws: "The sacredness of life must be protected in whatever circumstances it is found; whether the life endangered is in the womb of a mother in a New York abortion clinic or in the fear-racked body of a poor peasant in Southeast Asia." As a trained social worker Cooke's humanist concerns were broadly based, but he knew the proper hierarchy of values: "Improving the quality of life is surely a laudable purpose, but the quality of life movement becomes insidious and dangerous when it equates the quality of life with life itself." This is as good an argument as any *against* the unequivocal use of what later was to become the "seamless garment" argument.

When Cooke left New York for Washington, D.C., where the

179

NCCB's Pro-Life Activities Committee was centered, he entered a world in which he was not a controlling force. It was not that he was simpleminded about the USCC staff. He knew that some of the priests there were woolly-headed about contraception, but he was also confident of his ability to make them toe the line on the Right-to-Life. He did not have to try very hard because pro-contraception priests frequently oppose abortion to demonstrate that they do accept Church guidance in critical matters. However, there remains an unrecognized problem in their ethical approach. The moral system which justifies contraception readily justifies abortion. The contraceptive ethos links condoms, IUDs, and pills with sterilization and abortion as a complete family-planning package. From the Church's worldview all three were intrinsically evil. Indeed, if there is a "seamless garment" to be made, it is one that ties contraception into abortion inexorably. The argument that contraception prevents abortion has long since been discredited. Quite the opposite; failed contraception leads to abortion. The Church's position is different: Not only is life sacred and untouchable, but so is the process of giving life. Many years later (July 18, 1984) John Paul II would make clear that the moral norm governing contraception "belongs not only to the natural moral law, but also to the *moral order revealed by God.*[6] Even so, important USCC priests would not agree, and Cooke's confidence in keeping their hidden agenda in line would prove to be misplaced. He might have been less sure of himself had he reviewed the work done under his predecessor, Cardinal John Cody. An early *Respect Life Booklet* (1978–79) totally ignored the issue of contraception and its relationship to abortion, this in spite of *Humanae Vitae*'s connection of the two.

It is not surprising, therefore, that Cooke returned home from Washington somewhat embarrassed over NCCB's 1981 decision to abandon the drive for a Human Life Amendment and replace it with the ill-fated Hatch approach. He was a team player, and if the NCCB's "team" called for that shift, Cooke would go along, however reluctantly. The sadder aspect of this sequence was that many Right-to-Lifers in his own metropolitan area believed he had sold them out.

The Church's Americanizers (and these included important Bishops) made a judgment that their approach was better in the long run, arguing that debate would eventually turn public opinion around, while power plays would only exacerbate ecumenical relations. With four thousand abortions taking place each day, the argument did not even sound persuasive. It was the sort of gradualism these same elites rejected out of hand when the issue was race or "trickle down" capitalism. As for ecumenical relations, it all depends on the religionists to whom Right-to-Lifers need relate. Americanizers have contempt for the Jerry Falwells who stand against abortion and freely associate with mainline Church leaders who favor abortion. Joseph M. Scheidler, executive director of Chicago's Pro-Life Action League, took grave umbrage in 1986 at Cardinal Bernardin's Chicago Archdiocese's entering "an accord" with the Episcopal Bishop of Chicago with no Catholic attention paid to the Episcopal Church's position on abortion. After announcing how the Illinois Masonic Hospital reversed itself to permit abortions on the advice of the Episcopal Bishop, Scheidler had this to say:

> Those who actively fight abortion have discovered that there is a genuine ecumenism growing out of the battle to save the unborn. Catholics, Baptists, non-denominational evangelicals, fundamentalists, and members of all and no religion are united in a belief in God and the value of his creatures. This genuine ecumenism will last, and will flourish, because it accepts a positive, eternal value for its base. And we never sign an accord. We live one.[7]

By the time Cardinal Bernardin succeeded Cooke as Chairman of the NCCB's Pro-Life Activities Committee, the trend was away from abortion as a dominant political issue. Indeed, in 1985 the USCC submitted an *amicus curiae* brief to the U.S. Supreme Court accepting the reality of the Court's judgment that abortion is a constitutional right. In 1973 the U.S. Bishops had called the *Roe v. Wade* decision wrong and denied that abortion was a right guaranteed by the Constitution. Right-to-Lifers interpreted the latest USCC move as a sign that the Bishops' central headquarters had abandoned its attempt to overturn *Roe* at the very moment a non-Catholic President, Ronald Reagan, was asking the same Court to reverse itself.

All these shifts took place after Cardinal Cooke's death. But during his lifetime Terry Cooke was a single-issue Catholic, if that issue was Right-to-Life.

NOTES

1. *The New York Times Magazine,* October 13, 1968.

2. *The Education of Catholic Americans* (Garden City, N.Y.: Doubleday & Co., 1968).

3. *The New York Times,* April 16, 1968.

4. *The New York Times,* June 4, 1970.

5. The statement of Msgr. Molloy, made April 3, 1970, is recorded in *Government Aid to Nonpublic Schools: Yes or No* (Jamaica, N.Y.: St. John's University Press, 1972).

6. *Reflections on Humanae Vitae* (Boston: St. Paul Editions, 1984).

7. *The Chicago Catholic,* December 19–26, 1986.

FOUR

Terry Cooke and the Challenges of Vatican II

IT IS A SHAME that Terry Cooke did not come along when the Church was at her best, during the period of self-appreciation and internal peace, when the world outside looked at her with a certain amount of awe, when all Bishops looked ten feet tall and all Catholics expected them to solve any problems that came their way. He would have walked through that world with great grace and left in his wake great serenity. And a sense of God's presence. But that was not God's plan for the Church, nor for him. Instead he took over in the year of the Tet offensive, the year when both Martin Luther King and Robert Kennedy went to God the violent way. And the year of *Humanae Vitae*.

A Cardinal's job is tiring by itself because of the rounds he must make every day, of altars, of conference tables, of banquets,

183

and of wakes. But in good times routine makes it easy, even boring. Most people of good sense thank God for the structured life because it saves thinking up new answers every five minutes. Revolutionaries care little for routine because it gives them so little to fight about. Rebels like disorder because this is when they are the center of attention. Disorder may be the playground of the devil, but a little bit of hell is heaven to malcontents.

By the time Terry Cooke could call 452 Madison Avenue his permanent home, there was hell to pay in St. Patrick's Cathedral and at City Hall. The Archbishop of New York was expected to have control over the one and clout in the other. But by 1968 his influence in both places was at a low point, with protestors inside the Cathedral and a mayor who was not friendly to Catholics.

The loss of political influence would not have disturbed Cooke personally, or any other Catholic for that matter, save for the fact that Catholics made up almost half of the city population, and New York's Archbishop traditionally was their spokesman. Once upon a time he was entitled by informal agreement to name one or two of his own constituency to the Board of Education, to the Board of Higher Education, to the Board of Regents, and to various welfare councils. That was the era of the city's history when the three major religious bodies were respected in City Hall. The last mayor with whom that was possible was Robert F. Wagner. Then came the rule of unbelief among City Fathers.

Cardinal Cooke would have to deal with other unbelief, too, sometimes directed at his worthiness to sit where he sat, sometimes represented by a lack of faith in the Church herself, even the one defined by the Second Vatican Council. Whatever else he was, Cooke was a Vatican II Bishop. He accepted all of its demands as Gospel—attention to the poor and the causes which uplifted their status, outreach to those of different faiths and none, a more meaningful manner of liturgical worship, more listening to the pews by pastors, including Bishops, new structures to facilitate participation, and so forth. Although all of these fundamental objectives of the Council admitted of different interpretations and so of their nature would involve some differences of opinion about how best to achieve what the Council designed, the fundamental thrust was congenial to a man of Cooke's background. While ever the dutiful son of the Church, he had long since appreciated the advantages of a vernacular liturgy, had broad ecumenical contacts as a young priest, was a social worker by training and a friendly personality besides. The decrees of Vatican II of themselves were no challenge. What would test his mettle would be the turbulent spirit that followed in the wake of the Council among those who had other things in mind than a keener sense of the presence of God in the world, wider acceptance of the reign of Christ in human hearts, and holier Catholics.

THE CITY OF POLITICIANS

The Archdiocese of New York first began to lose its political clout when the Catholic neighborhoods in which its parishes were deeply rooted began to disintegrate. Ethnic populations, densely housed, usually wound up with political leaders who knew their people and represented them downtown where the City Fathers met. A goodly share of those leaders were themselves religiously affiliated or recognized the religious realities of their precincts. The opinion of the rabbi, the minister, and the priest had standing. However, in the decade preceding Cooke's ascension, five hundred thousand Poles, Irish, and Italians moved out or were forced to move, taking their family stability and their political muscle with them. Politicos like Daniel Patrick Moynihan and flibbertigibbets like Andrew Greeley trace the decay of New York to the lack of interest by Irish Catholics in the plight of the new poor, many of whom were Catholic. Their interpretation is cynical and a lie. New York neighborhoods were made and remade by one ethnic group elbowing its way slowly into another's turf, usually to the betterment of both. Owning two pairs of shoes instead of one made the difference. There was no rent control during the depression, and if you moved at the right moment, you earned one month's free rent. After World War II the young became exurbanites by choice, but little has been written about how many such migrations were involuntary, forced upon low- and low-mid-

185

dle-income families by political and business entrepreneurs, during the Wagner administration, interested in making a dollar. In one ten-year period, for example, one hundred thousand child-centered people, mostly poor or nearly poor Catholics of Irish, Italian, and Slavic background, were driven out of four-story walk-ups on the Upper East Side to make way for luxury housing mostly for singles and the rising Yuppie class. About the time Cooke was coming into his own, the larger Catholic family size in that area alone was 4.7 with a median annual income of $7,500, well above the city's birthrate and below its $9,273 median income. Both Wagner and Lindsay were advised by Catholic leadership to take note of what "bulldozing" and "city planning" were doing to integrated neighborhoods, but by this time each of these officials had other voting blocs to cultivate. The movable Catholics were disposable and Church authority, which was not given to public rowdiness, could be counted on not to threaten City Hall.

In any commentary on the municipal disarray and political corruption of the 1980s, the cultural values of those who dominated city politics after the Catholic departure are worth taking into account. These values were to have a profound bearing on the social behavior of newcomers. Earlier migrants, even though still poor as the data indicate, were products of the school of hard knocks, with closely knit family and religious ties reinforced by the public policy of government at all levels. Religious leaders were a welcome part of that public support system. In the new dispensation the emphasis went from duties to rights with newcomers promised, as if they were right around the corner, good housing, better education, and job opportunities, easier access to welfare benefits, family limitation procedures, including abortion, and a benign administration of justice. Side by side with what often became manufactured slums were the glass houses of upwardly mobile Yuppies, living alone, in pairs, but not in a family. The city began the new planning with noble ideals, but "Fort Apache" and "The Blackboard Jungle" were the result as much of a bad moral philosophy in political leadership, as they were of inept management ability. The "new planners" had no intention of sharing their newly acquired power with religious leaders, especially with Catholic ecclesiastics and Orthodox Jewish rabbis, the only leaders left in the city willing to speak up about the importance to the city of the Judeo-Christian moral and religious codes. Social science results were the new ethic, and they usually represented a low common denominator of people's wants. By 1986 social success was proclaimed not with the arrival of safe neighborhoods but when intolerable crime fell by two percentage points. In the face of the most dangerous social disease in modern times—AIDS—City Fathers proposed not a quarantine of carriers, nor a good dose of virtue reinforced by public law, but condoms, free condoms dispensed by public officials. Civic endorsement of fornication, adultery, and sodomy would have scandalized Boss William Tweed, the nineteenth-century scalawag who scandalized his people by making stealing respectable.

Cardinal Cooke's political involvement generally meant soothing sensitive feelings or gently rebuking unfriendly critics, keeping an eye from the outside on the nomination and election process, and defending Catholic interests or upholding public morality. For the most part he permitted his staff to do the political infighting whenever his visibility did not seem necessary. Still if there were important political stakes, like cementing the right friendships or punishing an enemy, this man of detail left little to someone else's chance, whether it was arranging a seat for Joseph Califano at the Al Smith Dinner, a papal audience for John and Mary Lindsay, or removing distinguished people from the Foundling Party's invitation list because they were pro-abortion. Cooke could even become irate, as he did when Agriculture Secretary Butz attacked Paul VI's position on birth control with a mock Italian accent no less: "He no playa the game, he no makea the rules." The Cardinal would not accept the Secretary's private apology and demanded that President Ford have Butz publicly "apologize immediately or resign." The Secretary later resigned after another gaffe.

Cooke was especially sensitive to the various forces within the local community, in particular to his wide network of Jewish friends. He recognized the fact that the Jewish community was large and appreciated the good relations the New York Archdiocese enjoyed with many of its leaders. When a Pope was to visit the U.S., Cooke was solicitous that the Jewish leaders participate and, when possible, meet with the Pope, even though he also knew that the Holy See had serious disagreements politically with U.S. Jews and the State of Israel.

Another knotty problem for him was the proper course of action to pursue in dealing with Governor Hugh Carey. In his congressional days the Brooklyn Democrat was an outspoken defender of Catholic interests, unambivalently so. Once governor, his constituency changed radically, now consisting mainly of the trade union movement, the Liberal Party, the Jewish vote, the Democratic machine, and certain minority group leaders. Because of some clouds on his private life, the Catholic vote was no longer locked into him. Still, Carey's churchgoing and his large family were persuasive for many of Cooke's flock. Cooke had to be careful, however, because Carey's position on abortion remained to be seen. Public funding of abortion and parental rights over the abortions of minors were Right-to-Life issues and Catholic Democrats like Carey were inclined to allege helplessness to do anything about them. Governors usually excused their weakness by pointing to the power of the legislative majority, or argued we should not forbid to others the freedom of the Constitution. Hugh Carey confessed this powerlessness and Cooke let him get away with neutrality on the issues. As head of NCCB's Pro-Life Activities Committee, he could have done more to confront cop-outs of the kind Jewish or labor leaders would never accept from their adherents. Pro-life activists, on the other hand, were prepared to fight Carey or anyone else over tax-paid abortions. And they were capable of fomenting a tax revolt among Catholics and Orthodox Jews. Carey, master of the legislative process that he was, stayed pragmatic, enough to avoid getting into difficulty with Cooke, the way Cuomo later did with O'Connor.

The New York Archbishop had his own in-house difficulties with Right-to-Life factions. Led by heady lay people, pro-lifers flexed their muscles more than once to Governor Rockefeller, and they did not mind upsetting clergy, all the way up to the level of Cardinal. Competing factions such as the New York State Right-to-Life and the Coalition for Life vied for contributed monies from Catholic sources, hurling charges at each other indiscriminately about the other's failure to represent the unborn effectively. Bitterness among these lay officials was more than enough to tax all of the Cardinal's patience. Furthermore, not even Terry Cooke could prevent the Coalition for Life from drawing a bead on the National Conference of Catholic Charities for its lackluster support of the antiabortion crusade. Privately, Right-to-Lifers regularly complained that the national leaders of Catholic Charities, like the USCC Secretariat, were more interested in what happened in faraway Chile or to the Panama Canal than they were in the destruction of unborn life in the United States. Cardinal Cooke took this in stride, but found himself in a tight spot when he heard that the Fordham University Graduate School of Social Service Women's Caucus supported "the right of all women to safe, legal abortions," some of the signers being employees of his own Catholic Charities' organization. The Right-to-Life people were prepared to publish the 199 names just at the opening of the Cardinal's annual appeal. This embarrassment somehow never became public.

In some of these controversies Cardinal Cooke did the best he could. He helped prevent the legalization of marijuana. Opposed to the jailing of youthful offenders for minor uses, he strongly opposed the drug's legalization because of its toxic effects on serious users. But he did not have influence when it counted. For example, the Mayor's Committee on the Judiciary, by then totally committed to a secular ideology, selected judges who often were a social problem themselves. Traditionally, work for the Democratic machinery was the major *sine qua non* for choosing new judges. Then, ideology became the norm. Attorneys who favored stiff punishment for crimes of violence were disqualified by nominating panels, while those who would give special treatment to homosexual pairs seeking to adopt children were viewed approvingly. One Jewish judge was rejected for the criminal court by the Mayor's committee "unceremoniously," it was said, because he sentenced the exhibitors of the obscene movie *Deep Throat* to jail. Shortly thereafter the same jurist was chosen for the federal bench, a slap at the ideological selectivity going on in City Hall.[1] Cooke had almost no influence here. He took part in private discussions during 1975 on the state's Equal Rights Amendment before that ill-fated constitutional amendment met its doom. Like the Bishops of the state, the Cardinal was favorable to political equality of the sexes, but his lawyers could not provide him with a definitive judicial prognosis of what the amendment might mean in practice. Drafting women into the Armed Services or into combat were peripheral issues, whereas the status of wives and mothers under such a law was by no means certain. The nation was not simply a complex of individuals. It was a society of families, whose well-being depended largely on women. Protective marriage and family legislation would surely be reinterpreted in the light of ERA, with the tradition of cohesive family life in more jeopardy than ever. A side issue, one surely not to be ignored, was the specter of homosexual pairs empowered by ERA to adopt children. The Catholic laity read the concerns correctly and groups like the Knights of Columbus worked to defeat it. The Bishops assumed a wait-and-see posture.

Archbishop Cooke also found himself in a political no-man's-land in 1976 when he wanted to lease the old Chancery Office on Madison Avenue. All sorts of politicians got in his way. The property once known as the Villard Houses, was a landmark and Harry Helmsley, the prospective buyer, was willing to keep it intact as part of his proposed Palace Hotel. The lease, which would guarantee the Archdiocese income for ninety-nine years, ran into objections from nineteenth-century sentimentalists, environmentalists, Helmsley competitors, and any politicians who could gain attention by opposing the move. After a three-year delay which almost ruined the project, Cooke won out.

He was less successful, however, on the West Side, where his enemy was profitable obscenity and more profitable sex exploitation. The Times Square area, the crossroads of the world, was and is a national disgrace. Once the center of what by today's standards would be tame burlesque houses, Forty-second Street in Cooke's time was the home of pornographers, pimps, dirty movies, pederasts, peep shows, sex, violence, and dope pushers. It also housed a $2 billion sex industry which drew runaways from the inner city and from the hinterlands, most of whom became prostitutes and objects of violence when they tried to break loose on their own. The amount of rehabilitative aid money poured into this ward by private and public agencies was infinitesimal compared with the pot of gold dug from the pits of vice. Forty years earlier, Msgr. Joseph McCaffrey, a New York police chaplain, used his pulpit at Holy Cross Church on Forty-second Street to shout warnings at City Fathers about a burgeoning social menace. Money grabbers laughed at him and the custodians of city safety shared in the loot. Thirty years later Msgr. Robert Rappleyea waged the same lonely battle, but by his time business and civic leaders were finally interested in a cleanup. Moral idealism did not push them as much as the desire to improve the city's looks and to beef up its tax base. To bring new hotels, new legitimate theaters, and convention centers into the area, the sleaze would have to be bulldozed out of existence. And this would require rezoning.

Once upon a time in New York dirty magazines were sold to dealers in small lots, as part of a package with *Life*, *Newsweek*, and *Time*. A dealer then could not buy the best sellers without buying the dirt, but the mores of the city were such that vendors did not dare put dirt on display. They took the loss. When *Playboy* broke the decency barrier, hard core porn became only a paper stand away. For many years Father Morton Hill's Morality in Media stood alone against the tide, but his efforts at voluntary reform had negligible results because municipal sanction was missing. Antipornography laws were looked upon as the offspring of the Neanderthal Man. Finally, the Codes Committee of the New York State legislature opened public hearings October 24, 1973. ACLU and its cohorts showed up in force, clamoring for a hands-off policy on obscenity. One novelist testified proudly that he allowed his six- and nine-year-old daughters to look at *Playboy* and other sex magazines. In the face of testimony of this kind, legislative leaders were determined to develop a strong antiobscenity law, but they also recognized the indifference in New York's voting community to the growth of the porn industry. Ordinary citizens had no clear idea of how deep filth and vice, including sexual violence, had dug into local communities. Prosecutions for obscenity in New York City were nil, even though police files were filled with cases of mutilated sex organs and butchered bodies, including those of children, at the hands of perverts wallowing in pornography and sex devices. By 1973 Albany looked to the churches to mobilize public opinion against pornography, seemingly unaware that following Vatican II, the Catholic Church had abandoned one of the country's more successful private instruments of media self-control—the Legion of Decency.

Although the Supreme Court had previously decreed that obscenity was to be defined according to local community standards, no one in New York was lifting a hand to ascertain what those community standards were. Community standards were at best whatever the District Attorney said they were, and Robert Morgenthau, elected in 1974, was not known to be exercised over obscenity. An Obscenity Center existed, whose attorneys were anxious to define obscenity and to develop supporting data from scientific and religious sources. The effort was complicated by a parallel Supreme Court ruling which allowed community standards to be determined by taking into account the extent to which citizens accepted or tolerated "adult use" establishments. Without concerted local opposition to such "adult use" centers, the courts might easily presume the legitimacy of their existence.

By March 1977 Cardinal Cooke undertook to drum up parochial support for an antipornography drive. "Adult use" establishments were called what they were, "sex exploitation operations," and pastors were directed to harness the opposition, especially since the attempt to solve the Times Square problem would mean farming out its excesses to the outer boroughs. Queens, called the "Borough of Homes," was already a county of porn houses, dirty movies, and massage parlors. The Planning Commission then began to revise zoning regulations to reduce the concentration of degenerate sex-oriented establishments on Forty-second Street. Mayor Abraham Beame called for rigid enforcement of obscenity laws by all city agencies and an investigation of the sex business by the FBI. On April 5, 1977, Cooke called upon

192

New Yorkers to require "civic leaders and law enforcement officials to seek swift remedies to restore city streets, entertainment and shopping areas to the citizens and not leave them in the hands of brutal degraders of sex and human life." By this time being against "massage parlors" was good politics, sufficiently so to inspire Queen's Borough President Donald Manes to call for an end to the "spread the filth campaign." The problem however, remained "the law," and convicting anyone of obscenity, even of pimping, was almost impossible. The sexual revolution had reached the Supreme Court and political-minded district attorneys were not about to challenge those nine wise men. Cardinal Cooke could not win fully against those odds, but to the extent that City Hall was now publicly against sin, and efforts were underway to drive porno activity off the street, Cardinal Cooke deserves some credit.

However, a larger question begged for an answer: Why had the Church not developed the research necessary to provide practicing attorneys with the tools they needed to lead the Supreme Court in different directions? Other minority group leaders had inspired the Court, successfully one can say, to overemphasize "the establishment clause" to the neglect of "freedom of religion." What were Catholics doing to tackle the meaning of the "right of privacy," used everywhere to protect vice. First invented in 1965 to declare unconstitutional a Connecticut law forbidding the use of contraceptives, the right of privacy was being extended to preclude local governments from dealing with pornography and its socially corrosive consequences. The Constitution did not mention such a right, yet here it was being used to prevent state and city governments from protecting the standards of moral decency which made their jurisdictions places where people wanted to live. The Court's concern for liberty had been so broadly interpreted that standards of decency to which twelve normal citizens could attest were impossible to maintain. Licentious practices became legally protected because they did not breach the permissible community behavior. Instead of ethical norms governing conduct, conduct determined the acceptable norms.

During these troubled years Catholic university law schools contributed little to raise the conscience of the Supreme Court. *Daily News* correspondent William Reel capsulated the social effects of judicial laxity (April 1, 1977) when he described decadence in the language of people: Citizens who stayed indoors because they no longer wished to be menaced by drunks and addicts, or have their money ripped out of their hands, or to be cursed, molested, raped, robbed, and otherwise driven to terror. This sick state of affairs has not been remedied to this day.

THE CITY OF PRIESTS

The Second Vatican Council in its *Dogmatic Constitution on the Church (Lumen Gentium* in Latin) proclaims (No. 2) that the local Bishops, whose authority is exercised personally in the name of Christ, have "a sacred right and duty before the Lord of legislating for and of passing judgment on their subjects, as well as of regulating everything that concerns the good order of divine worship and of the apostolate." Someone might well have reminded Terry Cooke of Harry Truman's crack as he watched "Ike" Eisenhower take the oath of office: "Wait till he rings the bell on his desk and finds that no one answers." There were many Catholics by 1968 who were unprepared to answer the call of their Archbishop to obey Church Law and/or diocesan regulations.

Archbishop Cooke was no "dictator," but neither did he lack a sense of who he was. He possessed all those qualities associated with "bridge building" without any confusion in his mind about where "the buck stopped." When he sought to institutionalize the authorized innovations of Vatican II—in diocesan reorganization, consultation procedures, ecumenical and political outreach, religious life renewal, Right-to-Life—he knew where to go for friendly support. He was also a shrewd observer of the forces which might spell trouble for his or the Church's programs. One of these was the recently established Priests' Senate. Shared consultation did not bother him (executive authority cannot be shared) since few Bishops had his qualifications for cooperative

194

enterprise. In Chancery circles he was known jokingly as "the group worker," a reference to his ability to sit with groups, listen, and with remarkable skill steer his audience toward an acceptable conclusion. The problem that would trouble Cooke most was the mood of a Senate leadership with a hidden agenda that might contravene Church doctrine or policy. Vatican II introduced the opportunity for change in the Church but not for denial. Cooke also sensed that he represented the general views of New York priests better than his Senate. And in this he was surely correct.

The diocesan activists had managed in the early days to manipulate their way into Senate leadership through a well-conceived system of proportional representation (which Cooke did not resist), at a time when most priests had little interest in the politics of diocesan management. The New York Senate was hardly different from other priest assemblies of that day—concentration on threatening Church structures and the promotion of social reform, deemphasis of those aspects of priestly ministry which concerned the Kingdom of God. Senate meetings spent many hours on how to limit Cooke's ability to make unilateral decisions, but little time on sin, penance, or the development of personal virtue among the flock. A number of the first Senate leaders favored public dissent from Church teaching, were anti-*Humanae Vitae,* and saw themselves mostly as the civil rights leaders of the Church. There was hardly a social action cause they did not espouse, hardly an action by Rome in defense of the Church or the priesthood that they did not ignore or oppose. Caesar Chavez's farm workers enjoyed wide support, and properly so. But priests who had no expertise in politics or had no responsibility for the defense of the country's welfare were also making political judgments about the federal budget or the B-1 bomber, which were hardly "Catholic" issues. Coming down on the side of optional celibacy or of general absolution, calling for the end of sexism in the Church, only made Senates irrelevant to the life of the average parish priest.

RETIREMENT OF PASTORS

Cardinal Cooke's genius consisted in fending away from him issues he considered harmful to the Church, e.g., civil rights for homosexuals or interference with his right to select seminary faculty. Otherwise, he collaborated willingly and sincerely on all matters that were solid Vatican II recommendations. At times, however, Cooke bowed to pressure needlessly or failed to be resolute when it was important to defend a well-established Catholic tradition against an innovation whose long-range ramifications were unknown. One example of this was his enforced retirement of priests at seventy-five years and his ready acquiescence to two terms of six years for New York pastors with no option for a third term. The other was the assignment of priests by a personnel board, not by the Bishop. Under these two new policies "voluntarism," i.e., the primacy of free choice, was out for older priests but in for younger priests.

The Church's common law held that a pastor could not be removed or transferred arbitrarily, and usually only for cause. Indeed, if the pastor insisted (hardly ever the case), he could demand a hearing before a competent judge. Under this law the Bishop was free always to "promote" a pastor to a better parish, usually by mutual agreement or as a result of the Bishop's persuasive powers. Involuntary removal or transfer, however, was permitted by canon law only for cause. Age alone or years in a given parish per se were not reasons Rome would accept as justification for forced removals or transfers. You could remove a sixty-year-old for senility or drunkenness, but not a vigorous seventy-five-year-old who was still about his Father's business and much beloved by his people.

After centuries of bitter experience with the harm done to the Church's mission by instability in the pastorate, Rome's inclination was to protect pastors. In exchange for a long celibate life and adequate service, priests could expect the reward of undisturbed tenure. Most priests at seventy-five had few family members left to assist them through the trying times of old age, and those of that generation had little money. Indeed, in their early years they were taught not to accumulate possessions and were paid accordingly. Now, after Vatican II, the rules changed, with forced retirement and a monthly pension of five hundred dollars, hardly adequate to replace the warm and useful rectory life they took for granted and by any reasonable title a reward to which they had a right.

During the nineteenth century, certain Bishops took advantage of priests by their arbitrary assignment practices. In those days, too, foreign-born priests scurried from diocese to diocese seeking "sweetheart deals" from needy Bishops. As the twentieth century was moving toward midpoint, Rome told Pittsburgh's Bishop Hugh Boyle to cease and desist appointing Administrators to parishes (instead of pastors) who enjoyed no tenure and were removable at the will of the Bishop.

The post-Vatican II policy of inviting pastors to retire, like the policy of setting terms of office, had advantages for priests as well as Bishops. Bishops who were helpless to find open parishes for "younger" priests (often fifty-year-olds), suddenly found themselves with enlarged opportunities for appointments they never expected. Older priests who so desired had an honorable way out of the burdens of office without seeming to be abandoning their priesthood. Term of office (six years, maximum of twelve in one place), was also a good thing, one which afforded both Bishops, priests, and people an opportunity to have a say in how they benefited or not by change at the end of a particular time period. Bishops and priests had honorable options which they never enjoyed before—to stay or to move. And for the first time the sense of the people was a factor.

Special difficulties developed when Cardinal Cooke made the new retirement system compulsory and the transfers after twelve years absolute. It was one thing to invite a man to submit his resignation, something else for a Bishop not to keep his own options open, not to retain specially qualified pastors in their posts on a year-to-year basis, as the Holy See did sometimes with Bishops, or respect a veteran priest's wishes. Cardinal Cooke had an indult from the Congregation of the Clergy allowing him to set terms for pastors *"ad experimentum,"* but nothing in the indult prevented him from granting a third six-year term, if circumstances warranted. He did make exceptions for minority-group pastors but not for the rest, some of whom were asked to uproot themselves and begin anew elsewhere at sixty-five years of age. Neither the common law of the Church nor the Roman experience were given much consideration, this about the time heads of state were beginning to manage governments well into their seventies, making it difficult to fathom why Cardinal Cooke would act against his own practical reason. It did not seem right to force out a virile seventy-five-year-old beloved by his people or to ask a healthy sixty-five-year-old, against his will, to take a new parish when all he and his kind wanted to do was to reap the fruits of their earlier labors. In practice, some effective pastors took the forced move as a personal affront and the new parishes were hardly enhanced by a move forced upon them. As events proved, absolutes about age and terms were no more helpful to apostolic parish life than the absolute permanency of the earlier decades.

What automatic removals and/or transfers did was to absolve the Bishop of personal decision-making and of explaining why he allowed one man to stay but insisted that another man go. The priests affected by the automatic rule were the ones most unlikely to think of appealing over the Bishop's head. One Brooklyn pastor, where the retirement rule was seventy-one, did appeal to Rome and was upheld, retiring finally at seventy-seven years of age. However, as Cooke began the last year of his life, John Paul II issued the New Code of Canon Law, NCCL—canons 522 and 538—which authorized the Bishop to set terms of office for pastors and to request those who are seventy-five years old to resign. The Bishop retains his authority to make exceptions to whatever general policy he follows.

ASSIGNING CURATES

The "assignment" system also became a casualty even though, strictly speaking, the Church depends on priests going where they are sent. The New Testament is filled with the word "sent"—it occurs so often that a small biblical concordance could be built around it. The Church by its nature is missionary, and the word "mission" means "sent." Yet after Vatican II the tendency developed to substitute mutual agreement for assignment. No system is ever perfect, of course, but the mission of the Church depends on the ability of the Bishop to place priests where they are needed, not where they like to go. Under Spellman, the Vicar General, first McIntyre, John Maguire at the end, regularly moved priests around, trying to balance the good of the parish and the overall needs of the diocese while mindful of the needs or preferences of the individual. It was a highly personal system, which fared well with officials like Edward Gaffney, John Maguire, and Thomas Donnellen, all of whom were priest-oriented. They would have fared even better with a Personnel Board empowered to supply more complete information than one official could carry around in his head.

Yet, when finally a board did come into the picture, so did new complicating factors. Personal option of the appointee became a commonplace ingredient, the priest usually invited to go see whether the place would suit him and whether the pastor would take him. If a younger priest did not receive what he wanted most, he never received what he wanted least. When taking a new "assignment," he knew his pleasure was an important aspect of the going. Hitherto, a real "assignment" involved a certain risk-taking. It could turn out to be very rewarding, and it might not work. In the Gaffney-Maguire days one could always return later with a request for another assignment, but in the meantime the priest did what he was told to do. The mission, i.e., the sending based on the Bishop's sense of the Church's need and the priest's obedience, was the important understanding.

199

In the new dispensation, the word "assignment" was virtually stripped of its meaning. Appointments were delayed for months because of the need to negotiate, as if the priest was a union all by himself. One Bishop, commenting on the process, said: "What used to be carried on in one man's mind for immediate decision is now wheeled out monthly in a filing cabinet for interminable dialogue." Cardinal Cooke, who was not obligated by the new system, appreciated its weakness. If a priest resisted the personal appointment which the Archbishop hoped he would take, Cooke was heard to say at times, "If you don't want this, you can go to the Personnel Board." The affected priest knew he might end up worse off. It is by no means certain that the post-Vatican II novelties in personnel management have advanced human happiness, certainly not for priests disposed to be unhappy. But it clearly made it difficult for pastors, responsible for service to the people, to "send" a curate to tasks and to insist that they be done, when the latter's preferences were built into the very system. Some pastors, perceived to be difficult, received no diocesan curates because no one wanted to go to them. The chief sufferer in the long run was the parish community. As a defense against the unreasonable pastor, the new stress on "personal option" only undermined hierarchy, i.e., the authority of the chief pastor to manage his portion of God's kingdom.

THE SEMINARY

Ominous to the future of the Archdiocese, also, was the division within the faculty at St. Joseph's Seminary. It was not so much political as doctrinal. During Cooke's early years young ordinands grew to hate their seminary training, hardly an auspicious beginning for a lifelong commitment to a demanding vocation. Seminary divisions came to public notice by 1973 when five professors at Dunwoodie complained about three other professors' views about what Jesus knew, and when He knew it, about His divine sonship. The issue was somewhat critical, as one might guess, because going the rounds even to this day is the view that during His lifetime Jesus did not know a great deal about His nature or His mission, at least if one depended on the New Testament for "proof." Eventually, the complaining faculty found their way out of Dunwoodie (with a little help from Cooke) but not before they disparaged the competence of those who supported the traditional Catholic reading of the scriptures.

The Dunwoodie case was symbolic of a large Church problem. How much did Jesus know about Himself? Did He really know during His public life that He was the Son of God? These were no abstract questions for future priests. Catholic biblical critics, following a Protestant lead, divorcing their exegesis from Church teaching, had begun to stress Jesus' humanity more than his "unprovable" divinity. The new exegesis also raised doubts (this is about all it could do) about Jesus Himself. Many seminarians had every right to wonder whether the Church's position as to His divinity might not be overdrawn. Squabbling among seminary faculty hardly reinforced Church teaching in the minds of ecclesiastical tyros. The situation was allowed to heal itself, but not before members of the Priests' Senate took sides, enough to forestall the Cardinal's intervention. In spite of all these difficulties, Dunwoodie by Cooke's death was one of the finest seminaries in the country.

THE PUERTO RICAN INFLUX

Diocesan problems with the Spanish apostolate also complicated Cardinal Cooke's life. Like every port city, New York received more than its share of Spanish-speaking migrants, mostly Puerto Ricans at first. During the 1950s, the diocesan response seemed simple enough—provide more of the same attention once given to the Irish, the Germans, and the Italians. The difference was that Puerto Ricans did not bring their own priests with them. In spite of this lack, remarkable things were done by individual priests. One, Irish-born, Maynooth-trained Michael Crowley, arriving in 1954, took the Puerto Ricans by storm. Assigned to St. Jerome's parish in the Bronx, this young priest found the routines of a declining "Irish" parish insufficient to fill the day of an enthusiast who knew there was more to the priesthood than going to wakes or writing out Mass cards. He learned Spanish in six months and even to play Puerto Rican songs on his little hand accordian, which he called "the squeeze box." Then he did what priests of old did regularly. He visited Puerto Ricans in their homes, day by day, night by night; all of these people lived in four-, five-, and six-story walk-ups. Crowley was a warm, gregarious man with a gift for gab and meeting people came easy to him. But he did not come to these poor people as a social worker. He was checking on the quality of their Catholic life as much as their human needs. To regularize their marriages, to get them to Mass, to baptize their babies, and to see that the young were taught the catechism, these were high on Crowley's list of priorities. He also found poverty, fatherless homes, young people in trouble with the law, families isolated from the culture around them. A large part of his day was spent in the streets with kids, in welfare offices, in police precincts, or simply playing his "squeeze box" for teenagers on a neighborhood stoop.

When the Irish apostle was called home by his Bishop in 1959, the parochial school was mostly Spanish, more than a thousand Puerto Rican children were under religious instruction, the large lower church was amply filled on Sunday with their parents, and St. Jerome's, for all practical purposes, was now a Spanish parish. His success may be called a personal triumph, of course, due to his special ability to integrate the demands of the sacramental priesthood with the human aspirations of the new poor. Nonetheless, he personified the priesthood at its best. He left for home in 1959 as beloved by St. Jerome's Irish as he surely was by the Puerto Ricans who were complete strangers to him five years earlier. In 1960 Father Crowley, now back in Ireland, was sent by his Bishop to Peru to found a parish on behalf of the diocese of Cork. And he left behind him in New York a large memory of what the Catholic priesthood was all about.

During the early post-Vatican II euphoria, the Archdiocese, with a view to improving the diocesan approach to the Puerto Ricans, accepted a proposal to create an "experimental parish."

This came into being before Spellman died. One such Manhattan parish was chosen because it was situated in a transitional neighborhood with populations as disparate as the Slav-Irish parishioners and Spanish newcomers could be. A "team" of priests, rather than a pastor, was assigned to revitalize the parish. The theory underpinning the experiment held that the mission of the parish was outreach to twenty thousand alienated poor Spanish of the area, not simply to serve the two thousand "elite" churchgoers and Church supporters present on the parochial rolls. The priests hypothesized that Puerto Ricans "find no place in a middle-class-oriented Church, nor do they care to seek one." The parish was to be adult-centered, not child-centered, geared to community action, not to schooling. Small meetings—in homes mostly—were expected to transform the neighborhood. A "Joy-Allegria Plan" of catechetics, with its emphasis on the "here and now" was better suited to the inner city, they claimed, than the traditional catechetics with its orientation toward eternity. (Actually, the Joy-Allegria Plan at the moment in question did not have a Spanish edition.) The experiment also called for the closing of the school. In fact, very early during the initiative the priests asked the sisters: "What do you think is the best educational service we can offer the children in our neighborhood?" To which the nuns responded: "Something other than the parochial school." In 1967 this school enrolled three hundred sixty-nine youngsters, mostly Puerto Rican, two thirds of whose families had an income of less than four thousand dollars, one half lacking an identifiable father. What was to be done with the school building? The priests had an answer to that: Turn the parochial school into a nonsectarian urban day school financed by a foundation. The priests had no idea how this could be done, but they argued: "The community will never believe the Church's selfless interest, if the Church allows its facilities to be used for schools which service their educational needs without their being afraid of being indoctrinated by Catholic doctrine." The sentence was poorly constructed, but the plan was clear enough. The urban day school was to be a witness of the Church's interest in the community, not a witness of the Church's faith.

Here, stated clearly, was an ideology that underlay many of the so-called "base communities" in South America, one which years later drew the fire of John Paul II. But in 1968 the experimenting priests were merely mouthing what they learned from their short stays in Catholic training centers in Puerto Rico. The approach was anti-Church and eventually led the experiment into disaster. Common sense should have indicated that priests cannot create a parish by separating adults from the needs of their children, or by fragmenting it into ethnic factions, or by disdaining the people who go to Church and who pay the bills, or by acting in the name of the Church while ignoring the Church's evangelizing nature. Unlike the Church in Europe or South America, the U.S. Church grew to be gargantuan precisely because of its school system. What merit was there in having teaching sisters deal in trendy causes or with people on a one-to-one basis, sometimes performing tasks better done by laity, when historically those same sisters had changed, and effectively changed, the face of neighborhoods simply by teaching forty children day after day? Where was the sense in a parish catechetical program without a specifically Catholic objective? One priest on the team complained: "There is a dichotomy between running a good school and religious education," just about the time he tried to dismantle the only religious education the parish had, viz., the school.

By 1970 the situation called for diocesan action. A new sister principal with a traditional love of educating children moved in, surveyed the scene, and summarized her difficulty as follows: "None of the priests presently part of the team wants to involve himself in the interest of our school as it is presently conducted, thus the school ceases to be truly a parish school. The sisters become the sole operators of the school." When two of the priests' team left the priesthood, new priests were assigned who restored sanity to the parish and gave support to the new Sisters of Charity. But not before the experiment wasted thousands of dollars and hundreds of hours of good people's time trying to cover up the mistakes of ideologues who had long since lost their sense of the Church. In one year (1967–68) the parish deficit grew from $41,000 to $62,000 with the new priests uninterested in fund-raising.

The original mistake was to create an experiment which was not an experiment at all. Nothing in the so-called plan was ever scheduled for testing. Instead, a trio of ideologue priest-cronies joined with a convent of radicalized religious women to set a new course for the Church of New York. They had nothing in mind save a theory which presumed that the existing Church was an evil institution. The Church of 1968 may not have been at its best, but its parishes and schools were established successes. The real problem was that priests and religious no longer worked them properly, or believed in them either.

The Manhattan experiment became a dramatic microcosm of the problems that would plague the administration of Cardinal Cooke to the very end. The "experimenting" priests were untypical of New York's priesthood, just as the sisters who finally saved the school were hardly the new religious then being programmed in their Motherhouse in Riverdale. As time went on the costs of parochial schools went up and up, aging pastors lost enthusiasm for raising more and more money for diminishing enrollments, parents were less motivated to choose Catholic schooling for their children at fancy prices, and Cardinal Cooke, for all his attempts to be nice, failed to persuade his religious communities to come back to educating the young.

Symptomatic also of the troubles that began to plague the new Archbishop in the late sixties and early seventies was public scandal caused by priest misbehavior with women. (A decade later police accounts of pederasty involving priests would only be another sign of the debasement of the once highly respected priestly caste.) But by 1970 it was neighborhood priests and parishioners who began to blow the whistle on miscreant clergy, a relatively new phenomenon in the U.S. Church. Prior to Vatican II the American priesthood was honored for the celibate state it really was. A small minority in those days might imbibe the fruit of the vine more than was good for the Church, and venal priests were not unknown, whose God was money and a good time. But, by and large, the Catholic priesthood was as respected for its chastity as for its celibacy. No one knew that better than the local constabulary, who routinely tipped their hats to priests and tore up their parking tickets just as readily.

By the time Cooke was into his second year, offending priests, still few in number, were threatening to create public controversy with him so as to render him nervous and ambivalent in his dealings with them. One such priest, exposed by his parishioners, actually accused Cardinal Cooke of injustice for suspending him, even though the Archdiocese was still paying his salary. This priest achieved headline status on the "Six O'Clock News" with his complaints against the Archdiocese, although the media editors evinced no interest in exposing the priest's sins and crimes against the Church. In earlier days such a priest would have run far from "a public trial," but the new breed of offender considered his misconduct no one's business but his own, and believed that the only ones scandalized anymore by a priest's extramarital sexual behavior were narrow-minded ecclesiastics. The Bishop's suspension, therefore, was the immoral act, not the conduct itself. It was this queer form of insanity with no relation to Catholic life which made some of Cardinal Cooke's days miserable.

Transcripts still available today reporting tales of priests who fathered children in the course of their Vietnam "peace ministry" illustrate how far Bishops and religious superiors lost control of their priests. Priests who chose to be identified more with the Catonsville Nine or with the local "liberal" Democratic congressmen or with the Committee to Free Angela Davis than with their superiors often achieved hero status in some communities. It is not possible to calculate the harm done to the Church by priest activists, such as the one who told a group of religious: "A Marymount Provincial is to be measured 'proper' to the extent that she becomes 'disreputable.' "

Even the suburbs were not immune from radical upheaval. Three priests out of harmony with archdiocesan policies and those of the Holy See tore one suburban parish apart. They looked upon themselves as the avant-garde force of the real Vatican II, making socio-political activity, not traditional Catholic pieties, the parish priority. When the parishioners rebelled and

206

demanded that Cardinal Cooke remove the priests, the pastor in his weekly bulletin suggested that "calmer days ahead now seem possible through the withdrawal of laity rather than the priests." Laity did go elsewhere and in due course the three priests were reassigned, but not before a prestigious parish was reduced to tatters, a condition from which it has never recovered to this day.

LOW PRIEST MORALE

In view of these goings on, so out of character to most priests, it was probably inevitable that those carrying on the Church's work would begin to ask, "What's the use?" Yet, Terry Cooke was the most unlikely prelate to preside over unhappy priests. He knew his diocesans better than any outsider would have and by temperament was inclined to say "yes" to people. Furthermore, he indicated very quickly that, though a son to his predecessor, he was not about to walk the trodden roads of Spellman. Still, five years into his administration, Cooke was up to his miter in clerical complaints. Key priests were abandoning their calling and his Priests' Senate leaders repeatedly nagged him about his failure as a diocesan therapist. They painted rectory life as so bad that priests were beginning to feel "homeless," blaming the Archdiocese for placing men in rectories with pastors and/or curates who were impossible to live with. The Senate went further, calling for "consolidation of rectories, for opportunities to enlarge the common life of parish priests and thereby prevent an ill-tempered personality from souring common life." The example of high school tables was put forth as preferable to rectory dining, because as many as ten or more priests broke bread together regularly and otherwise enjoyed a wider ambit of personal relationships. The Priests' Senate was convinced that Cooke should understand the reasonableness of this request and if he did not, he would be judged to be insensitive to the emotional needs of parish priests. In some quarters there was talk of "apartment living," an option that would reverse the Council of Trent's historic decision to reinforce celibacy by removing priests from the temptations commonplace to street living.

Many of the priests' complaints were legitimate, but hardly different from day-to-day difficulties of their married brothers and sisters. Rectory life often involved no more than three priests so that one difficult pastor or one irascible curate could wreak havoc with common life. But, then, even in the best diocesan parish house, there was little common life, even when the priests were friendly. The rectory was more often a house to sleep in than a place of common prayer or shared dining. Unlike the living quarters of religious communities, where many members were assigned and by rule called to regular exercises together, the typical priest's home functioned by laissez-faire. The days of the pastor acting as a religious superior had long since passed, leaving priests free to work out their own schedules, coming together only during funerals, administration of sacraments, at parish events, and irregularly at meals. No one called for a return to a pastor-regulated rectory life, although the evils of rugged individualism were there for all to see. Self-starting priests thrived in their freedom to build up parish solidarity in accordance with their personal preferences and those of the Church. Dependent or lazy types, who were good only for routine chores, usually were mere names to churchgoers, rarely in demand and only occasionally responded effectively when parishioners crossed their paths. It is not surprising that in this latter group one found the unhappy and the malcontents. Since the pastor had little supervisory authority anymore, the only device left to him and the curate was "downtown" or to the Archbishop himself.

In fairness to Terry Cooke, the "morale problem" went far beyond the Hudson River, and the person least able to cope with a Church-wide problem was the local Bishop. In part because the word "morale" was almost undefinable. Rugged living conditions in slum areas sometimes begot high morale, the noisiest complainers sometimes were found in the lush living of prosperous suburbs.

What really was "low priest morale?" One elderly pastor thought it was manufactured by elites, affecting mostly the young who were badly chosen and badly trained for the rigors of celibate priestly life. The old man recalled how at his ordination the Bishop did not ask him whether he was prepared to be happy, merely whether he was willing to work to build up the Body of Christ. The precise point at which seminaries (or Bishops) began to stress personal satisfaction over effective ministry as a norm of priestly success could not be pinpointed, but by Cooke's accession to New York, the revolution in priestly values was part of the post-Vatican II problem. Of course, agitators busy about stirring discontent within the priesthood were modest neither in their efforts nor their claims. Books and lectures poured out of publishing houses describing how unhappy priests really were. Even the National Conference of Catholic Bishops commissioned social science studies to explore the causes of the expected unhappiness, which according to form were identified with alleged loss of identity, institutional insensitivity, unrealistic expectations, or the failure of the Church properly to take up the cause of the poor. The charges against the institutional Church, despite their diversity, became so repetitious that Martin Luther King's response to Michael Harrington (reported in his little autobiography) was as good an explanation as any of what was happening to Catholic lives. Asked by the socialist writer whether he had read Harrington's book on U.S. poverty, the black civil rights leader said, "Yes, I didn't know we were so poor until I read your book." Similarly, with many priests and nuns who had been functioning satisfactorily for years, their new learning told them they were unhappy and they believed it.

Frequently their confrontations with Archbishop Cooke were indirect, rhetorical rather than face to face, and often revolving around trivial, not substantial issues. The complainers wanted to know what he was going to do about the shortage of priests, as if anything effective could be done about that in their lifetime. They wanted more authority to be given to Episcopal Vicars, more decentralization of services, at the very moment that "the diocese" alone could save poor parishes, subsidize schools, or deal with politicians on controversial items like abortion. They had a trendy interest in more black and Hispanic priests, and the return of ex-priests to the ministry, but even critics of the Archbishop knew these were annoying chips in a game of confrontation, not serious answers to the priest shortage of 1972.

JUSTICE TO THE POOR

Probably no issue exacerbated the relationship of Terry Cooke and his Priests' Senate more than his alleged failure to do justice to the poor. The 1972 Senate used the authority of recent papal encyclicals to demand the Archbishop explain what he was doing for "the liberation of all enslaved peoples and the gospel demand to destroy unjust social structures." This was the new party line directed at a priest whose early ministry always involved the poor, especially the young poor. The Senate's real argument was with civil society, not with the Church, which had small control over the politics of Lyndon Baines Johnson or Richard Milhous Nixon. Even then, if the Church could destroy unjust structures overnight, what new instruments did the agitators have to take their place? None of Cardinal Cooke's critics had gone this far in their thinking. It was a point Cardinal Joseph Ratzinger would raise thirteen years later: "Those who repeat all this [liberation talk] seem to have no concrete and practical idea how a society could be organized after the revolution. They limit themselves to repeating that the revolution must be brought about."

It is remarkable that Cooke finally in 1972 willingly took his critics on. And he chose to do so in his address to the Annual Priests' Assembly convoked by his Senate.

He started with their complaint about "priestly morale," the subject the Senate chose for discussion. While admitting that "a demoralized or unhappy man will rarely be a generous and effective priest," he placed the source of unhappiness in the personality, not in the circumstances of a priest's life.

The boyish Cardinal could become quite manly when he wanted to and he was never more the male than when he reminded them of priestly priorities: " 'Seek first His kingship over you, His way of holiness.' "[2] It was as close as he could come to

210

scolding those priests who were looking at the Church as just another social institution, a political instrument for dealing with civic concerns. "Our people have a *right* to find in our rectories and churches men who are devoted primarily to the work of religion." Here he reminded them of the decline in Mass attendance, of careless liturgies, of the obligation to attend Mass, of the apparent abandonment of sexual morality among the young, of the growing cynicism about so many social causes. And then as if speaking of politicians: "We must remind them and our people that in no way can Catholics compromise themselves by voting for or supporting any public figure who advocates abortion."

All in all Cooke, on that occasion, proved himself to be fearless of what discontented priests thought of him. "I have discovered that some priests have almost abandoned elementary manners." Rudeness and contemptible speech patterns were not the only offenses: "Respect for doctrine and for the teaching authority of the Church cannot in conscience be compromised publicly or privately in the work of a priest—I formally warn those who have been careless or wholly self-directed in these matters. Priests are not free to contradict the authoritative teaching of the Church."

Naturally, the reaction to such tough talk was mixed, but not in the way the voluble activists expected. Some priests resented the charge that morale was "low," although they readily admitted it was not "high." Complaints about "Downtown" were real, but not exactly the bitter charges made by the revolutionaries. Indeed, some priests thought Cooke paid too much attention to the pressure groups who were always haranguing him about diocesan failures, and not enough to supporting or inspiring run-of-the-mill parish priests. Cooke's surprising directness deflated his loudest enemies and this satisfied some priests that the Archbishop did not easily roll over and die. The problem for the rank and file was the suspicion that Cooke's hard line was merely talk. The words were reassuring—especially the demand that priests respect Church Law—but whether mavericks and scandal mongers would be disciplined remained a moot concern. Two priests ordained a dozen years said they would buy the Cardinal's whole package, "if he goes after some of the big ones in a few weeks." Another priest ordained twenty-two years said: "It was the greatest talk I ever heard on priestly practice, but if there is no follow-up, no one will believe the administration again."

One surprising result of the 1972 Assembly was the rising conviction among priests that the Archbishop could and should provide more vigorous leadership in the realm of civil politics, i.e., on those issues unconnected with institutional Church initiatives. They did not like the tone of the activists and they made the elimination of abortion a priority for Catholic activism. But the issues of housing, poverty, employment, prisons, drugs, crime, race, violence, peace, and child abuse also demanded new leadership from the Cardinal and vigorous involvement in the political process by which obvious social evils would be attenuated, even if they could not entirely be eliminated.

For the next ten years, until he became very ill, Terry Cooke danced around these priest problems and the aberrant behavior that was commonplace. One year after the 1972 "Back Talk," the Cardinal had to face another Assembly, for which the Study Papers for the event kept up the cry that priests felt "homeless." Nothing really had changed.

All this occurred during the pontificate of Paul VI, which was a time of drift. Once Cardinal Cooke complained to me that there was little he could do to bring things into line since the Pope was taking no action against dissidents. That was the way it was.

THE CITY OF NUNS

If ever there was an authority figure capable of making the claims of modern pop psychology work with women, it was Terry Cooke. If ever understanding and dialogue were the keys to engendering acceptable behavior and healthy social relationships, then Mrs. Cooke's youngest son was just the man to open those doors. And normally his easiest time should have come in his relationship with the religious women of his Archdiocese. By tradition and rule they were considered the revered helpmates of their Bishop. Spellman could be a cold person and at times something of a martinet. But even he did more for their institutions and to make them comfortable than any of his predecessors. If the religious women, therefore, began to be restive or acquired a need for a change in their life style, here now was just the man the Pope had ordered for them. But things did not turn out that way, not even with the Sisters of Charity, for whom he was traditionally the highest superior. The Archbishop of New York was obligated to abide by the Church's book on the nature of religious life. "The nuns," however, were not in *the mood* to accept this book anymore as their guide.

Merely placing apostrophes around "nun" indicates that something changed after the Council. The word "nun" goes back to the Latin for a "child's nurse" or nanny, but in modern usage among Catholics it was the affectionate term above all others for the teachers of their children and their own in days bygone. Those sisters were anything but baby tenders. "Nun" was used almost as often and as endearingly as "Mom." Yet, beginning in 1965, the religious women, indoctrinated by avant-garde priests, learned that educating children was beneath Vatican II's sense of liberated dignity. They relegated the word "nun" to oblivion and with the interment went the memory that she was the best part of the twentieth-century Church.

The first task performed in 1966 by me, as an eager Secretary for Education, was to bring Cardinal Spellman's blessing to a high school principal named Sister Mary Concepta Blake, O.P., the "boss lady" of Aquinas High School. Under her tutelage for over thirty-one years 5,612 young ladies received high school diplomas. By that day almost all of those, from 1935 onward at least, were well into motherhood, in that generation three and four children each. Sister Concepta was already on the way to establishing a record as the god-mother of at least twenty-thousand Catholics. The audience was asked to ponder what other woman but a nun could go to God carrying so many living gifts in her arms.

Sister Concepta's departure from Aquinas marked the beginning of another exodus. Many older religious continued in the classroom, but more and more nuns began to flee the arduous work of transforming little roughnecks into altar boys. The dissolution of religious orders, especially of women, cut the U.S. Catholic school system in half from its high point of 5,000,000 students in 1967. New York alone declined from 216,000 students in 430 schools to 130,000 students in 320 schools. The Sisters of Charity, a diocesan community, fell from a membership of 1,400 to 800, of whom only 380 by 1985 were in education. Whereas Catholic law still requires religious to live in community, the 1985 directory for Charity's lists 56 of their 124 residences as apartments containing only one or two sisters. Community life is not possible in these circumstances. The new constitutions of religious communities generally bear little resemblance to the mind of their Foundresses nor do they significantly conform to the New Code of Canon Law. New forms of government are in place without mention of the hierarchic Church, with preference for "personal option" over assignment to Church apostolates, tolerating conflicting life styles, the optional wearing of the habit, deemphasis on spiritual exercises in favor of social activism. Since 1965 many religious communities have rejected religious life without saying so in clear language.

While Spellman was alive, general agreement was reached that religious communities needed updating. Very few priests favored long skirts, ugly veils, restrictions on a nun's mail or travel. Even pastors agreed that the stipends for sisters were indecently low, considering their long hours and their status as educated women. Still, the American nun was far and away ahead of her European counterpart in status, level of living, social role, even freedom. Cardinal Leo Suenens, whose Belgian religious lived monkish lives, was good at telling American nuns, "Be free," until the car he was riding in one day was driven into a ditch when he was leaving Mount St. Vincent's College. Shaken, he turned to Spellman to ask: "What was that?" Spellman's gleeful response, "There go two of your liberated nuns," brought a Suenens' growl, "They're going too far." Suenens' own nuns in Belgium were not allowed to drive automobiles.

More than fifty thousand religious women have since departed religious life, leaving the modernized communities with the median age around sixty. Religious women still work very hard in schools and welfare agencies, but they do it now by choice and almost as solo operators, not as part of an institutional commitment by their religious community to the Church. Whether one listens to a rebel nun like Berkeley's Sister Sandra Schneiders, I.H.M., who thinks American religious women, because they now are lay persons, do not have to listen to Church authority, or to Sister Marie White, S.C., who after fifty years of still-dedicated service says ruefully: "Large numbers of religious women show little faith in the Church and the magisterium," the picture is dark.

What ought to be disabused, however, is the notion that all this came about through the uprising of oppressed religious women in the classrooms or of those out on the missions. These frankly were often innocent bystanders to the community revolution that began in the well-endowed Motherhouses, women's colleges, and huge charitable and hospital institutions where large numbers of "professional" nuns worked. Mothers General at Mount St. Vincent, Sparkhill, and Dobbs Ferry easily united with degreed sisters who had imbibed "enlightened" university wisdom, frequently from Jesuits. How could the sister-troops-in-the-field resist changes imposed from on high, when they were explained so thoroughly by sages who set themselves up as semiofficial interpreters of the recent Council. Freedom of choice and movement, personal fulfillment, social activism, humanist concerns became the new choices. The troops were told that feminism and anti-institutionalism were demanded by Vatican II. The conflicts which ensued within communities were not those between the old and the young at all. The first revolutionaries indeed were middle-aged religious holding office, those who lived in or near large institutional settings, such as Mount St. Vincent's College, St. Vincent's Hospital, or at the Motherhouse in Riverdale. Parochial school teachers scattered in small settings throughout ten New York counties (one hundred fifty miles to the diocesan line) were no match for the concentrated political power of those in these big houses. Furthermore, the college teachers and the social workers had easy access to high salaries, due to funds provided these institutions by government. Readily they were the sisters with moneys to spend on committee meetings, reports, handbills, the types of resources unavailable to the parish teachers. The times themselves were electric but so was the passion for change for those in religious life who already had status. Community study groups and reorganization cells came under the control of the change-makers, who used their new power boldly to freeze out of strategic committee positions defenders of the life they knew St. Elizabeth Seton had established.

What was the Archbishop of New York to do in these circumstances? Or any Bishop? Corrective action, if it came at all, was never proposed on time, arrived too late in most cases, and then only from faraway Rome. Cardinal Cooke and other responsible Bishops simply waited. The least contemplated course was that given by St. Paul to Timothy[3] "Preach the word, stay with this task whether convenient or inconvenient—correcting, reproving, appealing—constantly teaching and never losing patience. For the time will come when people will not tolerate sound doctrine, but following their own desires, will surround themselves with teachers who tickle their ears. They will stop listening to the truth and will wander off to fables." The virtue Bishops exercised in those days was patience, and it was not the relevant virtue. The stakes were high. Still, no one wished the Bishops or anyone else to be unkind to religious superiors. On the other hand, only they could have halted the Church's bleeding during those early days of revolution.

Cardinal Cooke did get angry three years late (March 11, 1973), when the Sisters of Charity announced they were closing St. Joseph-by-the-Sea High School on Staten Island. One year earlier he had warned Sister Margaret Dowling, the president of the Sisters of Charity, about selling off valuable Church properties, some of which were gifts of Cardinal Spellman or were held by virtue of Cooke's own "substantial gift." The sisters had received an attractive offer for the property from City University but Cooke thought they could solve their debt problem (said to be $3.5 million) by making St. Joseph's a coeducational institution. This would give them a larger student body. When the nuns

216

vacillated, Cooke wrote to the community president: "I would like to make it crystal clear that I deplore the action which has been taken and further that I am deeply troubled by the precipitous manner in which the decision not to accept a freshman class was announced." He further stated that he personally would "insure that the present students at St. Joseph's will be able to complete their education under Catholic auspices." He did this by reorganizing the school on his own terms. This course guaranteed the school's continued existence, but also absolved the Sisters of Charity of continued responsibility for the school.

Defiance within New York's religious communities did not begin overnight. It began with the post-Vatican II surge of humanist concerns and the influx of new minorities into the metropolitan area. Religious women were sent to Fordham University, to Manhattan College, and to the Catholic University of Puerto Rico to be educated in the Spanish language and Spanish culture. Msgr. Ivan Illich, one-time coordinator of Spanish-Catholic Action for the New York Archdiocese, set up think-tanks for religious in Mexico, long before "liberation theology" became a household word, with or without its Marxist overtones. He introduced them to the dynamics of revolutionary thinking and tactical training in how to upset institutions, including the Church. Those who went to study learned more than how to speak Spanish. If they arrived with veils, they were told to leave them behind. Off with the veil, out of the schools, off with common prayer, out of the convent, off with the rules, out on the streets. These were the new rallying cries. Power to the sisterhood, down with male dominance, freedom above all became driving forces. Old Catholic maxims (e.g., seek first the Kingdom of God) suddenly lost their meaning. Words like poverty, chastity, and obedience were eviscerated of their obvious meanings, to be redefined as "openness" to whatever individual religions understood humanity to mean to them.

In these first years of the 1960s, pro-abortion nuns or religious partisans of a woman's priesthood were unthinkable. Yet, if one regularly read the internal newsletters of these communities, the ultimate direction was clear. Motherhouses were awash with psycho-social reorientations, with Erich Fromm replacing St. Ignatius

Loyola. No one at the Bishop's level believed that the sisters meant what they were writing, but they did. Young postulants were told during their formation that women religious were lost in "a highly organized social structure," that having been trained defectively for personal relationships, they now, belatedly, must recover in small communities of twos and threes. Convents were out. Young nuns must learn to take charge of their own lives. To cease relying for their well-being on someone who "lorded" over them. The consulted experts never mentioned the Church or the community's Saint Foundress. Incredibly, but true, the Mother General used a community newsletter to disparage the "Good Community Woman" (her own age group), i.e., she who was "interested in all that concerned the Congregation, its members, its apostolic works," one ever "ready to sacrifice her preferences to serve the common good." The new community spirit, she now proposed, was whatever "motivates each individual sister." Loyalty was no longer to be expressed "in uncritical allegiance to the past." Seize freedom, politicize religious life on behalf of social causes, the community was told. Brother Gabriel Moran instructed the Sisters of Charity that leaders exist to do the will of the people, are those who disdain religious titles and dress, who demand full secular pay for religious work. Sister Francis Borgia Rothluebber, the Gloria Steinem of the Leadership Conference of Women Religious, blared a reveille for radicalized nuns. This is the lady, who after reducing the once great School Sisters of St. Francis to a shadow of their former selves, proclaimed in 1985 that never again would she live under a superior.

Reorientations such as these were going on under the inattentive eyes of New York's highest ecclesiastical authorities. Only twenty years earlier (1943) the Archdiocese had created the office of Vicar for Religious to help develop contemporary but authentic religious life. The new Vicar was to help religious develop formation programs and new modes of operation consistent with Church teaching. Suddenly after the Council religious superiors led the charge against higher authority, even when by doing so the Church's mission and community peace were placed in jeopardy. Deviation was considered the price of progress. Most major communities publicly declared their intention to be "self-directed," i.e., to ignore anything coming from ecclesiastical authority.

In many communities veteran religious considered their duty done when they complained to "higher" authority. A large number simply abandoned their vocations. Some religious looked for hiding places inside a system which now was a battle zone. At the end of my tenure as Education Secretary, three Sisters of Charity opted out of their parochial school for catechetical work in a country parish that had no need of them, simply to escape the tensions of their previous convent life. The pastor in question was a friend who was to become their innkeeper now that they were wayfarers. But the option they chose was a grievous misuse of scarce personnel and destructive of the diocesan school system. I denied their request. The Mother General protested and, even though everyone by this time was talked out, called for more dialogue. She argued that the difficulty was lack of communication. In response she was told that, on the contrary, the difficulty was her inability as a superior to say "no" to older nuns once her young ones were permitted to go where they pleased. A policy of floating nuns would be unacceptable to any diocesan official with a minimum of concern for the common good of the Church. But by 1970 the common good of the diocese was no longer an appreciated good in the higher councils of religious communities.

THE DISORDERED CITY

While Terry Cooke could be sanguine about his inability to turn the Church around, his blood would boil somewhat whenever the Church or any of her agencies came under attack from the outside. Catholic institutions enjoyed their good reputation for all the right reasons—good management and lower costs—although there was no shortage of antireligious bigots who resented their existence and the public moneys which came to them under municipal purchase-of-service contracts.

CHILD CARE

For more than a century city and state governments found it cheaper and wiser to consign the care of the aged or dependent children to nonpublic bodies. On November 11, 1974, however, the New York Civil Liberties Union decided to upset the relationship by bringing suit in federal court accusing foster-care agencies under religious jurisdiction of discriminating against minority groups and of spending more money on their own religionists than public agencies spent on their custodials. NYCLU also objected to placing children in agencies on the basis of their religion, a practice in effect since the first orphan asylums were built by churches in the early nineteenth century. The charges were based on a study that had been drawn up by academics with recognized political motives. Actually, a majority of the foster children under Catholic care were Protestant (Protestant wealth having deserted the field), with three quarters of them being black or Spanish. Although the *prima facie* case was ridiculous, the complaint worked its way through the court system for thirteen years. Ending with a federal judge's ruling in 1987 that all foster-child agencies must provide contraception and abortion counseling to children under their care. The chickens of government aid had come home to roost on the worst of secular terms. (As of this latter moment, Cardinal O'Connor is firm in his position that he will close Catholic foster-care institutions rather than comply with the order.)

The 1974 suit was only the beginning of the Church's new problem. *The New York Daily News* conducted its own private investigation of all child-caring institutions, with special interest in the Catholic centers which, their reporters assumed, were using public moneys to serve Catholic interests. They changed their tune later but not before the ins and outs of how investigative reporting is carried on came to light. *The News* was angry with the Archdiocese because *The Times* published the Church's full financial statement first, wrongly thinking Cooke had closed them out of a lead story. Worse still *The News*'s editors still rankled over the unwillingness of Cooke over a ten-year period to grant them a wide-ranging personal interview. Other factors also came into play. A nursing home scandal involving a rabbi had been fodder for the headline-hunting tabloid over many weeks. A good Catholic scandal might just be what *The News* needed to boost circulation. Officials in the city's Welfare Department, no friends of private charity, were not above feeding appropriate data to reporters anxious to "prove" that the Church did profit from child-caring rentals. There seemed to be a lively interest, too, in tearing down the image of "sisters working for nothing."

The News's series, finally published in 1975, turned out to be unbalanced. The Church was engaged in caring for children, and the devotion or the professionalism of the religious/lay staff never came through in a report that was skewed to suggest chicanery by Church officials in complicated financial transfers. *The News*'s staff was unpleasant enough to make something out of the sisters' using a portion of their salaries to make payments to the Social Security system, something which every employer does for every employee every week. The animus was simply an indication of how far reporters go to cast a shadow over nuns' generosity in giving the rest of their salaries to the care of children. For investing two hundred thousand dollars in their investigation, *The News* produced a series of wild charges and one major refusal on its part to examine the records of any three Catholic institutions it chose to cite. *The News* had its agenda and stayed with it.

The Catholic involvement in child care continues to this day, and Cardinal Cooke eventually took the investigations in stride. Tightened management procedures were one follow-up to what often had been a family operation. What made the encounter unpleasant was the handicap under which Church leaders function under public charges like these. How does a Bishop save dignity if he countercharges that the city is harming children by cutting back on payments for foster care, while city officials fatten the budgets of power brokers? Cardinal Cooke would have gained little by a public discussion of how the city was placing an increased number of disturbed children in Catholic institutions and how criminal types were being assigned to them by the courts. Furthermore, how could he with grace accuse the authors of scientific studies and investigative reporting of anti-Catholic animus? Then, ever present, were the various judicial opinions likely to be antireligious of their very nature. Cardinal O'Connor was to find how far this animus was prepared to go.

THE HOMOSEXUAL LOBBY

Cardinal Cooke's most publicized confrontation was with the homosexual lobby and undoubtedly remains the most perduring public controversy of his administration. *The Political Struggle of Active Homosexuals* by this writer (1974), written with Cooke's encouragement, was a summary of his efforts to frustrate the campaign of homosexual activists, under the pretext of seeking civil rights, from gaining social legitimacy for bisexuality and homosexuality. As early as 1971 the fight began to amend New York City's Administrative Code to outlaw discrimination by reason of "sexual orientation or affectional preference." Similar legislation banned discrimination by reason of race, religion, national origin, or sex. Such an amendment was intended to guarantee bisexuals and homosexuals equal access to employment opportunities, to public accommodations, resorts or amusements, housing and commercial space, and more. The city Commission on Human Rights was intended to be the educational agency obligated to promote toleration of this life style and to introduce homosexual activists into city agencies to facilitate the leavening process. No one questioned, least of all Terence Cooke, that overt homosexuals were objects of personal discrimination—but so were cultists, the unwashed, Amish, Hasidics, nudists, hippies, and various categories of citizens (e.g., Catholics) whose beliefs, behavior, or life style was considered contrary to the general norms of expected conduct in society, or which threatened the norms necessary for the maintenance of a civilized society. The important question was whether being homosexual by choice was the same as being black, whether antihomosexuality should be sanctioned by the public law the way racism was. The popular answers to both those questions were no, and the last thing homosexual activists wanted was a general referendum on the issue. They preferred instead to have government agencies, mostly unelected bureaucrats, force tolerance with the long-term expectation that acceptance of homosexuality and bisexuality would eventually come. The entire history of civilized society argued differently. No society, not even pre-Christian Greece, whose poets, dramatists, and generals idealized pederasty, ever endorsed or encouraged homosexuality. Common laws are adequate to protect individual homosexuals. What the activists were asking was much more—"privileged protection"—and their demands were usually rejected.

For Cardinal Cooke the issue was political—what life styles should public law encourage—not simply a religious matter, although religious principles underpinned his own moral philosophy. It required character on the easygoing Cooke's part to stand up to the pressure and the abuse heaped on him because he opposed the political aspirations of homosexual activists. Rome said it later: Homosexuality is "a more or less strong tendency ordered toward an intrinsic moral evil and thus the inclination itself must be seen as an objective disorder."[4] This had been taught by the Church from the beginning. And by the Torah and the Talmud.

Religious principles alone do not explain the universal resistance of civilized nations to the homosexual life style. While sexuality is not reducible to its biological aspects, it is beyond dispute that heterosexuality is the life style which biology dictates. By the nature of things people do not become fixed in homosexual relationships unless the normal process of development and acculturation is disturbed. Males and females complement each other, as do their organs of sexuality. The facts of biology lend powerful credence to the common view of mankind that heterosexuality is natural and normal, not only descriptively but prescriptively. Homosexuality, on the other hand, is universally considered the abnormal condition. People do not arrive at this conviction as a result of reading Moses or Jesus. It was thus understood from the beginning. God made man in his likeness and then woman—

"bone from my bones, flesh from my flesh." From that moment on the sex drive was a powerful force in human affairs, so much so that fidelity to God's plan has never been easy. Indeed, lust and infidelity are always the favorite themes of poets and dramatists, and the most excusable of sins. Even Christ warned about these deviations from the norm. But can one conjure a Christ feeling the need to decry, "a man who looks lustfully at another man"?[5] For similar reasons St. Paul called homosexual acts "shameful things"[6] and likened them to adultery and idolatry as grave offenses, not only against God, but against the nature of the human condition.[7]

This view has been structured into the fabric of nation after nation, whose basic cell has always been the family, a heterosexual institution, if there ever was one. It was the country's mores and the family itself which Cooke was defending, not necessarily or exclusively his religious convictions. While the political pressure on politicians began to mount in 1972 and 1973, the Cardinal enjoyed the support, if not of City Hall, then at least of public opinion. There were other considerations, too, one of which made the homosexual drive seem to be one more element in the urban decay of America. The assault at hand actually was aimed at the mores of cities. Rural neighborhoods were too family oriented to be challenged. Those old enough to have grown up in the old urban neighborhoods lived amid a good deal of vice, but not homosexuality. Priests served in those parishes for years upon years without coming upon rings of homosexual activists. During all the postwar years of the family life movements, the subject of homosexuality was never an item for discussion.

I was almost twenty years into the ministry, and transferred out of a low-income neighborhood to a middle-income two-family-home area in the Bronx, when I first encountered the phenomenon. The year was 1959 and it was two policemen ringing the rectory door to announce that they had uncovered pederasts in our parish molesting young boys (the children of working mothers) after school. About the same time the *New York Daily News* assigned investigative reporter Jess Stearn to look into the Mattucine and Bilitis societies, two obscure defensive homosexual organizations with roots more on the West Coast than in New York. In the mid-fifties the heading Homosexuality almost disappeared from The New York Times Subject Index, and even in 1960 there were only three cross-references to it. The idea of homosexual priests or nuns during this period was unthinkable. By 1964—the year of the civil rights law—the Homosexual entries filled a column of fine print, and the words transvestite and lesbian began to appear in headlines. Homosexual activism was on its way.

On May 24, 1974, *The New York Times* credited the opposition of the Roman Catholic Archdiocese of New York as the "key factor" in the defeat of Intro II, the first serious effort to crown the homosexual drive for acceptance in Gotham City. Intro II had looked like a shoo-in. Mayor John V. Lindsay lent his weight to the effort, but the support given by ex-Mayor Wagner and political bosses Meade Esposito and Pat Cunningham, all Catholics, surprised many. Typically, *The Times* made little reference to the powerful anti voices of the Orthodox rabbinate and black politicians. One black councilman, Samuel D. Wright of Brooklyn, explained his opposition by reciting his experience walking the streets of his district. He found 80 percent of the people against it. Indeed, the money, political organization, and public promotion for Intro II came only from Manhattan, not from the other four boroughs, and then only from affluent elites. The homosexual liberators were so enraged at losing that they conducted an all-night "sit-in" at St. Patrick's Cathedral and to symbolize their contempt for politicians, they subsequently unleashed a score of white mice on the floor of a council meeting in session.

Cardinal Cooke deserved credit, of course, although he would be the last to claim it. Yet the political reality was that Brooklyn's Thomas Cuite, Majority Leader of the City Council, and Aileen Ryan, a Bronx councilwoman, were the prime movers of Intro II's defeat. It was they, not Cooke, who rounded up the three votes necessary to keep Intro II off the city books by a vote of 22–19. As long as Cuite remained Majority Leader, the bill never passed. The year after he retired—1986—the bill, once more named Intro II, was signed by Mayor Koch into law. While Cuite was there, he had the authority to bottle the bill in committee, to keep it from the full committee, to postpone votes until he was sure of the results, to exchange favors for a favorable vote—all those tricks which are part of the legislative process and have been used so well for other purposes on the national scene by politicians such as Sam Rayburn and Lyndon Johnson.

Even so, Cuite could not have been so effective without grass-roots support. The Archdiocese used its own *Catholic News* and parish newsletters to spread the word and close relations were established with the Orthodox rabbis and Greek Orthodox clergy. A "Committee to Protect Family Life in New York City" was formed and legal counsels were hired. The Catholic Lawyers Guild and University Law Deans were persuaded to intercede, and a pamphlet on the moral-pastoral-psychological dimensions of homosexuality was designed and distributed. Every public relations device was employed. The sailing was not always smooth— as when the leading psychiatrist of Cooke's Family Consultation Service decided to support Intro II, the *Brooklyn Tablet* followed suit, and the only priest on the City Council voted for the bill. On the side of the Church, however, was the widespread public concern of most citizens over the employment of homosexuals in teaching and child-caring situations.

The 1974 contest was no sooner over than the 1975 battle began. By now every major institution in the city, including industry and labor unions, had become concerned about affirmative action mandates, requirements to hire a percentage of identifiable homosexuals or be accused of discrimination. It was for this reason that Catholic and Jewish populations continued during the year to speak out against any new bill that might be in the offing. A new "Committee to Protect Our Youth" came into being about the time homosexual activists were telling Democratic leaders of City Hall that if they did not get a bill passed in the spring, they would disrupt and make ridiculous the 1976 Democratic National Convention in August. The Archdiocese was not in that kind of business, but it did continue quietly to communicate with a large number of people about the moral dimension of all such bills. Labor unions were supportive because they hoped to function without unending litigation defending themselves from groups pressing claims for homosexuals. The effort cost money, but private benefactors were not wanting to supply the fifty thousand dollars needed annually to keep this communication going.

The homosexual activists were not idle either. The Democratic Convention was in the offing, and with all that media attention they saw the gains to be made with planned parades, demonstrations in front of St. Patrick's Cathedral, picketing of delegates' hotels all day, protests outside the National Committee headquarters, celebration of homosexual love in Foley Square, etc. Still, Tom Cuite, recognizing a public squeeze when he saw it, stood tall, strongly resolved to oppose any new bill. He made it clear, however, to Catholic and Jewish organizations that their people had to back cooperating councilmen in local elections. The Knights of Columbus was particularly effective in this kind of politicking. So was the Committee to Protect Family Life. In one Bronx district, largely Catholic, a councilman changed his tune quickly when he found a hundred thousand flyers passed to voters outside local churches one Sunday morning, identifying him as pro-Intro II.

In 1977 the situation changed somewhat when Mayor-elect Koch announced he was about to fulfill his promises to the homosexual community. Intro 554 would be for him what the Police Civilian Review Board was to one of his predecessors, John V. Lindsay. Koch demanded that the bill be forced out of the General Welfare Committee and expected the new council president, Carol Bellamy, to insist on its passage. He also threatened Majority Leader Tom Cuite with dismissal. With the new mayor actively on their side, the homosexual activists hoped for a backroom deal and, if that did not work, they were prepared to launch a major drive, to defame the opposition, as necessary, using Anita Bryant as the whipping girl. She had defeated the homosexuals in Florida. Still, the activists had money and access to the media. Their only opposition were Catholics and Orthodox Jews, and they were ready to vilify that opposition. Other religious leaders sympathized but did not participate because they did not care to face the homosexual firepower, now enhanced by its strength in the advertising market.

A sense was developing in the Catholic leadership that the combination of Koch and media would eventually force a bill through in spite of Cuite. So, a fall-back position began to emerge in Catholic leadership, viz., to exclude homosexual employment in positions where the clientele was under eighteen years of age. The homosexuals rejected the suggestion so it never became more than a private proposal of one county leader. The ideal political posture for Catholics and Orthodox Jews was to demand a referendum, of course, and such a possibility regularly made the homosexuals nervous. They surely would lose a general vote. But it remained important in any case that the moral aspects of this political fight never be lost, viz., that homosexual behavior is immoral. This was not merely a matter of preaching, but of making it clear to the public that Catholic leaders would protect their children from homosexuals, that they would contest the intrusion of government on the side of homosexuality or the use of tax-supported institutions, like public schools, to advance a basically immoral cause. The rising problem for Church leadership, however, was the presence of homosexual priests like Richard Ginder and John McNeil on the other side, along with groups like Dignity, which enjoyed partial episcopal support, even though its approach was not authentically Catholic. It was important that these dissidents be isolated because they were propagandists for the homosexual activists, not for the Catholic-Orthodox Jewish cause. The Church's difficulty continued to be money, especially since a homosexual "task force" was in the process of raising $1 million to undo in New York what Anita Bryant successfully accomplished in Miami.

Even so, 1977 passed into 1978 and Tom Cuite remained in command. *The New York Times* favored the latest bill—already defeated seven times—arguing that homosexual teachers who went too far could be disciplined or fired. But this claim was false. Once homosexuals obtained a "civil right" for their status, their legalized ability to harass their critics would be enhanced. By claiming equality with blacks, Jews, or Catholics, they would carve out a privileged sanctuary for themselves. Catholic leadership had never given credibility to *The Times*'s argument, the fear that all homosexuals were pederasts at heart. What Catholics wanted reinforced was heterosexuality, not homosexuality. They thus opposed any dilution of the proper formation due to children of tender years. Nor was the Church demanding that homosexuals be fired from schools, since few of them were very influential. What was important was preventing homosexuality from becoming a *bona fide* occupational qualification in summer camps and counseling situations. Another concern at this time was the right (granted under a loose law) of homosexuals and homosexual pairs to demand housing in two-family homes or in dormitories, etc., where they would be close to impressionable youngsters. Legal counsel thought two-family homes would be protected, but until there was a test case no one could be absolutely sure.

One subject recurring throughout these annual bouts, though never fully aired, was the extent to which homosexuality is a congenital given. Homosexual activists maintained that all roles, and nature itself, are simply learned experiences, which as far as heterosexuality itself is concerned is ridiculous. A boy and a girl isolated on a desert island would soon discover what boys and girls are intended to be. But homosexuality? Nature in the concrete is never pure, as Siamese twins give evidence, and "survival of the fittest" plays havoc with those disposed by nature to tuberculosis or alcoholism. But, in spite of all the recent writing on the subject, there are no scientific data available to "prove" that any human being is born homosexual. Hormonal imbalances are known to exist and early environmental or psychogenic influences do shape dispositions and tendencies in weak personalities, especially if they have been seduced. So does culture with its specific "do's and don't's." Gang behavior is commonplace in preteens and teens, and throughout life there are times when men and women prefer to associate with their own sex. None of these relationships are connected with orgiastic sexual behavior, unless something triggers the potential in every human being to pursue sexual pleasure, however immoral or deviant. In any event whether the end result was immoral heterosexual or homosexual pleasure, parents as well as Church leaders, and one could hope civic officials too, had every right to ensure that the teaching influences on the young were positive and moral. In the formative years when the imitative instincts of children are strong, teachers convey their values and their practices to children in more ways than verbally. If Intro 554 was passed as written—with its legitimization of "sexual orientation . . . the choice of sexual partner by gender"—the active homosexual could become an attractive role model for the young.

Of course, the nation was beginning to reap the final harvest of its contraceptive culture, by 1979 deeply embedded in popular thinking. Once the link between sex, marriage, and procreation was broken, it was a small step toward general approval for fornication, adultery, or sodomy, all of which by intent (and realistically for homosexuals) had no connection with procreation. Under the contraceptive ethos sex became an end justifying itself. "We gotta have sex," said one Canadian homosexual demanding free condoms during the later AIDS crisis. In the contemporary media little is mentioned about responsible use of the sexual faculties, within marriage and reasonably, only about safe sex. No sexual activity is truly safe once it is unreasonable, irresponsible, or driven by lust. Rarely do media give these considerations any time.

Nonetheless, by 1978 the homosexual movement gained political ground by constant media exposure. Intro 554 was defeated once more, even though the opposition spent three hundred thousand dollars and worked hysterically to force a favorable City Council vote. The Catholic troops were beginning to show signs of weariness because the eternal discussion of homosexuality was somewhat depressing. Other problems, equally distasteful to the public, began to appear—white slavery of male and female prostitutes, advanced pornography, and degrading standards in the entertainment industry. Existing law was not being enforced, an omission which smacked of corruption. Only large corporations possessed the wallop in New York to effectuate reform, but they would rather relocate than fight. Fighting might lose them customers. So the burden fell on the backs of the churches.

Between 1978 and 1983, the year Cooke died, the Holy See began to intervene. Part of the cause was an article which appeared in the magazine *Christopher Street* (September 1979), entitled "The Gay Challenge to the Catholic Church." This article, some twenty pages long, described the network of homosexuals, working alone or through groups like Dignity and New Ways, that had reached into dioceses and into Rome itself. On February 23, 1978, Archbishop Jean Jadot wrote Cardinal Cooke inquiring about three priests in New York, religious, who were involved actively with homosexuals. The religious superiors who were questioned confessed general ignorance of what their respective subjects were doing. The evidence, however, suggested they were sanctioning homosexual behavior. In 1979 Jadot forced Richmond's Bishop Walter Sullivan to suspend a homosexual priest. Rome reprimanded Father Pedro Arrupe for allowing Jesuit John McNeil to publish his book *The Church and The Homosexual*. It also silenced McNeil, who later was expelled from the Jesuits. But by now the infiltration of the Church machinery by active homosexuals had become a matter of serious concern to more than Paul VI—and a matter of scandal to the faithful.

In 1980 Mayor Koch, frustrated by his inability to win the council to his point of view, issued his own Executive Order No. 50, which banned discrimination in employment on the basis of "sexual orientation or affectional preference." The Archdiocese refused to comply and eventually the New York Court of Appeals declared the order void and unenforceable because it was an unlawful usurpation of the City Council's legislative power. On March 20, 1986, the city at last passed Intro II. In June of that year the city and Church-sponsored agencies reached agreement that the latter may rightfully make their employment decisions in the light of a "religious exemption" from the law's general demands. This exemption is presently under review by the city, so that the final word on the subject has not been spoken.

Homosexual insertion into the body politic is still far from a settled issue. What *New York* magazine once called "Gay Clout" (August 29, 1977) has been demonstrated, powerful enough, it was claimed there, to "have anything they want of this city," if they pulled themselves together. Yet, throughout all the public in-fighting the nature of homosexual activism and its significance for the American community was never fully explored. Few citizens read their literature, so they were unaware of the nature of the sexuality that was being offered as the alternative to marriage. The average parent had no idea what "rimming" or "fisting" was, nor how promiscuous practicing homosexuals are. For the vast majority of its practitioners, homosexuality is anything but a gay life, and police often report its violence. Yet "the 1972 Gay Rights Platform" demanded that "Federal encouragement and support for sex education courses prepared and taught by quali-fied gay women and men presenting homosexuality as a valid, healthy preference and life style, and as a viable alternative to heterosexuality." Police infiltrate "homosexual sado-masochistic slave markets" in Los Angeles or temporarily break up a "homo-sexual prostitution operation" in New York involving eight-year-old boys, and there is little follow-up.[8] The impact of the homo-sexual propaganda on adolescent boys and girls is ignored.[9] The activists, seizing upon their civil rights, have reached the point of power, where employers, at least in government, actively recruit a homosexual quota of employees in sensitive areas, like police-work.[10] This is one illustration of the power of a few strategically placed government officers to change the mores of a city.

And now there is AIDS.

ST. TERENCE COOKE?

This was all that many people talked about for weeks after he was buried. As the story of his last three months unfolded in the press, with all the gory details American reporters have begun to exact as due their natural right to know, great compassion was directed toward Cardinal Cooke. He was still "Terry" to all the priests who knew him, even though in personal meetings they paid him the respect due "Eminence." The sorrow that poured forth from the moment his terminal illness was announced was genuine. To learn that he was dying from the day he was made a

Bishop in 1965 came as a shock to many. Cancer of the lymph nodes sometimes moves slowly, in his case almost eighteen years before it killed him. But the helplessness and pain of the last few months, his courage, forbearance, and piety, acquired him a unique kind of stature at the end, which he did not enjoy in the early years. Even his successor made a point of extolling Terry Cooke's sanctity as his rite of passage from Scranton to New York.

The canonization process will, of course, go its ecclesial way, and who is to say at this juncture what possibilities lay ahead that Terry Cooke will join John Neumann as a second U.S. Bishop saint. The fact is, however, living or dead Cooke was a good man, a dedicated priest, and a very hard worker for the Church. These are the elementals of sainthood, even if no future Pope gives it public recognition. Speculating about his place in history is another futile guessing game, partly because he has not been dead long enough for his administrative record to be known, let alone evaluated. Since he was not a man given to controversy, his wins and his losses are still somewhat private and may remain so. On this basis historians are likely to judge him no better or no worse than the ratings given to his predecessors, once removed—John Farley and Patrick Hayes, also New Yorkers by birth, good men who did a number of fine things for the Church of New York but, as Cardinals, did not distinguish themselves with great deeds or eloquent proclamations. Anyway, Terry Cooke probably never saw himself as a great ground-breaker or reformer.

The New York Times looked upon the Archdiocese he inherited as "a lively scene, what with jazz Masses, financial crises, and liberal clergy bent on greater priest-power." Cooke's Archdiocese was a lively scene because New York is always lively, but there were hardly any jazz masses under Cooke, no financial crises, and the "liberal clergy," whoever they were supposed to be, never acquired any priest power from him. Although dissenting choruses frequently upset him, Archbishop Cooke inherited all the dislocations within the Church that followed Vatican II. Cooke left New York well off financially. The available resources ran well beyond several hundred millions of dollars.

Over and above the many activities with a plus component, described elsewhere in this book, for which Cooke deserves credit, tribute must be paid him for seizing national leadership of the Right-to-Life movement and turning it into a crusade. Some prominent Bishops were not as single-minded on abortion as they should have been, but Cooke, in spite of the political wrangling which always unsettled him, remained on the side of the angels. The new Chancery Office, the Inter-Parish Finance Commission, his aid for ghetto school children, pensions for all diocesan employees, these and many other accomplishments will be lost from the view of future historians. His interventions in the 1977 Bishops' Meeting, which saved the National Catechetical Directory from becoming a disaster, may have been his finest hour. When he personally became dissatisfied with the kind of training given at Fordham and Manhattan Colleges to future religious educators, he established his own Archdiocesan Catechetical Institute for that purpose. Cooke did not deal directly with the heresies and semiheresies often proclaimed in the classrooms of Catholic colleges, but in this he was no less careless than his peers in the U.S. hierarchy. One thing could always be said of Terry Cooke, and his priests knew it, he was a believer. And he followed the lead of the Holy See. The Archdiocese of New York did not abandon the Church's first confession-first communion sequence, did not become a center for wild General Absolution parties, nor did its Marriage Court become an annulment mill, as many others notoriously did.

In important respects the Archdiocese was worse off at his death than it was when he was installed, but so was the Church. The full effect of the flight of religious women from education cut his school system in half and his parishes increasingly were in the hands of aging pastors who had too little young American or too much foreign priest-help. The old enthusiasm in Motherhouses, rectories, and Chancery Offices seemed to be gone. Cardinal Terence Cooke was like Paul VI, the man who made him, prayerful and pious but incapable of recharging the system. There are few around yet who know how to do that. The times call for John Paul II's faith, a new dynamism, and a stiff dose of disciplining which few today seem capable of providing. One of the most complimentary things said about Paul VI and Cardinal Cooke is that they avoided schism. The truth which neither would face was the schism that was everywhere. Like cancer, it was a word never to be spoken. But whatever talents God gave both in the beginning, they used well. Perhaps that is all we should ask of anyone. The imponderables of history are best left to God.

Or, in His Providence, to John Paul II and John O'Connor.

NOTES

1. *New York Law Journal,* February 25, 1980.
2. Matthew 6:33.
3. II Timothy 4:2–4.
4. *Origins,* November 13, 1986.
5. Matthew 5:28.
6. Romans 1:26–27.
7. I Corinthians 6:9ff.
8. *New York Daily News* and *New York Post,* April 9 and 12, 1976.
9. John Harvey, *The Priest,* March 1980.
10. *New York Daily News,* May 18–19, 1987.

FIVE

The Roots of the Church: Parish Life

THE CONSULTATION conducted by the U.S. Bishops in preparation for the 1987 Synod of Bishops indicated that when people talk about where God is present in their lives, "the primary place they identify is their family. Next is their parish." Thus, Archbishop John May, president of the U.S. Bishops' Conference, was able to tell the Synod Bishops on October 5: "The universal Church is realized for most Catholics in the parish." Why such a statement should surprise anyone is itself a wonder.

In every corner of the United States there is a parish church, and its spire reminds the neighborhood that God is in His heaven and that its chimes call to Sunday crowds to give Him worship. The only Churchman most Catholics will ever know is their parish priest. If they know anything about the Church, it is from his likes they first learned it, and whatever raw feelings they have on that subject, good and bad, grew out of early experiences at the parochial level. Polls do not really tell the living story of the Catholic Church, nor do writers. Only parish life does. Like the family unit in a nation, the importance of a parish to the Church is oftentimes hidden under the routine things it does every day without fanfare. It is almost exclusively a living document, dying a little each time it loses a good pastor, leaving its life story only in the archive of God's infinite mind.

If a parish priest is good at shepherding, which is what being a pastor is all about, he comes to know his people, their wants and needs, their accomplishments, and their crosses, and he gives them all the support they need to live up to the requirements of their faith. This becomes easier if he (with others) is successful at forging a Catholic identity around the liturgy of the Church and her teachings. If he goes down to his people's lower level, it is to lift them up to a viable Christian norm. If he shows compassion, it is to suffer with them in their anguish, not to coddle their weaknesses or cover up their sins.

I was fortunate to spend half my priestly life as a parish priest. Indeed in only four years out of forty-seven have I been unconnected with a parish. Two parochial assignments in particular, one as curate, one as pastor, brought me into contact with the Church where Catholics really can be found.

ST. MONICA'S PARISH

Looking at a picture taken in 1954 of 760 school children standing on East Eightieth Street with their 17 School Sisters of St. Francis, one of whom, Sister Mary Evasia, was principal, is not simply an exercise in nostalgia. It is a reminder of how well the American Bishops built the U.S. Church. The occasion was the seventy-fifth anniversary of the founding of St. Monica's parish in midtown Manhattan, a significant milestone to be sure because by the centenary the parish school would be no more, and the School Sisters of St. Francis, once the glory of Midwest German Catholic achievement, would be decimated, in flight from schoolwork, from their founder's purpose, and from post-Vatican II norms for religious life.

But 1954 was their glory hour, beloved as they were by an entire metropolitan parish, and their contributions properly recorded in *The Story of St. Monica's Parish*, a volume I wrote to commemorate the giant works of three generations of religious and laity on behalf of Mother Church. Looked at today from the perspective of time, that record causes one to ask, how did the School Sisters do it with an average class size of forty-eight pupils, all from low-middle-income parents struggling to civilize their children even as they lived in what at best were nothing more than hot-water flats? And do it all the while the eight sisters who did not have Master's Degrees continued graduate work after school and on Saturday.

St. Monica's was my first parish assignment, one of four encompassing twenty-five years. Only St. John the Evangelist, where I served as pastor 1970–74, comes close to etching on me an indelible mark of the full significance of how much the Church depends on its parish priests and on those religious sisters who civilized roughnecks better than they lived to see.

In 1945 St. Monica's was a microcosm of what was to be a new problem for the urban Church of New York—radical change in rapid fashion. World War II had just ended, and shortly before, the pastor of thirty years had died, and in the same year New York's Sisters of Charity had withdrawn from the school they helped found in 1886. Nothing could be more devastating for a cohesive Catholic neighborhood. Baptisms were down to 203 from a high point of 489, marriages numbered 93 in 1944 compared to 222 a generation earlier, and the school population was half of what it had been. The people looked backward and they had every right to enjoy their past. Once the Selective Service program began in 1940, the social program of a very socially conscious parish became veritably nonexistent. The parish, deprived by World War II of its most active manpower, left parishioners mainly interested in praying for the safe return of their soldier husbands and sons. Indeed, when the new pastor arrived late in 1943, he was constantly told what a great parish this was before he came. Father John Moylan lacked the glamor of his predecessor, but the remarks were not intended to be unkind. The leading parishioners were simply embarrassed at what he found when he came; $3,000 in the bank and $10,000 in outstanding debts.

It did not take long to realize the importance of the pastor to the effectiveness of the Church's mission. Coming from the neighboring parish, I knew Msgr. Arthur Kenny by reputation, but it did not take long to appreciate how Father Moylan must have felt when he was constantly reminded that the Kenny era (1913–43) was "the golden age" of the parish, and Arthur Kenny was chiefly responsible. He was a veritable legend, cultivated in mind, a magnificent orator who used his pince-nez glasses in much the same fashion as Franklin Roosevelt, and a public figure quite comfortable with his position as a leader of men. He was a blend of regality, athletic prowess, and neighborliness, a priest of patrician bearing with the common touch. His rectory was a home for priests, a house of hospitality. Two of his curates lived with him for twenty years, and all of the seventeen priests he supervised spoke of him in admiring terms. The nature of his status was never symbolized better than in 1926 when, while in Rome, he was made a Domestic Prelate at a time when monsignors were few and far between. Upon his return his leading parishioners met him at the Hudson River pier with a band, and as his car drove up First Avenue toward East Seventy-Ninth Street, St. Monica's school children lined the streets waving their flags, as if he were a new Bishop entering his diocese for the first time.

We tend to forget—or underestimate—the qualities of and the training that went into these men to make them the dominant neighborhood figures they were. Debunkers, even in the priesthood, speak of those triumphal pastors as if they were all autocrats of the rectory table. Surely an occasional bully existed, but this was not the priest singled out for the encomiums paid those American priests who acquired special status in the Church because they exercised their role with unique style and effectiveness. Arthur Kenny's career would have been well nigh triumphal, without spot or wrinkle, had he been given an Administrator during the physical decline in the last years of his life. One notices how the parish declined with him, how Mass attendance, school population, parish income, number of converts, marriages validated, etc., went downhill when the curates had no one to direct or command them.

But in his heyday, which would span a quarter of a century, his parish hummed. I walked into that rectory in 1945 to find a filing cabinet of census cards, capsulating the religious status of more than thirty-five hundred families, the last card dated 1939. Every year of his best years, the Parish Visitors knocked on doors of homes in his parish block by block, often to meet people lost in the anonymity of city life. Working with the parish priests and another religious community, the Helpers of the Holy Souls, the Parish Visitors brought consolation, education, social work, and sacramental initiation to hundreds monthly, who would otherwise have been lost in the urban canyons of a parish whose territorial boundaries covered forty-two square blocks.

A new priest quickly learned what his parish was like by listening to the neighborhood veterans, most of whom had been born at the turn of the century. They belonged to the parish's Jimmy Cagney period. Cagney, who attended P.S. 158 around the corner from St. Monica's, was not looked upon then as such a tough guy. He danced, we were told, which made him something of a sissy to the middle-aged men telling the story. The sacristan and the president of the Rosary Society really ran the parish, the men said, a little case of sour grapes it would seem; but the lay people's admiration of the priests bordered on worship.

Two priests in particular, who together gave Kenny forty years of service, held that parish (with the pastor) in the palms of their hands. Edmond T. Harty and John W. Cunningham used to entertain young men, then just married or about to be, with wagers about which one of the two could specify the names of families living in any house in the parish on any street the laymen would choose. New Yorkers of this generation would know that each midtown street contained fifty five-story houses with ten flats each, five hundred families in all on a single block! Granted that the two priests in question were never as good as aging memories made them out to be, nonetheless the legends were at best only modest exaggerations. Going into those homes ten to fifteen years after these priests departed, the newcomer learned how well those priests knew their people. This intimacy was a large part of their success. This was what parish priests were supposed to do, and they did it or had someone like Kenny prodding them to do it, as much by example as by direction.

Not everyone was fortunate enough to come out of one good parish tradition and fall into another just as good, one indeed with a fuller line of dominating priestly personalities. We are not supposed to use that word "Dominus" anymore because it suggests lording over people, as if the modern world is *not* ruled aggressively by all kinds of activists. But in those days "Lording" meant "The Lord" and both Arthur Kenny and John Moylan were in different ways "Christ-like." Each of them knew what "pastoring" was about. Lately the word "pastoral" has been used to suggest that priests (or the Church) must cater to the "mind" of their flock, never pushing them to do anything beyond their seeming capacity or against their private judgment. The contemporary "pastoral" priest is thus set against the alleged pre-Vatican legalist or martinet. Those who so change the meaning of an important biblical word must contend with Jesus, who referred to Himself as the "Good Pastor," who shepherded His sheep into the fold, not one who let them go their own way. The Pauline Epistles to Timothy and Titus are called "pastoral" precisely because they provided practical directives to the early Christians on how to be good Christians. The long tradition of the Church itself has canonized the role of pastor to include the obligation to teach Christian doctrine, to administer the sacraments, and to shape people's lives toward the norms and ideals of their faith. Arthur Kenny and John Moylan tolerated large amounts of disobedience in their lifetimes and both were kindly confessors, but they would have had more drunks, thieves, and adulterers in their parish had they not been insistent on norms for and penance from sinners. Their parishioners even confessed the use of contraceptives, i.e., those who indulged, and it was a rare woman who thought of aborting a child.

By the time the new pastor arrived, and shortly the new assistants, the parish picture had changed as much in the work habits of the rectory, as in the neighborhood population itself. The two pastors I worked under between 1945 and 1956—Msgr. John J. Moylan and Bishop James H. A. Griffiths—were fine men and good pastors, different but exemplary. Whereas Kenny was ordained in 1892, Moylan left Dunwoodie in 1904. Griffiths came to the priesthood in 1927. Moylan's training was closer to Kenny's and Griffiths was more a ruler than Moylan was. Both ran good parishes, although Moylan's style was to let it run, Griffiths' to see that it ran his way. Without doubt Griffiths was the smartest Bishop I ever knew and something of a martinet. On his confessional box hung a sign "French, German, Italian, Spanish," indicating the languages he was prepared to absolve in, which prompted one observant priest wag to wisecrack, "I guess Griffiths doesn't speak English."

The one thing that everyone noticed about Msgr. Moylan (and his predecessor, too) was his personal discipline. Discipline came to him early in life, was reinforced by his seminary training, and remained with him until he died three days after his seventy-fourth birthday. A Jersey City boy from birth, John Moylan began to learn Latin and Greek from his pastor, beginning in the fourth grade once he manifested interest in becoming a priest. His later curates were always puzzled how anyone ordained in 1904 managed it at twenty-two years of age. One day Father Moylan broke his reticence long enough to explain that he had every intention of entering St. Peter's Prep after grade school until his Jersey City pastor, George Corrigan (brother of New York's Archbishop Michael Corrigan), told him St. Peter's College was about to open a new academic track (ca. 1895), the entrance requirement of which was a working knowledge of Latin and Greek. Fourteen-year-old Moylan took the exam and passed it! For the rest of his pastorate, whenever serious discussion arose at table, one of his priests, responding to something he said, was bound to add: "The trouble with you, Monsignor, is that you never went to high school."

The wonder of it all is not that a smart young boy could learn Latin and Greek so well, but that a nineteenth-century pastor was qualified to pass on such learning. The discipline required for this remarkable achievement never slackened. Father Moylan was never late for Mass, was the first one in the confessional and the last one out, never stayed out of his rectory overnight in twelve years as pastor, covered the rectory for his curates, visited the sick, buried the dead, and was still writing out his Sunday sermons every week, even as he was celebrating his golden anniversary as a priest. A shy man by disposition, embarrassed by public notice, he felt it necessary to ask Cardinal Spellman in 1949, when the latter called to tell him he had been made a monsignor: "Do I have to do anything for it?" Assured that he did not, he told the Cardinal: "All right." He was not a boss but nonetheless a good Administrator. He guarded parish expenditures with almost penurious attention yet gave generously of the little he had to those in need. One morning as I was going down to morning Mass and later out to visit my hospitalized mother, there on my study floor was three hundred dollars. I knew instantly it was from him. No note, but knowing that the hospital bills were piling up, Father Moylan made a typical unannounced gesture. When I saw him that morning, all I said was, "Thanks." His response was merely a nod.

If the biblical message, "The meek shall inherit the earth," means anything, John Moylan gave it flesh in his dying. This priest, who was often remembered for stoking coal into the school furnace at 6 A.M. whenever the janitor was drunk or for removing garbage from the rectory for the same reason, died with great public notice, in contrast to the majestic Kenny, who died during Holy Week when no funeral Mass could be said. Moylan died July 10, 1955, while most of his parish was on vacation or still celebrating the national Independence Day holiday. Nonetheless, they returned from the beaches in droves, filling his twelve-hundred-seat St. Monica's with their presence at his funeral. After Cardinal Spellman departed the church that morning, one hundred automobiles assembled outside to follow John Moylan's body to Paterson, New Jersey, where he was laid to rest with his parents. This pastor, who never accepted a pastor's salary during his tenure, was mourned by no one else close to him—save the only family every good priest leaves behind.

When I walked into Father Moylan's rooms that first Saturday afternoon, October 1945, not yet having reached thirty years of age, he treated me with the respect I saw him give the oldest of his curates, a Father James Riordan, a senior citizen in my judgment of forty-seven years old. Without apology and with no room for dispute, the pastor placed his new priest in charge of the school, the altar boys, the Holy Name Society, the Children of Mary, the CYO, the Irish Night show, and as I discovered later, everything and anything the older priests no longer wished to handle. The schedule allowed me to be free Wednesday night and Friday after lunch. A day or so later Father Riordan, who was responsible for the public high school students, said, "I can't handle them alone. Will you help me?" It was easy to say yes, but also the end of a free Wednesday night. This same senior curate also suggested he and I would guarantee coverage of every wake, every grave, every baptism or wedding party, every Sunday Mass outside church, and every parish event in order that no parishioner would feel neglected. We worked together for four years on all the programs he indicated. Do you know how many people you come to know merely by appearing at those ritual events? When Riordan went on to become a pastor in 1949, the ritual practices continued so that by the end of ten years the priests were able on Sunday morning to address practically all of the 3,500 parishioners coming out of Mass by first name.

In strict territorial terms St. Monica's parish was gigantic. A 1950 demographic study done by Cornell Medical College turned up 49,200 people living within its confines, half of whom by birthrate computations were Catholic. Thirty-five percent— 17,000—were foreign-born, only 7 percent of whom came from Ireland. The rest were Germans, Bohemians, Slovaks, Hungarians, and very few Italians. What saved the Catholicity of this mass of people was the fact that eight parishes in and around St.

Monica's geography, six of which were national, served their combined religious needs. The neighborhood was knee-deep in churches and clergy. (Their combined Sunday Mass attendance was in excess of 20,000.) Why so many churches? Gossip had it that an indiscrete remark about Italians early in his career prevented Msgr. Michael Lavelle, Rector of St. Patrick's Cathedral for more than fifty years, from becoming a Bishop. In the hope of undoing the damage, it was said Vicar General Lavelle became an expert at founding national parishes. The effort did not get him what he probably wanted, but the Catholic people of Yorkville were richly served thereby, a blessing because most of them were lower middle class or poor. The same Cornell study showed just how low, with its breakdown of monthly rental groups in the parish:

$80 and over	2,500
$79 to $40	10,000
$39 to $30	20,500
$29 to $20	16,000

It is little wonder that the pastor had difficulty making ends meet. As one might also suspect, the religious difficulties of the underprivileged turned out to be as acute as their social problems. One great advantage, however, was the neighborhood itself. Beside the churches, Yorkville housed eleven hospitals, one settlement house, two day nurseries, three nursing schools, two youth centers, three serviceable political organizations, a dental clinic for the young, a Community Service agency, six Catholic high schools, four Catholic commercial high schools, one Catholic college, two visiting communities for the sick, and two residences for women. With institutional setups like that around the corner, parish life was a snap for any priest willing to work.

But how does one energize a parish that looks backward? It turned out to be easier than it first appeared. It was the parochial school which opened the door to the parish. The title "School Director" was new to me, but apparently it came out of a tradition which began in St. Monica's with Arthur Kenny, but originated in St. Michael's on the West Side at the turn of the century. The

School Director was the pastor's representative in all school matters, saving a busy pastor who had little time for the school but did not want the religious women or the children neglected. It was also a gem of an idea, because the school was not a disembodied entity of the Church, but an arm of the parish mission. Fortunately, too, this young curate arrived on "Open House" day, when parents came with their little darlings to inspect the classrooms and to say hello to the nuns. After making a tour of the sixteen rooms, saving the eighth-grade boys for last (hoping most of my first altar boys could be found there), I visited the principal, Sister Mary De Padua, to ask: "Is this the local public school?" Not knowing me, she hesitated. My next statement, understandable enough to anyone who knew Yorkville boys, broke her up: "Where did we get that crowd of football players in the eighth grade? Some of them look like they should be in jail. And your nun up there hardly makes five feet." Being a Hurley out of Washington, D.C., not a German girl from Nebraska, she recognized the anomaly. Her School Sisters, mostly of German background and used to the disciplined ways of German pastors, already had experienced a bellyful of East Side roughnecks. They surely could use a little masculine support. Sister De Padua and I hit it off immediately and this made all the rest easy.

St. Monica's priests thereafter became involved in the school on a daily basis, familiar faces to the children who carried home good-humored tales and made the priests' names household words. What is more, priests visited the convent on a regular basis, at a time when this kind of friendliness was uncommon. Beautiful to remember is how these friendships became deep without any of the familiarity that offends the sacredness of the respective roles.

While the priestly presence in the school was important (even those eighth-grade ruffians knew better than to ruin Sister Berchman's day), those nuns, and they were almost all young, Sister De Padua herself being only thirty-eight, became involved with lay people in the parish on matters other than schoolwork. Busy schedule or no, the School Sisters became helpmates of, and were helped in return by, all the lay activists in the parish. By rule they were not permitted to visit homes, but in time the parish came to them. Mother Corona, the major superior of a community 3,000 strong in 1950, once remarked that at transfer time no nuns left a mission with greater regret than those stationed on East Eightieth Street. It was the full complement of their staff, a School Sister in every classroom, that enabled the parish to give every child a free education at a cost to the pastor of only $50 per child per annum. The annual outlay for educating 760 children was under $40,000, the price of what 2 good lay teachers handling 20 children would be today.

St. Monica's school was the pipeline to the outer parish. Years later chronic complainers and anti-Church religious ridiculed the spending of so much money on children. They chose to ignore that each school family, usually practicing Catholics, lived in the same house with people of little and no religion. These parents were the leaven in the parish. The School Sisters, simply by being there, brought a similar inspiration to the families of public school pupils. Not only did they promote family devotional practices everywhere, but they distributed medals and booklets by the thousands, and through their contacts the priests were apprised of neighborhood situations which would have otherwise escaped their attention.

Once the process began for a priest to interview each parent who enrolled a child in the school or the CCD program, the religious performance of the family was followed as closely as the learning life of the child. Within ten years hundreds upon hundreds of parents had developed a close working relationship with both priests and School Sisters. The school also became the means of promoting convert classes (which at one point brought fifty newcomers to the Church each year) and an entire network of apostolic activities such as those carried out in the name of Sodality, St. Vincent de Paul, Cana Conference, etc. St. Monica's even had its own Labor School for workingmen. It was from the above-mentioned groups that new parochial leadership came to the fore.

Still, nothing came easy when the task at hand was finding, motivating, and training new leadership. Most people are not joiners and, even if so disposed by personality, the ones a priest would like to attract were already oversubscribed by the nature of their work or the size of their family commitment. Then, there was always the "old guard," which protects every parish status quo. A newcomer found out early that nothing much goes on against it. Like the sexton who did not want to make an extra set of keys to the parish buildings for a new priest. Parish councils today surely formalize lay participation in the conduct of Church business, but even in pre-Vatican II days, every good parish was "run" by a corps of leading lay lights. The more active the parish, the more laity were involved in the doing.

Going through a shakedown period had its humorous side. Once the Holy Name Society heard there would be no beer permitted at the next Irish Night entertainment, three prominent officers came to the pastor to complain. Father Moylan listened to a long harangue with his usual reserve until the delegates threatened that without beer no one would show up. The pastor quickly replied: "Yes, at least twenty-four, five priests and nineteen nuns." When the men persisted he arose and said firmly but not meanly: "I have only been here a short while but am fascinated that the Holy Name Society sends to me as petitioners for beer, three men to whom I have already administered the pledge." With that he walked out. Irish Night was a great success and went on without beer for five years, until the parish's public drinking habits were stabilized.

Three new groups—Sodality, St. Vincent de Paul, Cana Conference—became the spearheads of all the parish's recovered apostolic activity. The traditional societies remained to serve the valuable role of encouraging sacramental regularity and parochial camaraderie, benefits particularly important to the older parishioners. The new groups appealed to parishioners in the twenty to forty-five age range and to those ready to plan an active role in the apostolic work of the parish. The Sodality never grew to have more than a hundred and fifty members. St. Vincent de Paul work was confined to twelve carefully selected men, while twenty-five Cana couples ran the parish programs for married couples and participated in the diocesan Pre-Cana instruction of engaged couples. Together these two hundred-odd lay people all under forty-five became the sparkplugs of energy in every program of parish life.

The secret of leadership vitality—in Communist cells or old-time Jesuit Sodalities—is the existence of "the book," which leaders follow dutifully. Cana Conferences were new instruments during the 1950s, and their "outlines," first developed in Chicago, begot immediate enthusiasm and helped Christian marriage become the Church's "in" thing. The first Cana Conferences in St. Monica's brought into active parish membership people who hitherto were unknown to the priests. Here was an example of meeting parishioners at their level of need and motivating them to enlarge their vision of what it meant to be a Catholic. It was an apostolate that grew out of the family needs created by World War II, as parochial schools had been the Church's response to the Protestant Crusade against Catholics in the nineteenth century. Today Cana as a movement does not exist.

But today neither "the Sodality of Our Lady" (a Jesuit creation) nor "the St. Vincent de Paul Society" (an obvious offshoot of the French saint's apostolate) are effective apostolates of the Church. The Jesuits abandoned the Sodality because it was too churchy, while the Vincentians never had responsibility for the apostolate which bears their patron's name. Yet if one follows "the book" for both movements, one finds there the Church's spiritual tradition at its best. Both associations seek first the sanctification of their members, who then are invited to exemplify their holiness in deeds consonant with the goals established by the founders for their respective organizations. The Sodality, though co-opted by women in St. Monica's as elsewhere, could theoretically just as easily have been a man's or a mixed association. The program of spiritual formation was quite detailed and the committee work reinforced the formation process. The Sodality became a way of life for them, whether married or single. One young man confessed he found his future wife on a subway. She was one of a number of young ladies he observed each week engrossed always in taking notes as they conversed. He discovered that they usually prepared their weekly meetings going to work! These women took over the visitation of the neighborhood sick, especially those in cancer hospitals, and provided support for family life in the parish by linking their activity to the leadership in the Vincentian and Cana apostolates. At their urging and twice a year on two of Mary's Feast Days (December 8 and August 15), the parish celebrated in church the Solemn Benediction of Expectant Mothers. Both events became part of the parish support system for mothers, at a time when parenting was considered a noble but difficult Christian vocation.

The reorganized St. Vincent de Paul Society also became a source of joy to the pastor. Even Bishop Griffiths on his arrival in 1955 was impressed, and he did not lavish praise easily. Twelve men, between the ages of thirty and thirty-five, all married but two, followed their "little book" (as old as Frederick Ozanam), weekly meditation, spiritual reading, prayer together—as part of their readiness to carry on in the parish name the corporal and spiritual works of mercy. Beside this weekly meeting of two hours to review the scope of their activity, two Vincentians took duty each night to make an average of three home visits and continued doing this every week of the year. In the course of one fifty-two-week period, they regularly assisted eight hundred families, most of which related to some economic need such as food, clothing, employment, camp for the children, etc. But almost two hundred of those house calls in a given year dealt with situations arising in the school, the CCD program, or in the various adult programs. Each house call dealt with the total family situation not simply the narrow economic need. By virtue of their activity a large number of irregular marriages were rectified, parents were induced to send their children to the parochial school or released-time classes, to attend Sunday Mass, or to become active in parish affairs, to join the parish AA group, etc. Those twelve men became the eyes and ears of the priests and created a network of relationships which helped turn St. Monica's into one large family gathering.

You can judge a parish spirit by observing how many parishioners linger outside or around the Church property on a Sunday morning to say hello to the priests, to visit with the nuns, or merely to chat with each other. Parish social events can merely be a congregation of revelers seeking entertainment or the meeting place of people who know each other in the celebration of their common faith and in friendship. In 1945 the annual parish outing brought less than a hundred parishioners in two buses to a favorite campsite. By 1955 more than thirty buses were needed to carry one thousand denizens of the barbecue pit to their annual outdoor meeting place. And it never rained.

One advantage of living long and keeping in touch is the satisfaction of knowing that relationships forged with the Church and among people, which began on East Seventy-ninth Street, have lasted to this day.

THE CHANGING PARISH

By the time I became pastor in 1970, the parochial system itself had been weakened. What was once considered the "highest achievement of the American priest" had begun to show signs of age, losing status among young clergy, and becoming more the haven of the saved than a missionary arm of the Church. In some respects the very productivity of the system helped debilitate it, because parishes not infrequently became victims of benign enterprise by the priests who lived off the rich legacy left by nineteenth-century predecessors. Pastors were seen less as shepherds of souls, more as Administrators of the parish economy. Curates were priests known for their ritual performance more than as dominant public figures in local communities. In the post-World War II period the best services provided the faithful, after daily Mass, were provided by nuns, whose convents after hours were often busier than the next-door rectory. Still the system existed, if no longer fully utilized. The pastor was the boss, deferred to and, when push came to shove, obeyed. Priests appeared for daily Mass with remarkable fidelity, were always in their rectories at night, unless excused by the pastor, and they appeared together for routine tasks or whenever the pastor set a schedule. No priest ever absented himself for Saturday confessions and evening supper. They treated each other with respect in public, wore their clerical garb in the rectory office or when otherwise performing priestly duties, and recognized in theory, if not in practice, that they were subject to authority. The system, therefore, was intact, even if priestly life had become formalized in the process and priestly work less creative and less missionary. The abundant fruits pouring out of the system after World War II—high rates of religious observance, extraordinary expansion of religious institutions, vocations, convents, etc.—the result of the solid institutional motivations and procedures established by their predecessors, made it easy for other institutions to replace the parish as the center of Catholic life. The Catholic educational system had succeeded so well that building schools became more important than building Gothic churches. Religious women assumed ascendancy in the parish, at least as far as people's daily experience was concerned, while a parish priest's daily work load was light, unless he was a workaholic, as many were.

My generation of priests grew up reading French Abbé G. Michonneau's *Revolution in a City Parish* (1949), the book which made him famous worldwide. We were going to give the parish system new energy, make it more prayerful and more human, more truly Catholic, community-minded too, less parochial but more missionary, a social center for people but still apostolic. In response to one of Michonneau's pet peeves, we surely intended to reduce "the clink of money around the altar." And we thought our chances of success were better in the United States because our people, in contrast to the French, were churchgoers and priest lovers.

By 1970 there was a "new system" in place and to old-time Catholics, it was somewhat disorderly. A verbal picture of what transpired in the rectory life after 1965 is not easy to draw. One aging parish "pro" said it slyly: "My first pastor told me that he wasn't interested in how much theology I knew, but whether I was prepared to work. Recently the Chancery sent me a curate to do what I can to make him happy—if he's willing to accept the assignment." The emphasis had moved, he said, from the Church's mission to the priest's needs. The old "pro" was correct.

The shift was more therapeutic than pastoral and did little to enhance constituted authority.

The "new system's" fundamental assumptions—the supreme value of personalism, subjectivism, smallness, consensus, and the evil of structured living—had become the sacred cows of Catholic elites bent on fashioning a new Church. But in the doing they undermined the corporate purpose and priestly (religious) discipline. Church bodies became hostage to individualists, often those with little regard for tradition or official policy. One mother superior summarized the change as follows: "I rarely heard the word love used in my early days, but our convents saw a lot of it. Now we hear 'love' *ad nauseam* and I've never seen so much hostility."

The transformation, almost overnight, became a matter of large significance for parish life: first, because it undermined the role of pastors, who are responsible for God's revealed word, the sacraments, and governance of the Church; and secondly, because it reduced in value that which keeps the ecclesiastical machinery functioning smoothly, viz., the moral virtue of its chief officers.

Once our vocational commitment and obedience were attenuated, the priestly mission suffered. If the Pope came to be disrespected, or looked inept, over a long period, lower pastors found it almost impossible to maintain the Church's standards, let alone preserve the Christian patrimony. And this is the particular danger of our time. Unlike the religious orders, the parish is tied into the Bishop by direct connection and for the most part is still in the hands of a diocesan priest, who also has a special relationship with the Bishop. The revolutionary movements which have substantially broken the ties of religious communities and the colleges they once managed faithfully have their eyes on the Bishop connection of parish priests and their faithful. *The Notre Dame Study of Catholic Life* (1987), alleged to reflect what is currently happening in 195,000 parishes, claims that a new parish style is emerging, one which unfolds the mind of Vatican II and one which legitimates "pick and choose" Catholicism, where rejection of Church teachings is as appropriate as faithful religious observance. The summary of *The Notre Dame Study* by Joseph Gremillin and Jim Castelli insists that the "emerging parish" has two new ingredients—(1) a "Vatican II engendered sense of lay ownership of the Church" and (2) "Growing reliance by core Catholics on their own consciences in deciding what is moral and what is best for the Church."

In actual fact neither of these objectives can be legitimized by anything said by the recent Council, by Paul VI or John Paul II, or by the New Code of Canon Law. The parish is still the universal Church in miniature, designed to make disciples in the local neighborhood and to make those disciples as faithful as possible. We have only to read the gospels to know that in the parish vineyard we will find the hard-hearted, the fickle, the worldly, and apostates. The Church cannot expect to be any more successful with these than Christ was. However, the facts of Catholic life do not justify the conclusion that wandering Christians are thereby new prophets who dispense from Christ's demand that they live in accord with His teachings and keep His commandments—or forfeit eternal life (cf. John 8:31–32; Matthew 19:17). The present agitation for women priests and lay-run parishes is part of a strategy to undermine the hierarchy of the Church, as the birth-control controversy a generation ago separated Catholics from the Church's sexual ethic.

ST. JOHN THE EVANGELIST

By the time I took over as pastor of St. John the Evangelist Church on September 27, 1970, the niceties of system were all but gone, and a large part of the parish too.

The church, school, rectory, and convent were being razed to make way for a new Chancery Office and the relocation of Cathedral High School. The proposal to strip this 128-year-old parish had been discussed during Spellman's time as an abstract question, but Terence Cooke, almost immediately upon his installation as Archbishop, decided to move this project. The last person to be consulted was the old pastor, Msgr. William R. O'Connor, one of New York's distinguished priests.

Today, almost twenty years later, a twenty-one-story building graces First Avenue between East Fifty-fifth and Fifty-sixth streets, a symbol of Cooke's determination to replace dying institutional settings with new ones, and without cost to the already overburdened people of his Archdiocese. Even St. John's parishioners are happier today than they would ever have been remaining in their old and half-empty church quarters. But the birth of what is known today as "1011 First Avenue" was painful, unduly protracted, and at one point in danger of miscarriage.

In the spring of 1968 the diocesan takeover began to take flesh because the old Cathedral High School had to be abandoned without delay. In order to meet the requirements of the city's new safety code, the Archdiocese faced repair costs running to millions of dollars. Furthermore, the Chancery Office on Madison Avenue had outworn its usefulness. Archbishop John Maguire favored replacing St. John's properties during the Spellman regime and it remained Cooke's favored option. The midtown parish was accessible to public transportation. Its complex of buildings was underused. It was free of debt and Sutton Place never again would be a family neighborhood in the old sense. And new real estate in this area would have involved an outlay of $8 to 10 million. The Sisters of Charity, teaching in Cathedral High School, were involved in the remote planning from the beginning, but only on December 5, 1968, did the new Vicar General find time to inform Msgr. O'Connor officially about what Archbishop Cooke had in mind. All hell broke loose on East Fifty-fifth Street.

It was bad enough that the pastor and the people were upset, and legitimately so. But the Area Conference of the Priests' Senate, then a new diocesan structure and inclined to be antiestablishment, made things worse by agitating against the move, without its officers knowing anything about the complexities of the proposal and without sensitivity to the Archbishop's difficulties. To the new Archbishop, who was trying to find his way amicably through a tough but unpopular decision, the Area Conference became a source of annoyance. Finally, Cooke sent Msgr. Francis M. Costello, chairman of the Building Commission, to tell the priests they were wrong.

The pastor and the parishioners were critics of a different order. Msgr. O'Connor asked that no announcement be made until after January 1, 1969, arguing that the parish family was entitled to a peaceful Christmas holiday. The "truce" only provided a normally mild pastor the opportunity to get his dander up. All his life he was known to be a man of principle, as Bishop McIntyre and Cardinal Spellman had learned years before. He was not prepared to fight his Archbishop, even one twenty-five years his junior, but he was determined to place his views on the record. So, on Sunday, January 28, he mounted his pulpit at all masses to announce officially what Archbishop Cooke had in mind, with an advisory of his own that he disagreed with that judgment, that he had not really been consulted, and that the Archbishop's decision was final. One need not have sat in the pews that day to guess the stream of anger that was directed at Archbishop Cooke, especially by the parents of parochial school children.

The pastor's letter to Cooke (January 23) expressed "bewilderment and dismay." "The irony of the situation," he said, "is that with new apartment houses, our parish numbers will increase." His closing lines were words of protest: "No one ever asked me to present my views on these changes. Since, however, they affect our parish so vitally, I feel that, as pastor, I have an obligation to present my views quite frankly." The parishioners took up the cause with a vengeance, telling the Archbishop that they would hold a public meeting on Sunday, March 2, and demanded: "Inform us through our pastor who will attend this meeting." The fact sheet they distributed at all the masses on February 23 asserted in part: "It is hard to believe in today's social structure that such arbitrary, bureaucratic means can still be employed. At no time during this period of planning was anyone in the parish consulted or advised." Outrage that their properties, valued in the millions, purchased and improved by the generosity and exertions of many generations of parishioners, were being expropriated knew no bounds. They thought that Vatican II had put an end to this sort of thing.

Archbishop Cooke was distressed, and as Secretary for Education I was sent to meet with Msgr. O'Connor, an old friend, and to give him a sympathetic ear. In truth, we met to discuss the transfer of property rights. Where will the Church services be held? Who bears what costs? Will the parish priests be involved in the planning? No one, not even the Archbishop, could assuage the people. Cooke then sent Msgr. Francis M. Costello and me to the March 2 meeting of parish parents, which turned out to be stormy, indeed. The venom directed at Cooke's legates stopped short of the parishioners' hurling tomatoes. We returned through a back door to the rectory with the pastor, happy to remain there until the cover of darkness eased the leaving.

Archbishop Cooke continued to have problems. The original plan to have three distinct buildings—a church and rectory on East Fifty-fifth Street, a school on Fifty-sixth Street, a tall tower on First Avenue to house a Chancery Office—was scrapped for reasons of high cost. In its place a single twenty-one-storied multipurpose building with three internal components was substituted. Parishioners considered this further evidence of bad faith. They were now to be given a hundred-seat chapel for three years, then a permanent chapel in a building, not a traditional church of their own. Then, Mayor Lindsay intervened to deny variances that might have jeopardized the entire proposal, which originally called for an income-producing component. The Sutton Place community was also unfriendly to the idea of a high school in a fancy neighborhood, where the median income was thirty-three thousand in 1970 dollars. The natives were disconcerted, to say the least, by the prospect of black and Puerto Rican teenage girls roaming their streets before and after school hours. At one point, Mayor John V. Lindsay offered Archbishop Cooke city property on the West Side, out of harm's way as far as Sutton Place residents were concerned. But Cooke was determined—the parish property had been used for Church purposes for almost a century, the high school had functioned in midtown for more than forty years. It was also a perfect place for children of the poor to find part-time work which would help to pay their monthly tuition. Without further ado and considering the inability of anyone to deter using the property for religious purposes, Cooke proceeded to demolish the ninety-year-old church.

As he trotted off to Rome to receive the Cardinal's hat (April

28, 1969), Cooke rested easy with the thought that Mayor Lindsay no longer would give him trouble. Not so the churchgoers of St. John's, who were still waiting for him upon his return. The average parishioner might have been poor by Sutton Place standards (a median income of twelve thousand dollars), but in this context, each was a determined watchdog of his parochial rights. They even blamed Cooke for the stroke which later confined Msgr. O'Connor to a nursing home. What no one at the time anticipated was that Cardinal Cooke would send to St. John's as the new pastor, to heal the breaches there, one of the two people who sounded the death knell of the old church—his Secretary for Education. Overnight I went from a role as promoter of the Cardinal's interests to defender of the people's claims.

My first appearance in St. John's pulpit on September 13, 1970, was an occasion for Catholic people to show their best side. There was no advantage in pussyfooting. At all the masses that day my opening line was: "I know that I am speaking to a lot of you who hate my guts and who would prefer anyone else to be your pastor." Taking the bull by the horns, I recounted my long friendship with Msgr. O'Connor, apologized for all diocesan sins, reassured them of Cardinal Cooke's promises: "When our new church is built and our parish is fully restored, you will then see that Cardinal Cooke was right in moving St. John's into the twenty-first century, even though his decision caused pain to all of us in the twentieth." After the eleven o'clock Mass I heard one lady say to her companion: "I still hate him." Within the first week I created a Parish Advisory Team (later the Parish Council) to serve as a sounding board for the people and to be an instrument of communication with the Cardinal.

The role reversal from Cardinal's Secretary to pastor was not without its problems, however. Convincing an angry people that the Bishop's decision was sound became as difficult as guaranteeing that the Archdiocese would fulfill its commitment. The Cardinal did not need a distinguished parish remaining in a perpetual state of war with him. Yet not even he could foresee what diocesan middlemen, who neither heard the promises nor felt the people's anguish, might do in the name of cost cutting.

The presence of Msgr. Francis M. Costello, chairman of the archdiocesan Building Commission, made the double-role playing easier. He and his technical adviser, James Clavin, Philip Mitchell, the builder of the tower, Anthony Genovese, the architect for the church, and I were close friends. These relationships were extremely helpful since the diocese was in control of the entire construction, as if the parish did not preexist. The first priority for the diocesan officials was to build the high school. Naturally, building the parish church was placed on the back burner, a state of affairs which annoyed what now was a functioning Parish Council. Its members recalled in detail the promise made by the Cardinal that they would receive a church commensurate with their traditions. In those early days the parish prospects did not look auspicious. The space allotted looked like empty garage space—a rectangular area two stories high, flat-ceilinged with four square metal pillars driving down through the center of what would be the church's altar area. The story of how this tawdry space was turned into a beautiful church must begin with the genius of the architect, Tony Genovese, who created the design, and his selection of Benoit Gilsoul as the sculptor-painter of all the artifacts. Even the spiral staircase to the balcony was an artistic touch drawn into the plans by Genovese, although at one point one of the Cardinal's bookkeepers tried to eliminate it in the interests of saving fifteen thousand dollars.

The fundamental problem for me, however, was not simply the nickel-and-diming which regularly went on in the name of cost accounting. Understandably, lower officials think they please higher authority by controlling costs at the lowest level, regardless of the values involved. With the departure of Msgr. Costello from the Building Commission, the parish ceased to have an important role in determining the form and style of its own church. When questions were raised, the Cardinal intervened to ask for greater flexibility in dealing with the parish. One official was so shortsighted as to say that "perhaps the only identification needs to be the name of the church on the wall of the building." A complete year passed (1970–71) without consultation between diocese and parish. There was no published estimate of the budget set aside for church adornment, nor a list of what the budget included, no provision made for "parish space" within the tower for meetings, social affairs, etc. (The final diocesan expenditure came to $250,000.) Six months after the church opened (October 16, 1973), the Ecclesiastical Assistance Corporation, which managed the building complex, tried to charge St. John's parish $48,258 for rental space. Since the parish used 4 percent of the building space, it was scheduled to pay 4 percent of the operating costs. Once reminded, Cardinal Cooke understood that if either he or the pastor arose in the parish pulpit to suggest that St. John's people now must pay a "proportionate share of the base operating costs of the New York Catholic Center," both he and the pastor would need to go into hiding. A case might be made ten years later that the reconstructed parish should pay usage costs. But not in 1973 when the archdiocesan obligations to St. John's had not been rendered adequately, particularly when the Parish Council was fully aware that the parish's million-dollar properties had been signed over to the Archdiocese for the "mythical" one dollar. The members also knew that $150,000 of parish money was spent to clean up and improve the chapel and rectory space allegedly "given" to the parish in lieu of the properties taken by right of eminent domain.

The other difficulty we faced was the change in the parish population by virtue of the four-year hiatus from old to new church. A parish that serves less than a thousand people in New York has to justify its existence when contiguous parishes could supply neighborhood needs just as easily. Actually, fifteen thousand Catholics lived within the territorial confines, most of them worshiping elsewhere, including two thousand of old-time St. John's parishioners. The first gambit was to organize a parish census. Letters were mailed to a large number of locals drawn from parish records and the telephone company's street list, notifying them that a priest would be visiting them. A dry run on fifty families demonstrated how easy census-taking is to those who are comfortable doing it. Most Catholics welcome a priest who says he would like to bless the home. Actually, some of the visited parishioners had rarely seen a priest in their building, let alone within their home. A good amount of good will was created in the first months as the visitations multiplied. However, this parish census was never completed because the priests were not interested. Such visitations had never been part of their training or priestly experience. And there was nothing left to Church discipline to make them do it. Excuses were always the same—census-taking was not possible in New York. Yet the loss to the Church when priests remained rectory-bound continued to be incalculable.

Inaugurating an Open House on Sundays and having the priest standing outside the church before and after all the masses, also paid dividends. It still fascinates me how much outreach to people is accomplished on weekends, the only time when the faithful have ready access to priests, if the latter make themselves available. People are appreciative of service, and when the little chapel was dolled up to look more like a House of God, even the singing and the collections improved. For Catholics it is still the liturgy that counts, whether celebrated in St. Peter's Basilica or a basement church. Carefully celebrated, the Mass is sheer drama, as surely as was the Crucifixion of Christ. Preaching remained a problem whenever the celebrant was a poor speaker or had little worthwhile to say. But it was the Mass that still mattered.

The most difficult part, however, of reorganizing a vital parish without a school is to decide what ought to be done for the people between Monday and Friday. A well-run parish depends on a sense of purpose, a plan and a team. If a parish has a school population of eight hundred, a CCD audience of eight hundred more, four hundred baptisms annually, two hundred funerals, and two hundred weddings, the pastor need not worry about work. In such a parish the priests almost knock each other down moving in and out through various doors. But in a parish like St. John's, going out to the people with service, being available to them, planning religious rites and lectures on their behalf, organizing the activists to widen the parish apostolate, knowing how to respond to people's need, how to suffer with them in their time of pain—these are the initiatives which create a parish. The memorable priests are those who are there when it counts most, who can turn a ride to the cemetery into a spiritual experience. The great parish priests are always outstanding social apostles: they bless sterile wives who go on to become mothers; they open parish doors to Alcoholics Anonymous and Daytop; they reach down deep for the money which pays someone's rent; they follow their criminals into the jailhouse; and they know where to find jobs. Knowing where and how to find a job for a parishioner is an important skill for any parish priest. All it takes usually is to be on friendly terms with the heads of the local employment agencies, who are as much interested in quality people as any pastor.

Since Vatican II the Church has been laying great emphasis on the social apostolate, even at the parish level, more than it once did. The parish is not the diocese, of course, so there is a limit to what its lay leaders can do to alleviate situations of national or international import. But they should be involved in the social concerns of the neighborhood, and whether they be Parish Council members, Vincentians, or Legionaires, there are needy people out there, needy in soul as well as body, whose social situation requires correction before they are ready to be addressed on matters usually called religious. In St. John's a tradition developed of working with the Salvation Army, the local synagogue, and the Lutheran pastor on a variety of civic and ecumenical interests. Probably the most important service the parish rendered in a wealthy section of the city to the concept of social reform was to raise the consciousness of Catholics about the social issues— peace and poverty, mainly—through meetings and sermons. About the time we were midway through the parish-building program, Paul VI was speaking of "new poor," i.e., those who do not easily fit into society, of "minority groups" too, i.e., those without equality before the law, and "migrants," who find it difficult to claim their legitimate social rights. Personal service still was the parish's high priority, but its social dimension was not neglected.

One of the most memorable situations arose in St. John's one Saturday afternoon in 1971 when a young German immigrant named Carl showed up at the rectory looking for someone to pay his rent in the nearby Sutton Hotel. The Sutton Hotel was not the Waldorf, but in its day it was a prestige home away from home for Hollywood stars. A Catholic but no churchgoer, Carl opened his dealings with the pastor somewhat arrogantly and demandingly. But every veteran priest knows the con game very well. The professional panhandler presents a sad story at the tail end of a Friday afternoon or on a weekend, when all agencies are closed and stories are difficult to check. Carl was asking for a considerable amount of money to forestall a dispossession. His tale was good—an immigrant who broke his leg (it was in a cast). Because of it, he lost his job as a chef, and now was alone in New York and about to be put out on the street. The story sounded too flimsy to be true. The hotel manager, however, confirmed that up to this moment Carl had been a sober well-behaved resident, sufficient reason to give Carl momentary relief and rent at least for the weekend. To test his sincerity, however, he was asked to return on the following day, which he did. Did he know anyone in New York who could verify his claim. No. Nobody. But he did have a doctor friend in Los Angeles. Did the doctor have a telephone number? Yes. Carl's medical friend proved to be within phone's reach and his account of Carl's post-World War II life proved to be heart-wrenching. A boy of thirteen in 1945, Carl was thrown out of his home by his mother's new husband, forced to wander Germany during his teenage years, eking a living as best he could. He was a bitter man, the doctor said, but good, one who deserved better from life, and if he now had a broken leg, it would be another typical catastrophe for a very sad and perhaps an unbalanced man. Could we get him to Los Angeles, the doctor asked, assuring that he would take care of Carl from there. Within hours Carl was on his way west, a paid ticket and a little travel money in his pocket. Nothing more was heard from Carl until one day six months later his German voice was heard on the other end of the telephone. He was back in Frankfurt with relatives, courtesy of his doctor friend. He was calling now merely to say thanks.

The dedication of the new Church of St. John the Evangelist, April 14, 1973, was called "the fifth spring of St. John's parish." The blaring trumpets announced that a church in Sutton Place was alive and well. The overflow crowd of parishioners, all ages and various social classes, celebrated the rebirth with hardly a

memory of the dying that went before. Indeed, the four-year tra-
vail had only quickened both the interest and the pride of the
faithful in their own parochial origins and traditions, duly reported for the occasion in the pastor's book-size history. St.
John's had been born and reborn five times, beginning in 1840 on
the site where St. Patrick's Cathedral now stands, bumped from
place to place around what later became Madison Avenue until,
after the Cathedral opened its doors for Catholic worship in 1879,
it finally arrived at its present site.

The anguish of the rebirth process from 1969 onward was
small compared to what was endured by the first pastor and his
people in 1839 when John Maginnis was told to create the first
midtown parish, midtown literally in the widest sense because his
live-in parishioners were mostly two or three miles to the north
and south of East Fiftieth Street. We moderns tend to forget, if we
ever knew, how pioneering those nineteenth-century priests and
laity were. Maginnis often operated out of a tent. How fluid the
times and the Church were in that century is seen in the fact that
after serving St. John's for two years, and St. Andrew's at City
Hall for ten more, Maginnis crossed the country by way of Cape
Horn to found the first English-speaking parish in San Francisco,
not surprisingly named St. Patrick's. His late-in-life friendship
with Archbishop Joseph Alemany kept him in Golden Gate territory until he died in 1864. Michael Curran, one of his successors
at St. John's on Fifth Avenue, later commenting on what his
priesthood was like in those days, spoke of his early experience
with rural farmers, among whom "he could find no shelter except
the hallway of a tavern, with his valise for a pillow." The 1850
pastor, James McMahon, in almost no time at all faced six thousand churchgoers every Sunday morning, often without the help
of another priest. Those parishioners, too, were scattered over
three square miles of a city already moving northward. In his
spare time McMahon was expected to minister to the religious
needs of prisoners incarcerated on an island in the East River!

It was easy for the 1973 pastor, therefore, at the rededication
to remind his reborn parish that the strength of the Church, as
well as its weakness, "is due more to what went on within the

264

Church than without, as much to the faith, the conceptions and the workmanship of an unusual corps of Catholic leaders as to Catholic oppressors. The pioneers of the American Church knew what they were to do and did it with a relish." Then, as if to drive the point home for my 1973 audience, I added: "It is less than fair to find the explanation of or lay the blame for contemporary malaise on social pressures from a hostile American environment. As our strengths are our own, so are our weaknesses." The Church of St. John, I concluded, had contributed a great deal to the lives of the seven hundred and fifty thousand people it had served over one hundred thirty-three years, and its recovery should be taken as an omen of what awaited the U.S. Church in the twenty-first century.

A TIME TO GO

Into every life there come moments for making important decisions. When that person is a priest, serious thought about an assignment or employment cannot be entertained by him alone. During the spring of 1970 the Vincentian president of St. John's University, Father Joseph T. Cahill, C.M., sent word that he was interested in having me take a new professional chair he was about to create. The John A. Flynn Chair in Contemporary Catholic Problems, to be named after one of Father Cahill's predecessors, was an attractive offer, although academic life up to that point in time held no great charm. But circumstances do alter cases and Father Cahill's "chair" seemed to be the right size. And the timing was right.

By 1970 the Church's burning issues were national in scope, not parochial. Indeed, parish life was being adversely affected more by what was going on within the National Conference of Catholic Bishops than what was happening in "452" or the local Chancery Office. A Secretary for Education to a New York Cardinal by the nature of things is involved in those problems too. But it was also clear that Catholic colleges were contributing most to the Catholic crisis in every diocese.

265

St. John's University was well known to Cardinal Spellman, especially after the 1965 strike of its faculty against the Vincentian leadership. In 1966 Spelly sent John Meng to my office for a discussion of the issues involved in the strike. Meng, then president of Hunter College, was counselor to the St. John's administration, and this meeting was my introduction to the internal affairs of the university. Spellman expressed his sympathy with the Vincentians but, since the university was located in Queens (the Staten Island campus of SJU was still four years away), the Cardinal was not involved. However, when Father Cahill explained to him that the Vincentians intended to resist a takeover by an outside union, led by non-Catholics, Spelly got off one of his typical cracks, "Father, if it's war, it's war." The St. John's president was then, as he is twenty-odd years later, firm in his commitment to the institution's Catholicity. Later, in 1966, he attended a meeting in Spellman's New York education office to explore the post-Vatican II threats to the religious affiliation of all Catholic colleges, and it was there that I first met him.

When Father Cahill's offer to me was made known to Cooke, the Cardinal's response was positive, but cautious. He recognized the time had come for change in Education Secretaries, but he also liked to keep his priests, where possible, close to home. Customarily, Bishops alone choose which of their priests go to "outside" work—in Washington, Rome, or elsewhere. Cooke sometimes used "elsewhere" as a way of ridding himself of troublesome priests who had "marketable" doctorates. Oftentimes, this merely meant his moving troubles out of New York to "elsewhere." When he offered the pastorate of St. John the Evangelist as part of his agreeing to my professorship, the understanding was mutual. Taking two posts at one time was not uncommon in the New York Archdiocese. My four years as pastor turned out to be an enriching experience. Several aspects of that pastorate involved a little derring-do, one of which was persuading a distinguished Montreal firm to build a ninety-thousand-dollar pipe organ worthy of the parish history and the local churchgoers. The organ stands today as one of the church's well-remarked features. The other was the establishment of what became the James J.

Flood Scholarship Fund for the education of poor children. The parish contributed a hundred thousand dollars to this fund, named after one of St. John's great pastors, who worked East Fifty-fifth Street from 1880 to 1923. This priest's pastorate was so long and distinguished that it is still spoken of as "The Era of the Great Flood."

By 1974 the parish was alive and St. John's University was deeply involved with the Vatican in the contest over Catholic higher education. If ever there developed a case where no one can serve two masters, it evolved in the growing tug of war between the pastor and the professor. It was not possible to be both successfully, once the scope of each developed to demand complete commitment. This was especially true of the pastorate, where the availability of effective associate priests was by then hard to come by. No one knew this difficulty better than someone who had spent twenty years in the pastoral ministry. So, on May 30, 1974, on the thirty-second anniversary of my priesthood, I resigned to become a full-time professor and ten days later the Cardinal accepted it. His words were generous:

> I wish to thank you for your dedicated service as Pastor during these years of transition and development. When I appointed you Pastor four years ago, I felt sure the people of St. John's would find in you a good shepherd and they have—and, therefore, they will miss you very much.
>
> I am also grateful for the excellent contribution you are making to Catholic higher education at St. John's University. I understand, to some extent, the great work that must be accomplished and I am proud of the talent and experience that you bring to this important mission of the Church. I guess it cannot be done part-time.
>
> Under the circumstances I accept, with regret, your resignation as Pastor of the Church of St. John the Evangelist.

SIX

From Teaching
to Controversy

THERE IS A WELL-TOLD STORY—and true—about a seminarian who successfully plied his way through to the diocesan priesthood by pretending to be a hippie. He grew a beard, wore jeans, and walked around looking disheveled. On one occasion in preparation for his final exams, he boned up on all those propositions condemned by Pius X during the Modernist Controversy (1907) and fed them back as true to his post-Vatican II faculty, later to find he passed with flying colors! Once ordained, he cut his hair, shaved his beard, donned his black suit and Roman collar, and went out to perform his ministry in accordance with the strict Roman Catholic agenda. He insists to this day that if he gave evidence during seminary days that he was a "Catholic square," he would have been sent packing.

The story is weird, I know, but not so atypical of what has been going on in many quarters of the Church in recent years, where Catholics who want to do the right thing have to fight their way through a bad system.

It was not always so. During the pre- and post-World War II period, it was fun to be a Catholic and more fun to be a priest. And it was easy to teach the faith to non-Catholics and a joy to explain it to our own. I had an adult instruction class from 1945–55, which attracted the attention of the local Jehovah's Witnesses, newcomers to our area. They liked to harass Catholics with a superabundance of usually irrelevant biblical citations, but once they came to accept the rules, we enjoyed having them and acquired a few converts along the way. Between 1955 and 1965 Brother John Egan ran a marriage preparation course for his four hundred seniors at Iona College, all young men then. It was a breeze to outsiders like myself. The Irish Christian Brothers did a good job of preconditioning these twenty-one-year-olds about sex. Still, discussing marriage, contraception, and babies with them was quite a relaxed experience, often very funny, as the young men roared whenever the tables were turned either on Brother Egan, me, or some wiseacre in the audience. They may not all have been, but their girls, if not their training, would have helped the vast majority to maintain their virginity.

My first articles for *The Sign,* then the widest-read Catholic magazine in the U.S., or the Jesuit *America,* known and respected for its political judgments and for its fidelity to Church norms, were harmless little things like "How to Be a Good Husband," "How to Be a Good Wife," "Responsible Parenthood." The content was less pop psychology than the reinforcement of Catholic principles and values. Even my first "controversial" articles in the 1940s on white-collar workers or calling for more openness to blacks by trade unions or on the right of government workers to strike, written for *Commonweal,* were inoffensive and hardly argumentative. The Church's social teaching may not have been widely known or appreciated, but if the Pope said it, you were not going to get much of an argument from Catholics. In spite of the great success of my marriage books during the pre-Vatican II period, by 1963 when Doubleday published my *Birth Control and Catholics,* the Catholic market for books with an *imprimatur* had just about disappeared. The sexual revolution was underway and antiestablishment Catholic authors were the ones dominating the sales of publishing houses. The era of anti-Catholic polemics had begun—this time led by Catholics. As Robert Kaiser explained the reversal: "Loyalty to the Church, as newly defined by Vatican II, did not necessarily mean loyalty to the Pope or to the crowd that played on his fears. The Church was now the people of God."[1]

It would be a mistake, however, to think that the revolutionaries popped out of nowhere, or that Catholic malcontents did not exist in the World War II period. The Church was too big not to have them, although the systems of control and the internalized discipline of the membership made them hardly noticeable or looked upon as deviants. Later on, Jesuits like John McKenzie and Daniel Berrigan would complain about their Catholic training either at the hand of parents or of Jesuits. Greg Schneider, son of that great and pious Fordham psychologist Alexander, and aide at one time to candidates Jimmy Carter and Mike Dukakis, publicly damned the Church for "screwing up" its people better than anyone. And, hardly anyone in the United States has been left in ignorance of Phil Donahue's venom about his Catholic formation process, although the TV huckster knew his sainted mother would not approve. But most of us were very proud of our large families and of our large parishes, of the Church which brought the likes of Avery Dulles into it and Louis Budenz back to it.

It is not surprising, perhaps, that the Church was run over roughshod during the turbulence of the 1960s. It is less understandable that the Church's "pit bulls" were allowed to chew her body to bits with no one in authority having the sense to call the ecclesiastical cops. The savagery with which almost the most sacred of Catholic beliefs and moral norms were doubted, disparaged, or denied by internal enemies, with no comparable counterforce from those who were the sole legislators—executives—judges of things Catholic will give rise to volumes uncountable by historians in centuries to come.

My active and major entry into the world of post-Vatican II polemics came in 1976 when Dale Francis, editor for Our Sunday Visitor Press, persuaded publisher and Maryknoll priest Alfred Nevins to accept a book to which he gave title *Who Should Run the Catholic Church?* The small volume suggested that theologians and social scientists were running the Church, a thesis which unfolded, not as a result of the birth-control controversy, but during the controversy over first confession for children. Here was a strange battleground, more symbolic of the Church's real problem than the birth-control fight ten years earlier. After all, a fight for unrestrained sex at least involved primitive urges. But first confession for children? Why were Catholic educators so anxious to get rid of it?

Subsequent events would reveal that the principle under attack was not a necessary ritual for eight-year-olds, but the right of the Holy See to determine the religious formation of Catholics.

First confession for second-graders, the new scholars said, only began with Pius X in 1910 and (theologically speaking) was not really required for the reception of Holy Communion at so young an age. Eight-year-olds were incapable of serious sin and, if forced to confess sin at an early age, were likely to develop psychological problems—excessive guilt being one—when they reached adulthood. Critics of the discipline conjured up stereotypes of sixty-five-year-old Catholics who still confessed disobedience of parents or who accused themselves of sins which were not sins at all. Many mature Catholics, it was said, though sinless, abstained from communion if they were not able to confess. Millions of Catholics, who lined up every Saturday night for absolution, would hardly have recognized themselves in these stereotypes, but they were repeated so often during the first-confession controversy that by the end of the 1970s Saturday night confessional lines all but disappeared.

In this particular confrontation between the Church and her new theologians, two different views—of nature and of Church—faced each other in opposition. Catholic tradition called for the Christian person and the Christian community to find their fulfillment in the Church. Christ commanded apostles to "make disciples of all nations," so what was more eminently reasonable than that the Church would be the source of norms for both personhood and community. By this shall all men know that you are my disciples: Worship God, be baptized, do penance, celebrate the Eucharist, live good lives, love one another, etc.

Doing penance was an important mark of the Catholic Christian from the first days. Christ who died to save His people from their sins instituted the sacrament of Penance as His instrument for helping weak men and women to attain holiness and salvation. Christians were expected to internalize concepts of sin and programs of remedy as well. And they were to have an urgent concern about both. The Catholic, therefore, was called upon to learn the proper norms for Christian life and should he deviate he was to take the proper steps to return himself to "the state of grace." This formation process normally began within the family under the tutelage of parents. In 1910 Pius X brought the Church into children's lives when he initiated what up to the twentieth century was unprecedented—the reception of the sacraments of Penance and the Eucharist at the tender age of eight. The practice became a normal and acceptable element in the religious training of young Catholics during the remainder of the twentieth century.

Who Should Run the Catholic Church? was an effort to demonstrate how contemporary social science theories were used to undermine the penitential discipline of the Church. The fight over children's confession and the attempt to popularize general absolution were little more than efforts by scholars to make private confession and private absolution a matter of personal choice, not something necessary to ordinary Christian life. Indoctrination and obedience (i.e., "teaching them to observe all that I have commanded you") became well-nigh universal no-no's among religious orders and in the Catholic schools they dominated: "If you do not get anything out of Mass, you do not have to go," became a new adage. Concern for eternal life, adherence to Church norms, and Catholic identity were being replaced by a training for human betterment in this world, for freedom of conscientious decision-making by Christians presumed to be mature, and for openness to other Christian bodies. Several inherent contradictions in the new catechetics became obvious immediately. How does one intensify Catholic social consciousness on the basis of Church teaching while exalting the sanctity of the individual conscience against Church teaching? How can the Church impose new social obligations on a people being retrained to pick and choose their own way through the demands of the universal Faith? Or, why should anyone take the Church seriously if Christ never really established a church at all?

John Cardinal Wright, Paul VI's Vicar for Catechetics, understood better than anyone the significance of the first-confession fight. Priests like Father Alfred Nevins, M.M., needed no special urging from Rome to take up the cudgels on behalf of the General Catechetical Directory (1972), which insisted on the continuance of the practice of first confession first. (The New Code of Canon Law, promulgated eleven years later, specifies that first communion be preceded by sacramental confession.) Father Nevins wanted an article for *The Priest* on the subject and I wrote to his specifications with a question: *"Confession before First Communion?"* (October 1972). What is fascinating about the dispute is that the "experts," who insisted on parents' involvement in the first-communion process, were also prepared to ignore parents should they insist on first confession. Once any diocesan office decided there was to be no first confession, children were to be denied the opportunity to confess their sins. It was as simple as that. What turned out to be the novelty was the refusal of pastors to interfere with teachers or diocesan educators who insisted on scuttling the established and still authorized discipline.

By 1976 the battle for the soul of the U.S. Church had reached a serious stage. David Tracy, then an upcoming president of the Catholic Theological Society, wrote a book maintaining it was no longer possible for a Christian to justify his doctrinal beliefs by an appeal to the Bible or to the official teaching of the Church. The editor of *Commonweal* attributed the Church's dwindling constituency to Pope Paul's preoccupation with the so-called "deposit of faith," which he reputedly handled "as if it were a lump of gold in a strong box to which he jealously guards the key." The New Catholic Encyclopedia made bold to advise its updated constituency that dissent from authoritative Church teaching was "a legitimate option for Catholics." The National Catholic Education Association battled on two fronts—against Rome's efforts to restore its oversight of catechesis and Catholic higher education. Andrew Greeley devoted one of his syndicated columns to a piece I did in 1976 for *The Critic*, called "The Uncertain Church: The New Catholic Problem." He called it "demented drivel," sneering at any effort to divide the Church into "good and bad guys," he being completely comfortable with his "good guys," i.e., those engaged in dismantling Catholic institutions. The article could not have been published in a more appropriate place, since its reading public included the leading members of the Catholic revolution then in progress. Nothing ever wrote stirred up so much anger in the right places in a short space of time. Avery Dulles in an article for *The Long Island Catholic* thought Msgr. Kelly used "slick debating tactics to discredit his adversaries" and invented "a scapegoat as a fifth column conspiring against the Church from within." Dulles' basic argument against the article's thesis was that ecclesiastical discipline would not restore the Church's credibility: "Msgr. Kelly's magisterium of popes and bishops carries very little weight with the vast majority of Catholics." Arguing that the Catholic crisis was brought on by changing times and the mass media, Dulles advised: "The credibility of Catholicism must be established in some more effective way than by crozier thumping or by the rather bland statements that generally come out of Roman Congregations and National Bishops' Conferences." The monsignor's problem, Dulles thought, was Kelly's passion for "cheap certitude," the kind that accepts every Roman document as if it were the very Word of God.

That the Church's problems were the fault of the mass media was an oft-used rationalization by those who were calling important Church teachings into doubt. They never explained satisfactorily how the Church lost its credibility with its own faithful within ten years. What about those protest meetings, press releases, newspaper advertisements, TV appearances, and well-publicized lectures to Catholic audiences by dissenting Catholic professors? One would be rash, indeed, to speak of a "fifth column" in Marxist terms, unless Charles Curran's activity at Catholic University in 1967 and 1968 qualified. Organized every moment or not, post-Vatican II dissenters regularly reinforced each other often enough to qualify for the description "conspiracy." In the early years after the Council, Avery Dulles was an active participant. It will take many years before the Church recovers from his 1976 advocacy of a "second magisterium" residing in theologians, with the complementary suggestion that teaching statements of bishops be "co-authored." Father Dulles was also president of the Catholic Theological Society when the notorious book *Human Sexuality* was in production. By 1976 Father Dulles' *Models of the Church,* a popular manual for college and seminary ecclesiology courses, became a much more serious assault on the institutional Church. Not only did he assert there (in a book incidentally which did not qualify for an *imprimatur)* that there was "a comparatively meager basis in scripture and in early Church tradition" for an institutional Church, but the ecclesiology on which such a Church was built was, he said, "out of phase with the demands of the times." Said Dulles:

> In an age of dialogue, ecumenism, and interest in world religions, the monopolistic tendency of this model is unacceptable. In an age when all large institutions are regarded with suspicion or aversion, it is exceptionally difficult to attract people to a religion that represents itself as primarily institutional. As sociologists have noted, we are experiencing in our age the breakdown of closed societies. While people are willing to dedicate themselves to a cause or a movement, they do not wish to bind themselves totally to any institution. Institutions are seen as self-serving and repressive and as needed to be kept under strong vigilance. In our modern pluralistic society, especially in a country such as the United States, people do not experience any given church as a necessary means of giving significance to their lives but they may prefer a certain church as providing services that could not equally be obtained elsewhere. Fulfillment and significance are things that an individual usually finds more in private than in the public sphere, more in the personal than in the institutional.[2]

In this year when The Fellowship of Catholic Scholars came into being, Dulles was asserting in ecumenical workshops that

275

Christ's Church was not adequately identical with any existing ecclesiastical organization. In formal lectures to various Catholic and ecumenical audiences, here and abroad, (which he finally published in 1982 as *A Church to Believe In),* Dulles admitted his uncertainty about Christian origins, about whether we can speak of revealed doctrines, about the time at which the episcopate came into existence, what the precise meaning of papal primacy might be, whether every believer need confess the solemnly defined truths concerning Mary's Immaculate Conception and Assumption, and so forth. *A Church to Believe In* is little more than activist advocacy of political positions in opposition to important Church positions reiterated time and time again by the Church's highest authority.

Doubleday's well-known Catholic editor John Delaney telephoned one day to enquire whether I would like to expand *The Critic* article into a book. *The Battle for the American Church* became that book in 1979. Those dubbed "right-wingers" liked *The Battle,* except Lefebvrites, who said it spoke lies about their hero. Those who considered themselves "bridge builders," because they took no sides in the guerrilla war, argued that theologians like Charles Curran or Avery Dulles or Richard McCormick were misunderstood. The issues, they said, were much more complicated than I described them. Those who prided themselves on their "liberal" affiliation hated the book, because its five hundred pages gave chapter and verse against the various claims of dissent.

The Crisis of Authority: John Paul II and the American Bishops (Regnery Gateway) was a natural follow-up to *The Battle,* although it would never have come into being without Dale Vree, editor of the *New Oxford Review,* then an Episcopalian. He telephoned from the West Coast one day soliciting a major book review. He expressed appreciation for *The Battle.* When I said, "There's a new ball game with John Paul II," Vree became intrigued with the notion that the election of the new Pope shifted "the battle" to a new arena, i.e., the halls of Bishops. What would they do to reinforce the objectives of the new Pope, who seemed to mean business? Dale Vree thought this would make a good article for his magazine. When several months later he received a draft of the proposed article, Vree telephoned to say the story was too depressing to publish. At the time he was trying to move his Episcopal diocese toward Rome, so that any suggestion that the Catholic Church had problems little different from Episcopalians hardly helped his cause. The proposed article then developed into *The Crisis of Authority* and argued that U.S. Bishops and John Paul II were on different wavelengths in matters of teaching faith, morals, and Catholic discipline.

The Crisis brought Jesuits out of the closet as *The Battle* never did. *America* magazine dismissed the earlier work with a one-liner —Kelly consigns the post-Vatican II Church to a position somewhere between a rock and a hard place. But for *The Crisis,* Jesuit editor Joseph O'Hare called upon Msgr. George G. Higgins to be his battering ram. Higgins, a longtime critic of Bishops even while employed in their Washington office, appeared as a defender of Bishops against Kelly. "With a heavy heart," Higgins accused Kelly of "theological hatred," of writing "an intemperate, even vituperative book." Said Higgins: "It gives me no satisfaction to be crossing swords with a friend of such long standing." Actually Higgins was simply an associate in a common cause of social justice, not always on the same side. He had a long record of shouting down his critics and was, therefore, a good choice to cut the book to ribbons, to choose words like "vigilante" to describe me, and with enough information about mutual friendships to manipulate his evaluation to my disadvantage.

Msgr. Higgins simply denied the thesis that the Roman ball was now in the U.S. Bishops' court. (Subsequent ecclesial events prove how wrong he was.) But to discredit my thesis, Higgins had to discredit me, to show what a scoundrel I really was: "Kelly's crude slap in the face at [Msgr. John Tracy] Ellis in his new book is his way of telling his old friend to get lost—that his orthodoxy is in question." Factually, Ellis' name never appeared in the book. The book merely notes that the U.S. Bishops in 1970 chose six known critics of things episcopal to research questions on the Catholic priesthood, reports which for the most part turned out to be disasters. Ellis wrote one of those reports, a piece of information which normal readers of *The Crisis* would not have known. The question of someone's orthodoxy never arose, even with the mention that four of the selected researchers eventually left the priesthood. (Only Ellis and Greeley remained.) But by introducing Ellis' name Higgins hoped to gain credibility for his long-standing membership in the academic circles I was criticizing. His final judgment was that the book was, "an unmitigated disaster," a conclusion not necessarily demonstrable if the later judgments of John Paul II and Joseph Cardinal Ratzinger (whose conduct in office Higgins later deplored) are taken into account.[3]

It was strange for Higgins to introduce the "orthodoxy" issue at all, because he himself was somewhat vulnerable. For many years he had aligned himself with dissenters in many areas, although before Vatican II he was a typical representative of the prevailing mood of Catholic actionists, "Have papal encyclical, will travel." After 1965, however, his approved papal letters would not include *Humanae Vitae*. I sent *America* a reply to the Higgins' critique—through Regnery-Gateway—the opening paragraphs of which editor Joseph O'Hare, S.J., failed to publish:

> I respond most reluctantly to questions about Msgr. George Higgins' rage that anyone should state publicly that the Church in the U.S. is in difficulty or marshalls publicly known facts in defense of this thesis. He does not seem to admit there are such problems, except in the minds of vigilantes. His intemperate, and even vituperative review of *The Crisis of Authority* in *America* magazine is not altogether out of character. But I am pleased to see him emerge as a defender of bishops since a good part of his priestly life has been spent criticising, sometimes opposing, them.
>
> The last time we confronted each other was 1965 one night in the Staff House of what would become the *United States Catholic Conference*, where Fr. Higgins was asserting with certitude, because he wanted it so, that Paul VI would change Catholic doctrine on contraception. We know how wrong he was then not only on a point of fact but on a point of Catholic doctrine as well.

Difficult for outsiders sometimes to understand is the nature of the core issues in dispute, viz., questions of faith and morals, not simply differences of opinion about Church policy, and also the punishing power priests like Higgins had acquired to protect the turf of dissidents, most frequently by disparaging their critics. Msgr. Higgins also defended Richard McCormick's moral views as legitimate, even though they were contradictory to Church teaching. When Charles Curran was called to Rome to defend himself (and failed) before the Congregation for the Doctrine of the Faith, his companion and counselor was George Higgins. As early as 1976 that punishing power of subalterns was used against Archbishop Bernardin when the president of *NCCB* in that year made a public statement on abortion which seemed to favor Republican Gerald Ford's run for a presidential term in his own right more than that of Democrat Jimmy Carter's aspiring candidacy. Higgins and some of his USCC cohorts threatened to resign from USCC and make public protest if that statement stood. Bernardin ate crow, and Higgins remained at his USCC post until retirement. It was not surprising, therefore, that O'Hare chose Higgins to bury *The Crisis* in 1981. Three years later with an assist from Avery Dulles, he bullied the Ethics and Public Policy Center in Washington, D.C., into not publishing James Hitchcock's *The Pope and the Jesuits,* threatening to conduct a nationwide campaign against the center. Although paid in advance to write the critique of the Jesuits, Hitchcock was forced to find another publisher.

In any event, even with *America* doing its best, *The Crisis* received more attention than *The Battle* did, particularly from Jesuits. One well-known Jesuit at Georgetown wrote: "Your *The Crisis of Authority* is excellent. It is exactly the shot of intellectual and religious adrenalin I need." How did he come upon the book? In the Woodstock Library, where it was jutting out of the stacks irregularly because Msgr. Higgins' review had been pasted into the book's cover! Said he: "What you say about the various state of my beloved Society is too true, though you touch only the tip of the iceberg." Another Jesuit, this time from the West, whose letter to *America* never found its way into print, told Father Joseph O'Hare that the Higgins review was "irresponsible" and accused the editors of "bias." Editor O'Hare took his confrere sufficiently seriously to respond to his complaints with a personal note, calling Msgr. Kelly's view of Catholicism "exotic," a word meaning "from a strange country" (or from a strange Church), "alien" or "outlandish." O'Hare's choice of words was purposeful, suggesting that the insider was really an outsider, if he followed "alien" positions from Rome. However, another Jesuit, Kenneth Baker, explained the crisis this way: "There is a crisis in the *exercise* of authority because an elite group of theologians and journalists has terrorized the bishops into silence and inactivity." This was the major point of *The Crisis.*

Toward the end of his vitriol about *The Crisis*, Msgr. Higgins appealed to the authority of Father Raymond E. Brown, to demonstrate (in the latter's words) that "the bishops do not see disagreement with theologians to be such a great problem—certainly not as great as militant vigilantes would make it." Brown is further called upon to assure the unwary that the theologians who are criticized "are openly praised by the magisterium both here and abroad." Kelly and "his soul mates," therefore, are absurd.

Little did Msgr. Higgins know in 1981 that my next book would be *The New Biblical Theorists: Raymond E. Brown and Beyond* (Servant Publications). *The Battle* had ignored the biblicists' role in the shaping the internal conflicts with magisterium. For one thing, hardly anyone blames a bad house on brickmakers, which is what biblicists are to theology. For another, it was not easy for me in 1979 to make a solid case against biblical critics. Even two years later when *The Crisis* hit the bookshelves, an interlocking directorate of Catholics and non-Catholics, of theologians and academic freedom fighters, was heaping praise on the critical exegetes and fending off complainers with charges of fundamentalism or scholarly ignorance. Father Brown and Father McCormick, each time they would suggest a change in a Catholic doctrinal position, would defend themselves by appealing to dogmatist Father Dulles, who at the time was calling his critics "right-wingers" and accusing Rome of making doctrinal statements which evaded "in a calculated way" the findings of modern scholarship.

Earlier, these same arguments were Richard McCormick's fashionable defense of his personal antimagisterium moral views, he who considered authoritative magisterium an invitation to dialogue, not an exercise of authority calling for simple acceptance or rejection. McCormick had long since abandoned taking his dissent exclusively to scholarly audiences, taking it instead by 1975 to popular audiences, even to seminarians. When I remonstrated with his views on homosexuality in a March 1976 article for the *Homiletic and Pastoral Review,* McCormick wrote me two bitter letters (April 21 and May 11) baring not only his principles but his pique. He did not like to be criticized. He did not like his oral views published without his permission, and anyway his views on such things as homosexuality were only "probes," as if he and his peers somehow had a special right to go among the faithful hawking what he liked to call "tentative" antimagisterial views. In the letters he had no apology for contesting magisterium publicly. Indeed, he claimed support for his dissent among certain Bishops. The people who do most harm to magisterium, he averred, were those who take Roman statements uncritically. For my "sin" of criticizing him, allegedly "smearing" him, he said, McCormick promised to chastise me in the next issue of *Theological Studies.*[4]

Here was a classic case of a theologian crying foul in the face of criticism, alleging he was incorrectly reported, even in his "probing," but whose entire methodology before and after 1975 permitted exceptions to absolute moral norms, the ban on homosexual activity only being one. In my original complaint, I drew on a report on a lecture McCormick gave New York's Douglaston Seminary, written by sympathetic *Brooklyn Tablet* columnist Father Howard Basler. Prior to publication I read Basler's report to several priests who heard McCormick that day, each of whom confirmed that the summary was accurate. In a column entitled "A New Catholic Attitude Toward Homosexuality," Howard Basler reported the Jesuit moralist as follows:

> Jesuit moral theologian Richard McCormick proposed a revision of pastoral life ranging from full acceptance and sacramental ministry (except marriage) for the irreversible homosexual living in a stable, exclusive union to [civic justice] . . .

Priests and counsellors must do more than just urge conformity to norms beyond a person's capability. Ministry does not ask a person to strive for what is unreal to him or her, but seeks a solution in terms of individual ability and circumstances.

Then Basler quoted McCormick:

To urge a person incapable of more than a stable exclusive union, is not to violate our obligation to proclaim the Christian ideal of covenanted marriage.[5]

This position was criticized by me in *Homiletic* as follows:

Moral theologian Richard J. McCormick, who spent half a lifetime teaching seminarians in Chicago and now operates out of Georgetown University, has joined forces with Charles Curran of the Catholic University of America, prepared to accept sacramental ministry [except marriage] to irreversible homosexuals living in a stable exclusive union and counsels priests to do more than merely urge conformity beyond a person's capability. Apparently it is not good pastoral practice to ask a person to strive for what is unreal to him. If love-making with a regular partner is an improvement over promiscuity, this becomes a morally acceptable solution.[6]

Three months earlier the McCormick view was rejected by the Holy See.[7]

Not only was the Jesuit reported correctly but the "probing" he espoused at Douglaston was consistent with the proportionalist views he had of Christian morality before and since, according to which no human acts are always and everywhere intrinsically evil. What is remarkable about the McCormick letters, apart from the anger, is the role he usurps for himself (and his dissident peers), viz., to save the Roman magisterium from itself and, as he clearly stated in his May 11 letter to me, "from the people who now seem bent on destroying it—sc. those who are captives of a single formulation." Such a single formulation would be—"Thou shalt not commit sodomy." Whatever else the McCormick worldview represents, it surely makes him and his peers the final judges of Catholic truth, and entitles them to decide when and how often doctrinal interventions by the Holy See are (in his words) "unexplained, unjustified, unilateral, ill-timed, or all of these."[8]

It was not easy then, nor is it now, to win over organized scholars bent on reinforcing their own willfulness or using their media power to browbeat their opposition, even a Roman Congregation established to protect the Church's faith. One veteran biblicist confessed he no longer wrote, because he could not take the heat of controversy. Whenever the Franciscan exegete Father Manuel Miguens asserted that modern biblical criticism lacked a scientific base and raised unconscionable doubts about important articles of faith, he was abused. Indeed, he lost his university post. Several years later Miguens went home to his native Spain depressed, wondering how many prelates realized the seriousness of what was happening to the biblical underpinnings of Catholic Christianity, which as late as 1981 were not being subjected to evenhanded scholarly debate. And Joseph Cardinal Ratzinger, Prefect of the Congregation for the Faith, was still many months away from the first of his many devestating criticisms of the historico-critical method.

It was at this point a seminary professor of the New Testament suggested that if I wanted to know what was wrong with much contemporary Catholic theology, I should read everything that was ever written by Father Raymond E. Brown, S.S. I did and the end result was *The New Biblical Theorists,* adorned with a preface by internationally acclaimed theologian René Laurentin, who insisted to me in advance that the book would raise questions that needed raising.

The New Biblical Theorists was projected as an evaluation of contemporary biblical theories personified best in the writings of their chief American exponent. One of the Church's leading theologians early warned me to be prepared for the "inevitable attacks." A member of Rome's Biblicum said it was urgent to make these views known. A member of the International Theological Commission added, "I am happy you will publish a study of the biblical positions of R. E. Brown." A non-Catholic theologian thought Father Brown's views "should receive the kind of careful analysis you give," and in many quarters *The New Biblical Theorists* was gratefully received.

Father Brown, however, did not ignore it. During his Thomas Vernon Moore lecture (September 29, 1984) at the Catholic University of America he explained his reasons for choosing to lecture at this time on René Laurentin: viz, George Kelly's book, which he regarded as nothing more than "ultra-conservative propaganda." Nor could he resist adding: "It was astonishing to me that René Laurentin had written the foreword to such a book." Brown, in vindication, cited a review of the book by his friend Jerome Murphy-O'Connor, O.P., as *prima facie* evidence of the low quality, not only of Kelly's book but Laurentin's foreword, as well. The Murphy-O'Connor paragraph reads as follows: "Kelly's book generates anger; the thinly veiled animosity, the incessant slurs, the pervasive bitter righteousness." Later, the same Murphy-O'Connor accosted Laurentin in Europe at a meeting of the Board of the International Concilium, where he expressed indignation that he should write such a foreword, one which, he said, placed the internationally known Frenchman outside the mainstream of American biblical scholarship. The threat did not go unnoticed by Laurentin.[9]

Labeling their academic adversaries as "ultra-conservatives," "literalists," "right-wingers," "fundamentalists," a debating ploy right out of the French Revolution, the avant garde of post-Vatican II theology gained control of the terms of what should be a debate governed by the rules of civil conversation. Misuse of labeling was most noticeable in controversies over scripture. Catholics who marshaled arguments against the misapplication of the historical method and its predetermined conclusions were usually denied equal time in academic circles. Father Brown remained as always wide of the mark whenever he applied the epithet "ultra-conservative" to his critics. Most of those did not propose any particular reading of the Bible at all. They merely objected to some of his "arbitrary conclusions," simple deductions from what he once called his "detective work." Those outside the academic establishment found it hard to believe the intensity of the punishments that were inflicted on Catholic professors who swayed away from the party line of the "new theology." Cardinal Ratzinger became only the most prominent of those abused for his "conservative" opinions about the historical critical method. One leading Protestant called him an "overeducated peasant."

Why were these controversies so bitter? It is difficult to say. Perhaps because the new "knowledge class" in theology has acquired a power within the Church which its members resent having challenged. Perhaps because biblical critics see ecumenical gains from a common reading of scripture, based on "science," rather than on sectarian traditions, and they do not want those gains, such as they are, since Vatican II to be lost. Most likely, passions rise higher over historico-critical exegesis because the stakes for the practice of the faith are higher. Whatever the reason for the hostilities, defenders of the Faith are surely correct when they maintain that the conflicts over faith and morals following the Council, are related to scholarly obsession with the historical method divorced from Church tradition. Historicists argue that all human propositions (in scripture, in dogma, in morals), including those about Christ and the Church, are conditioned by the historical situation from which they derived, limiting their value or truthfulness for later centuries. When historicist exegetes so interpret scripture, independently of anything the Church has said about it, they assert for their class an authority over the final determination of what God, Moses, and Christ really said or did or they raise doubts about the truth of Church determinations which they cannot resolve by their "science." Within this framework whatever is historically relevant to Christianity, indeed to religious life of any kind, no longer belongs to the successors of the apostles to determine.

Consider Father Raymond E. Brown's present position on the virginal conception of Jesus. He believes it to be true as a matter of faith. Further, he presumes it has been infallibly defined by the Church's magisterium. But, because some Protestants and some Catholics deny it, we must study the question again, he says. Brown studies only to find that the "scientifically controllable evidence" leaves Mary's virginity an unresolved problem. (Challenged by other scholars for ignoring the place of dogma in Catholic exegesis, Brown later modifies his scholarly doubt by locating the problem in the lack of "scientifically controllable *biblical* evidence.") At the end of his final analysis he raises one more question, asking whether the doctrine of the virginal conception, which he earlier called infallible, is in view of the new acceptance of historicist study really infallible, after all.[10]

Father Brown thus leaves his audience, if not himself, in what biblicist Dennis McCarthy, S.J., once called a "squirrel cage," running round and round in a circle, always returning to the same place, doubt.

There are other alleged scientific discoveries which have been expounded and defended by Father Brown in the past fifteen years before young audiences. Among the better known are the following taken from his writings in *Theological Studies,* and his books, *Birth of the Messiah, Virginal Conception, Priest and Bishop, Critical Meaning of the Bible,* and *The Community of the Beloved Disciple:*

- The stories of Christ's birth are dubious history.
- Early Christians understood themselves as a renewed Israel not immediately as the New Israel.
- We must nuance any statement which would have the historical Jesus institute the Church or the priesthood at the Last Supper.
- In the New Testament we are never told that the Eucharistic power was passed from the Twelve to missionary apostles to presbyter Bishops.
- Only in the third and fourth century can one take for granted that when "priests" are mentioned, ministers of the Eucharist are meant.
- The Twelve were neither missionaries nor Bishops.
- Sacramental powers were given to the *Christian community* in the persons of the Twelve.
- Presbyter-Bishops described in the New Testament are not traceable "in any way" to the successors of the Twelve.
- The episcopate gradually emerged but can be defended "as divinely established by Christ" only if one says it emerged under the guidance of the Holy Spirit.

- Peter cannot be looked upon as the Bishop of the Early Roman Church community. Succession to his church role fell to the Bishop of Rome, the Bishop of the city where Peter died. However, that concentration of authority produces "difficulties such as we are now encountering within Catholicism," says Brown.
- Vatican II was "biblically naive" when it called Catholic Bishops successors to the apostles.
- It is dangerous to assume that second-century structures existed in the first century.

Most of these statements are not "facts" but unprovable biblical theories based on internal data in the New Testament, interpreted without regard to what the Church has said about these matters. The deleterious effects of these "theories" on the faith of Catholics are recognized by more than illiterate "right-wingers." Thomas Sheehan, a veteran scholar at Loyola University in Chicago, traced the origins of the existing Catholic crisis to the rejection of traditional readings of the New Testament by Catholic intellectuals. Sheehan made the case that there is no solid biblical foundation for the Catholic Church and its doctrines. Jesus went to His death without knowing (or wishing) that His followers declare Him the founder and titular head of a new religion, let alone that He was the consubstantial Son of God. Jesus knew nothing about the Trinity, never mentioned it in His preaching, did not know His mother was a virgin, and, though a faith-healer, did not perform miracles, ordained no priests, consecrated no Bishops, did not know He was supposed to establish the Roman Catholic and Apostolic Church with Peter the first in "a long line of infallible popes." He is supposed to have instituted the Eucharist and Holy Orders, but He would not be allowed in the modern Church (should He somehow be reincarnated) to receive first communion or priesthood because He would fail the required examinations, and might even be condemned by the Holy See for not believing that He Himself was God.

The conclusions of modern biblical research, Sheehan avers, also demonstrate that the Christian Church was really instituted by Simon Peter, not Jesus. Catholic doctrines as such come, therefore, not from Christ, but are derived from the circumstances of the Church after He was buried. Sheehan further asserts that this revolutionary approach to the Bible is the result of a "liberal consensus" which today dominates Catholic theology, even the seminary teaching of future priests. ("The folk religion of most practicing Catholics still lives on the pre-revolutionary fare that generally is served up from their local pulpits and especially from the one currently occupied by the conservative Pope John Paul II.")[11]

We owe a debt of gratitude to Sheehan for directing the Catholic debate to crisis over doctrine, rather than crisis over structures. Doubts raised among the faithful about divine revelation, the Church's proclaimed Word of God, are commonplace. We may thank him, too, for locating the source of Catholic doubt in the so-called "liberal consensus" of modern biblical critics. Those who earlier raised questions about modern biblical criticism are usually denigrated as fundamentalists, whereas Sheehan, obviously, neither a religious fanatic, nor a theological vigilante, nor a crony of the Roman Curia, asserts that biblical critics have undercut the credibility of substantial Catholic claims. The Catholic problematic, therefore, takes on a more serious tone.

How did Brown and company respond to Sheehan? Well, if they were hostile to Laurentin and Kelly, they were respectful of Thomas Sheehan. In *The Bible Today* (March 1985) Joseph A. Fitzmyer, S.J., and Raymond E. Brown replied to Thomas Sheehan in an article entitled "A Danger Also from the Left." While they consider my *The New Biblical Theorists* a "blatant and easy to recognize" assault on modern biblical scholarship from "the right," the assaults from "the left," in their judgment, "are sometimes more subtle and less apparently offensive." This is a curious assessment, but also a telling clue to the mind-set of the Fitzmyer-Brown school. Laurentin and the company which includes Kelly merely complain that modern biblical theorists leave Catholics unnecessarily doubtful about the Church's origins and the validity of her doctrines; Sheehan and company say modern biblical research demonstrates that Christians, Protestant or Catholic, have no rational or historical reason for their beliefs at all.

Should not this latter conclusion be considered more blatant and the most offensive charge against modern biblicists? But, then, Sheehan and company, though agnostic about Christian faith, represent the scholarly community autonomous from Church authority. This is the constituency, more than the Catholic community at large, with which Fitzmyer and Brown have curried favor, at least up to now.

A question that constantly arises is the following: Where was magisterium while these radical discussions were being transported into Catholic classrooms? For the most part U.S. Bishops stood mute on biblical criticism, or were supportive of Father Brown. Only the late Lawrence Cardinal Shehan was bold enough to dispute Brown's exegesis not only of scripture, but of Vatican II. Undeterred, Father Brown kept pointing to his one-term membership on the Pontifical Biblical Commission as evidence of the acceptability of his views in Rome. However, this claim has no significance for the authenticity of Brown's exegesis. Those whose Roman association goes back further, to membership on groups like the papal Birth Control Commission (1964), or who worked with the Sacred Congregations of Catholic Education and of the Clergy from the days of Cardinals Garrone and Wright (from 1970 onward)—can testify firsthand that labor on behalf of Roman dicasteries does not mean endorsement of their personal views by the Pope or the Holy See. Someone below the Pope makes a nomination or extends an invitation or seeks assistance. The consultant is brought in for input, certainly not for endorsement. Indeed, beginning with the Birth Control Commission and until this very day, many Americans who have worked with offices of the Holy See were anti-Roman, if they were not also antimagisterium.

By 1982 the Holy See was building a case against the misuse or overuse of the historico-critical method in deciding the truth or meaning of doctrines. Cardinal Ratzinger, on behalf of the Congregation for the Doctrine of the Faith, which he heads, criticized an Anglican-Roman Catholic dialogue in that year for its failure to state clearly that "Holy Orders is a sacrament instituted by Christ" and for its failure "to measure up to the truth of Catholic faith on the primacy of Peter and his successors." Explained the Cardinal: "It is not possible for the Church to adopt as the effective norm for reading the Scriptures only what historical criticism maintains, thus allowing the homogeneity of the developments which appear in tradition to remain in doubt."

A few months later (January 1983) Ratzinger traveled to Paris to lecture French catechetical leaders about problems with post-Vatican II religious education. On that occasion he told teachers of French students: "Dogma is nothing else, by definition, than the interpretation of Scripture; but this interpretation, derived from the faith over the centuries, no longer seems capable of agreeing with the understanding of the texts to which the historical-critical method, in the meantime, had been leading. Consequently, there co-exist two forms of apparently irreconcilable interpretation: the historical-critical and dogmatic interpretations. This latter interpretation, according to the viewpoint currently in vogue, could only be considered as being a pre-scientific stage in the new interpretation . . . when scientific certitude is considered the only valid, indeed, possible form of certitude. The certitude of dogma had to appear as a now bypassed stage of an archaic idea or as the will to power of surviving institutions."[12] The German Cardinal-scholar was suggesting that biblical scholars were setting themselves up as the *de facto* court of last resort for interpreting scripture. The effect of this procedure on religious education was by then so obvious that little more need be said.

Later still in 1983, Ratzinger addressed Church officials in Rome about the effect of so-called biblical research on the development of liberation theology. The only relevant section of that lecture to this discussion is Ratzinger's assessment of the critical biblical question: "How to read Holy Writ correctly? The Council has been read in public theological opinion as if it had simply given enlightened assent of the Catholic Church to the so-called historical-critical exegesis. With it legitimized, then, all the rest follows from it . . . The question of the correct reading and understanding of the Scriptures has urgent need, therefore, of clarification. It must once again become evident that the Church (even scientifically) is the legitimate depository of the Bible. For this, in the present state of the question, a declaration of the magesterium seems desirable."[13]

Late in 1984 Cardinal Ratzinger aimed his heaviest charge against biblical criticism, the substance of which is as follows:

> The link between Bible and Church has been broken, Historico-critical interpretation of Scripture has made of it an entity independent of the Church: The Bible is read not starting from the Church and in company with the Church, but starting from the latest method claiming to be "scientific." Only thus it is asserted, can the Bible be read correctly. This independence has gone the length of becoming, in some, a counterposition, since the traditional faith of the Church, her dogmas, no longer seem justified by critical exegesis, but seem only obstacles to an authentic understanding of Christianity.
>
> This separation, however, tends to empty out both the Church and Scripture from within. More: a Church without biblical foundations becomes a casual historical product, no longer, surely, the Church of Jesus Christ but that human organization, that mere organizational framework we were talking about. Further, a Bible without the Church is no longer the efficacious Word of God; rather it is a collection of multiple historical sources from which one seeks to draw out, in the light of modern times, what one deems useful. Thus the final word on the Word of God no longer belongs to the lawful pastors, to the magisterium, but to the expert, to the professor, to everchangeable hypotheses. We must begin to see the limits of an exegesis which really is itself a reading conditioned by philosophical prejudices, by ideological pre-understandings, and which does nothing but substitute one philosophy for another."[14]

Once Cardinal Ratzinger entered the picture, Father Brown changed his tune somewhat. During a March 1985 lecture in New York he went out of his way to assure his audience that the authority of the Church must be trusted because biblical study by itself cannot provide all the reasons why the Church teaches what it teaches. He expressed concern that Catholics, who believe that all dogmas are biblically based, might leave the Church over such things as the ordination or nonordination of women, whichever way the Pope decides. Father Brown encouraged his hearers that night to accept the authority of the Church, advice that is surely on a Catholic track. Yet, how and when did Catholics come to believe that Bible readings were the essential determinants of Catholic Faith? Protestants believed this to be the basis of their affiliation, but the average Catholic knew that Church teaching on the Assumption of Mary, to cite one example, could not be demonstrated as true from a biblical text. Catholics were never disturbed by this understanding until recent times. Why, therefore, should they be disturbed today about the Canon 1024 which prescribes that "only a baptized male validly receives sacred ordination." Until a dozen years ago Catholics accepted this proposition as a matter of divine law. Along came Father Brown and the Catholic Biblical Association to suggest seriously, and everywhere, that biblical studies offered reasons for thinking that the last word of the Church on this subject might not have been said. And, as well on other Catholic doctrines, including Christ's establishment of the Church.

The contemporary Catholic crisis did not develop from questions such as these, because most of them were rather old questions. The new difference was the late Catholic biblical establishment. Unchallenged by any hierarchy, save Rome, this group of academic elites allowed many established Catholic positions to remain in doubt, especially among the young who did not recognize the difference between biblical nuance and real doubt. Scholars did not warn these innocents then that academic research did not determine the faith-meaning of biblical books. Nor did they indicate to hearers that they were speculating well outside the Catholic tradition or acting as if that tradition had no role to play in the use of their scientific method. This biblical establishment also scorned those who contested the validity of their speculations, scorn which manifested itself in the frequency with which their critics were boycotted from the halls and journals under their control. In 1983 Servant Publications sought to advertise *The New Biblical Theorists* in *The Catholic Biblical Quarterly*. Publishers do this all the time. On May 16, 1983, *CBQ* advised Servant that this particular advertisement was "not suitable."

Edward Gibbon's maxim, "I sighed as a lover, I obeyed as a son," does not quite describe the average Catholic academic today. If John Paul II conveys a notion of what is acceptable in a doctor of theology, it is a Henri de Lubac or a Hans Urs von Balthasar, each a critical thinker in our time, both raised to the Cardinalate, a rare honor for Catholics whose only claim to fame so far are their books. If the Church is to dig her way out of the morass of today's mendacity and animosity prevalent in her university and religious ranks, it will be as a result of a renewed respect for a hierarchy which knows what the Catholic Faith entails, has a sense of its responsibility to protect its integrity and to instill its meaning in the lives of those entrusted to its care. Intrafamily fights are the normal spillover from close ties among members. They can be stimulating, creative, and fun as long as the adherents unite against their common foe, whether it be the world, the flesh, or the devil. And as long as they do not treat each other as the enemy.

Dissenters argue that ongoing dialogue and negotiations with Bishops will bring about such harmony, but this is not and has never been so. The suggestion not only reduces hierarchy to their level as determinators of Catholic truth, but experience going back to Adam demonstrates over and over again that those whose response to God's revelation will always be "I will not serve" are and will remain numerous. Let the willful dissenter go his way if his only value is human freedom. However, in the Church's life, the care of the sheep is the supreme value, and this is the job for shepherds. These latter must command respect for the quality of their lives and for what they believe; but they must also command obedience to the law from the Church's troublemakers, from those who divide the flock. At the beginning of Christian time Peter said it well:

> You had gone astray like sheep. But now you have come back to the Shepherd and Bishop of Your Souls.[15]

This is not an easy role to play in a culture which aggrandizes rights while liberating subjects from essential responsibilities. But it must be played exactly as Christ scripted it for Himself.

NOTES

1. Robert Blair Kaiser, *The Politics of Sex and Religion* (Leaven Press, 1985).

2. Avery Dulles, *Models of the Church* (Garden City, N.Y.: Doubleday & Co., 1974). See entire treatment of this subject, pp. 188–91.

3. For the Higgins reaction, see *America*, June 5 and July 31, 1982.

4. The letters and my responses are in the Archives of St. John's University. And the McCormick chastisement can be found in *Theological Studies*, March 1977, p. 85 (Notes on Moral Theology). It is of some interest that in the chastising Father McCormick did not refer at all to our disagreements over his view of the morality of homosexual acts, but to my Fall 1976 article in *The Critic*, "The Uncertain Church," about which he said the following: "One commentator [Andrew Greeley] referred to this article as 'demented drivel.' To this Kelly responded that 'the article is serious.' One hates to be confronted with such desperate alternatives; but if pressed, I would have to say the article is not 'serious,' represents the collapse of theological courtesy."

5. *Brooklyn Tablet*, August 7, 1975.

6. *Homiletic and Pastoral Review*, March 1976.

7. See the *Declaration on Sexual Ethics*, December 29, 1975, No. 8, republished by the *United States Catholic Conference*.

8. See Richard J. McCormick, *"The Chill-Factor: Recent Roman Interventions,"* America, June 30, 1984. Editor Joseph O'Hare's summary of the article is as follows: "The evidence is accumulating that some Roman congregations are listening to archconservative complaints. Their responses jeopardize not only due process but lead to theological confusion."

9. See Father Brown's *Thomas Vernon Moore Lecture at the Catholic University of America*, September 29, 1984.

10. Raymond Brown's *Virginal Conception*, (Ramsey, N.J.: Paulest Press).

11. Thomas Sheehan in *New York Review of Books*, June 14, 1984.

12. *La Documentation Catholique,* March 6, 1983.

13. *FCS Newsletter,* June 1984.

14. See *The Ratzinger Report* (San Francisco: Ignatius Press). He expanded on these criticisms in a New York lecture, January 27, 1988, *Origins,* February 11, 1988.

15. I St. Peter 2:25.

SEVEN

The Fellowship
of Catholic Scholars

THE BEGINNINGS

THE FELLOWSHIP OF CATHOLIC SCHOLARS would never have come into existence in normal times. It was conceived in 1976 because the major scholarly organizations of the Church were anti-Roman and were havens for dissenters who no longer believed much of what the Pope, any Pope, was teaching. What was more ominous, their chief spokesmen were instructing the Catholic faithful to dissent, too. Charles Curran openly said in 1986 what he insinuated ten years earlier: "I'm saying there is a right for the Catholic Faithful to dissent."[1] Had the Catholic Theological Society of America, whose president Curran became in 1968, remained true to the purposes for which it was established after World War II, there would have been no need for The Fellowship of Catholic Scholars.

In December 1976 I met with Jesuit faculty at Loyola University in Chicago and the University of San Francisco, and with St. Louis University's James Hitchock to explore the possibilities. Four dozen "founders" met later in St. Louis' Kenrick Seminary August 23–24, 1977, and *The Fellowship of Catholic Scholars* was born. The first president was Ronald Lawler, O.F.M. Cap., of the Catholic University of America, assisted by vice presidents James Hitchcock (St. Louis), Earl Weis, S.J. (Loyola), Sister Janet Fitzgerald, O.P. (Molloy), Joseph Graham (St. Thomas), Joseph Fessio, S.J. (San Francisco), and me.

The Statement of Purpose read in part:

1. We Catholic scholars in various disciplines join in fellowship in order to serve Jesus Christ better by helping one another in our work and by putting our abilities more fully at the service of the Catholic faith.

2. We wish to form a fellowship of scholars who see their intellectual work as an expression of the service that they owe to God. To Him we give thanks for our Catholic Faith, and for every opportunity He gives us to serve that faith.

3. We wish to form a fellowship of scholars open to the work of the Holy Spirit within the Church. Thus we wholeheartedly accept and support the renewal of the Church of Christ undertaken by Pope John XXIII, shaped by Vatican II, and carried on by succeeding pontiffs.

4. We accept as the rule of our life and thought the entire faith of the Catholic Church. This we see not merely in solemn definitions but in the ordinary teaching of the Pope and those bishops in union with him, and also embodied in those modes of worship and ways of Christian life and practice, of the present as of the past, which have been in harmony with the teaching of St. Peter's successors in the see of Rome.

5. The questions raised by contemporary thought must be considered with courage and dealt with in honesty. We will seek to do this, faithful to the truth always guarded in the Church by the Holy Spirit and sensitive to the needs of the family of faith. We wish to accept a responsibility which a Catholic scholar must not evade: to assist everyone, so far as we are able, to personal assent to the mystery of Christ as made manifest through the lived faith of the Church, His Body, and through the active charity without which faith is dead.

One would think that the arrival on the Church scene of a scholarly group friendly to the Bishops would be greeted with salvos of applause or at least with outpourings of good wishes. The Fellowship as yet had no record to criticize and most of its "founders," though firmly based in their respective colleges or universities, were far removed from the saber rattling that had been going on since 1967. The *St. Louis Post Dispatch* reported blandly on August 24, 1977, that "No specific scholarly project or publication was to be started by the Fellowship." But skepticism also existed from the beginning. One contributor to *America* (November 26, 1977) expressed anxiety about "those who want to be more papist than the Pope." The well-disposed *St. Louis Review* speculated: "If the new group does not project a reactionary image, we can hope it will be an important instrument of the Church."[2] The reason for the new organization's existence received almost no attention. My first letter to Cardinal Cooke on the association (August 29, 1977) described the mood outside: "Prior to the St. Louis meeting and desiring to have a reasonably safe account of the first meeting go out through *NC News,* I called someone in USCC, whom I knew reasonably well, asking how I could protect the Fellowship from a bad first story. My adviser suggested I go through Cardinal Carberry's press office because there was no certainty that a direct request for coverage by *NC News* would not result in a hatchet job. This meant in practice a story which would leave the impression that the new organization was being launched by 'right-wingers.' "

Far from being right-wingers in the customary understanding of that term, the only motive that brought theologians to collaborate with social scientists, philosophers with liturgists, canonists with medical researchers, was a common commitment to the magisterium. No one at that founding meeting knew anyone else's political ideology; all were committed to renewal of the liturgy and religious life as the recent Council dictated; a number were already involved in ecumenical dialogue; and many were social activists. Some like Germain Grisez, John Sheets, Paul Quay, Henry Sattler, Joseph Farraher, William May, William Lynch, and James Hitchcock, were recognized scholars in their respective fields and needed no convincing about the Church's need of sound scholarship. But, together, they were opposed to public dissent against magisterium and opposed to research undertaken with a view to challenging Church teaching. Some Fellowship members became quite good at researching dissent itself, as a valid line of scholarly inquiry. And, indeed, it was.

One item on the first agenda received little attention that August 23–24, 1977, viz., the suggestion that faithful scholars who were harassed by dissenters within their institutions or their religious orders receive Fellowship support. Diocesan priests, especially those in large metropolitan centers, rarely found themselves in "the doghouse" because they stood with *Humanae Vitae* or with Church teaching on infallibility or priestly orders. The same could not be said of religious orders where obedience to the Holy See was flouted by major superiors, but enforced on inferiors who bucked the "revolution" or were too noticeably papist. Frequently "young Turks" quickly assumed command posts in Catholic higher education and used their power against anyone who stood in the way of what they called progress. Henri de Lubac, eyeing this activity in France, remarked in a letter to me how, "the post-Conciliar Church was almost immediately called upon to fall into line, not with what the Council said but what it should have said." The exile of the Jesuit loyalists was particularly noticeable: John Ford from CUA, Joseph Farraher from *Theological Studies*, John Lynch from *Weston*, Frank Canavan and Thurston Davis from *America*. Denying tenure to the popular Franciscan Manuel Miguens at CUA was a particularly cruel act, because he was the only doctor of sacred scripture they had and his sole offense was that he was a critic of Raymond E. Brown. John Hardon received an invitation to teach at the Gregorian University in Rome, later to see it withdrawn. Religious communities of women were even worse off.

The scholarly organizations were no better. In 1976 Redemptorist Henry Sattler rose at an annual meeting of the Catholic Theological Society to ask Anthony Kosnik, the chief author of CTSA's forthcoming book on *Human Sexuality* (which later would be condemned by Rome, as well as the U.S. Bishops) why his committee excluded theologians who favored *Humanae Vitae*. Kosnik unashamedly confessed: "We didn't want people with a closed mind." A Catholic Biblical Association study of the role of women in early Christianity without membership blessing was turned into a report in favor of women's ordination (1979), two years after the Holy See had said such ordination was not possible.

Such was the mood of Catholic academia when the Fellowship, encouraged by forty bishops led by Cardinals Carberry, Cooke, and Medeiros opened for business. Within a few months membership grew to a hundred and fifty, with inquiries from Canada, Ireland, England, Australia, India, and from Rome.

FATHER JOSEPH FESSIO, S. J.

The Fellowship's first year was uneventful, but not necessarily the lives of some of its members. Bold Jesuit Joseph Fessio dared to convoke a symposium commemorating the tenth anniversary (1978) of *Humanae Vitae*. He also created a St. Ignatius Institute within the University of San Francisco, which, he said, "emphasizes fidelity to the teachings of the Church, stresses classical Catholic teachings, provides Catholic formation with Catholic teaching." This was enough for *Our Sunday Visitor* to call him "the controversial Jesuit," who "comes off as too Catholic for some."[3] Some of his Jesuit confreres were even more unsympathetic. Berkeley Jesuit John Coleman, later a great defender of the Dutch Church, regretted the narrowness of Fessio's Symposium, viz., no dissenters.[4] USF confrere Vernon Roland let a broadside go against Fessio's faculty, student body, and program, calling them an Ottaviani-like effort to inculcate "pure logical Catholic truth," whereas everyone knew after Vatican II that the Church

300

only dealt with "a developmental truth that is ragged, experimental and uncomfortably fallible."[5] In view of the fact that Jesuits Cornelius Buckley (USF), John Hardon (SJU), and Richard Roach (Marquette) were later censured (Buckley silenced) for criticizing fellow but dissenting Jesuits contrary to house rules, the record must show that no such restrictions were placed on those who attacked Fessio.

Related to this story was the investigation by USF's president into the complaints against Father Fessio's Institute. The final report, based on purely secular norms, evaluated Fessio as follows: The Institute "represents one of the most potent generating centers for new funds in the whole USF complex; USF loses some students because of its perceived liberal theological positions, just as surely as it gains others and would lose more except for the St. Ignatius Institute." The critics of the Institute are far more narrowminded than the views they project on the Institute. The final observation of the evaluator (Michael Scriver) focuses on the real issue, one still pertinent today: "In the press coverage of the St. Ignatius Institute this year (1978), the most obvious fact was that the critics were vociferous and hostile, while Fr. Fessio was judicious and temperate. It is not quite persuasive for these critics to make it a major thrust of their criticism that Fr. Fessio is intolerant and intemperate." But so it would continue, with the Berkeley faculty continuing to be reported as "moderate" and Father Fessio, in spite of his solid accomplishments and his friendship with Cardinal Ratzinger, continuing to be called a "right-winger." The real dividing line was the definitions of the Catholic faith by Rome.

The president of USF, Father John L LoSchiavo, S.J., was persistent, however, because on June 11, 1987, he fired Father Fessio for "mismanagement of funds." The charge was not true, of course. Father Fessio called the firing a "setup." By 1987 his Institute was well able to survive without the Fessio presence; and in the year of his greatest defeat, he became the recipient of the Cardinal Wright Award for outstanding service to the Church and was tapped by John Paul II as an "expert" for the 1987 Roman Synod on the Laity. *Newsweek* magazine later credited Fessio with scuttling an American effort to gain Roman approval for altar girls.

PROFESSOR WILLIAM MAY
AND FATHER RICHARD ROACH

To those who were determined to find reactionaries in those early Fellowship members, the applications of one layman and one priest were significant evidence to the contrary. Professor William May reached the front page of the *National Catholic Register*[6] with a retraction of his dissent from *Humanae Vitae.* The motivation which prodded him and others to join Charles Curran's chorus ten years earlier makes interesting reading today: "Many of the persons who had signed it [Curran's list] enjoyed outstanding reputations, and I wanted to be counted among them; among the 'elite,' the illuminati, the bold, courageous advanced thinkers in Roman Catholicism. I wanted this particularly at a time I was in the publishing business [Bruce], aggressively seeking new authors and books reflecting the theology of the future. I thought that signing the document would help me secure these authors and these books." May continued: "[I] began to repent this act almost immediately," explaining "the strength of my wife, her faith, her true love and her goodness helped bring me to my senses, finally."

Father Richard Roach, S.J., had a more difficult time. Marquette's president wished to send Roach as a delegate to the first Fellowship convention in Kansas City (1977). He was allowed to come but only after he was made aware that his article for Planned Parenthood was well known in Fellowship quarters. It was a tribute to Roach's good humor that a little later he appeared at a CUA conference convoked by Fellowship members with this opening line: "I am here to speak on Catholic moral theology to which I am a recent convert."

TAKING POSITIONS

The Fellowship was three years old before it issued its first public statement on a controversial question. A second intervention would soon follow. Politicking for partisan advantage within the Church was distasteful to the founding members. Ward-heel jousting for patronage or for this or that institutional policy also smacked of the vulgarity that regularly characterized U.S. neighborhoods every election year. The Church, on the other hand, was looked upon as a community of grace and charity, with Bishops empowered by Christ to teach, rule, and sanctify, and so beyond rowdy displays of rivalry and bitter confrontations. Still after 1965 substantial power over Catholic institutions fell into the hands of dissenters simply because they treated the Church as just another human social body, one which could be moved in their direction by intimidating Bishops with discomfort or embarrassment for maintaining the Church's status quo.

The first controversial Fellowship statement, published November 11, 1979, was entitled "The Catholicity of Catholic Universities and Colleges." It was the Fellowship's answer to the National Catholic Educational Association and a defense of John Paul II's assertion of the Church's right to establish institutions in which its teachings are proposed authentically in a spirit of devotion to the Church itself. The Fellowship analysis ended on a questioning note: "Why the corporate body of Catholics that constitute a university community cannot make a Catholic commitment is difficult to understand. Personal witness to the faith by Catholics at secular and State universities is commonplace. The private witness, however, is not what defines a Catholic university. By definition a Catholic university must be a corporate moral person committed totally to the mission of the Church—the pastoral mission no less than the intellectual."

Within weeks (January 7, 1980) the Fellowship was back in the public forum defending John Paul II's censure of Hans Küng. The Curia had been after Paul VI for several years to discipline

Küng without avail. The action of the new Pope, which was praised by William Cardinal Baum, Archbishop John Quinn, and the then Bishop James A. Hickey, became necessary (said the Fellowship) because "by his writings and lectures Fr. Küng has unsettled the faith of innumerable numbers of the Christian faithful." Here again, the Fellowship was somewhat alone. Many well-known academics, Bernard Cooke, David Burrell, Avery Dulles, Andrew Greeley, Richard McBrien, Charles Curran, Raymond E. Brown, expressed concern over the Roman action, disturbed because "authority" interfered with "scholarship." Sixty self-styled Catholic theologians appeared on the front page of *The New York Times* with their affirmation: "We publicly affirm our recognition that he is indeed a Roman Catholic theologian."

A third intervention followed on June 1, 1980, when the Fellowship challenged the Catholic Biblical Association for its study of priestly ordination. CBA concluded that the New Testament evidence "points toward the admission of women to priestly ministry." This group went beyond the assertions of the Catholic Theological Society of America, which earlier settled for saying simply that no biblical evidence stood in the way.

The Fellowship report called the CBA report defective on four counts:

1. Its conclusion favorable to the priestly ordination of women goes beyond the New Testament evidence.

2. It mistakenly confuses women's participation in several ministries of the early Church as a title to priestly ordination, while these ministries were of a different character.

3. It errs by confusing Paul's assertion of the basic human equality of both sexes before God with an argument favoring a basic sameness in roles in the Church.

4. It distorts the obvious Role of the Twelve and the manner in which the early Church made decisions concerning the priesthood and the Church's leadership.

One did not need to be an exegete to know that scripture alone was not going to settle the question of whether women could be ordained priests, anymore than it could settle the truth of Christ's divinity or papal primacy. Indeed, scripture when joined to tradition, especially to the ancient testimony of the Orthodox Christian Community, pointed to the opposite of CBA's proposed conclusion. Subsequently, Msgr. Jerome D. Quinn, the only American member of the Pontifical Biblical Commission, concluded that "the New Testament authors opt theologically for ordaining only men to the Apostolic ministry . . . And this they did because the Lord willed it."[7]

By 1979 leading members of both CBA and CTSA were no longer abstract scholars but ideologues. The original CBA committee was chaired by Milwaukee priest Richard J. Sklba, and was designed to study the role of women in early Christianity, not women's priestly ordination. Over the objections of many CBA members, including several former presidents, Sklba moved to make his study a political issue for the Church. The "Sklba report," which was not submitted to CBA membership for debate or official endorsement, reached the public about the time Rome announced that Sklba was to be the next auxiliary bishop of Milwaukee. Called to Rome two days before his scheduled consecration (December 19, 1979) to explain himself, Sklba pledged fidelity to John Paul II with the following affirmation: "I accept the teaching of the Holy Father on the question of the ordination of women fully and without reservation." A week later Sklba, now a Bishop, returned to the headlines with a new declaration favoring women's ordination: "I don't intend to back off anything I believe in."[8]

Jesuit theologian John Sheets looked upon these scholarly gymnastics and concluded that Catholic scholarship had long since been politicized. He criticized the report of the Catholic Theological Society, which was milder than that of CBA, as follows:

> How does the CTSA expect professional respect when it loads a task force with people who have the same opinions on the subject, and who call in consultants who share these opinions? Much the same thing happened in the study on human sexuality. Has the CTSA ceased to be a body of professional scholars interested in the serious investigation of the truth or has it become a politicized advocacy group? Every serious body of scholars realizes that truth is not

served by simply turning up the volume, hoping to drown out other points of view. Again, has what is supposed to be a body of theologians begun to assume a more direct and extensive pastoral role not only in competition with the bishops, but sometimes in contradiction of them? These are serious questions."9

THE FELLOWSHIP BOOKS

One expects scholars to be scholarly, and within ten years the leading Fellowship members among them had written a hundred books dealing with faith, morals, biblical exegesis, contemporary problems, catechetics, spiritual formation, socio-political issues, and charismatics. My book *The Battle for the American Church* and Hitchcock's *The Pope and the Jesuits* received a great deal of attention because they were research into the extent of dissent within the Church. Books of this genre are controversial of their nature. As exercises in polemics on behalf of the Church, they were bitterly resented by those who were conducting polemics of a different kind. Some Fellowship publications were intended to identify divisions within the Church in order to clarify issues that were often befogged under various footnote systems. It was not possible to stand in the middle of contradictory positions, if one of the sides happened to be taken by the Holy See. So-called middle-of-the-roaders were always on someone's side, the fearful usually on Rome's side, the coy often on the side of dissent. Once upon a time, the name "fellow traveler" was used to identify closet radicals who played the Communist Party line without signing a membership card. "Fellow travelers" of dissent also existed all over the Church by the time Fellowship members began to publish their books.

Against this background of scholarly polemics the literary activity of the Fellowship members must be judged. The most influential publication by anyone is a catechism, *The Teaching of Christ* by Ronald and Thomas Lawler, with Donald Wuerl. *Theological Studies* called this book, "undoubtedly the best manual to date for adult catechetical instruction." On the other hand, USCC's catechetical magazine *The Living Light* did not like it because it did not pay sufficient tribute to the dissonance among contemporary theologians, a disapproval which did not prevent it from selling a million copies in little more than five years and in ten languages, even in Chinese.

The *magnus opus theologicum* of the past ten years is Germain Grisez's *Christian Moral Principles,* the first of a series of volumes scheduled to be published under the general heading *The Way of the Lord Jesus.* Not only is this Grisez's most impressive work, but it is one which the critics of the Holy See will be contesting for years to come. William May's multiple volumes easily offset the production heritage of Charles Curran. Manuel Miguens, while he was in the United States was a vigorous prosecutor of sound biblical exegesis with his treatises on the *Virgin Birth* and *Christian Ministries.* Father James O'Connor became a powerful scholarly spokesman for Vatican II's sense of the Catholic Church and the Pope's infallibility with *His Father's Son* and *The Gift of Infallibility.* Paul Vitz, William Kirkpatrick, Janice D'Avignon, Robert Levis, Eugene Kevane, and Michael Wrenn were no mean defenders of the Church's authentic catechetics. But because the broadest attacks on Catholic teaching came in the moral sphere, it was the Fellowship's moral theologians who bore the brunt of articulating authentically the norms of Catholic behavior. Beside May and Grisez the Fellowship moralists included John Ford, Joseph Mangan, Joseph Farraher, Richard Roach—all Jesuits, and Edward Bayer, William Smith, John Finnis, Joseph Boyle, Orville Griese, and John Haas. These were among the best of their kind in the Church. May, a prolific scholarly layman, was for many years held up for tenure in CUA's Theology Department because he wrote "polemic" material. In a department notorious for the presence of Charles Curran and others, his controversial offense was defending the magisterium against the school's dissenters.

What is significant about this lineup is the concentration of Fellowship attention on those aspects of Catholicity on which its credibility depends. James Schall, Donald Keefe, Brian Benestad, John Guegen, Frank Canavan, Charles Dechert, and Rodger

Charles were well-known protagonists of the Church's social gospel here and in Europe. All of these in one way or another were involved in the construction or the rewriting of episcopal pastorals.

Gone were the days when Bruce, Sheed and Ward, Herder and Herder, Ave Maria Press, and the Paulists could be counted on to turn out books in support of the Church. Their places were taken by Crossroad, Seabury, and Glazier, who traded on dissent, and the Paulist Press, whose brochures were a veritable Who's Who for the Church's leading revisionist thinkers. Maryknoll, which once sold the missions, now sold revolution via Orbis Books. This state of affairs explains why Father Kenneth Baker's *Homiletic and Pastoral Review* was so important throughout the post-Vatican II period. Even Lawrence Cardinal Shehan turned to *HPR* when he wished to update his thinking on contraception or to contest Raymond Brown's views on the priesthood and episcopacy. Where else was he to go? Not any longer to *Theological Studies, Catholic Mind,* or *Thought,* each a one-time Jesuit outlet for solid Catholic thinking. Father Mark Hegener, with almost no money assets, put together a library of first-rate scholarly Catholic works (Bouyer, Schall, Grisez, Molnar, etc.), often with no help from his Franciscan superiors, who removed him in 1986. If one examines the major scholarly works published in the past ten years (Balthasar, Feuillet, O'Connor, Miguens, etc.), one finds them published by small publishing houses—St. Bede, Alba, World, etc.)

The "phenom" of the Catholic publishing business today is another of the Fellowship's founding members—Father Joseph Fessio. What this young Jesuit has accomplished in ten years is remarkable. By now he may be the largest publisher of authentic Catholic literature in the United States. Ignatius Press's list of titles is verily Catholic (Christopher Derrick, G. K. Chesterton, John Cardinal Wright, Joseph Cardinal Ratzinger, Jordan Aumann, Henri de Lubac, Jean Galot, Thomas Dubay, Hans Urs Van Balthasar, Louis Bouyer, Rodger Charles, Paul Johnson, Humberto Belli, etc.) Other Fellowship members who have expanded the literary options of magisterium's defenders include Ralph McInerney and *Crisis,* John Miller, C.S.C., and *Social Jus-*

tice, Timothy O'Donnell and *Faith and Reason,* all respectable and well-received new issues.

JOINT SCHOLARS

By 1976 "the scholars" were aware of their power over Catholic Institutions. If they lacked the title that belonged to those who sat in episcopal chairs, they surely had acquired a "veto power" over what Bishops could and could not do. What is more, they taught Bishops to speak their language, to accept the scholars conceptual framework, to play the game of dialogue without challenging the rules laid down for their participation. *Fides Quaereus Intellectum* was an old Catholic procedure, a Catholic tradition going back to St. Anselm, at least. But Christian dialogue ordinarily began with Christianity's "givens," with the beliefs "revealed" and expressed in the creeds of the Church. This meant that the speculation of Catholic scholars began and ended with that which was taught firmly and universally by Popes and Bishops in union with Him. "Development of doctrine" simply meant new insights or new explanations of words like "salvation, "redemption," "resurrection," "grace," and "Heaven and hell," never suggestions that the words were meaningless or untrue. The theological method adopted by many post-Vatican II scholars was a throwback to that which dominated the writings of Alfred Loisy at the turn of the twentieth century. For him dogmas were not truths revealed by God but interpretations of religious facts "acquired by the toil of mental labour." Human reason exploring mankind's religious experience was the main source of whatever we knew about "God." Empirical data (scientific testing) were the best supports, i.e., proofs, of religious claims.

In this scheme of things "givens"—such as the "deposit of faith"—or abstract philosophical reasoning, are no longer looked upon as valid methods of knowing truth of any kind, including "truth" allegedly originating with a God-person. Church statements are seen as equally flawed because, in spite of their presumption of truth based on traditional wisdom, they have not been tested by the fire of scholarly debate. Consequently, historic ecclesial declarations (in this view) remain unreliable or at best tentative bases for religious convictions, whether proclaimed by Moses, Christ, or a Pope. The proposed solution to this ambiguity (so scholars say) is the application of a new methodological principle—*Intellectus Quaerens Fidem*—a procedure of free enquiry which aims at grounding faith in verifiable reason and empirical data. However, in spite of its pretensions the new methodology, lacking a faith substratum, leads at best to the personal theories about religious facts created by enterprising scholars who are often at war with each other for reasons that have little to do with science. Conflicting philosophical systems lead different theologians to useful, if contradictory, explanations of natural religious behavior, but without faith themselves they are helpless in the presence of "a deposit of faith" purporting to contain divine revelation which only a Moses, a Christ, or a Pope can interpret correctly.

The best exposition of this "new" method at work is Jesuit John O'Malley's article in *Theological Studies,* which argued that Catholics come to see all truth as relative, conditioned absolutely by the historical circumstances of its formulation.[10] Nothing is absolute. All is relative. Even the Second Vatican Council is only a breakthrough, not an answer to the meaning of Christ. What O'Malley argued forcefully was that the Council liberated the Church from its logical and closed mind about God and salvation. Modern man accepts nothing that is absolute, because he knows only what science has taught him, viz., all "truth" is only a stage to the "truth" still to be discovered. What O'Malley wrote, if taken seriously, marks the end of anything which can be called Christian. There is no omega point. Only search. One aspect of the *Theological Studies'* presentation is unexplainable from an institutional point of view. Why was O'Malley not challenged? And he was not. Not by fellow Jesuits. Not by Pedro Arrupe. Not by a Bishop. But he was amply answered a century ago by John Henry Newman, whose search for religious truth led him to Rome. Asked Newman: "Why yield to the authority of the Church in the questions and developments of faith?" The future

Cardinal answered: "Some authority there must be if there is a revelation given, and other authority there is none but She. A revelation is not given if there is no authority to decide what it is that is given."[11]

The O'Malley concept of "revelation" came to the fore in 1977 during the controversy over what was going into the U.S. Bishops' *National Catholic Directory*. Gabriel Moran, a Christian Brother who for a time dominated the training of religious educators, expressed disappointment that the final version of NCD confined "revelation" to "official Christian sources." Moran said, "The language of natural and supernatural revelation had become inadequate by the nineteenth century."[12] Eugene Fontinell, reviewing Philip Keane's book *Sexual Morality,* whose *imprimatur* was later withdrawn by the Holy See, saw "human morality not as a slavish carrying-out of the eternal unchangeable orders of a divine potentate, but as a sharing in the creative life of a loving creator who invites us to a struggle with him to bring forth a new world richer in realization and possibility."[13]

Can any serious student see Christ saying this? "Ideas," even for the founder of Christianity, were not simply rationalizations of mental states. They were often political, as the Jews and Romans considered His to be. The proposal, therefore, that Catholic theologians were autonomous from the supervision of or correction by the Pope (or even by a Christ or a Moses) strikes at the heart of the Catholic understanding of revelation, or of a Church based on a given "deposit of faith." Theologians know this better than Bishops, although all recent Popes know best the institutional significance of theology divorced from Church authority. Regularly since the Council the U.S. theological establishment has refused to concede substantial authority to Pope or Bishops over their deliberations. They have come to resent the "intrusion" of papal contributions into what they call "the domain of the theologian," which they would like to maintain as free intellectual territory.[14]

These preliminary remarks are one way of explaining the problem faced by the Fellowship of Catholic Scholars when it became a recognized member of the "Joint Committee of Catholic Learned

Societies and Scholars" (JCCLSS). In the year of the Fellowship's founding, a proposal was made to unify the relationship between the Catholic scholarly community and the National Conference of Catholic Bishops. The most observable function of the JCCLSS was to hold annual colloquia with Bishops, which began in 1978. But JCCLSS looked for more—to be the agency formally recognized as the source of research data for episcopal pronouncements or decisions. The first two colloquia (1978–79) indicate how quickly the leadership in these joint meetings fell to the scholars. While JCCLSS membership included the Fellowship, the Biblical, Philosophical, and Mariological Societies, it was spokesman for the Catholic Theological Societies who dominated the discussions and the official report.[15] One would think, given the state of the Church a dozen years after the Council, that the first items for discussion might have been the transmission of the Catholic Faith. Instead, the first two colloquia discussed scholarship and pluralism.

Some of the views expressed in 1978 were as follows: By Father Joseph Komonchak: "It is usually prudent for bishops to avoid taking a position when the theologians have not reached a conclusion"; by Father Avery Dulles, S.J.: "Could theologians, individually or at least corporately, be acknowledged as possessing true doctrinal or magisterial authority?" The notion, he insisted, was well founded in tradition. He criticized the excessive privatizing of theology as if theologians indulge in nothing other than airy speculation. He suggested that statements could occasionally be issued jointly by Bishops and theologians.

These were the prevailing views by members of the *Catholic Theological Society* whose leading members a few years earlier had published *Human Sexuality,* a book which flatly contradicted the Church's sexual ethic and was condemned by Rome and the U.S. Bishops.

The 1979 colloquium stayed with pluralism. CUA's William Hill, O.P., made the case that a pluralism of Catholic theologies exists today. No longer does there exist the monolith which many Catholics inherited from Neo-Scholasticism and which they took

312

to be normative. CUA's Dean Hoge seemed to suggest that the Church could support considerable cognitive dissent.

In October 1980 Cincinnati's Father Donald McCarthy was brought in to present a paper on the difficulties presented to the Church by a "proportionalist" theory of moral theology. Proportionalism denied the existence of moral absolutes, arguing for moral choices based on practical judgment about the good or bad effects of particular actions. This theory justifies contraception and abortion in certain circumstances, and other forms of sexual deviance as well. Father Komonchak added the point that the *de fide definita* propositions of the Church are few in number, leaving scholars the role of articulating what the Faith means to modern man. At this colloquium defenders of the Church's standard teaching (e.g., Father Dennis Bradley, S.J.) counterargued that no one can legitimately import into theology his own philosophy and do justice to the revealed data. He insisted one must first believe in the proclamation of the Church and then think philosophically.

The general thrust of these meetings with Bishops was to reinforce the status of dissenting theologians, ultimately leaving to Rome the unwelcome task of making appropriate corrections of doctrinal errors wending their way through the institutions of the U.S. Church. But, if that be the case, of what value is there to a Committee on Doctrine within the NCCB?

Continued resistance to the proper exercise of hierarchical oversight characterized these JCCLSS meetings into 1984. Earlier that year (February 28, 1984) Rome requested the Archbishop of Newark to withdraw the *imprimatur* from a Paulist adult catechism entitled *Christ Among Us*. After seventeen years of popular use (the *imprimatur* first given in 1967) Cardinal Ratzinger decided the book was not "suitable as a catechetical text" and was not to be reprinted because even with "substantial corrections," it would still not be suitable. What was wrong with this book? To quote Archbishop John Whealon: "The book is shot through with dissent." Among the specific shortcomings Whealon found were the following: the virginity of Mary is of small consequence (page 68); the baptism of infants is questionable (page 195); intercommunion is tolerable (page 264); mortal sin is not a particular action (page 285); Catholic conscience is described without the magisterium (page 285); premarital intercourse seen only as not the ideal (page 323); etc.

One would think that serious scholars, fully Catholic, would have developed means of extirpating these errors and shortcomings from catechetical texts posing as presenting the Church's teaching accurately and with conviction. Instead, Father Thomas P. Ivory of the National Conference of Diocesan Directors of Religious Education (and a Newark priest) persuaded JCCLSS to express its "grave concern" over the removal of the *imprimaturs*. His argument was that the withdrawal was arbitrary. Father James Provost, a CUA canonist, maintained that a work can be given an *imprimatur*, even if it holds positions opposed to authentic Catholic teaching, as long as the advocacy or contradictory position is presented as the personal opinion of the author and not "authentic Catholic teaching." Fellowship representative at JCCLSS meetings William May pointed out that since the printed *imprimatur* contained the advisory that the approved book was free from doctrinal error, no such exception could be permitted. When the JCCLSS moved to take its complaint to the National Conference of Catholic Bishops, only May voted negatively. (While the scholars were calling Rome's action arbitrary, Newark's Archbishop Peter Gerety told the public that Rome had been negotiating over the Wilhelm withdrawal for several years, hardly evidence of arbitrariness.) The remainder of this meeting was spent discussing new ways of "dialoguing" with the Bishops. Participating members generally hoped that the Bishops would come to accept the "consensus" of theologians on critical issues. The NCCB resisted this concept, although the Bishops themselves showed no interest in taking command of the dialogue. From the discussions it was clear that JCCLSS was experiencing difficulty with such Archbishops as Bernard Law. The members then expressed preference for dealing with Bishops such as Kenneth Untener and Richard Sklba.

Unhappiness with these colloquia emerged as early as 1981. The theologians were not making the headway they wanted with the Bishops. But neither were the Bishops successful in persuading theologians that, like everyone else in the Church and as John Paul II indicated many times, they owed assent to the truths of the Faith. There were other complaints about the Joint Committee. *The American Catholic Historical Review*'s representative raised the question of imbalanced membership—too many theologians and too many social scientists—and only one Church historian! Robert Emmet Curran, S.J., called for "less reliance on the wisdom of the behavioral and social sciences" and "a more equitable representation of the member societies." By 1986 a new working relationship with the Bishops was sought. A memorandum sent to the Bishops' Committee on Doctrine suggested restructuring the meetings, this time excluding the American Catholic Philosophical Association and The Fellowship of Catholic Scholars, the only two scholarly organizations on record with support of Rome's declarations on Catholic higher education. If ever there was indication of the direction toward which the scholars would like to lead Bishops, this exclusionary move was it. One year later (1987) this small group of dissenting scholars got their way when the Committee on Doctrine developed a set of guidelines for dealing with doctrinal controversy involving Bishops which seriously compromised the Bishops' role as the Catholic teachers *par excellence.* It was evident by then that the mixed Catholic signals coming from Church headquarters involved more than academes and ecclesial bureaucrats. The national machinery of Bishops was itself involved.

THE UNITED STATES CATHOLIC CONFERENCE

The Fellowship of Catholic Scholars began its work in 1976, expecting to be of service to the Bishops, who operated on a day-to-day basis through the United States Catholic Conference (called USCC), a national Chancery Office of a sort, responsible for reinforcing Catholic doctrine and moral norms throughout the Church and representing Bishops in national affairs. It was precisely to assist Bishops to determine what might be done to assure authentic teaching that the Fellowship was founded.

However, establishing working relations with the USCC proved to be no easy matter. On May 30, 1978, our first president, Father Ronald Lawler, and I arranged to meet with the then Bishop Thomas Kelly, O.P., the General Secretary of the Bishops' Conference. He was cordial, apologized for the many interruptions which made serious conversation impossible, but clearly had no interest in help from Fellowship scholars. A year later, Lawler's successor, James Hitchcock, arranged to meet with Archbishop John Quinn, the president of the Bishops' Conference, prior to its November 1979 meeting. This get-together was also unproductive, a waste especially for Professor Glenn Olsen, who flew in from Utah specifically to share his convert's view of the contemporary Church with the nation's chief Bishop. But the Archbishop manifested no interest in anything the Fellowship leaders had to say about the state of Catholic higher education. Indeed, the same John Quinn, who two years earlier placed great stress on the importance of the Holy See to Church teaching, became testy when doubts were raised in his presence about the quality of episcopal consultations which unduly featured dissenting opinions. The 1979 meeting was the last effort made by Fellowship leadership to deal directly with the top officers of the Bishops' Conference or with its civilian arm, the USCC.

What was wrong? Most of the prominent Fellowship members were decent Christians and many of them (Grisez, Finnis, May, Lawler, Hardon, Miguens, Olsen) were leading scholars. Dr. Hitchcock was a veteran researcher into Catholic dissent and a gentleman besides; my *Battle* was not yet published and the Fellowship's quarterly *Newsletter* had not yet adopted any public positions. Furthermore, while Fellowship charter members were not the darlings of the National Catholic Reporter, neither did they rate highly with *The Wanderer* or the fanatic followers of the schismatic Archbishop Marcel Lefebvre. What, then, was Quinn afraid of? Here were academics committed to the integrity of the Catholic Faith and obedience to Church Law offering their service to the nation's episcopal body and their contributions were rejected. Why?

It did not take long to discover that the USCC leadership by

316

1979 was committed to other scholarly associations, which the Fellowship considered to be the headquarters of dissent.

To the surprise of few a dispute occurred very early between the Fellowship and Bishop Thomas Kelly. Dr. William McCready, a senior research assistant at Chicago's National Opinion Research Center received an appointment to a USCC Commission on Marriage and Family Life. McCready, a known critic (with Father Andrew Greeley) of the Church's teaching on contraception, should have been an unlikely consultant to Bishops who presumptively believed Church teaching on the subject to be true. Kelly was asked for an explanation, which, when it arrived, said, in part, that the sociologist was hired for his scientific expertise, not for his theology. The excuse was lame. Sociologists correctly argue that "birds of a feather flock together," and it was the Mc-Creadys, not supporters of *Humanae Vitae,* who had status in the USCC machinery. The editor of *The Long Island Catholic,* Msgr. Daniel Hamilton, phrased "the main question" by asking whether Church authorities should appoint to official Church commissions persons who have publicly rejected some element of the Church's authentic teaching on faith and morals. He thought that the answer was clearly no." In response McCready denied that he publicly rejected any authentic teachings of the Church or that he positioned himself publicly on the morality of birth control. Yet three years earlier (1976), he coauthored a study entitled *Catholic Schools in a Declining Church,* which relentlessly criticized the Church's teaching on contraception. McCready also had told an NCEA audience (April 2, 1976): "Most of us mature when we admit that we have made a mistake and have taken steps to correct it. Why can we not assume that the Church too would grow and mature if it could admit that the rigid prohibition against artificial contraception was an honest mistake."[16]

Fellowship founders came to realize that a pattern had already developed within the USCC which favored selective reinforcement of Church teachings and ecclesiastical discipline. Papal social teachings with their large stress on social controls of economic life found a happy home in the Bishops' Washington bureaucracies, but not other Church demands, especially those which would regulate personal, religious, or academic life. Rome had little trouble with U.S. Bishops over matters of justice and peace, certainly not by comparison with the "liberation" hierarchies of South America. But the bane of Catholic life in this country became "liberation" of a different kind—of religious men and women from their superiors, of college presidents from Bishops, of Catholics in general from the strictures of the Ten Commandments. And in this latter fight to loosen the ties of magisterium over Catholic consciences, the USCC machinery was often on the side of the recalcitrants. How else can we explain the alienation of the U.S. Church from Rome on one issue after another—from the first Confession of eight-year-olds through the Charles Curran debacle to the refusal of Bishops to enforce Church Law on religious communities.

In one sense, however, the "McCready flap" was only a minor lapse in Bishop Kelly's administration of the USCC. Dissenting theologians had made the rejection of the Church's sexual ethic a "litmus test" of the "new Catholic" programmed by the Second Vatican Council. *Humanae Vitae,* especially in its negative attitude toward contraception, was never USCC's favorite papal statement. When, for example, the Bishops' bureauracy turned their attention to sexuality, the chosen authorities were social scientists, not Paul VI or John Paul II.

In this connection the *pièce de résistance* out of the USCC machinery was the 1981 publication *Education in Human Sexuality for Christians,* a sex education curriculum for preschool years through high school written, as the book said, "from a Catholic perspective." Ostensibly, it was the Church's answer to secular courses whose readiness to explain in great detail the joys of sexual pleasures was well known, as were their guidelines for playing house responsibly (i.e., to avoid pregnancy), but especially for breaking away from taboos about sex passed on by parents or "old wives' tales." Claiming to reduce unwanted pregnancies, secular sex education largely taught the mechanics of sex, while debriefing the young of any sense of guilt about sex. In spite of such instruction, or because of it, young America by 1981 was more sexually active than ever before, illegitimate births and teenage abortions were running into the hundreds of thousands each year, and one divorce annually for two marriages was now the national norm. Growing up with one mother still married to the same father with more than one brother or sister was a declining American social pattern.

Catholic parents had the right to expect that sex education under Church auspices would counter this culture at the least, and be wholly in conformity with the Church's complex of teachings at best. Still, the USCC guidelines omitted elements absolutely essential for a Catholic approach to sexual education. For example, they failed to take seriously the consequences of original sin and the serious reality of personal sin in sexual matters. The first draft of this document did not even mention original sin. The Second Vatican Council taught: "The whole life of man, both individual and social, shows itself to be a struggle, and a dramatic one, between good and evil, between light and darkness. Man finds that he is unable of himself to overcome the assaults of evil successfully, so that everyone feels as though bound by chains. But the Lord came to free and strengthen man, renewing him inwardly and casting out the prince of this world[17] who held him in bondage of sin."[18]

The USCC guidelines did not fully reflect this teaching. They spoke frequently of God's love and His willingness to forgive us, but were not specific about the reality of sin, nor of sin's effect on relationships (with God and others), nor of the place of repentance in the life of Catholic youth. How is it possible to teach about sexuality in a Catholic way without indicating that sexual sins gravely offend the Lord, endanger eternal salvation, and make authentic Christian life impossible. The USCC guidelines did nothing of the kind.

Ambiguity about sin also leads the USCC guidelines into ambiguity about moral norms in general. Catholic teaching about sexual morality was presented as something to be considered, but not as a demand of faith. Since many allegedly committed Christians claim today that contraceptive intercourse, genital activity by unmarried couples committed to one another, homosexual activity by homosexually oriented persons in a stable relationship, are morally good responses to given human situations, any document purporting to represent the thinking of the American Bishops would normally confront these deviations from Church teaching directly. This booklet ignored these problems.

The weakness of the USCC sex guidelines is perhaps best indicated in the way the authors handled contraception. Any informed Catholic (1981 vintage) knew that "the pill" no longer was the hot religious issue it had been in 1961. Dissenters had long since marched from freedom to use the pill to the freedom of people's consciences to determine for themselves right or wrong on any sexual choice. Instead of facing the reality, the USCC guidelines ended up weaker on contraception than most other Church documents. In 1979, for example, the National Catechetical Directory spoke of "the evil of artificial contraception and sterilization for that purpose" and condemned "the view that sterilization and artificial contraception are morally legitimate means of family limitation." One would expect that an official text published later, especially one restricted to sex education alone, would be more specific since it was designed to assist teachers and students about how best to apply the approved teaching in their lives. Yet hardly any guidance at all was given in this booklet on how to deal with contraception, sterilization, or abortion. Not only was there an absence of detailed information about the abortifacient aspects of contraception, but Natural Family Planning was just about ignored. The booklet drew its moral guidance from controversial psychological theorists (Lawrence Kohlberg, e.g.) rather than from the wisdom of Catholic spiritual writers and, as if to add insult to injury, called for explicit instruction on the physiology and biology of sexual relations to be carried out in mixed classes, even for children whose sexual interests are generally latent. This was an encroachment on parents' rights, and even on the privacy of the children, if there ever was one.

Far more serious than the faulty sex guidelines was the determination by a Bishops' body to publish them in spite of serious advance criticism of a doctrinal nature. Msgr. Richard Malone, the Bishops' "watchdog" at the time on doctrinal matters, considered the advance draft defective. The Fellowship of Catholic

Scholars wanted the booklet reviewed and strengthened before distribution. How was it possible for an official Church agency to disseminate guidelines which never proposed acceptance of the Church's teaching nor invited readers to shape their lives accordingly? Who in this leadership chose to flaunt his dissent from established Church norms?

Then the rain of public complaint fell all over the project. The National Federation of Catholic Physicians' Guilds criticized the USCC for its ambiguity, demanding that Catholics "be fully versed in the many errors prevalent in society and they must know why these views are false." *Our Sunday Visitor* saw the document as unhelpful—"another sign of the fogged cliffs that stretch between the various factions in the Church."[19] It turned out that various Congregations in Rome were unhappy, too.

The closest the USCC came to acknowledging that a major blunder had been made was the subsequent decision of the November 1981 meeting of the NCCB requiring all future USCC books to specify the authorship and the precise responsibility of the Bishops' Conference for the content, if any. Had such regulations been in force a year earlier, the USCC sex education guidelines could not have been presented as an official document of the American Bishops. However, these new regulations still do not guarantee that the content of such books will reinforce Catholic doctrinal and moral norms as these are enunciated by the Holy See. Time would demonstrate further that forces within the Bishops' body would make further efforts to dilute the Catholic message on marriage and sexuality.

The end for the USCC was still not in sight. On November 1, 1983, the Sacred Congregation for Catholic Education issued Rome's outlines for sex education. Its manual, entitled *Education in Human Sexuality for Christians*, recapitulates in summary fashion what the Church historically has taught and still teaches about the training of the young for proper male-female relationships, for marriage, chastity, and virginity. The primary rights of parents are recognized and every contemporary sexual disorder comes under its purview. The doctrine of the Church is clearly stated in all instances, including stress on "the necessity of transmitting to the young at an appropriate age the teaching of the Church on artificial means of contraception, and the reason for such teaching, so that the young may be prepared for responsible marriage, full of love and open to life."[20]

Shortly thereafter word quietly filtered out of USCC that its sex guidelines were in the process of being revised. No such revision has been made to this day.

The chasm between Rome and the spokesman for several of the Church's Washington bureaus was further demonstrated during a September 1982 meeting of the National Institute for the Family, which assembled for the purpose of analyzing John Paul II's recently published *Familiaris Consortio*. This Apostolic Exhortation was the direct result of a 1980 Roman Synod on the Family and reaffirmed most of what the world knew to be the received Catholic teaching on sex, marriage, and parenthood. The National Institute, by virtue of the composition of its leadership and invited speakers, provided important evidence of how far removed leading lights of the USCC infrastructure were from the thought and moral norms of the Holy See.

The *National Institute for the Family* was convoked under the leadership of Father Donald B. Conroy. Who was he? Conroy was the recently resigned director of USCC Family Life Programs, an adviser to the U.S. delegation to the 1980 Family Synod, a priest described by Bishop Thomas Kelly as someone who played "a leading role in the development of the [USCC's] pastoral plan." Who were those invited to give papers at this meeting as part of what the conveners said was a consultation on *Familiaris Consortio?* Dolores Leckey (also a USCC delegate to the Roman Synod), Robert Kinast, Joseph and Mercedes Iannone, Paulist James Young, Mary G. Durkin (Andrew Greeley's sister), Monika K. Hellwig, Robert Friday, David M. Thomas, Jesuit Richard McCormick. No one of these was known to be a defender of the Church's integral teaching on Catholic family life, even though they were associated with the USCC in one form or another. Some, like McCormick, were virulent dissenters.

What did they have in common? They were all unhappy with *Familiaris Consortio*. For Leckey, John Paul II was insufficiently feminist. Robert Kinast did not like the Pope's ecclesiology. The Iannones wondered if the Church could tolerate mature believers, that is those who were independent of Church authority. Paulist Young opposed denying the Eucharist to divorced and invalidly remarried Catholics. Durkin wanted more of married people's sexual experiences included in the document. Hellwig thought that ecstatic sexual union, licit or illicit, could be sacramental, even if hierarchy said no. Robert Friday faulted John Paul's ecclesiology, too. Imagine, he said, *Familiaris Consortio*'s expectation that the Church's value system is to be incorporated in and taught by the family! David M. Thomas disapproved of the exhortation's tendency to talk down to the family rather than learning from the experience of families. McCormick thought *Familiaris Consortio* would add to the decline of respect for the Church's authoritative teaching in the sexual area. He prophesied the complete silence of most American Bishops on the matter.

It would be hard to conceive of another modern institution in which so many "experts" who owe whatever status they have to their establishment, and often remain on payroll, are simultaneously free-wheeling members of an opposing party, without the normal penalty for dissidence. Father Henry Sattler, one-time Bishops' family life expert and a Fellowship founder, who participated in the National Institute sessions, was appalled at the extent of "rejection" at the three-day meeting—the assertion of the laity's equal authority with hierarchy in determining the content of the Catholic Faith. This position is heretical. Sattler's report[21] summarized the meeting as follows: "Most of the speakers took diametrically opposite positions to *Familiaris Consortio* in the areas of contraception, indissolubility, the sacramentality of matrimony, the right to the Eucharist for invalidly remarried divorcés, on celibacy and virginity, on the right of the magisterium to teach authoritatively." *Hardly* any other institution functioning in the U.S. today would tolerate such a one-sided assault on its chief officer from within the ranks and leave him undefended.

THE IDEOLOGY OF THE USCC

It has always been difficult to understand why "defenders of the Faith," at least some of them, were not welcomed after Vatican II into the inner councils of the U.S. Bishops. Certainly there was evidence by the Council's end of rebellion in the ranks—even within the ranks of the Bishops. Under the leadership of Detroit's Archbishop John Dearden, the old National Catholic Welfare Conference became the United States Catholic Conference, with Bishop Joseph Bernardin, auxiliary to Archbishop Paul Hallinan of Atlanta, moved to the nation's capital as USCC's first General Secretary. Hallinan was hierarchy's first defender of Charles E. Curran. Years later as Cardinal Archbishop of Chicago, Bernardin would confess his debt to both Dearden and Hallinan. Whereas the NCWC was hardly a place where dissenters lived comfortably, the same could not be said of the USCC after 1966.

Msgr. George Higgins makes a good case that the USCC staff does not run the Bishops. He dismisses critics who "blame" the Church's Washington bureaucrats for the shortcomings of the early drafts of episcopal statements; calling them "neo-conservatives," who are simply objecting to the Bishops' social teachings. Higgins' own interpretation of what those teachings demand may lead him to miscalculate the views of his so-called neo-conservatives. But he is right in saying Bishops' control the USCC machinery and, insofar as its ideological proclivities are concerned, Bishops set the tone for USCC, and choose or approve those named to the staff of the National Conference of Catholic Bishops.

But the unasked question, and one rarely answered with candor, is: Which Bishops? While a real effort has been made since 1965 to rally round the elected episcopal leadership, there are obvious ideological differences within the hierarchy. Some Bishops are unhappy with the policies and management of the USCC. How could it be otherwise? The U.S. Church is continental in scope. Historically, American Bishops were unified in their commitment to Rome but were often at odds with each other when their diocesan or regional needs differed radically. Does anyone expect the Polish Bishops to see the Catholic world through the eyes of the French hierarchy? Why should New York and California Bishops be of one mind about practical Church judgments, separated as they are by wider distance and differing histories? In the immediate pre-Vatican II period, priests jokingly spoke of the rivalry between New York's Francis Cardinal Spellman and "The Axis," the latter being the ecclesiastical leaders of three Midwest Sees, Chicago, Detroit, and Cincinnati. These three Bishops had virtual control of the National Catholic Welfare Conference, while Spellman's ecclesial influence derived from his personal relationship with Pius XII. "The Axis" never had the power in Church or national affairs that Spellman had, but the "Midwest" Bishops relished their influence within the NCWC. Once in 1944, for example, there was a double opening for Executive Director of NCWC's Department of Education and for the National Catholic Educational Association. Msgr. George Johnson, who held both posts, died unexpectedly a few months before. At the subsequent Bishops' meeting, Spellman became restless over the apparent infighting about the successor, to the point of offering New York's entire education staff (three priests) to replace Johnson. But before he knew it, two Midwest priests (Father Fred Hochwalt of Cincinnati and Father William McManus from Chicago) were brought to Washington overnight to take command of the USCC and NCEA posts by orders of "The Axis," as if to show Spellman who ran things in Washington. The New York Cardinal really did not care, but his disagreements with his Midwest counterparts are replicable in episcopal divisions forty years later. With one difference: "There is less freedom of debate among Bishops today than during the years of Cardinal Stritch and Cardinal Spellman." So said one major Archbishop to me in 1986.

"Neo-conservatives" may be opposed to the Church's social teaching, as Msgr. Higgins suggests, but when that is the sole issue, there is no reason why an informed Catholic should opt for Higgins' understanding of this teaching. Well-instructed Catholics accept the Church's right to be concerned about people's human condition, especially of the poor, and of her right to help liberate the oppressed, and to mitigate warlike tensions among nations. Even with the teaching in mind, they are still free to disagree with the USCC's socio-political platforms, especially if these are oriented more to government activism than to creative free enterprise. While politics always begets enemies, the hostility to USCC programming goes further, as much to its ambiguous treatment of certain Catholic doctrines, as to its politics. The USCC can afford to be wrong about Nicaragua so that Mass-attenders will hardly notice; but about sexual morality? About the essentials of religious life? About *imprimaturs?*

Only Rome—Popes and Sacred Congregations—has maintained the Catholic doctrinal balance with some consistency. The Bishops' machinery, on the other hand, has been strong on the social issues, but woefully weak on the dogmatic issues. Even as the U.S. Bishops were making authoritative statements about war, about poverty, about MX missiles, and food stamps, U.S. theologians were freely teaching priests and religious, often under the auspices of Bishops, that Christ did not establish the Church, the Papacy, the episcopacy, or the sacrificing priesthood.

Why, for example, was Richard McBrien's two-volume summa of alleged Catholic belief, *Catholicism,* allowed to move into college classrooms for five years (1980–85) before it was censured? Published without an *imprimatur* and demolished almost immediately by the Australian Bishops (September 7, 1980) as unworthy of recommendation for primary/secondary school teachers or to ordinary lay people, *Catholicism* was judged very late by the NCCB's Committee on Doctrine to be ambiguous about the virginal conception of Jesus, the perpetual virginity of Mary, the foundation of the Church, and the binding force of Marian dogmas. The two volumes also did not support the Church's authoritative teaching on contraception and the ordination of women. If these were critical neglects by McBrien, why was no one in the U.S. Bishops' Conference paying attention to Rome for the better part of twenty years, as the Holy See issued one dogmatic statement after another, on average one a year, rebutting one or the other doctrinal truth being denied, doubted, or rendered ambiguous in books like McBrien's?

On another occasion, the president of the Fellowship wrote to Msgr. Daniel Hoye, General Secretary of the USCC (April 18, 1986), asking "why Charles Curran and the Association of Catholic Colleges and Universities (ACCU) appeared on the front page of *Origins* with their responses to the Holy See *before* Cardinals Ratzinger's and Baum's positions were presented to the reader?" *Origins*, of course, is the USCC's documentary service, which makes available to the public speeches, reports, and critiques which pertain to the conduct of Catholic affairs. At the time two serious controversies were going on between Rome and U.S. Catholic leaders—Ratzinger vs. Curran, Baum vs. Theodore Hesburgh and company. Their outcome would eventually determine whether or not magisterium is the final judge of what is Catholic about theology or a university. *Origins* gave front-page coverage in two issues[22] to Curran's and ACCU's answer to Rome, *before* the uninitiated reader had any opportunity to know from *Origins* what Rome was saying on both subjects. Richard Daw, the editor-in-chief of NC News Service, on behalf of Msgr. Hoye, answered my questions. His defense of placing Curran before Ratzinger and Baum before Hesburgh, et al., reads as follows:

> *Origins* is a news publication and decisions are made on that basis.

Further:

> In the edition related to Father Curran, the news was clearly his statement. The entire matter came to public attention because he held a news conference. From a news standpoint, that was the point at which to begin.
>
> The same was true of the edition relating to Catholic universities. The document by the Congregation for Catholic Education came into the news at that particular time because 110 college and university presidents made an issue of it. As a matter of fact, the Congregation's document most likely would not have appeared in *Origins* at all at this point had not an issue been made of it, because it is a draft and we rarely publish drafts of anything.

Daw concludes:

> Nothing is done in *Origins* (nor at NC generally) for reasons of ideology. We are neither liberal nor conservative. We are profes-

sional journalists trying to provide information to a public greatly in need of it. We leave the ideological jousting to others; our hands are quite full trying to report it.[23]

The fact is that *Origins* is not "a news publication," as Daw asserts, but the Bishops' documentary service—the Church's instrument for making available documents relevant to the Church's work of evangelization and the formation of public opinion, especially among Catholics.

It is appropriate to point out, in spite of Daw, that the real "news" was Rome's "crackdown" on both Curran and the ACCU. This is precisely how the secular press described the confrontation. Even Curran said the Roman action was unique, alleging that the American Bishops recognized public dissent by him (and *a fortiori* by Hesburgh and company). If the "man bites dog" norm is Daw's prevailing standard, then surely Ratzinger biting Curran and Baum biting Hesburgh were the real news. Dissent by the Curran-ACCU factions was stale news by March 1986. Moreover, since NC News was "leaking" Curran material to the Catholic press (obviously made available by Curran himself), it was clear that only Curran, not the Church, was benefiting from the revelations. Readers of *Origins* were given the opportunity of examining Ratzinger-Baum, only after going first through Curran-ACCU criticism of the Roman positions, including the assertions that the American Bishops were at odds with the Holy See. (Actually, some in high places were.)

The Daw contention that the NC News Service does not normally deal with "drafts" is a peculiar argument, because drafts of every major U.S. pastoral were published by *Origins*. Cardinal Baum's draft had been public property for almost a year when the ACCU response was made. The Baum document was a historic document of its kind. Why was it not worthy of Daw's attention much earlier? Surely the U.S. Bishops would have benefited from widespread knowledge of Rome's positions without automatic rebuttal from dissenters.

Strangest of all is Daw's assertion that his "professionalism" places him outside the conservative-liberal jousting over people like Curran or organizations like the ACCU. Is that what Rome's efforts are all about, ideology based on mere differences of opinion? Here Daw brings into focus one of the most serious Church problems of modern times—the self-proclaimed and alleged neutrality of "the Catholic professional" (editor, teacher, catechist, college president, etc.) toward Catholic truth or Catholic institutional interests.

"Professionalism" like "academic freedom" is an abstraction. It never works out in practice as it is defined by its practitioners. It is not an absolute because it bows to truth for one thing and to the virtues of knowledge, understanding, and wisdom for another. Furthermore, "professionalism" is conditioned by the finality of the institution it serves. In the Church's case this finality is the magisterium which governs the Church. Even newspapers have institutional objectives and editorial policies, otherwise why are there so many perceptions of news and truth? Burying stories in the back of a paper is commonplace, even for *The New York Times,* but one ought not expect to have Rome buried behind dissenters in an episcopal organ of communication.

Richard Daw simply placed Charles Curran and ACCU up front in *Origins* apparently without any thought of the greater good of the Church. No committed institution (AFL-CIO, NAACP, etc.) would turn its chief media over to an editor who makes himself an independent judge of what is good for the institution. Even the editor of the *Washington Post* responds to the policies of the publisher or he looks for another job. Or was Daw suggesting that he was free to ride his own track, even if it was no help to the Holy See's effort to get the Church's moral teaching back on track? Can one imagine the AFL-CIO or NAACP featuring attacks on their policies by Jerry Falwell on the front pages of their official magazines, with Lane Kirkland and Benjamin Hooks drawing up the rear?

The ideology of the NC News Service and its parent organization—the USCC—and the cozy relationship of both with major dissenters was once more in view a month later, when Msgr. Daniel Hoye, the NCCB General Secretary, announced the appointment of Father Michael Buckley, S.J., as Executive Director of NCCB's Committee on Catholic Doctrine and Pastoral Research. The Committee on Doctrine was particularly crucial because it had been established to keep an eye on the theological aberrations disturbing the Catholic faithful, errors which Rome had catalogued over two decades. Msgr. Richard Malone, a Philadelphia priest whose priestly service included a stint in Cardinal Ratzinger's Doctrinal Congregation, had held the post for ten years and was known to be disenchanted with the doctrinal course USCC followed. USCC watchers knew that Hoye and company were unhappy with him. There were no recognized pro-Roman partisans in this national Chancery Office except Malone. Suddenly, he was notified his contract with the National Conference of Catholic Bishops would not be renewed. Just as quickly, a California Jesuit named Michael Buckley was named to take Malone's place. Hoye was the appointer of record, but Buckley had more important sponsors. He was known to enjoy the confidence of San Francisco's Archbishop John Quinn.

The nomination immediately ran into a buzz saw of complaint from Bishops-in-the-field. While bylaws of the USCC gave General Secretary Hoye a quasi-absolute control over the hiring and firing of his staff, it was commonly understood that Hoye, like his predecessors, was subject to the president and the major officers of the NCCB. After 1968 the key official in this national apparatus was Bishop Joseph Bernardin, first as General Secretary (1968–72), then as president of NCCB (1974–77), and later when subsequent presidents, Quinn, Roach, Malone, and May, were considered members of the "Bernardin party." Very few Bishops outside this circle had any direct influence over the USCC bureaucracy. Indeed, General Secretaries have been known to tell individual Bishops that their choices for committee assignments were not acceptable to staff. Phyllis Schlafly was denied one such appointment on a Family Life Committee which a new Bishop-chairman from the Midwest thought overrepresented the feminist ideology. Another Bishop-ordinary from the industrial East, when he objected to an unsatisfactory panel of which he was expected to be chairman, was told by the General Secretary: "You Bishops have to learn you're not running the USCC." This is particularly the mind-set with which the opposition to Buckley would eventually be forced to deal. The USCC establishment, reinforced by the nation's chief Bishops, was not used to contradiction by Bishops-in-the-field no matter how many prestigious Sees they held, and the Bishops who objected to Buckley as the "watchdog" of Catholic doctrine in the United States were not minor figures in the Church.

What was their concern? Jesuit Michael Buckley had a well-developed record of dissent from Church teachings. Some Bishops knew this of themselves, and those who did not were so advised by Buckley's fellow Jesuits. His most publicized nonconformity came on March 16, 1977, when, with his confreres at the Jesuit Theologate at Berkeley, he asserted Rome erred in its case against the priestly ordination of women. The dissent was published in *The Los Angeles Times,* even before their letter of protest was received by Apostolic Delegate Jean Jadot to whom it was directed. Part of their reasoning contained the following rationalization: "Dissent in our culture is the protest of those who belong. It is the loyal opposition of those who feel their very identification is leading them into a situation in which they seem to acquiesce in what is evil."[24] This mode of thinking was akin to that expressed in another letter (1985) Buckley sent to Apostolic Pro-Nuncio Laghi, when he called Rome's dealings with recalcitrant religious who signed a 1984 advertisement favoring abortion "materially sinful." These judgments are irreconcilable with his self-professed "love of the Church and the Vicar of Christ."

The record also showed that Father Buckley identified with another Berkeley pronouncement on *Humanae Vitae* which asserted that Paul VI's teaching "does not seem to us to require internal assent to its conclusions as true," a remarkable prejudgment in view of later statements on the subject of contraception by John Paul II's *Familiaris Consortio* and the Roman Synod of 1980.[25] As a member of Archbishop John Quinn's Committee on Religious Life, Buckley praised forms of religious life which rejected Church Law and the charisms of the founders of well-established religious orders. His vague understanding of Catholic truth also came to the fore when he criticized Archbishop John

Foley's address to the presidents of Jesuit universities in December 1985. Foley had made a point of the "truth already possessed" by the Church, which he said the Catholic university was obligated to transmit. This was not satisfactory to Buckley:

> What the Archbishop calls "truth already possessed" can be more deeply understood, purified from its accultural accretions and steadied in its assertions of the message of Christ, only if its reflections occur in an atmosphere in which its questions and its evidence are taken seriously and challenged with academic care and freedom.[26]

Buckley also placed himself on record in opposition to Cardinal Baum's schema on Catholic university life.

Simply stated, Buckley's expressed views claim that no statement of magisterium stands until university professors accept it. In his way of thinking no Catholic institution of higher learning can be anything more than a debating society in which pros and cons about the Faith are eternally argued, with the debaters acting as their own judges without the intervention of the "outside" authority, called magisterium. His approach was considered unsatisfactory a century ago by no less an authority than Cardinal Newman.

Many Jesuits looked upon Buckley's appointment as a slap at the Holy See. They knew him to be counter-Catholic, not the counterculturist one might expect a Jesuit to be. They also had concerns about the degree to which Buckley affirmed the declared teaching of the Church.

When four weeks after the Hoye announcement (June 1986) the U.S. Bishops met in Collegeville, Minnesota, for their mid-year meeting, important Bishops made their objections known and without much argument from NCCB's officers the appointment was rescinded. This unprecedented move startled many, but it represented a first effort by informed Bishops to have, at long last, input into an agency whose public positions were not infrequently at odds with Rome and with their view of proper Church priorities. The complaining Bishops went home to their respective dioceses consoled in the knowledge that their voices were heard, only to find later that they had been mousetrapped.

Before the month was out San Francisco's Archbishop John Quinn led a charge to have the appointment reinstituted. In a three-page letter to Msgr. Hoye (dated July 15, 1986), Quinn fulminated against the Buckley critics, defended his protégé's "orthodoxy and loyalty to the Holy See," saw the objections as an attack on the hierarchy and the USCC itself, and demanded some new "process" to reaffirm the Buckley appointment. Although the Quinn letter was circulated widely at his request, it did not lack for episcopal criticism, even on the West Coast: (1) of the process which proposed Buckley for a sensitive episcopal post, almost out of nowhere and without any broad consultation among Bishops, and (2) of the failure to select (as one Bishop phrased it) a theologian "who has an unqualified allegiance to the Holy Father and to the Holy See and whose past record contains absolutely no deviation from this highest level of fidelity." He did not think Father Buckley passed this test.

One would think that the issue was joined and that if the administration was to renege on its Collegeville recall, there would be a full-scale adjudication of the differences, involving the complaining Bishops and especially those Jesuits who did not consider Michael Buckley an apt candidate for the role of doctrinal "watchdog" of the U.S. hierarchy. A report prepared by Jesuits for the complaining Bishops contained this paragraph: "The grave wounds which have been inflicted on the Jesuit Community in the name of false reform have come for the most part through our formation program. No institute has personified these evils better than the Jesuit theologate presently located in Berkeley, California. Buckley has played a primary role in the life and work of this theologate. He is sometimes called 'Mr. Berkeley.' Two principal evils have emanated from that theologate. The *first* is a revisionist view of Catholic doctrines of faith and morals. The *second* is a principled or determined rejection of liturgical discipline."

Instead of a full-scale investigation of the doubts, Msgr. Hoye, acting on behalf of the Bishops' ruling body, convoked a committee of three Bishops of his own choosing, headed by Archbishop Daniel Pilarczyk, one-time auxiliary to Cardinal Bernardin in Cin-

cinnati and his successor there. Without calling any outside witnesses and, as far as one can judge, solely by reading the complaints and interviewing the controversial Jesuit himself, the
three Bishops in less than a month decided that Buckley's "position on the question of the ordination of women is one that is
theologically sound and in accord with Church teaching." They
further asserted, "We have no evidence that Fr. Buckley had ever
publically dissented from the teaching of the magisterium, or was
in any way disloyal to the Church, the Holy Father, or the Holy
See." Michael Buckley was rehired forthwith.[27]

If Archbishop Pilarczyk's committee did not appreciate the significance of the issues raised by the original Bishop-protesters,
others did. Sister Mary Augusta Neal, Catholics for a Free Choice,
Daniel and Marjorie Maguire, Frances Kissling, Mary Hunt, and
the *National Catholic Reporter* favored the appointment, each one
of these being a proponent of dissent within the Church. One
tongue-in-cheek endorser of Buckley had an unusual reason:
"The more they do things like this, the sooner the Holy See will
realize it has a monstrosity on its hands." Even Msgr. Hoye tried
to explain Buckley away: "He will retain the right to his own
opinions in the field; when he's working for the Conference, he'll
possess the qualities of a good staff person."[28]

The most important aspect of the "Buckley victory" was the
determination of the top leadership of the NCCB to have their
way, even against notable Bishops-in-the-field, and to insist on
perpetuating the USCC's ambiguity on important doctrinal issues.
While those "other" Bishops were not directly attacked, Archbishop Quinn took note of their presence within the Conference
and dismissed their significance in his search for scapegoats. He
directed his fire instead at "an author who has written a book
attacking the American hierarchy and the Conference," a reference to my 1982 *Crisis of Authority* (Regnery-Gateway), which far
from being "an attack" was a catalogue of the programs and
people favored by the USCC and the contrast of those choices
with the ones made in Rome under Paul VI and John Paul II.
Similar outrage was not manifested by the San Francisco prelate
against those academics or religious superiors who equivalently

decimated major religious communities by their dissidence. *NC News* correspondent Jerry Filteau picked up the Quinn charge, in his effort to find a scapegoat for the brouhaha over Buckley, pointing to Msgr. George Kelly "a noted advocate of conservative positions on theology and Church authority."[29] The only role I played in this controversy was to respond to concerned Bishops who looked to The Fellowship of Catholic Scholars for background on Father Buckley. A graduate student's search of the Catholic Periodical Index elicited enough data to confirm the doubts of those Bishops. If the appointment had been to a sensitive post in government, e.g., FBI, a periodical index would only be the beginning place for a security check. But not even this minimum clearance was looked upon with favor by those in charge of the Bishops' Conference, when a decision with profound doctrinal significance to the Church was called into question by Bishops! While there were those, like the *National Catholic Reporter,* who saw the Buckley reappointment as a defeat of the Church's "right wing," the real loser was the freedom of Bishops-in-the-field to play a major role in the conduct of their own Conference. Not only were they ignored, but they were not made to feel influential enough to initiate the kind of investigation that is commonplace in similar civic situations.

The long-range meaning of the Buckley appointment would shortly be clear. Executive Directors of anything, including a Committee on Doctrine, are not chairmen of the Board, but as the day-to-day functionaries, they control who does what research, who sees the morning mail, and a large amount of what those decision-makers in the Chair get to examine. They are also in a good position to readjust broad policy decisions whenever details are given over to lower levels of management to work out.

THE SUPPORTING BISHOPS

After a Labor Day Mass 1986 in the lower sacristy of St. Patrick's Cathedral, William Cardinal Baum remarked how fortunate it was for the Church that The Fellowship of Catholic Scholars existed. The Prefect of Rome's Congregation for Catholic Education was prompted to make this remark after saying how encouraging the Fellowship's earlier report was that fourteen hundred Catholic academics supported the Holy See's effort to restore authenticity to Catholic universities and to their theology departments. For months Rome had been bombarded with negative headlines suggesting that the recent censure of Charles Curran and Baum's new guidelines for Catholic higher education were offensive to the vast majority of Catholic scholars in the U.S. Factually, there are at least twenty-five thousand professors teaching in the U.S. Catholic college network and no one knew for sure what most of them thought. Curran and Hesburgh used the media effectively to pressure Rome by the sheer weight of alleged antimagisterial numbers. The Fellowship survey appeared as a beacon of light in what to Rome looked like a dark night, so hostile were the Curran-Hesburgh forces to whatever the Holy See did to guarantee that those institutions which traded on the name were truly Catholic. The results of the Fellowship's instant survey were no more scientifically accurate than the polls organized against Rome within the Catholic University of America. But it was encouraging to the Pope and to the Bishops in communion with him.

The Fellowship for ten years and more has supported every definition and policy of the Holy See, covering a wide spectrum of decisions, from very sacred matters to the kind of attire suitable for priests and religious. While certain Catholic academic institutions following Vatican II undertook to place themselves in a critic's role vis-à-vis Church authority, this was not the Fellowship posture. Of course, there were those occasional exceptions among some Bishops who made themselves counterpoints to or rivals of the Holy See. Such Bishops surfaced first during the Council and achieved a certain notoriety in the media. Many dissenting scholars would not have achieved power over Catholic structures without the active collaboration or passive acquiescence of anti-Roman Bishops. Nonetheless, as a general rule the Fellowship supported Bishops and was supported in turn by them.

One other difficulty complicated the Fellowship's task. The foundational doctrines of the Church, its supernatural basis as it were, were of a different order from its social teaching. There were more legitimate differences possible to Catholics over how to lift the poor out of poverty than how to protect the life of the unborn; over making peace as against making war, about reorganizing socio-political life in contrast with reorganizing the sacramental life of the Church. A Catholic scholar could have socialist or capitalist inclinations but he could not be party to a move to have doubts about Christ's divinity or His Real Presence settled by a vote of the people. On worldly issues the Fellowship member could be "liberal" or "conservative," but by faith he normally was committed to all that the Catholic Church believes and teaches doctrinally, even though media perspective often consigned him to conservative rank. (It is strange that many of those who rejected Catholic teaching were called "liberal," even though there was nothing liberating for a man of faith in breaking his ties with the Pope.)

During the short life of the Fellowship, therefore, members contributed to perfecting Church documents, even though this meant criticism of this or that draft. On the other hand, if a particular Bishop or a Bishops' agency maintained positions against a definition or a policy initiated by the Holy See (e.g., on religious life), it was no surprise to anyone that Fellowship members would stand with the Holy See. The affected Bishops or agencies were not pleased, of course, but the general policy of the Fellowship to support magisterium remained normative. Most Bishops understood this, as did the Holy See, which usually was familiar with its own critics within National Conferences.

Four Cardinals helped The Fellowship of Catholic Scholars come into existence and 150 Bishops, about one half of the U.S. hierarchy, sustained its ongoing operation. John Wright, Prefect of the Congregation for the Clergy in Rome, as early as 1974 began to speak of the need for a counterforce in the U.S. Church to offset the usurped power of dissenters over the Church's professional associations. Terence Cooke, Archbishop of New York, became the first benefactor, and John Carberry, Archbishop of St. Louis, offered his Kenrick Seminary in 1976 as the foundation center for the Fellowship. And so it happened, with a friend from

Australia, Karl Schmude, making a suggestion that the association be called a "Fellowship."

When one examines the list of Cardinals who have corresponded with, or otherwise expressed their interest in the Fellowship over the years, the coverage is rather remarkable for a scholarly group which began on the outside of the reigning academic establishment and whose public role until this day is resistance to dissent. Cardinals Aponte, Baum, Carberry, Cody, Cooke, Hickey, Krol, Law, Manning, Medeiros, O'Boyle, and O'Connor were very supportive. (Only two U.S. Cardinals showed no interest.) Also in the forefront were the hundred and more Bishops led by Hartford's Archbishop John Whealon, Dubuque's James Byrne, Omaha's Daniel Sheehan (who attended the first convention), Military Archbishop Joseph Ryan, New Orlean's Philip Hannan, St. Louis' John May, Baltimore's Willian Borders, Mobile's Oscar Lipscomb, Philadelphia's Anthony Bevilacqua, Portland's William Levada, Atlanta's Thomas Donnellan, and New York's John Maguire and Fulton Sheen. (Only three major Archbishops kept their distance from the Fellowship.)

It would be less than honest, however, to leave the impression that friendly Bishops were closely involved with the daily doings of the Fellowship. Many Bishops do not always see their own mail, nor do they have any desire to be caught up in academic associations. In view of what has gone on within Catholic schools since 1965, this may have been a costly oversight. But it is a fact of their life. Unquestionably, some Bishops were at odds with the Holy See and from the beginning were suspicious of the Fellowship's role and function. In 1986, for example, one Bishop summarized his feelings this way: "I struggle with the spirit of The Fellowship of Catholic Scholars." He considered its chief spokesmen were "too careless with the truth and too self-righteous in your approach." Most of its scholars "left him cold." In a hierarchy of more than three hundred Bishops, it would be unusual not to find some in the U.S., as in every critical doctrinal controversy throughout the centuries, somewhat critical of Roman partisans. Only time will tell on which side the uncounted Bishops stand. The Fellowship of Catholic Scholars has been useful to some

Bishops and to some Roman curialists. This does not mean that the Fellowship is right in all its determinations or that Catholic Bishops need agree with Fellowship interventions in academic squabbles. But what forever will remain a conundrum is why the U.S. Bishops' national machinery displayed almost no interest in what might be called friendly scholarly associations. Had a broad range of scholars been consulted in the 1962–64 period, Bishops would have found majority support for the Church's teaching on contraception. By 1968 scholars, left to their own devices, drifted away from magisterium. Even today, the teaching of the Church is sustained in more Catholic academic circles than newspaper headlines indicate by such organizations as the American Catholic Philosophical Society and the Mariological Society, along with the Fellowship. Their officers are rarely brought into the councils of the U.S. Bishops.

The tendency in this situation is, of course, to blame, the Washington bureaucracy. This is not a legitimate explanation and Bishops rightfully resent the implication that they are pawns of young bureaucrats. A similar process of disassociation is at work when critics of the Vatican blame the Curia because they dare not make frontal assaults on the person of the Pope. No, sub-institutions are what leadership wishes or allows them to be. If bureaucracies are big enough, such as is the case with the U.S. Government, they can in the long run outmaneuver short-lived political leaders, and often do. However, Church bureaucracies are not that large and they could be dismantled overnight by strong episcopal leadership willing to suffer media pain. But if national episcopal leadership is concentrated in a "little circle" of Bishops willing to give time to the Washington bureaucracy, it is the Bishops involved, not the staff, who deserve the credit for the successes or blame for the troubles which ensue. If the U.S. Church is in tension with Rome at any level, responsibility rests with the Bishops in control of the NCCB and perhaps negatively with those Bishops who complain about the national policies and programs but are unwilling to devote the energy necessary to making their influence felt. The number of Bishops who wash their hands of the Washington apparatus are not few.

NOTES

1. *NC News,* June 4, 1986.
2. *St. Louis Review,* September 2, 1977.
3. *Our Sunday Visitor,* August 13, 1978.
4. *National Catholic Reporter,* August 11, 1978.
5. *America,* September 7, 1978.
6. *National Catholic Register,* July 2, 1978.
7. *America,* September 6, 1980.
8. See George A. Kelly's *The Church's Problem with Biblical Scholars* Chicago: Franciscan Herald Press, 1985.
9. *Communio,* Winter 1978.
10. *Theological Studies,* December 1971.
11. *Development of Doctrine.*
12. *NCR,* June 1, 1979.
13. *Commonweal,* June 8, 1979.
14. See this "autonomy" developed at length in "The Bulletin" of the Council of Societies for the Study of Religion," April 1988.
15. *Origins,* February 7, 1980.
16. *Origins,* May 16, 1976.
17. John 12:31.
18. *Gaudium et Spes,* No. 13.
19. *Our Sunday Visitor,* January 3, 1982.
20. *Education in Human Sexuality for Christians,* No. 62.
21. *Newsletter* of The Fellowship, 1982.
22. *Origins,* March 27 and April 10, 1986.
23. Memorandum of Daw to Hoye, April 24, 1986.
24. *Origins,* April 7, 1977.
25. *America,* September 7, 1968.
26. *National Jesuit News,* May 1986.
27. See Msgr. Daniel Hoye's August 22, 1986, letter of explanation to the U.S. Bishops.
28. *National Catholic Register,* June 10, 1986.
29. *NC News,* June 24, 1986.

EIGHT

The Coming
of John O'Connor

There was a man sent by God whose name was John.

THIS GOSPEL LINE was written for the Baptist, of course, but it could just as easily explain the appointment of John O'Connor to the See of New York. By all human accounting John O'Connor should be a pastor in Philadelphia. The circumstances of his detour to New York are nothing short of extraordinary.

In 1978 Msgr. O'Connor was Chief of U.S. Naval Chaplains, a rear admiral, and on the brink of retirement from military service. At fifty-eight years of age his next port of call normally would be Philadelphia, his home diocese. He did not seemingly have the good fortune of his close friend James Killeen, a New York priest and a Naval captain, who at retirement time in 1975

341

was tapped by Cardinal Cooke to be auxiliary Bishop for the Military Ordinariate. The MO, as it was called at the time, was an adjunct of the New York Archdiocese and the only upward ecclesiastical move available to an experienced chaplain. Even then only a few ever made the episcopal grade. (In 1986 it became an independent Archdiocese for the Military Services—U.S.A.) The fact that Cardinal Cooke took so long to fill this slot with Killeen made it unlikely that another opening would occur for years. Then, suddenly, on September 8, 1978, Bishop Killeen died. O'Connor came to St. Patrick's Cathedral to preach over his dead friend, and almost as if enough time had been wasted already, Cooke named O'Connor to take Killeen's place overnight.

On April 24, 1979, O'Connor became Auxiliary Bishop to the Military Ordinariate in New York. Of itself, the appointment was not especially significant, since in the sixty years of the organization's history, no Auxiliary Bishop, save one, achieved prominence. John O'Hara became Cardinal Archbishop of Philadelphia, but he had been Bishop of Buffalo after his service in the MO. The new Bishop O'Connor would serve under Coadjutor Archbishop Joseph T. Ryan, who played the O'Hara role for Cardinal Cooke. Ryan, who today heads the Military Archdiocese, had been a Navy chaplain, Archbishop of Anchorage, and for a number of years the U.S. Bishops' representative in the Middle East. During Ryan's tour of duty in Lebanon he became friendly with the young Msgr. Pio Laghi, assigned to that hot spot as part of his diplomatic apprenticeship for the Vatican's Secretariat of State. In 1979 O'Connor could look forward perhaps to assume Ryan's position in the MO if the Coadjutor retired, but by and large the post itself was normally considered an ecclesiastical dead end.

Enter Archbishop Joseph Bernardin, then of Cincinnati, chosen by the NCCB's president to chair a committee destined to draft a pastoral letter on the moral and religious dimensions of war. Bernardin immediately created a committee of five Bishops, four of whom were recognized as peace advocates and John O'Connor, military man and author of a 1968 book *A Chaplain Looks at Vietnam,* a book considered at the time to be "a ringing defense of the [President] Johnson administration policies." To NCCB watchers the pastoral's orientation was clear from the start, designed to be written under the guidance of four episcopal "doves" and one alleged Bishop hawk seemingly chosen to lend credibility to the final document's objectivity. What appeared to be a shrewd tactical move by Bernardin—to involve an obscure military Bishop in a preordained process—turned into a historic opportunity thrust upon O'Connor. In an important respect O'Connor owes his Cardinal's hat to Joseph Bernardin.

Bringing a pastoral from draft to official document is difficult enough, but "The Challenge of Peace" (1983) evoked more controversy than was necessary because the thrust of the message was skewed from the beginning toward pacifism and against American defense strategy. The political disagreements need not concern us here. They are amply reported in George Weigel's *Tranquillitas Ordinis,* which criticized the Bishops' preoccupation with nuclear weapons, when they should have been more concerned with morally appropriate uses of military force in defense of freedom.

What was incredible to many acquainted with the Catholic moral tradition was the inclusion in the first draft of a proposed episcopal judgment that "the deterrence relationship which prevails between the United States, the Soviet Union and other powers is objectively a sinful situation because of the threats implied in it. . . . [yet] . . . we reluctantly tolerate the American government's reliance on nuclear deterrence because unilateral withdrawal from this reliance has its obvious and grave risks." This statement placed the Bishops on record as maintaining the immorality of the mere possession of a vast nuclear arsenal because of the implied threat that it would be used, if necessary, to kill innocent Russians. The Bishops' committee was willing, however, to tolerate at least for a time the possession of the nuclear arsenal because *de facto* it did deter the Russians from warlike activity. Any unilateral disarmament by the United States posed a threat to world peace, thus justifying at least temporarily the continued use of nuclear weapons as a deterrent force against world conflict.

The line of reasoning in this first draft incorporated not only bad logic but, what was worse, bad theology. First, the possession of nuclear weapons did not of itself mean the U.S. would use them to kill innocent Russians. For Bishops to cast doubt on the proposition that deterrence of itself was objectively evil was itself an iffy judgment. Worse, however, was the follow-up conclusion that deterrence was objectively evil, but it might be tolerated in the interest of continued peace. In other words, we could do evil as a means to good. This was totally opposed to the moral teaching of the Catholic Church, going back to the days of St. Paul, who condemned the proposition that evil could be done that good might come of it.[1] If the end never justified the means, when the means themselves were evil, what was a Bishops' committee doing saying it could be done.

Enter John O'Connor. He not only knew the difference between military weapons and moral principles, but he knew his Catholic theology. And from the earliest stages of his participation on the Bernardin committee, he worked to move the Bishops' committee away from preoccupation with military technology and toward the fundamentals of the Catholic tradition. At the very least any trace of proportionalist theology had to be removed from the pastoral. Why? Because if you can justify one intrinsic evil, you can justify all such, providing you have a proportionately good reason. You can justify contraception, abortion, divorce, racial discrimination, etc. As for the per se evil of deterrence, someone failed to be in touch with Rome. On June 11, 1982, John Paul II said to the United Nations: "In current conditions 'deterrence' based on balance, certainly not an end in itself but as a step on the way toward disarmament, may still be judged morally acceptable."[2]

There is no doubt that the controlling forces within the Bernardin committee, and these included USCC staff personnel, were comfortable with the first two drafts and with the bad theology contained therein. John O'Connor recognized the disorder. About this time too, someone asked a USCC official how proportionalism —the theory that given satisfactory reasons you can choose evil to do good—could survive two drafts of a Bishops' pastoral. The answer came back: "Because Bernardin wants it there." At the minimum someone on staff wanted it there. And staff (obviously with Bernardin's consent) had assuredly skewed the list of episcopal consultors to favor pacifist and/or proportionalist theologians, including Joseph Fuchs, S.J., Richard McCormick, S.J., and Charles Curran. John O'Connor was not only outvoted by four Bishops, but by four or five staff as well. He made recommendations about new consultants but was generally ignored.

In spite of these handicaps, the correctness of his theological position and his military common sense came to the attention of Apostolic Delegate Pio Laghi. Working under Laghi's friend Archbishop Ryan did not hurt O'Connor either. But the urgency of O'Connor's concern (at one time he feared he might have to vote against the final document) meant that Rome eventually would have to become involved. Bishop O'Connor was now playing in the big leagues.

The critical issue at stake was the nature of the Catholic Church and the truth of its message. Father Donald J. Keefe, S.J., summarized the crisis for the Fellowship of Catholic Scholars' *Newsletter*[3] as follows:

> If American Catholics accept without discussion the notion that intrinsic evil can be tolerated to gain some good end, then consequentialist moral theory is in place and, with it, the politicization of Catholic morality and worship. In such an eventuality an ideologically-grounded *praxis* will replace doctrine and this *praxis,* rather than the Church's worship in truth, becomes the one responsibility which remains to Bishops, whose magisterial function will have been abandoned. Consequentialism is not merely a moral theology, it is an entire ecclesiology, for it submits all the concreteness of the Church's historicity to the single notion of *praxis.* This *praxis* supplants morality, doctrine, and sacramental worship. Once admitted into the Church, it must dissolve the Church, and that dissolution begins, as it must, with the episcopal office.

Well, it did not take long for Rome to move in on the situation. On January 18–19, 1983, a meeting was held in the Old Synod Hall of the Vatican. Curial officials of the highest order and leading Churchmen from five European hierarchies convened, with

Joseph Cardinal Ratzinger sitting in the moderator's chair. Early in the session the German Prefect of the Congregation for the Doctrine of the Faith insisted that Bishops' conferences did not have a *mandatum docendi,* that is, a teaching mandate from the Church. (This, he suggested, belonged to the individual Bishop or the episcopal college with the Pope.) He also raised a question about placing pacifism and the Church's just war principles on the same level. Pacifism claims there is no justification for force at any time. The just war theory says there is—under certain circumstances. The draft mistakenly tried to place them on an equal footing. Pacifism, while an option for individual Christians, was never recognized by the Church as a choice for states obligated to protect their people from unjust aggression. Ratzinger also questioned the judgment made on deterrence. When the meeting ended it was clear that this high-level ecclesiastical group had difficulties with the U.S. Bishops' proposals on the technical and military factors associated with war making. Not only were they weakening Bishops' teaching authority by overextending episcopal claims of competence, but also the laity's freedom of choice in free matters seemed to be circumscribed by unnecessary offical moralizing. It was wrong, the Roman assembly said, ever to propose Bishops' teaching as a basis for debate. Nor should Bishops propose as doctrine of the Church what pertains to prudential judgment involving alternative choices.

Less than three months later (May 3, 1983) the Bishops' pastoral letter was finally issued under the title "The Challenge of Peace: God's Promise and Our Response." John O'Connor voted for it, and almost all U.S. Bishops as well. The document no longer contained a reference to deterrence as a tolerable evil. Instead, the statement provided "a strictly conditioned moral acceptance of nuclear deterrence." (No. 186.)

One week later (May 10, 1983) John O'Connor was appointed Bishop of Scranton. There was little question in anyone's mind that his role in shaping the pastoral brought him a diocese of his own and that the promoter of the change was Archbishop Pio Laghi, with an able assist from his MO "boss," Archbishop Joseph T. Ryan. As everyone knows now, the story did not end there. Six months later, on October 6, 1983, Terence Cardinal Cooke died of acute leukemia, the result of his eighteen-year bout with cancer of the lymph nodes. The not-so-surprising choice to succeed him, made on January 31, 1984, was John O'Connor. The rise from obscurity to international prominence in one year was complete and remarkable.

Although he was ensconced in Scranton less than six months when Cooke died, O'Connor was a natural candidate for New York from the start. Subsequent news stories credited Cardinal Krol with placing his man in New York, and surely the Philadelphia Ordinary was consulted. Yet, the process of selecting Cooke's successor was more complicated. The consultations were wide, across the country considering the importance of the New York See. The influence of Archbishops Laghi and Ryan was not to be discounted. High-level politics went on, of course. Undoubtedly, the powers-that-be in control of the national Church machinery had no reason to be happy with an O'Connor in New York. News reports suggested that Archbishop Thomas Kelly of Louisville was their favorite candidate. He had succeeded to the Bernardin chair as General Secretary of the USCC in 1972 and was in direct line with all the NCCB presidents going back to Cardinal Dearden. Archbishop Kelly in New York would be more of the same and would have nationalized the influence of Bernardin. The internal game play was intense but Rome, i.e., John Paul II, had something different in mind. Pio Laghi prevailed. On the day of his installation (March 19, 1984), when we met after the ceremony, it amused me to say to O'Connor: "It pleases me to welcome a non-Kelly to New York."

In many ways O'Connor was a natural for Gotham City, the media center of the world. The teaching possibilities of a good communicator in St. Patrick's Cathedral were obvious. And, considering the catechetical confusion rampant in the U.S. Church, Rome needed a clarion voice there if it intended to follow through on the preachments of John Paul II. What the Holy See could not afford was an appointment to a powerful See like New York of a weak Bishop, one weak in convictions or weak in his ability to reform the Church in the Vatican II mold. Church rebels had been having a field day with such Bishops since the Council. Neither could the assignment go to an ecclesiastical climber who reveled chiefly in pomp or circumstance.

From discussions that were carried on during the post-Cooke interregnum, it was evident that Rome would send a signal to the U.S. Church by this appointment. (Shortly before, Holland Catholics received such a message with the assignment of Archbishop Adrian Simonis to Utrecht.) But to accomplish this in New York John Paul II had to go outside the normal procedures, to do the unusual, to reach for a "personality," yet one totally committed to the Holy See.

John O'Connor had several things going for him. Two of New York's greatest Archbishops—John Hughes and Francis Spellman —had come from the outside, from Philadelphia (1838) and Boston (1939), respectively. O'Connor enjoyed worldwide pastoral experience and already a national reputation. He had a trained mind and scholarly credentials besides, including an earned Ph.D. He knew the New York scene but was not tied into its bureaucracies. He was an eloquent preacher with good media presence.

These considerations impressed more than Archbishop Laghi, because eight months after O'Connor left the military ordinariate for Scranton, he returned to New York fully aware that a Cardinal's hat awaited him.

THE CARDINAL ARCHBISHOP OF NEW YORK

When the New York See was "open" in 1902 and the potential candidates to fill the slot lived as far away as Peoria and as nearby as Brooklyn, canonist Richard Burtsell opined that "New York belonged to the whole country and should look for the best man in it." By the turn of the century New York was an ecclesiastical plum, and as the new century grew old, it became bigger than life, unique enough to prompt a new Pope to greet the new Archbishop O'Connor, "Welcome to the Archbishop of the Capital of the World!" Outsiders have often been accused of envy when dealing with the inmates of "Fun City," especially when the territory is aggrandized by the likes of an Ed Koch. In national ecclesiastical affairs New York has always been something of a loner, and its Archbishop has rarely been identified in alliance with other prelates. Indeed, the major Eastern Sees have rarely been linked together politically. Certainly not the way Chicago, Cincinnati, and Detroit have been, and now St. Louis. Can anyone imagine Philadelphia's Dennis Daugherty, Boston's William O'Connell, or New York's Patrick Hayes—all Cardinals—forming a Catholic troika? New York has had six Cardinals, more than any other, yet today Los Angeles is larger, Chicago is more assertive, and Philadelphia has more class. Not every New York Cardinal cut a prominent figure on the pages of Church history, few did, but any appointment to New York after 1902 automatically brought a Cardinal's hat with the man, the sign of papal favor for the See and approval to the prelate who sat in its Cathedral Chair.

If one overlooks his public function as a leading American citizen, the Cardinal of New York performs three important ecclesiastical roles. He is:

1. The Pope's adviser and confidant on matters pertaining to the Universal Church. The word "cardinal" means "hinge" and the use of the word to describe the Pope's closest advisers goes back to the sixth century, when leading priests in Rome were tapped to assist the Pope in administering a Church that was becoming ever more universal. The present College of Cardinals was constituted in the twelfth century and is regulated today by Canons 349–359 of the New Code of Canon Law. A Cardinal is usually appointed to one or more of the Holy See's nine Congregations, three Secretariats, three Tribunals, and to any one of the seemingly endless Roman Councils, Commissions, or Offices.

The first three New York Cardinals (John McCloskey, John Farley, and Patrick Hayes) were New York priests and Roman loyalists, but had little input to *the administration of the Universal Church.* After the Concordat with Mussolini in 1929, New York was the right place for the administrators of Vatican City to find professional counsel on money matters. The Holy See was by then a world enterprise with universal obligations. There was great wealth in Church holdings, art works alone running to hundreds of millions, but the value of these assets was cultural, irreducible to cash flow. And it was cash flow the Pope needed after 1930 to support his far-flung missionary endeavor, now bereft of income from the Papal States. Peter's Pence from Bishops all over the world assuredly could not pay the mounting annual bills. Income from investments, therefore, became a major source of the papal patrimony, and New York Cardinals going back to Hayes's time were involved in maximizing returns to the papal treasury. Cardinal Cooke was brought into the Vatican's budget crisis during the 1980s and was rewarded with special appointments to several Roman Synods. But beyond this role and choosing Bishops, all the above-named prelates had little influence in Rome.

Cardinal Spellman, of course, was the exception. From the appointment of Myron Taylor in 1939 as FDR's special representative to the Vatican through Spellman's last visit to U.S. soldiers in Vietnam, the year before he died, he was "super-delegate" for the Holy See. Fund-raising for papal causes was only one of his special roles, as everyone knows, but whether the matter was Hungarian Jews oppressed by Hitler, the trials of Archbishop Stepinac and Mindszenty, War Relief, the needs of the Philippine Church, intervention with U.S. presidents on behalf of the Pope, or the internal affairs of dioceses, Spellman was Rome's chief ambassador. In this sense "the Little Man" was unique, Popes finding in him a prelate whose counsel was generally sound and who knew how to get things done.

The sum and substance of the matter, therefore, is that the man makes the job. Because an Archbishop, even in a prestigious See like New York, wears a Cardinal's hat, is no guarantee he will have unusual influence with the Pope or become a Papal adviser in more than name only. Only time will tell how Cardinal O'Connor fills these shoes.

2. A potential leader of the U.S. Church, by office if not by election. The impact of New York's Archbishops on the Church of the United States is more easily measured, although again it varies with the times and the man. John Hughes in the mid-nineteenth century made his fellow Bishops nervous by the boldness of his defense of the Church and of poor Catholic immigrants against their enemies. Yet he was just what Catholic immigrants needed in the midst of the Protestant Crusade against their arrival and their fervent expressions of Catholic Faith on Protestant soil. Hughes became a lightning rod of Catholic identity, and by the sheer force of his personality created a well-disciplined diocese, in spite of the ragamuffin nature of his flock. Critics he had, but most of them died in obscurity, whereas Hughes remains heralded by many as New York's greatest Archbishop. He created a model diocesan machinery, copied by other Bishops, fought efforts (correctly it seems) to colonize the priestless Midwestern dioceses with "his" immigrants, and established the patriotism of Catholics, once but not for all, with his public support of the Civil War. In his time New York priests began to take over distant Sees so that eventually a New Yorker presided over Chicago, New Orleans, Philadelphia, San Francisco, Los Angeles, Anchorage, and other places.

Twenty-one years after Hughes the only other non-Cardinal Archbishop of New York, Michael Augustine Corrigan, also a much beleaguered prelate, turned out to be a national Church leader in several important respects. His defense of the parochial school system was critical at a time when important Bishops were almost successful in persuading Rome that there were other acceptable substitutes to parish-owned and -operated schools. Corrigan's Dunwoodie Seminary, opened in 1896, was another pacesetter, considered in those early years a more demanding professional school than West Point. Furthermore, he was more correct on the subject of Americanism than other Bishops, at least in seeing its dangers. When Leo XIII's letter *Testem Benevolentiae* was issued on January 22, 1899, Corrigan was only one of two U.S. Bishops who thanked the Pope for addressing errors that Rome saw creeping into the body of the American Church. Catholic elites still insist on calling it a "phantom heresy," and perhaps it was such at the level of churchgoers. But Catholic opinion-molders of the day, and important Bishops, were convinced that the time to accommodate the Church to the American milieu and to have a face that looked less Roman had come. In practice this turn-of-the-century adaptation required a more positive approach to the Protestant culture and mores. Leo XIII, however, saw this trend as a dangerous American preoccupation with the practicalities of life on earth to the loss of life's spiritual meaning, a preference for activity over contemplation, a stress on freedom in religious life more than on the evangelical vows, and an illicit accommodation with Protestantism in general. Archbishop Corrigan shared the Pope's anxiety, although he was not joined at the time in this sentiment by a majority of his fellow Archbishops. Three score and more years would pass before these "errors" would make their way into the ranks of ordinary Catholics.

Disagreement between Rome and American Bishops, and among Bishops, during the nineteenth century reflected differences about strategies and tactics, not about the meaning of the Catholic Faith. There were no easy answers on how best to institutionalize the demands of the Church among multitongued constituents, most of whom were poor. The questions were subject to endless episcopal debates. Oneness of the Faith remained unchallenged at all levels during this era of Cardinal Gibbons' *Faith of Our Fathers* (1876) and the *Baltimore Catechism* (1884), whereas questions about national parishes, national tongues in catechesis, public aid to Catholic schools, intercredal cooperation with Protestants, establishment of a national Catholic university, etc., created a veritable babble of episcopal tongues. The arguments between Bishops, and the rivalries for Roman favor, were not always carried on with episcopal grace, but there was a wide spectrum of opinion expressed, with newspaper editors like James Gordon Bennett and James McMaster equally eager to tell Bishops where to head in. In spite of the cacophony a remarkable parish life had developed in the United States by World War I. Different though the styles of episcopal ruling seemed to be and argumentative the voices, too, Bishop leaders were plentiful. The results drew admiring glances from every Pope from Pius XI onward.

The chances of a John O'Connor, or a reincarnated John Ireland, John Lancaster Spalding, or a Bernard McQuaid, achieving similar prominence in the post-Vatican II Church are not the certainty they were in that nineteenth century called the age of the individual. All U.S. Bishops today are conscious of their membership in the National Conference of Catholic Bishops and the restraining influence it has on any episcopal voices contrary to group proclamations. Even after 1923 when the National Catholic Welfare Conference was finally in place, after misgivings in Rome, individual Bishops were not bound by its decisions and powerful Bishops simply ignored it. Little account was given, as in all forward movements, to warnings that a collective body of Bishops could short-circuit the relationship of the individual Bishop with the Holy See or would speak only for Bishops who represented the few who ran the NCWC. More significant perhaps was the remark attributed to an early NCWC staffer in 1923 to the effect that, "You can make Rome do whatever you want if you get a crowd behind you." This *obiter dicta* meant nothing in Roman-U.S. hierarchy relations until 1966 when the National Conference of Catholic Bishops (called the NCCB) replaced the Administrative Board of the NCWC.

A great deal has been written about the NCCB in the past twenty years and most of the commentary is extremist, lavish praise or not-so-faint damnation. A Conference which allegedly speaks for more than three hundred Bishops is not easy to pigeonhole. The best the outsider can do is to speak about perceptions. Since we are interested here only in the effect of a national bureaucratic institution on the individual Bishop, it is appropriate to ask: Is it possible for John Irelands or Bernard McQuaids to rise to national prominence in 1989 from obscure diocesan posts without the blessing of the national machinery? Would James Malone of Youngstown have made it to the front pages of *The New York Times* if he had not been president of the NCCB? Contemporary journalists like to counterpose Bernard Law of Boston to Joseph Bernardin of Chicago, as rivals for national ecclesiastical influence, but these prelates are Cardinals, with one leg up on prominence by nature of their super-status. Is this an accurate twentieth-century contrast to the Corrigan-Gibbons rivalry a hundred years ago? In 1989 obscure Bishops like Thomas Gumbleton (Detroit) or Raymond Hunthausen (Seattle) receive more media attention than Glennon Flavin (Lincoln) or Adam Maida (Green Bay), simply because they seem to be Rome bashers, not because they are considered outstanding ecclesiastical achievers.

There is little question that the NCCB is a more dominant force on individual Bishops than the NCWC ever was. Nor is there little doubt, either, that the machinery which was created by Detroit's John Cardinal Dearden is today firmly in the hands of Chicago's Joseph Cardinal Bernardin, himself brought to national prominence by Dearden in 1968. One noticed this influence in the 1986 Bishops' meeting where the five delegates (beside-Bernardin) chosen to represent the U.S. Church at the 1987 Roman Synod were identified with Chicago's Archbishop, as were the four Bishops (besides Bernardin) selected later to explain the U.S. Church to John Paul II, when the Pope arrived on the West Coast in September 1987. At that moment, at least, there was no serious challenge to the Bernardin hegemony in the national Bishops' machinery, even though many Bishops, and many here would be a large minority at least, are opposed to his general drift. How large a minority among the voting Bishops? Perhaps 120 against the 160 who might vote with Bernardin, if the 1986 elections for Conference president are a fair norm.

The important aspect of the national picture is not who dominates but what does the dominance mean. For the better part of forty years James Cardinal Gibbons of Baltimore was the country's leading prelate, but he had many rivals in Rome and in the public forum. No such serious public alternatives to Bernardin have yet emerged in recent years. The semblance of national unity among Bishops has been demanded as an attribute of the Conference, even though the media are aware of serious differences within the institution.

During the Gibbons era there were two distinct parties in the U.S. hierarchy whom commentators variously called Liberals or Americanists opposed by those called Conservatives or Romanists. Whether or not you read scholars like John Ellis, James Hennessey, Gerald Fogarty, or Jay P. Dolan, this is the ecclesiastical division you are given for that period. "Liberals" are generally written up as "good guys," while "Conservatives" are generally portrayed on the wrong side of every Catholic controversy. Old-time prelates like Gibbons and his allies, John Ireland or John Lancaster Spalding, usually receive favored treatment from the above-mentioned historians because they are perceived as "Liberal," but they were never so "Liberal" with Church teachings as the modern writers who praise them. Prelates like Corrigan, McQuade, and the German Bishops were strong opposing voices on major Church issues in those days. "Liberals" and "Conservatives" lost an equal amount of battles over the Romanization of the U.S. Church, but the Church prospered because all Bishops agreed on the Faith. Furthermore, although Gibbons could promote the cause of John L. Spalding for the Philadelphia See (he lost) for the reason that the latter "intimately understands the public spirit of the Republic," the Baltimore Cardinal was a staunchly orthodox Catholic. Even John Ireland, who would have permitted the state to operate schools built and owned by Catholic parishes, a politically avant-garde step if there ever was one, concurred with Pius X's condemnation of Modernism. Indeed, months before the Pope's condemnation of Modernism (1907), Ireland wrote that either Loisy was to be condemned, or Pius X would have to fold his tent and hie himself and his illusion of a divinely established Church into the nebulous regions of fable.

The situation after Vatican II was somewhat different. Bishops seemed to retreat everywhere before the backward movement (to Modernist days, at least) of the Catholic academe. The NCCB made every effort to accommodate itself to "experts," who looked upon Council documents as reasons enough to push the Church back to the undogmatic first century. Indeed, some Bishops (not just their experts) also seemed willing to turn the Church's clock back to less precise days of Catholic discipline, much to the shock of other Bishops. In any case, the majority of voting Bishops followed the NCCB leadership, although there always existed some rumbling in the tents.

This is not an ecclesiastical problem peculiar to the United States. The Dutch Bishops were surely the first offenders, followed in due course by Bishops of the First World, where most of the affluent Catholics lived and where Catholic academics seeking their worldly due often flexed their muscles in the face of hierarchy. In turn, Bishops in England, on the Continent, in Canada, and Down Under ran a good part of the way with their academic elites. Even when the latter seemed to go too far, Bishops were persuaded not to use counterforce because the media would make them look bad. Or, as many of them reasoned, little effective action could be taken if Paul VI himself was not doing much against dissent, save to make rhetorical protests.

Still, the time arrived, not long after the Charles Curran debacle in 1967, when it was clear that the U.S. Church's direction was professedly in tension with Rome. Cardinal Bernardin candidly admitted this "tension" only in 1987 when he discussed "the Hunthausen case." But the backbiting with Rome was evident in 1970 over the first confession of eight-year-olds. Decisions that should have been properly made in the U.S., if the national machinery followed the Roman norms, were finally honed out in the Vatican belatedly, making the Pope look like a traffic cop and Washington bureaucrats (among others) to be disobedient. In its doctrinal and disciplinary responses—on the average of one statement a year—the Holy See was clearing up the ambiguities about first confession, general absolution, *imprimaturs,* seminary training, religious life, sterilization in Catholic hospitals, Catholic higher education, the peace pastoral, and Charles Curran and company. None of these issues should have required the intervention of the Holy See.

Still, as far as the public perception was concerned, there seemed to be no major divisions within the NCCB. There were Bishops who disagreed with the ongoing policies, to be sure, but these rarely made it into the upper echelons of the NCCB machinery. And the few who did, being Ordinaries, made it obvious that they would not spend the time that was necessary to change the national course. They had no hand in appointments to the USCC bureaucracy, nor at times influence enough to obtain advance copies of controversial statements by NCCB with which they often disagreed. The public irenicism of Bishops only protected the "ins" at the Washington headquarters. USCC proposals which appeared to be out of synch with universal Church norms confused the pastoral situation at the diocesan level no matter how much a local Bishop wished it otherwise. What individual Bishop can insist within his diocese on the enforcement of papal teaching or directives if the public posture of NCCB is open-ended on that teaching? Mr. NCCB himself, Cardinal Bernardin, gave the clearest expression of the contemporary ecclesial situation, when on April 30, 1987, he defended John Paul II's teaching on artificial insemination, test tube babies, and surrogate motherhood as morally wrong. In the course of his presentation, however, he suggested to the laity that such conduct may not be sinful and anyway, "in the end, after prayerful and conscientious reflection on this teaching, they must make their own decision."[4] This is how dissenting theologians have been handling Church teaching, for years—stating it but indicating that private judgment about its relevance to life is the final arbiter. The wrongheadedness of this line of reasoning is not its assertion of a fact, viz., people ultimately do make their own personal decisions, but in the implication that when they make those decisions against the magisterium, they are acting in good conscience, rightly, and without sin —even when they are doing what the Cardinal readily admits is morally wrong. Bernardin's statement represented good Protestant theology, not the theology based on the Catholic Church's role in mediating Christ. It is also an approach to moral issues that one might have thought was settled—for Catholics at least— at the time of Martin Luther's excommunication. The same "theology of compromise," or "realism" as it is sometimes called, would come up again in 1988 when a Bernardin-approved "AIDS Statement" permitted factual information on condoms in public information programs about AIDS.

Even though the contemporary differences among Bishops are hardly peripheral to the Faith (like those which plagued their predecessors in the nineteenth century—German catechisms, the colonization of the Midwest, clerical attire, state aid to parochial schools), today we rarely see public rousting among them. U.S. Bishops who realize the depth of contemporary dissidence and its effect on Catholic mores are not visible critics of their own leadership, which prefers to let Rome deal with the problem. It can be granted that public squabbling by Bishops caused a good deal of scandal a hundred years ago and opened certain divisions among the Catholic faithful; but the present situation is no less scandalous on parish streets and in diocesan institutions, and the divisions are no less real because they are doctrinal, not simply political. There is an aspect of the present situation sufficiently different to make the contemporary crisis more ominous. Those old fights were truly Bishops' fights, only occasionally involving organized blocs of academics or laity. Today a hard core of Bishops is fronting for large blocs of Catholic dissidents who think the future Church belongs to them already, with only Rome standing in the way of total takeover. Washington-based columnist, Colman McCarthy, in reviewing *The Battle for the American Church* put it this way: "What's the battling about? The war is over." Disagreeing Bishops, therefore, especially those with status, cannot afford to stand on the sidelines. It took Rome the better part of two centuries to survive Gallicanism. The U.S. Church should not have to suffer more of the same from anything closely resembling Americanism.

The Archbishop of New York by nature of his Madison Avenue residence finds himself in the middle of all these controversies and without all the ready tools which simplified the life of his predecessors. There are also added strictures on his role-playing which they never had to face. Once Church authority gave up its strongest instruments of enforcement—excommunication, suspension, interdicting, oaths, silencing, etc. —it placed itself at the mercy of its internal enemies, who proceeded to use with abandon the most powerful instrument of social control in our time—labeling. Everyone knows, especially a sociologist, that a political battle is half won when the public becomes convinced that one side in the contest is deviant. French Revolutionary pundits, like Voltaire, helped bring down a King by sneering at him publicly. Since he had abused his self-proclaimed divine right of ruling, "right" therefore became wrong and "left" became right. "Liberal" was good because it meant change, "conservative" was bad because it protected privilege and tradition. The terminology has so burrowed its way into language everywhere that today no controversy over good and evil can prevent the media from dubbing one Bishop or another as liberal or conservative, with liberal always better because it is antilaw or antiinstitutional. Few Bishops either, especially if they are young, like to be called conservative.

Four score and seven years ago, few American leaders would have been scared away from their responsibility by bad mouthing of adversaries, certainly not Abraham Lincoln, perhaps the most vilified President in our history and usually recognized as the best. In 1900, no Catholic Bishop worth his miter would have compromised the Church's interests for a good headline or for popular approval. But, then, TV cameras were not peeking into private conversations with hidden microphones. Furthermore, the old code which guided turn-of-the-century pressmen, those who were not yellow journalists, that is, those who respected the offices of parenting, priesthood, and presidency, is no more. All public figures are fair game for hostile investigations and put-down if the result is news, any kind of news, even if by Judaeo-Christian standards it is unfit to print.

One has to be a man of great courage, therefore, to withstand the unpopular label and astute enough in matters pertaining to faith to avoid giving the media handles on which to hang the stigma—conservative, fundamentalist, right wing, whatever. The label is the ideologue's (or the lazy man's) way of scapegoating his opponent. A great deal is made out of Joe McCarthy's use of stigma to cower Communists and alleged fellow travelers in government, while similar outrage has been rarely manifested for the belittling of Herbert Hoover, Barry Goldwater, or Jerry Falwell. By whomever used, the wrong labels are a social albatross on the back of a public figure. Once called reactionary, racist, labor baron, anti-Semite, pinko, homophobe, misogynist, etc., a politician has an uphill fight to win or stay in office. Few do it, with FDR and Ronald Reagan being the exceptional masters of media. Tom Dewey, on the other hand, lost a sure-thing election in part because he was depicted as nothing more than a little man on a wedding cake. Archbishop O'Connor felt the sting of labeling when he dared challenge the so-called "liberal" mind-set on abortion.

Catholic Bishops by training and role are not geared to suffer negative media coverage. If they stand four square with the teaching of the Church, they will surely be stigmatized. Media favorites are those Bishops who are outspoken on exotic issues (e.g., the MX missile or liberation theology). Media nonpersons are the known critics of the secular agenda or those who are identifiable with John Paul II's theology. Archbishop Rembert Weakland of Milwaukee is a liberal, while Bernard Cardinal Law of Boston is a conservative prelate. So-called "liberal" Bishops can mitigate the full force of papal statements without media scapegoating. Archbishop Raymond Hunthausen once welcomed (May 18, 1984) notorious dissenter Richard McCormick into Seattle, telling his priests that "instead of having one clear set of moral norms upheld by all, we now have different schools of moral thought within the same mainstream of Catholic moral theology." The media gave high profile to Hunthausen's peace activity but ignored the posturing which brought Seattle into trouble with the Pope.

Few Bishops have the stomach for public brawling through media, so they bend over backward to avoid being labeled "conservative." Some even go out of their way to give high praise to scholars whom they know are troubling the faithful, while they keep at arms' length the very supporters who in times of trouble are normally welcome allies. After the Council of Trent seven Popes in a row reached out for any group that would help them save Germany and Poland for the Church. Since Vatican II similar supporting groups, whose numbers are legion, are on the outside of Bishops' chanceries, while important Church offices and conferences are staffed by the very people who have diluted the Church's Faith. John Paul II, repeatedly asks local Bishops to curtail dissent. Yet major Church institutions remain in the hands of prelates who have made peace more with "The American Catholic Experience" than with Roman management of the universal Church. A book carrying this very title by Notre Dame's Jay P. Dolan concludes with a chapter called "A New Catholicism." Predictably, the approved modern Church lays great stress on freedom in sex and marriage, private judgment in religious rites, and large doses of social action. The book does not explain how the "American Catholic Experience" leads to eternal salvation. The matter never comes up in the book nor in the centers of Catholic life where this kind of thinking prevails.

3. Chief pastor of souls in New York. These forces compound the difficulties which face every Bishop, including Cardinal O'Connor, *in their primary role as chief pastor of souls in their diocese.*

It is no simple matter these days for a newcomer to provide focus and system in what he has every right to consider his ecclesiastical machinery. To run a good grocery store you must first know what it is supposed to do. If there are a lot of automobile tires by the cash register, but no cornflakes, and the grocery store is losing money besides, a new manager has a big problem on his hands. The Church today seems to be expending a great deal of effort on consultation without evidence at this time that Vatican II has led to better doctrinal focus or a more effective system of evangelization. Good bishoping requires both. Scholars like to rate prelates for their identification with special causes, but a mitered cleric's ministry has to do with good parishes, good schools, good social welfare, better Catholics, converts, more committed clergy and religious, and in the last analysis the salvation of souls. Pastoral accomplishments among the masses, not approval from elites, is what bishoping is all about. The prelate cannot stand above conflict, he must resolve it on the side of truth. He cannot be neutral about right or wrong or allow both to coexist in his own institutions. He cannot show how evenhanded he is by taking no sides on issues of faith and morals. And he ought not reward or give the semblance of rewarding those who do wrong, or turn his back on Catholic apologists. If anything like these become a pattern of his administration, his legacy to his successor will be slews of postponed trouble. Every modern Bishop has inherited more than a fair share of that.

In 1966 Bishop Francis Furey, recently transported from Philadelphia, took over the San Diego diocese with instructions to bail it out. His predecessor, a wonderful old Bishop named Charles Buddy, had found himself after thirty years of service on the brink of bankruptcy, in large part because of his patronage of the University of San Diego. Furey brought in Cardinal Frank McIntyre of Los Angeles to use the financial skills he was known to have to save the university. When finally San Diego's debt was stabilized, McIntyre turned to Furey and said: "Frank, forty years down the line no one will remember we were here. They will only speak of Bishop Buddy's great vision." Such is the fate of most good pastors. McIntyre himself will always be second-guessed about his confrontation with the Immaculate Heart of Mary nuns, but long after someone decides the old curmudgeon was right on that issue, the 250-plus parishes, schools, and agencies McIntyre created and paid for in Los Angeles will still be serving hundreds of thousands of Catholics day after day, after day. One would have to look very hard for anyone else who could have transformed Los Angeles so effectively into one of the country's premier Sees.

Cardinal Patrick O'Boyle carved a niche for himself in history by standing up to priests who would not subscribe to *Humanae Vitae,* but his more enduring contribution to the Church was the creation of the Archdiocese of Washington, D.C., of which he was the first Ordinary. Few researchers may find time to analyze the effect on the Church of the majority of those 128 parishes which O'Boyle had built or the diocesan schools and child-caring homes, although some will remember that long before the 1954 Supreme Court decision, the transported New York prelate integrated his schools, in a border town no less.

If a majority of churchgoers in New York at the present moment are Italo-Americans, credit must go to Cardinal Spellman, who motivated Italian pastors to build elementary schools for their people, something which for many years they resisted doing.

These prelates were merely building on the pastoral patrimony bequeathed them by predecessors like John Hughes and Michael Corrigan. People forget what a model diocesan Bishop Corrigan really was, the man who created one quarter of today's New York parishes by his personal visitations. Much is made of the relative calm of New York priests during all kinds of Catholic crises. One does not find New York priests in any significant way leading charges against Church authority. Although many of them have always been involved in social movements, they have generally demonstrated good sense and large doses of reverence for whomever was Archbishop of New York. For that the Church can thank John Hughes who began with "the offscourings of the Irish nation." Peter Guilday described what the Church was like about the time New York's first Archbishop arrived:

> Uniformity of discipline was the principal need of the Church during the score of years which followed the (bishops') meeting of 1810. It was not easy of attainment, for misrule had spread under incompetent leadership in New York, Philadelphia and New Orleans. The Church here during the period of its infancy was sadly hampered by the presence of priests who knew not how to obey and of laity who were interpreting their share in Catholic life by non-Catholic church systems.[5]

John Hughes managed to make rebellion a risky business in New York and so it has remained to this day.

John J. O'Connor made the transit from Washington to Scranton to New York, from black cassock to watered silk with incredible speed. As a Cardinal he sits on some very important papal commissions, not the least of which have to do with making Bishops or guiding the public affairs of the Church. But when he goes to God, it will be the spiritual condition of the 2 million Catholics who live between Tottenville and Kingston, and their neighbors, who will be the norm by which he will be judged. When the Church in the United States was established on November 6, 1789, six months after George Washington was inaugurated as the first President of his country, Pius VI had this to say to its nation's pastors about their role:

> . . . Support must be given by that heavenly authority which is entrusted to the Catholic Church, as to a steady pillar and solid foundation which shall never fail . . .
>
> . . . That from her voice and instructions mankind may learn the objects of their faith and the rules of their conduct, not only for the

obtaining of eternal salvation, but also for the regulation of this life and the maintaining of concord in the society of this earthly city . . .

. . . This charge of teaching and ruling first given to the apostles, and especially to St. Peter, the Prince of the Apostles, on whom alone the Church is built, and to whom our Lord and Redeemer entrusted the feeding of his lambs and of his sheep, has been derived in due order of succession to Bishops, and especially to the Roman Pontiffs, successors of St. Peter and heirs of his power and dignity, that thereby it might be made evident that the gates of hell can never prevail against the Church, and that the divine founder of it will ever assist it to the consummation of ages . . .

. . . So that neither in the depravity of morals nor in the fluctuation of novel opinions, the episcopal succession shall ever fail or the bark of Peter be sunk.

Two hundred years later John Paul II hardly writes to modern Bishops any differently.

HE CAME, HE SAW . . .

When he was installed as Archbishop of New York, March 19, 1984, Archbishop O'Connor seized more than the day. He seized the pulpit, too. The Mets' cap exemplified his informality and making Ed Koch a foil for the mayor of Scranton only bespoke his actor's talent. Reaching out to a little altar boy in the front pews told us something about his paternal instincts, and when he spoke of the Church, you saw the passionate priest. Wherever you stood or sat in the Cathedral on that feast of St. Joseph, you knew instinctively that New York had a media personality in the Cardinal's Chair.

It is too early, of course, to measure what his long-range effect will be on the Archdiocese of New York or on the Church of the United States. The ecclesiastical situation is too complicated and the pieces to be returned to place, even in New York, are too damaged. One thing is clear; New York has an eloquent communicator of the Church's message. He has already seen how easily first enthusiasms fade, leaving only the things he does, not what he says for the stuff of future history. The enemies of a truly Catholic voice like his are lurking everywhere, in Catholic editorial offices, in religious monasteries, and among professors, even in seminaries. The heat of Harry Truman's kitchen has only begun to singe John O'Connor. As the Man from Independence learned—"public leaders grow or they die." Eventually, if they are good, they stand alone with their entire community rising or falling as a result of their decisions or their inability to decide.

Two statements by John O'Connor set the tone for his early archepiscopacy. Speaking to *The New York Times*'s religion editor, he made it abundantly clear that he was witness to the teaching of the Church:

> We are completely open to the widest variety of ideas and opinions and enthusiastic about listening to others discussing issues of interest and concern. At the same time, certain teachings of the Church are quite clearly determined, and while we are anxious to dispel misunderstandings, we raise unfulfillable expectations if we pretend that such teachings can be changed through discussion."[6]

In this he was merely echoing Cardinal Newman's suggestion that Bishops proclaim "a definite message to high and low from the World's Maker, whether men would hear or whether they would forbear."

Another statement was even more provocative because it seemed to invade the political sanctuary which secularists thought they had all to themselves. Though directed to Catholic politicians, it shot like an arrow through the hearts of officeholders and aspirants who piously proclaimed their only obligation was to voters: "I don't see how a Catholic in good conscience can vote for a candidate who explicitly supports abortion."

Archbishop O'Connor made this statement at a press conference three months after his installation, just as the 1984 presidential election campaign was heating up and about the time one of the candidates, Geraldine Ferraro, was discovered to be pro-abortion.

365

For both these declarations he was consigned by Kenneth Briggs to the lower regions, among those Bishops "who place a very conservative construction on the Council's preachment," whose "politics are farther to the right than more liberal Bishops."

These different thrusts to O'Connor's initial sortie into public affairs—one internal to the Church, the other *ad extra* to secular society—doomed him immediately, not only with the so-called "liberal establishment," which knows how to punish those who threaten their dominance of the American enterprise, but also with a large segment of Catholic opinion, including that of many Bishops. It is difficult to decide, even now, which group endangers him most. A Bishop's first priority is the good of souls, the souls of his flock, but since Catholics are not given to isolation from the society in which they live, O'Connor as their chief spokesman in New York could not sit idly by and permit Catholic politicians to compromise or deny, even by indirection, an important Catholic absolute—the right of the innocent to life, even if unborn. No less an authority than John Paul II had warned Bishops only the year before, while O'Connor was still in Scranton, that compassion for people was not to deter them from proclaiming "without fear or ambiguity the many controversial truths of our age."[7]

What his boldness did for him, whether he foresaw the likelihood or not, was to project him overnight into the role of Catholic apologist. Those of us who worked with him on the "peace pastoral" were not surprised. He was not long in New York, when he applied for membership in the Fellowship of Catholic Scholars, the one association of academics at the time committed to the Church's magisterium. It was on the basis of his own Catholic commitment that elements within the New York apparatus sought to bring him back to the "Big Apple" as their Archbishop and so worked to accomplish the objective. To Catholic churchgoers, who did not know him, he came as an angel of light. It had been more than a few years since they had heard such a vigorous voice on the side of Catholicity. Indeed, the decrease of Catholic identity was said to be a necessary fallout of Vatican II, which, even if it were only partially true, contributed to the ennui of those whose weekly contributions to the collection plate paid the salaries of the elites doing their best to Americanize the Roman Church. Had he been the Bishop of Bardstown, his Catholic speech-making would hardly have merited national attention, but from those first moments in "Fun City" he was a voice from Rome and a marked man with the Catholic latitudinarians.

Latitudinarians are generally defined as devotees of freedom of thought and behavior in matters religious, but the Catholic elite so described are not likely to be generous with their favors to the likes of O'Connor. They moved almost immediately to whip him into line. "Co-opted by the right" was one of the comments overheard the day of his installation. Before very long he would be called worse than that, such being the bitterness of those who mistakenly think that American Catholicism has at last outmaneuvered papal efforts to keep it Roman. If nothing else, they would try to neutralize his national influence. Historically, the Archbishop of New York, all by himself, was a force to be reckoned with, no matter who else claimed leadership in the U.S. Church.

Archbishop O'Connor's natural constituency was the faithful, the people who still attended church on Sunday, and who believed. Only once during the post-Vatican II period were they consulted by the national body of Bishops—about the removal of holy days from the Church calendar—and then they overwhelmingly rejected the proposed plan to cut back on their holy day obligations. Harry Truman in 1948, at the low point in his political fortunes, once asked a priest: "Hey, Father, who talks for the people?" It was later demonstrated that he did, and so did John O'Connor on those first days of his remarkable ascendency. In 1984 there were few Catholic apologists to rival him. And apologists for the Catholic message were sorely needed.

Archbishop O'Connor's root difficulty in preaching the unadulterated Catholic Word was the dissidence within his own Church. The support systems for the Catholic creeds had all but collapsed. The creeds were still true and were so proclaimed in Rome, but the Church world which made them livable, indeed enjoyable, had been shattered. The old pious signs of internal faith—blessing oneself passing a church door, making six o'clock Mass even if the party lasted all night, praying for a baby the first year of marriage and "churching" when it came, concern for the state of grace, praying at night for the grace of a happy death at twenty— were gone. And with their going went a large amount of trusting faith. Mass attendance was down, the confessional lines had dried up, and large numbers of the new Hispanics were becoming fundamentalist Protestants.

New York was not Seattle, however. It had its problems, but no one could accuse Cardinal Cooke of tolerating violations of Catholic norms concerning marriage, the administration of the sacraments, or the moral norms of the Church dealing with homosexual behavior. There were priests, to be sure, who deliberately bypassed first confession for children, gave general absolution in violation of Church norms, encouraged immoral homosexual behavior, "blessed" invalid second marriages, and misused the sacred liturgy. But by and large these were underground activities and the exception to normal practice. If there was any common abuse that was aboveboard in New York, it was the practice of many priests and religious to be anti-Chancery Office and more concerned about the state of people's pocketbooks than the state of their souls. The purpose of evangelization—to preach the kingdom of God and save souls—remained in the background of many priests' lives. The Church had lost its focus. The more general problem facing the new Archbishop was false teaching everywhere. He had a dozen colleges in his Archdiocese which years before had foresworn their allegiance to the Church, but whose presidents still smiled under the Catholic banner for the benefit of benefactors and potential students. The horror stories coming out of these institutions by 1984 were legendary, frequently involving ex-priests and ex-nuns on the faculty. Whatever else can be said about these institutions, their presidents were more interested in defending professors' academic freedom to teach whatever they wished, than in seeing the faith protected or their students graduating fully committed to the Church and practicing their faith. Only a generation earlier the best believing and practicing Catholics were the graduates of Catholic colleges. Contemporary bad teaching had muddied what was left of the Catholic mind among the young, especially the potential teachers who would eventually make their way into the Catholic school system. To offset this, Cooke established in 1970 a Director of Religious Education for his catechetical operations, but that office did not last long. The professionals resented the overview. Then in 1976, distressed about the products he saw coming out of Manhattan and Fordham, he set into motion his own Archdiocesan Catechetical Institute to certify teachers for his own system. The Institute worked, but it had acquired enemies whom the new Archbishop eventually would meet within his own household.

During those first days John O'Connor told the press that the Church is a hierarchical structure with doctrines fixed by the great Councils of the Church, and by bishops in union with the Pope. But all around New York he would find a "second magisterium" working against him. *Commonweal, America,* the Paulist Press, and columnists in religious newspapers would be only a few of those contesting in their pages whatever he said in St. Patrick's pulpit. Episcopal hierarchy had been enervated, except on paper. Catholics, no less than other Americans, were ruled not by leaders but by veto groups, those infrastructures of elites who paralyze government by terror of one kind or another. Young Catholics were no longer taught, even in Catholic schools, to respect their elders, let alone their pastors. Priests and the religious who flouted their vows, particularly of obedience, were the last ones to teach the Ten Commandments effectively.

The measure of how a system can be used to undermine system was in evidence during the interregnum—i.e., while O'Connor was still in Scranton. In 1983 New York's Dunwoodie Seminary, one of the country's best, was subject to the same investigation that John Paul II had ordered for all such training centers. Two prelates on the roving committee expressed "culture shock" at seeing clerical dress prevalent in the seminary corridor and preoccupation among Dunwoodie students with orthodox belief. Later one of those Bishop investigators defended Charles Curran at the very moment that Rome was indicting him. The pressure toward a kind of pluralism that organizations like the AFL-CIO or the

NAACP would find objectionable was strong, even among those responsible for the full Catholic training of future priests.

Rebuilding the Catholic support system will not be easy, therefore, and no Bishop can do it alone. Three quarters of the nineteenth century went by before the U.S. Bishops began to appreciate the quality of American Catholicism that later would be so widely admired elsewhere. Dissenters sneer at the idea of a Golden Age of piety in America. But it existed, as anyone who did parish work in the first half of this century can attest. Archbishop Hughes would have been proud of the Catholic grandchildren and great-grandchildren his poor uneducated immigrants of the pre–Civil War period begot. It was the methodic teaching and discipline initiated by Bishops like Hughes that bore its fruit in good time. Success did not come overnight, because getting priests to live in rectories or to behave themselves in public or even to reserve the Blessed Sacrament in church was no easy task. But the Bishops won out in the end. Internalizing the goals of Vatican II, while intensifying Catholic piety, will demand the same kind of episcopal determination and more than a few outstanding Bishop leaders, of which the John O'Connors can be paradigms.

John Paul II does more than preach "One Lord, One Faith, One Church" to a flock that has become inured with factional Catholicism. He has begun to shore up Catholic truth with appropriate institutional supports, going out of his way to endorse and bless the faithful sons, daughters, and movements, while expressing displeasure, even censure, of those who war against the Church internally. The Church's conduct must always reinforce belief in what she teaches. Theologians must not gain favor if they insist on autonomy from the Church's catechesis. Religious educators cannot be sources of alienation and impiety. The Catholic Church is more than a complex of credal affirmations and moral interdictions. It is a way of life, a state of mind, a culture. St. Paul once advised, "Let that mind be in you which is in Christ Jesus, Our Lord."[8] Catholics are those who know their prayers and worship, but they are also a people stamped for life with a particular set of priorities, with a manner of knowing, living, playing, suffering, dying that marks them as different. They form an identifiable subculture or a counterculture in any civilization that is Godless. And at the heart of their world is the Catholic faith, supported and reinforced by Bishops to whom they are committed and who to the faithful are Christ.

Archbishop O'Connor's special difficulty remains the Church's uncertain voice on substantive Catholic matters. How far is it possible for an ecclesiastic to rally support for a Bishop-sponsored political judgment (itself not binding in conscience because it involves more than principle), when the very principle is questioned by his own, including some peers in the episcopacy? Mario Cuomo threw this gauntlet at the Church while defending himself against his New York Ordinary:

> There are many people, including some Catholic theologians, who do not accept the assumption, who do not believe the fetus is a person from the moment of conception, and who therefore find nothing immoral in aborting a fetus or, at least, find abortion a morally defensible act in many circumstances.[9]

The governor might not likely have made this assertion prior to *Roe v. Wade* (1973), when the national consensus was still against abortion-on-demand, and certainly not had he remained in private life. However, after he began to chase voting constituencies, Cuomo read the Catholic press carefully and was well advised by his clerical and/or episcopal friends on how to offset O'Connor's influence.

The Archbishop's conundrum was not how to deal with a Catholic governor who placed himself in opposition to Church authority. Mario Cuomo as the best practicing Catholic in recent years to acquire political fame, normally would be against abortion, politically as well as morally. And if he had to face a united Church, in office he would not likely waffle on the issue. All things being equal, Archbishop O'Connor was perfectly correct in wondering aloud how a convinced Catholic politician could in good conscience "explicitly support abortion." The trouble in 1984 was, and is today, that all things are no longer equal. Once upon a time the Cardinal Archbishop of New York was by himself "the powerhouse." He spoke the one voice of the Church, and while he never controlled the Catholic vote the way the anti-Catholic pundits said he did, he was not without influence politically—not so much at election time, because Catholic Bishops traditionally kept out of voting politics, but because he did have a large constituency that might act up if a Catholic politician seemed to be abusing the Church or denying Catholic doctrine. Even when a Spellman wanted a favorable vote on school aid, Catholics knew they were free to judge otherwise. And they often did. However, the measure of the Church's involvement in politics and the obligation of Catholic politicians to follow an informed conscience, not naked political expediency, always depended on the issue. In 1948 Pope Pius XII threatened to excommunicate all Catholics holding formal and willing allegience to the Communist party in Italy. At the time the existence of the Church there was at stake. In the United States no such pressure was ever placed on Catholics, even though Church authority in modern times made political judgments many times—on child labor laws, on labor and civil rights legislation, and on military matters. Mario Cuomo was perfectly correct in saying that political tactics were his to decide, not Archbishop O'Connor's. But on the abortion issue the bottom line was principle, not tactics. The trouble was that the hierarchy's national machinery provided the "out" that the expedient politician in Cuomo could seize. And the loophole would favor dissenting theologians, not Archbishop O'Connor.

Something must be made very clear about the abortion issue. In Catholic thought this is not comparable to the nuclear war issue, where disagreements concerning the best tactics for preserving peace are normal. The Supreme Court may have made it virtually impossible for statutory law to forbid abortions, but many options are open to politicians as to the ease of their availability, about how and where they are to be performed and who is to pay for them, etc. A number of legal options also exist, although they are not necessarily viable politically, to overturn the Supreme Court by constitutional amendment—either to outlaw all abortions (Hyde) or to remand the matter to the states (Hatch), or to legislate any one of many restrictions government officials normally invent to circumvent an unsatisfactory judicial decision.

Even so, when the one clear issue is the basic right of innocent life, including that of the unborn, the sound conscience of a Catholic is compelled to decide against direct killing and against direct abortion. The Church, which gives wide leeway to theologians and the faithful to judge circumstances where they might exercise proper freedom, has never permitted the use of theological opinions in such a matter as direct killing. The opinion of this or that theologian is of no account when the issue is the right of innocent life. And the human embryo or fetus is innocent human life, beyond the moral power of anyone, including the state or the mother, to destroy it. When one considers the 20 million and more abortions performed since 1973, those killings have now assumed the proportions of a holocaust, one that does not need an Archbishop to call it "widespread destruction" of human life.

It serves no purpose to recount the solemn statements of the Church which bind Catholic politicians, no less than Catholic mothers and Catholic doctors. From the "betrayal of human life" by Pius XI in 1931, to Vatican II's 1965 description of abortion as an "unspeakable crime," to the New York bishops' declaration in 1984 that "officeholders cannot escape their responsibility in this matter," the path of the informed Catholic conscience was clear. Whatever the political bind for the Catholic officeholder, he had no choice, if he were a convinced Catholic, but to follow the teaching of the Church. Why not on this? No one expected anything less when religious convictions were the main reasons for undoing racial discrimination or for supporting the farm workers and their boycott of nonunion lettuce. Abortion is a question of public order, but it is a question of human life first.

No issue in our time symbolizes more the intersection of the sacred with the secular than the direct and deliberate destruction of the unborn child. Our country was born out of a declaration that all men are created equal and are endowed by their Creator with certain inalienable rights. The right to life is not just one tenet in the American creed, it is the primary and predominant right, the *sine qua non* of all other rights. It is granted, according to this creed, not by the state, not even by parents, but by the Creator himself. The U.S. Bishops said as much in 1987, when they found Congress contemplating amending the 1964 Civil Rights Law in such a way as to allow abortion to be considered a civil right to kill a helpless human being.

Yet in 1976 the NCCB leadership gave Catholic politicians and others the loophole they needed to circumvent universal moral law. They boxed themselves into a "seamless-garment argument," later to be called "the consistent life ethic." Up to this year the Bishops as a body and individually assigned a higher priority to fighting abortion than they did to combatting other social evils whose remedy often admitted varied and complex solutions. The seamless-garment approach reduced abortion to a political level of importance hardly different from a concern about the war in Nicaragua or affirmative action at home. By going this route the Bishops appeared more ecumenical and less obsessed with "single-issue politics," that shrewd political ploy (as Cardinal O'Connor once called it) to embarrass Right-to-Lifers who held candidates responsible for their abortion votes. Single-issue voting was never a matter of controversy when Jews or Blacks or Sharecroppers made anti-Semitism, racism, or a hostile attitude toward the welfare system their sole reason for voting against a candidate.

The "seamless-garment argument" permitted the likes of Mario Cuomo and Ted Kennedy to hide under its umbrella to profess their Catholicity and their pro-abortion posture, too. The "seamless-garment argument" also took the wind out of the sails of the Right-to-Life Movement—a lay movement if there ever was one, an ecumenical movement too, and one that by 1976 had made abortion-on-demand the number one civil rights issue in the country and had made legislators conscious of a growing consensus against abortion-on-demand. This movement is today but a shadow of its former self, and generations of American youth now take for granted four thousand daily abortions as a constitutional right and safer than childbirth.

In summarizing the argument between Mario Cuomo and New York's new Archbishop, the *New York Times* headlined the story as follows: "Governor Finds Chicago Prelate an Ally in Debate with O'Connor."[10] The account quoted Cuomo as "calling on Catholics to attack a wide range of social welfare ills and, in effect, to avoid the narrower, single-issue focus some associate with Archbishop O'Connor." The governor then embraced the "seamless garment," stated "eloquently," said Cuomo, by Cardinal Bernardin at a Fordham University address the year before.

But Archbishop O'Connor was right and Mario Cuomo was wrong. For the Catholic—and all those Protestants and Jews who take the moral code seriously—the issue is truth. Political priorities are determined from this intellectual point. The truth—scientifically no less than morally—is that what is terminated in the womb is human life.

We have been told for decades, lately by some priests and a few Bishops, that if only we outfitted our girls with contraceptives, the nation would avoid unwanted pregnancies and abortion. This is a lie. Contraception, sterilization, and abortion are three platforms of a party which denies that human life and the life-giving process itself are sacred, of a world view which suggests that there is no principled limit to the taking of innocent human life. If we are looking for a seamless garment, one that is really seamless, not a garment basted together by loose political or partisan stitching, it is that which packages contraception, sterilization, and abortion. Forty years ago the Church was called divisive because she was anticontraceptive, twenty years ago the Church was censured because she opposed sterilization, a device that will depopulate the American future better than any condom. Today, her antiabortion and antihomosexual teachings stimulate additional anti-Catholic venom because Americans no longer like to feel guilty about their sins or their crimes. Still they cannot hide from the Catholic Church. Tomorrow's divisive issue will be, without question, antieuthanasia, the kind of violence on helpless creatures for which we once condemned Adolph Hitler.

This is the real seamless garment which, from contraception to the killing of the aged, is undermining the character of our people —a garment which bishops should do everything they can to tear asunder.

The Catholic Church cannot escape its truth or the consequences of its teaching. Our contemporary shame, for twenty years, at least, has been our quiet voice on the Church's sexual ethic, a silence which made John O'Connor in 1984 sound like a voice crying in a Catholic wilderness. He struck the right nerve. Catholic Americanizers already edgy about prelates who contest prevailing mores (usually theirs) or who sound too Catholic—i.e., like John Paul II—will be his enemies. They will subvert him or lambaste him for destroying consensus, unmindful that consensus against truth is irrelevant and immaterial. The first Philadelphian to head New York withstood similar opposition, but his reputation as a first-rate Bishop perdures a hundred and more years after his death. Indeed he turned New York into such a prominent See that Hughes's successor almost of necessity in Rome's view became the first American Cardinal. The newest Philadelphian to sit in Hughes's chair already has his fair share of the Church's enemies against him. Still Winston Churchill's words in the House of Commons on June 4, 1940, during Britain's darkest hour, if applied to a harassed Church, seem apt:

> Victory at all costs, victory in spite of all terror, victory however long and hard the road may be; for without victory there is no survival.

The Bishop's function, after all, is to build and maintain his Father's House. Only there do he and his people find their fulfillment. The Catholic Bishop must help warm people's lives with the fire of his faith, but above all he must make sure that under his leadership they save their souls. The direction of his activity is set by the Church, never more eloquently defined than in these words:

> The Church aims not at making a show but at doing a work. She regards this world and all that is in it as a mere shadow, as dust and ashes compared with the value of one single soul. The Church holds that unless she can in her own way do good to souls, there is no use in doing anything.

The first Cardinal to say that was John Henry Newman. The last Cardinal to say it was John J. O'Connor.[11]

NOTES

1. Romans 3:8.
2. *English L'Oservatore Romano,* June 21, 1982, p. 4.
3. *Fellowship of Catholic Scholars' Newsletter,* March 1983, p. 10.
4. *Chicago Tribune,* April 30, 1987.
5. *History of The Councils of Baltimore,* 1932.
6. *The New York Times,* Sunday, February 5, 1984.
7. *Origins,* September 15, 1983.
8. Philippians 2:5.
9. *The New York Times,* October 4, 1984, editorial page.
10. *The New York Times,* October 6, 1984.
11. Lecture for the Milton Eisenhower Symposium, Johns Hopkins University, October 14, 1986.

INDEX

social status, 49

Baker, Kenneth, Father, 280, 308
Baker, Oliver E., 31–32
Ball-Russell-Wherry rider, 54
Balthasar, Hans Urs von, Cardinal, 293
Barry, William, Msgr., 33
Bartholome, Peter, Bishop, 71
Basler, Howard, Father, 281–82
Battle for the American Church, 276–77, 279–80, 306, 358
Baum, William, Cardinal, 304, 335–36, 338
Bayer, Edward, 307
Benestad, Brian, 307
Bennett, William, 173
Bernardin, Joseph, Cardinal, 178, 181, 279, 324, 330, 333–34, 342–45, 354, 356–57
Bevilacqua, Anthony, Bishop, 338
Biblical evidence and faith statements, 292
Birth Control Commission, 74
Birth Control and Catholics, 270
Birth of the Messiah, 286
Blaine Amendment, 98–107, 109–11, 162–63
Blake, Mary Concepta, Sister, 213
Blumenthal, Albert, 159
Board of Catholic Education, 155–56
Borders, William, Bishop, 338
Boyle, Joseph, 307
Bradley, Dennis, Father, 313
Broderick, Bishop, 121
Brown, Raymond E., Father, 280, 283–89, 291–92, 299, 304
Buckley, Cornelius, Father, 301
Buckley, Michael, Father, 329–35
Bundy Committee, 157, 159
Burrell, David, 304
Butler, Bernard, 156
Byrne, James, Bishop, 338

Cahill, Joseph T., Father, 265–66
Call to Action, 66
Calvary Cemetery strike, 56–61
Cana movement, 67, 70, 248–49
Canavan, Frank, Father, 299, 307
Cantillon, Joseph, Father, 67
Carberry, John, Cardinal, 300, 337–38
Cardinal of New York's role, 349–64
Carey, Hugh L., 169, 188
Castelli, Jim, 253
Cathedral College, 2
Catholic Biblical Association, 300, 304–5
Catholic Charities Campaign, 141–42

Catholic Church
  anti-abortion activism, 176–82
  bureaucracies, 339
  child care institutions, 220–22
  discipline, 16–17
  disobedience within, 24–25
  dissent within, 92, 274–93, 299, 306, 334
  experiments within, 205
  foundational doctrines, 336
  fund-raising, 141–43
  government regulation, 101–2
  inner workings, 150–53
  just war theory, 346
  media problems, 174–75
  new theology, 284–89
  origin, 286–89
  pacifism and, 346
  parish censuses, 32–33
  political activism, 101–8, 110, 226–27
  self-criticism, 23
  social activism, 62
  teachings, 70–71, 325–26
  unfair labor practices, 57
Catholic colleges
  controversy, 266–67
  secularization, 133, 159–60
Catholic Committee, 163
Catholic education
  government aid, 157–75
  lay leadership, 135
  malcontents, 270
  reform, 146–49, 151
  regarding sex, 318–23
Catholic ethos, 10, 17
Catholic Evidence Guild, 13
Catholic Family Day, 72–73, 75
Catholic Fertility in Florida, 31
Catholic identity, 16–18, 271–72
Catholicism, 326
Catholic Labor Alliance, 47, 65
Catholic politicians, 371–74
Catholic publishers, 308–9
Catholics
  attributes, 186, 370–71
  consciences, 254
Catholics and the Practice of the Faith, 31
Catholic Schools in a Declining Church, 317
Catholics for a Free Choice, 334
Catholic Theological Society, 305
Catholic Welfare Committee, 101–4, 108
Catholic Worker, 42, 52
Census-taking, 32–33, 260–61
Charles, Rodger, 307–8

GEORGE A. KELLY, ordained a priest in 1942, holds a Ph.D. in Social Science from Catholic University of America. He was parish priest and pastor during the first half of his ministry. Later, he was director of the Institute for Advanced Studies at St. John's University, New York. Presently, he is a research professor there for Contemporary Catholic Problems. Founder of the Fellowship of Catholic Scholars, he was named a consultant to the Holy See in 1983.